SERENDIPITY AND THE AMERICAN DREAM

United States' Foreign Policy in a Changing Global Order

PREAMBLE

Tom Hanks says in the film, Forrest Gump, "Life is like a box of chocolates, and you munch them one by one." Chris Kyles, in his autobiography, titled as *American Sniper* says, "Mommy prevents me from killing and says violence is not good for humankind, but I say that it solves a lot of human problems". Chris Kyles is an ex-Navy Seal who functioned as a Marine sniper with the largest number of victims through his guns, Lapua and Winmag, in his various operations in Iraq since 2003 till 2009—his last engagement. This is part of the American Dream and US Policy around which the narrative will be woven.

SERENDIPITY AND THE AMERICAN DREAM

United States' Foreign Policy in a Changing Global Order

Dr. Manan Dwivedi

Faculty, International Relations and International Administration,
Indian Institute of Public Administration, New Delhi

Foreword by

Prof. Chintamani Mahapatra

Rector, JNU

PENTAGON PRESS

Serendipity and the American Dream: United States' Foreign Policy in a Changing Global Order

by Dr. Manan Dwivedi

ISBN 978-81-8274-894-1

First Published in 2016

Published by
PENTAGON PRESS
206, Peacock Lane, Shahpur Jat,
New Delhi-110049
Phones: 011-64706243, 26491568
Telefax: 011-26490600
email: rajan@pentagonpress.in
website: www.pentagonpress.in

Printed at Avantika Printers Private Limited.

Contents

Foreword

One of the most difficult tasks of an international relations scholar is to explain the role of the United States in global affairs without drawing criticisms of unadulterated bias in favour or against the United States. Significantly, one of the easiest ways to criticize the US foreign policy is to read an array of scholarly books, articles and media commentaries authored by Americans themselves. There are Americans who have condemned US policies in starker terms than the Russians, Chinese and scholars from developing countries. What is difficult perhaps is to find non-American scholars who admire the Americans for their "Dreams", actions, behaviour and even culture, certainly not because of lack of adequate knowledge but by seeking to understand America in different perspectives.

One such Indian scholar is Manan Dwivedi who has attempted to explain the US foreign policy going beyond the text books, research articles, archival documents and looking at American history, politics and foreign policies by adopting a cultural perspective. This book is neither a text book of US foreign policy nor a detailed research on any particular aspect or issue of US foreign and national security policies. It is neither a chronological history of American engagements with the rest of the world nor a geographical analysis of it. It can, in fact, be described as what it is not, than what it is. It is up to the readers to discover a different perspective adopted by an Indian scholar to understand the United States.

The author himself says that he has made an attempt "to festoon the Comic Book super heroes such as the Man of Steel-Superman, the web slinger-Spiderman and the effective collectivity of the Avengers, as, part of the American rationale for doing good to the humanity and rendering benevolent service to the larger comity of nations." Every American speaks of an "American Dream" and many foreign scholars have commented upon it. What is this dream all about? Has it been realized? Does it remain a dream? Does it clash with other nations' dream? Should "God Bless America" or the whole world? The book is a complex mixture of politics, economics, foreign policy, national security, foreign interventions and many more written in not so simple English but worth reading.

Prof. Chintamani Mahapatra
Rector, JNU

Preface

> *"Born into a New age, we are witnessing, the vicious vicissitudes of past rivalries being thrown away into the heap and rubble of History."*
>
> —Author

Is it "God Bless America"?

The presented work to follow is meant to be a treatise on the hallowed American dream along with the fundamentals of the US Foreign policy. The Book encapsulates the theme of US foreign policy and its varied ramifications in the context of various regions and nations of the international system. The author's central argument is that the infallibility of the grandiloquent American dream and the founding principles of the American nation need a revalidation which are originally very well intentioned and well pedestalled. The author has attempted to classify the counter American perceptions, appellations, apparitions and quintessential criticism of United States in order to weave together a narrative which generally sheds positive light on the American way of leading life, the general veneer of the life of its citizens along with the functioning and the various balance of power equations, which permeate the nook and cranny of US foreign policy making. The grand idea about the "American Republican experiment" and the utility of rhetoric and verbiage in the norm setting principles of the American dream, have been brought to the fore by the author. If the work emerges as a paen to the American cause, it does not harm the purport of the work.

The work to begin with, in the initial chapters, engages the readers with an enunciation and a descriptive analysis of the American founding principles and the nation's myth and lore and their eternally transcendental nature. The author makes a strident effort to posit the American values in the larger scheme of things. The work argues that all is not vile, trepidatory and commercialized about the American founding principles by enlarging and highlighting upon the founding principles of the American, "Way" which is infact a celebration of the "Antiquity" and "the Agrarian". The first few sections highlight the lore and the myth of the American revolution and the historical legerdemain of the hallowed Federalist papers along with a detailed analysis of the International Relations theory's percept of, "Idealism". President Woodrow Wilson and the Fourteen Points enunciated by him receive a great iota of space in the Book's narrative which once again ends up highlighting the infallibility and the benevolent nature of US foreign policy. The core argument which the book will engage the reader with, is, the idiom that there is a great utility about the core American ideals of liberty, fraternity, pursuit of happiness, constitutionalism and the efficacy of the benign and facilitating rubric of the rule of law. Rhetoric and propagandist verbiage has been known to engender a positive vibe about the nation state of America and its Citizen Cain's leading their lives and functioning in tandem with the rubric of the American dream. The need to espouse larger-than-life guiding and driving credentials in order to highlight a nation's comprehensive power and vitality, gets a generous rendering in the Book's narrative. The amplificatory functionality of the work is of significance here as the palaver about the greatness, humanity and the stolidity of the chosen nation, such as United States of America, has been stressed and re-emphasized in the narrative's rendering of a new manner of carrying on Politics and resuscitating the idea of the American dream. The symbolic and emphatic quality of the visual, cinematic, literary and cultural imageries concerning United States of America, leads to the spawning of a new narrative which need not be equated with a narrow denomination of neo-conservative tenets prevalent in the American nation as part of one section of its political discourse. The work highlights the central argument that the Realist take on the decisions and the actions-inactions of the White House in the realm of domestic and foreign policy making, needs to be enumerated and highlighted as being the indubitable rationale behind certain wars, military and diplomatic interventions, which have been undertaken by the American nation, in countries such as Korea, Vietnam, Iraq and Afghanistan. The notion of the American schism in its foreign policy making has been amply highlighted in separate chapters on Iran, Iraq, Afghanistan, Vietnam, Columbia and others. The entire text is an academic and a popular assertion and reinstatement of the nom de plume of the direction of the all pervading political and official schism between the strains of Isolationism and Interventionism in the American foreign policy making firmament.

Apart from the first few chapters which highlight the efficacy of the grandiloquent American Dream and the historical foundations of the establishment of the American nation, there are contemporary vignettes on present day world affairs describing the Raison' D Etre of American interventions in the confines of countries such as Iraq, Iran, Vietnam and others all placed in a deft chronological account of the way the American Foreign policy has progressed through the ages. The last but the most interesting attribute of the work refers to and utilizes the instrumentality of Cultural, Cinematic and literary metaphors to deftly highlight the profundity of the American experience. An assiduous attempt has been made to festoon the Comic Book super heroes such as the Man of Steel—Superman, the web slinger—Spiderman and the effective collectivity of the Avengers, as, part of the American rationale for doing good to the humanity and rendering benevolent service to the larger comity of nations. Thus, I hope the Preface prepares the august and adventurist reader to explore the academic renderings and quintessential American-Universalist flights of fancies, that lie ahead in the Book's pages. The work is an experiment to unravel the myth and lore of the "American experiment" and to strengthen it in all its pristine oeuvre.

Acknowledgements

The Project can be earnestly and safely termed as "Project America" which has been my elegant and Royale pet lecturing and research theme since the last two decades, when I as a neophyte scholar and intellectual—academic intervened upon the tedium of talk on US and its Foreign Policy with the ballast of an unwelcome iconoclast. My Pa, Bhupendraji, was my avid supporter as I now have filled a part of his American fantasy with academic and popular evidence and excerpts from primary and secondary sources to lead to a deft but late realization of his pogrom of, "Middle Class Americanization". What Bhupendraji, meant was that an Utopia can be achieved by the likes of President Reagan and President George Bush Senior along with UN Secretary General Javier Perez De Cuellar, in the hallowed portals of United Nations. This Utopia would provide the middle class with a more learned and cultured oeuvre due to an avid watching of the Hollywood's Cinematic constructs with special significance being attached to the Comic Book super heroes such as Superman, Spiderman, Tarzan, The Star Wars pantheon and the Avengers. This was Bhupendraji's notion of bridging the class divide as an individual middle class riposte to the Commitern's notion of Communist Internationale. Pa's solution was never meant to be academic but immensely popular and locally appreciated, it definitely was. I dedicate this work of mine to my Pa, Bhupendraji, as I too have militated academically and popularly to validate his American Dream and the Oregon trail of names, as a standard film star cast travels away and disappears away into unexplored spaces, in the initial credit sequences of Star Wars: The Force Awakens. Pa's Red Dhoti was often utilized as the "Cape" for the author riding his various fanciful flights as Kal-El aka Superman. It also dutifully became the cape for my earthly cousins in their trajectory of being ordained with super powers by Monto, that is, the author. It is to that surreal experience of camaraderie and phantasmagorical detail that I dedicate this Book.

I also dedicate this work of imagination and academic utility to my daughter, Pal Dwivedi for whom the loud and garish Super powers remain a sad enigma till date. She can relate to the bright haired Barbies and classy, colorful and tousled Cindrellas, but not to the American Dream as signified by the likes of Superman and the Avengers belonging to the Justice League. Only the charm of owning talking Barbies, diaper-draped babies and the American Mermaids from film constructs, such as, "Splash" have endeared her to the American Dream. Though not being much of a Dreamer, the Child yearns for toys with American origins and preferably, American characters with a sincere, sombre and beatific air. It is to that 'manufactured dream' that I dedicate the Book.

Pojs Dwivedi and Ma also need to be congratulated in the work's conceptualization who gave wings for me to fly with. My Ma's, strident warm walks in the hearth with unregulated cuppas of tea, coffee and masala oats gave me the strident wherewithal to complete the work and beautify it. Pojs diverted the attention of my Daughter, Pal Dwivedi to story books and moral readers to leave the sole word processor in the house, unoccupied for me to spawn a new benevolent narrative on America. It is to that domesticity that I dedicate "our" Book. Prof. Sushma Yadav encouraged the author immensely with her immense erudition and Yeomanly tenor and a part of my dedication goes to her benign self. Mam was a shining beacon of light for making me traverse the odyssey. Yogendra Narain sir was a like an astute beam of light and hope in my academic odyssey.

I religiously attribute the completion my book to Prof. Chintamani Mahapatra who routinely encouraged me with his singularly, pertinent poser in front of his room with a Chinese Cup picture, "Yes. So which recent Book you are writing these days? You have written three Books na?" Such filial affection kept me going as I matured academically reading Chintamani Sir's tweets and posts on Facebook along with meetings with him at his office at the School of international studies in JNU. His one time corrections in the sequencing of the chapters enabled me to posit the content in an ordered, sequenced and organized manner. Yogendra Narain Sir always encouraged me with his kind words and vast experience in administration.

I dedicate the work to Shri T.N. Chaturvedi, Dr. T. Chatterjee and Prof. B.M. Sharma who provided the tangible platform for the author to enter the proud and hallowed portals of the pristine and historical, Indian Institute of Public Administration. It is their intellectual tutelage and the strident urge to simplify the "lingo" of my write ups that I managed a decent manuscript. Gone was the verbiage due to the "Training Day" at IIPA! My American Dream and the assiduous Oregon Trail, practically began at IIPA with my superheroes filled collage room at IIPA.

I owe a lot to the Gujarat National Law University, where I partially won my Super colors with the affectionate well wishes and fun-filled academic froth of the Gnlu Denizens, that is my students in Gnlu.

1

On the Grandiloquent American Dream

The Founding principle can be that America is the greatest nation in the International Firmament. The counter appellation amounts to the fact that US is in decline in the post mortgage economic crisis and the scenario of multipolarity in the global comity of States.

The *United States of America is the quintessential liberator; the regulator nation on a tormented and besmirched Earth.* The counter appellation amounts to the statement that the United States of America is a hegemonic and crassly domineering state.

America is the ideal amalgamation of all imaginable races and ethnic clusters and is the land of milk and honey with an amalgamative experience for all and sundry. The counter appellation is that the United States of America is marred with racial discrimination and gun violence.

Finally, the American Dream is constituted by an unfettered stream of 'Demos'; liberty, egalitarianism, freedom of speech, religion and the pursuit of happiness. It is the idea of the grand pursuit, where-in, idea of the grandiloquent American Dream lies ensconced in. The final counter appellation is that the American Dream is a first-world formulation which reneges on the entire promise of humanism and philanthropy. Strange. The debate between the good-world charm of America and the vile ministrations of United States subsist on the same Planet Earth! Solution: A caped crusader, a Superhero bearing the 'S' insignia of hope and liberty and let it be the much tried and tested, Kal-El aka Superman, leading on with the torch of helping the American denizens and the rest of humankind. Kal El festoons himself upon a troubled Earth with a fervent appeal to liberty, egalitarianism, fraternity, equity, freedom of speech and the love for the founding myth and cherished values. These are the litany of ideals of the founding fathers in United States which an often targeted and ridiculed nation and its processes, strive for, earnestly in surreptitious and persistent manners.

The refrain from the movie, ***Mackenna's Gold*** is rather speculative but aptly symptomatic of the trajectory of the dream of the American Growth. The Hollywood construct bespeaks of the rise and ebb in the tide of America. The theme song reflects the Gold Rush and the exploratory lore of the American Dream in the nineteenth century. The epoch is depicted by the ditty, "*The Red Indian Bustard, which flies through the Californian skies and below it are present the train of ants like labourers who flit across the semi arid mountain tops dunes in search of Gold.*" The song ends with the refrain that the Government is there to take care of all the tangibles and the denizens can bask in its all pervading glory and chutzpah. That is the American Dream as the group of adventurers, led, by Gregory Peck, compete with the gang of the gangsters in order to win the trail of gold in the wide wilderness. The spirit of adventurism and entrepreneurship, is a chief trait of the American experience and the Dream which leads to a well-made and mulled-over Public Opinion about 'the American way and the attendant Dream'. This is also the spirit behind the much deliberated upon and narrated Oregon Trail across the Rocky mountains near the quintessential Wild West.

Thus, voyage and discovery are part of the audacity of the myth and lore of the grandiloquent American Dream. Willaim Bradford reported in one of the annals of American History, "The pilgrims of the Mayflower Pact were supposed to land in Virginia but they indeed landed on the tip of Cape Cod. Eventually settled west in Plymouth, but Now they must of their necessity go to their own lots."[1] Other places which were occupied were the regions near Massachusetts Bay, Hartford Dorchester, Medford and New Haven. Behind the search for a new found land lay the desire for a safe haven from European persecution, religious intolerance, along with the fear of contiguous disease and the clamour for expansive lands. Thus, the pact of the mayflower children was juxtaposed with the genre of adventure and experimentation with the idea of migration and settlement in a New Foundland. This initial foray into North America soon led the way to the developments in constitutions, nationalism and revolution and a sense of being part of a different community, far removed from the European mainland. The spirit of enquiry is thus, a part of the timelessness of the American Dream. In Steven Spielberg's, cinematic venture, *Back to the Future*, released in 1985 along with its two other sequels, the entire mythical ambit of the American Dream can be traced out. For instance, the first part reveals the whacky and the roving seventies and the *Grease* generation in a mode when the male protagonist Michael J. Fox, arranges for his mother to fall in love for his boring Pa, after he travels back in time in a time-travelling four wheeler invented by a crazed scientist in 1985. Thus, the original tale of BTF-1, sets up the quintessential lore of the American Dream with a car, a pug and a girlfriend amounting to stolidity for the larger nation. Rather strange, but that's how the mundane domesticity of the American Dream attains its meaning and rigor from the commonalities of the routinised rituals. The movie furthers the soft power of the American Dream, where-in, the American finesse, clean Parisian cities, happy chirpy youth, colourful and feisty citizenry along with the 1980's fame, Police Jaguars with humane and stylish cops lording over civic security, was transported across seas to the deprived and neolithic societies. These neolithic constructs still laboured in the age of black-and-white television sets with fume-spouting Vespa scooters. Part Deux of the *Back to the Future*, depicts a slightly dystopian world, wherein, the narrative is premised in 2015 when the populations have started moving in flying cars and consume food-tablets instead of burgers, hotdogs, rams and pizzas. This sequel did not catch on much with the American dreamers and failed to entice the international audience too.

The final part of the Trilogy on time traversing, had a narrative which was premised upon the nineteenth century Wild West all replete with the ideals of the Oregon Trail. The crack of six guns and the sound of the hooves, rent the air as the bounty hunters clashed in the city square in the same town square which was witness to the antics of Michael J. Fox hundred years on in 1985. The tale is complete with the semi vegetated desert and arid canyons, buffalo races and the gunslinging matches between the city sheriff and the absconding cowboys. Their war cry still remains as the clarion call in the twenty-first century, "Where's My Lasso?" as part of an acquisitive, domineering civic and political strain of the American way. This is a celluloid saga and a cinematic depiction of the standard and quintessential American dream indeed which is dabbled in by scholars such as Roland Barthes and Cynthia Weber. They create and reiterate a myth out of the vast expanse of inspirational and aspirational life that the American Union is all about. Thus, the Dream is all about a burning desire and a rags-to-riches story, if not excelling in an exactitude of detail, but, in the sentiment of aspiring to become a Great Society as conceptualised by President Lyndon Baines Johnson, on the lines of Roosevelt's New Deal.

The American Dream is also about directness and straight forwardness of life and the honesty of purpose. For instance, President Abraham Lincoln, chose the ubiquitous Union over the practice of slavery, pretty discreetly and unambiguously. Lincoln is remembered to have said," My paramount object in this struggle is to save the Union, and is not either to save or to destroy slavery. If I could save the Union without freeing any slave I would do it, and if I could save it by freeing all slaves then I would do it, and if I could do it by freeing some and leaving others enslaved, then, I would promptly do that too."[2] Thus, the entire jurisprudence of race relations and racial discrimination proffered by the American nation is premised upon this pragmatism, where-in, the unity and integrity of the nation along with the workability of the "Dream," is a key 'achievable' for the American establishment and the constituent citizenry. *Antiquity* is another argument which permeates the matrices of the American political thought and way of doing Politics. The contemporary American stress on referring to the traditional aspects of American ideals such as passion for freedom, liberty, fraternity, constitutionalism and egalitarianism is all traced back to the idiom of history and "Antiquity". The Americans since the war of independence have always referred to the idea of passion in seeking freedom from the British rule. Though some of the American observers maintain that America utilizes the rhetoric of human values to an exaggerated level in order to carve out a rationale for its foreign policy and domestic acts and policy decisions. Still, in the author's view, all nations inclined towards greatness and progress have to take recourse to national ideals and underwritten and publicized national principles in order to serve the cause of national interest. The same moral truth holds true for the American nation, too. Thus, the larger-than-life-ideals of American idols might be a natural concomitant to the idea of how a progressive and powerful nation state takes prides in its prestige and power and intends to showcase it before the rest of the international community. Race is a different case in point where the arguments are pitted against United States of America but harking back to the founding ideals of the American freedom runs, one can account for the ingrained reminiscences of the American ideal of 'freedom and liberty' traditions.

Talking about race as an impediment for the grand success of the Democratic Dream, Malcolm X, too was part of the tenet of upward mobility and the *trance* to own a house for his wife and children in the Long Island. It was a move to move beyond the black neighbourhoods which sported one bedroom houses with a common room and large kitchen wherein, an apron clad Mama would flit around in haste to prepare a quick breakfast for her four fat, rotund and cute progeny. Thus, the challenged classes too were married to the idea of owning a house which was not a political statement but an economically viable decision too, in order to usher in a stability in the living standards and thus, "living up" to the grandiloquent American Dream. It is about how a nation is built around a set of morals and principles keeping in view the fissiparous trends which permeate the nook and cranny of a challenged nation astride difficult domestic and external challenges which are socio-political and economic in nature. It is not a platitude about simpleton nationalism and popcorn-domestic pelf, but, about how the Star-Spangled Banner got unfurled after the community of people in America decided to take charge of their "collective and special destiny".

Simon Serfaty, writes in *A World Recast* that while the critiques of the

American vision can be cynical, then why cannot the idiom of cynical optimism be developed as a defence for the American way and the country's foreign policy? George Santayana wrote that cynicism is the mark of great intellect and it is shameful to surrender it to the first comer or the first impressive gust.[3] Maybe that is the explanation behind all kinds of ridicule and exasperated criticism often bordering on to lampooning of the American way though its material prowess, which feeds a multitude of lives all across the militant global system. Bismark, too said, "My ideal for Foreign Policy is the freedom from prejudice, the independence of our decisions from impressions of dislike or affection for foreign states and their Governments."[4] Serfaty argues that it is about morality in pragmatism because the final test is about efficacy.[5] The mission to get rid of Osama bin Laden was a wager and a bet which would have been a risky mess in terms of diplomacy and military strategy had the Seals-led mission been unsuccessful. The American Dream also came through the Hollywood movie, *Zero Dark Thirty*, directed by Katherine Bigelow, which showcases the ten-year-long American investigative operation spanning the entire globe which culminated in the raid on the Abottabad sanctuary in Pakistan to liquidate Osama bin Laden on May 11, 2011. Thus, similar to President Bush's decision to invade Iraq, Obama's decision to give a nod for the Seal act in Pakistan and the 'taking out' of Gaddafi's sons in Libya, all amounted to a realistic and pragmatic wager which never had too much of a connect with, internationality and a nonaligned vision of being an "above-the-belt-nation". The Lone Superpower has always had it alone in the vicissitudes of conflict resolution and the 'invites' which were not commonly doled out to America.

Self-doubt is a self-seeking exercise which belittles the larger-than-life projects at national stabilisation and does not amount to blatant eulogisation as might be concluded about the rationale and the efficacy of the American Dream. The American youth in consonance with the studies undertaken by the national dailies such as *The Atlantic* have fretted and fumed about the rationale about the efficacy of the American Dream. The young Americans might be tempted to nomenclature it as, ***the 'American Dream-2.0'***, which has a great iota of scepticism and self-quizzing as part of the domestic and the external visage of the nation of milk and honey that America prides itself on. It might be a youthful fad after all, as the youngsters in the United States perceive upward mobility not as a well-paying vocation in Manhattan with tree lined houses in the Suburbia. The availability of wealth in coarse material denominations, is wrongfully regarded as the ticket to happiness and upward mobility. This might be a youngster fad which might be pinpointing towards a deleterious strain amounting to a dissenting strain. This once again questions the Mainstream moorings of the established popularity bastions in United States. Still, the notion of "the American Dream-2.0" is not a transition on to a decline as it can be invariably aligned with the troughs in any great power's odyssey to betterment, self-realisation and novae experimentation.

In *The Purge*, societal view happens to be very dystopian in its pictorial narrative and the script line. The storyline impinges upon the idea that the American Government decides in a national decree that the citizens can go ahead with killing and maiming their arch antagonists in the country with whom they have rivalries. Violence, beheadings and slayings are allowed on that particular day. The scenario is a scare scenario, which forecasts a dystopian world which can emerge as a putrid real-time scenario which will feature rule-ordained killings in tandem with the Hobbesian Anarchy and the stealthy State of Nature. Another futuristic Hollywood creation titled as *The Hunger Games*, pinpoints towards a state demarcated by the Government which is following hidebound environs of rebels who are militating against the American establishment with apocalyptic aims for themselves. The, entire scenario, can be conveniently brushed aside as a 'purgatory scenario,' which reeks within a post-civilisational world. The Americans thus, need not turn sour if the threat presented by insidious and perverse human strains are controlled before they take an unbridled and 'un-cocooned veneer,' in the near future. It is once again a myth justified. *The Purge* can be very much establishment-oriented to ascertain the longevity of the original, sepia-tinged and *Bugsy*-styled American Dream. No need for an American Dream-2.0 after all! ***The public sphere is still to be counted for a lot despite the mainstream misgivings with the web world in America.***

Since the earliest times, the public sphere is replete with instances of nations and populations yearning to find a voice for themselves. ***America was never an exception to the rule. This points to the simpleton and mortal existence of the nation before it attained super powers draped in the star and striped star-spangled banner.*** Nations also yearn for their formed staple public opinion to make an impact upon the domestic polities and the foreign and strategic policies for themselves. Taking a central pot shot, the United States of America, too, has a propensity of spawning of a MIM (Military Industry Media) complex. The MIM complex is a mutually co-habitative and supportive edifice which is part of the nation-building striving since the years United States of America has intervened in international conflicts and vitriolic situations in yonder nations. Since the historicity of Paul Revere going downtown to Lexington and the other principalities of Concord and Medford across the dark river to alert the Patriots, messaging and signalling have played a primordial role in settling the ferment of the American Republic. The Americans are a putatively proud nation with an avidly witnessed 'Rally around the Flag' phenomenon. These patriotic and stellar enunciations constitute the grand and cumulative American Dream with its attendant debates and deliberations which as one prismatic vision, pinpoint the specialty and greatness of the homeland and on the other, imbue the narrative with an innate critical overview about, what all is undesirable in the quintessential American dream. In the 21st century, contemporary amendments and improvements upon the fundamental stock of the American Dream, are a need of the hour. In the author's view, it is only then that the Universality and the global acceptability of the American Dream can be achieved. In the author's view, it is not at all essential that all nations accept the functionality of the Dream. Still, the fact that among the larger corpus of the developing world, the Dream still retains a pathway to be followed and in a multipolar World it can be further adapted to the changing realities in order to retain the utility of the American Dream at least as 'a key reference point'. The pursuit of dignity and the attainment of good life with self-respect and all-round acceptance for the American myth and lore is what the American Dream can be comprehended as. It is also the domesticity of the American Dream which should naturally hold attraction for the developing world apart from the divisive discourse on equity as apparent through the economics of international relations.

When one talks about the American Dream, then, apart from the sustainability of development, the looming skyscrapers and the honey-sweet domesticity of life in the land of milk and honey, wars and how to be triumphant in them, too wins our erudite and critical attention. The various genre of American wars can receive our special attention. Often castigated as 'manufactured consent' at the hands of the mechanics of the American establishment, the raw force of serving up and arranging for the love and sacrifice for the nation at the time of a crucial hour is a noble exercise. National interest's fulfillment demands efficient Public Opinion management which serves a benign purpose. It is the utilitarian role of the American establishment akin to any Government of the day to unabashedly serve and fulfill the national interest of the country in all perceivable ways, which can be naturally brought to relief.

The tale of the American 'Mt Sianism', maximalism, formidability, stupendous serendipity and preponderance, can be earmarked with the instance of the US–Spanish war in 1898. It was here that the owner of the *Hearst* chain of newspapers, William Randolph Hearst spawned a clarion call to his war correspondents to provide him with real pictures of the war and maiming. His journo war cry was, "You give me the pictures, I will give you the war." The Dirty War, that is the Vietnam war, is a case in point which witnessed the souring of the American dream, where-in, the visage of the American GIs' burning the Vietnamese hamlets with Zippo lighters and the gruesome imagery of choppers circling over the My Lai village atop the stale, stack of human corpses did enough damage to the US strategy of 'red containment' in the South East Asian frontiers.

Though, the tumult of the Veteran war veterans and the Persian Gulf War veterans, left some of them as questioning and shattered souls, still, the potency of the threat of insurgency and terrorism, cannot be relegated to the back-burner which is now being universally taken up, especially by the global community in tandem with the December, 18, 2015 Resolution of the UNSC. It is led by the likes of US Secretary of State, John Kerry in the context of Syria and the Daesh in the context of its defeats in Tikrit and parts of Ramadi in Iraq and in Kobane and Al Abyad in Syria. There has to be an intentional and deliberate effort in media and public opinion management in order to rev up the national intent but definitely it should be tempered with a human delimitation, where-in, the transgressions of life and liberty should not make the mandarins scurry for cover. The jokes and tirades aimed at President George Bush are a case in point, wherein, the Bush Regime received a Manicheastic portrayal of its decisions and policy-making in Iraq and elsewhere. Though it is undeniable that a randomisation of the matrix-like-public sphere, took place with President Saddam Hussein too getting a demonised veneer at the hands of the American Public Diplomacy.

The Iraq War's instances of President Bush alighting upon the USS Abraham Lincoln in a soldier outfit and addressing the marines is part of a larger maritime-diplomatic tradition which resonates well with America's domestic and international audience. The same 'halo-landing' has been attempted successfully by President Obama too in Iraq and Afghanistan's 'long wars'. The incident of American Private Jessica Lynch falling prey to the Iraqi fire and fighting on till getting grievously wounded and being finally rescued by a group of American GIs in the dangerous streets of Baghdad, is another case in point. This sheds enough light on the role which the mainstream media portals such as the *CNN*, *Fox News* etc. played in spawning an 'echophonic impact' for a strong and potent America with serendipitous impact and rightly so.

Granted, that Mainstream Media are part of a Monopoly as observed by Ben Bagdikian, still, the unifying and the 'rallying role-playing' have a crucial role to play in communicating the national sentiment and its meaningful communicable intent. This is what the grandiloquent American Dream is all about. In the context of the Syrian war and the US policy vis-à-vis countering ISIS in Iraq, too, the lethal group has ignited sentiments all across the global firmament. The utility of brutal and inhuman 'imaging' as part of the virtual 'Simulacra,' cannot be overemphasised in the present narrative of the US policy in West Asia. Guantanamo might be insane but the public slitting of throats by the ISIS terrorists is an exercise in heinous man slaughter. It is their Public Diplomacy, and the American establishment too wages its own mechanics of Public Diplomacy. President Obama made up for what had transpired earlier in his Al Azhar Speech in Cairo in 2009, where, he offered an explanation and a hand of friendship to the besieged West Asia. In his later day statements, he declared the closure of Guantanamo and it is he who sketched the American withdrawal from Iraq and Afghanistan. Thus, a revision and a refurbishing of the US policy was attempted with mixed domestic and international responses. The point is that the Presidential speeches and the symbolic and the tokenish value of the policy statements too make for a more than a 'plane jane messaging' as the idiom of Public Diplomacy is served by these public utterings and meaningful posturing.

What President Franklin Delano Roosevelt initiated in Buenos Aires in Latin America in 1935 finds its indelible imprint through the posturing and the Media-Establishment interface even in the twenty-first century amidst a resurgent but cautious US in a post-recession reality. Communication through imageries and imaginative and colourful star-and-striped narratives is an exercise in the nation's image projection. In the author's view, it is this Public Diplomacy part in the context of the American image projection which is an essential element of advancing the country's national interest. The propagation of a country's myth and tales in the author's opinion is a matter of great pride and has a utilitarian role for the nation. In the author's view, the projection of comic book superheroes and Cinema bearing patriotic storylines was systematically carved out as a foreign policy and Public Diplomacy instrument during and after the World War-II days. The Superman's 'S' insignia might be of a Cold War origin, but, the post-September 11 times have meant newer flights and unfathomed trajectories for the superhero in a 'kryptonite'-ridden pathway.

The same narrative runs true for the theme of the American Dream, the mythical Oregon trail to the Wild west and its tale of inception through the founding myth of the United States. Dreams are the origins of all greatness and extraordinary human endeavours and their veritable outcomes. This stands truly tested through a look at human evolution. Still, the critiques of the myth and the lore of a national dream, hit out at all the emotive and subjective aspects of it. This criticism is accompanied by ridicule and finally an acrid acceptance when the intent of great nations, such as the United States, are realised by the larger mankind. That national arriving at greatness might be an Asian nation such as India, too. In the author's view, the only roadblock being that the critiques of national ethos and nationhood theories should believe in the idea of a country being a nation. The same runs true for the quintessential discourse of the American Dream and the related criticism and the vitriol which is attempted at the American nation and its hallowed Dream. Every citizen is a dreamer who wishes to attain the good life and its related accouterments for himself or herself. In the author's view, Dream chasers thus, should not be castigated and belittled because of the supernatural and supinely subjective quality of their uprightness and hard-working but expectant ethos and the ethics of self-improvement. This brings us to the fact that dreams are a rare mettle and nations such as America cut out their own exceptionalism and ordinary mortality through this exercise of dreaming aloud and strong with global and universal conviction. In the author's view, Americans utilize a great deal of grandiose vocabulary and rhetoric along with bombast in order to communicate with the rest of the comity of nations. In the context of the American revolution, the American revolt was often castigated as being aimed against British rule which was not exploitative and oppressive. In the light of the reality of British scheming in United States, the words such as, "Liberty", "fraternity", "anti-corruption" and "equality" which were utilized by the American Patriots were no misnomers. These words and adjectives were a passionate expression of the way the American dream was forged in the initial days of the American Republic.

In relation to the American Dream, the American narrative emerges from the emphasis on the social and political strains and class cleavages which permeated the colonies and even the happiest and the most egalitarian colonies such as Virginia. John Adams during the Philadelphia convention in 1787, spoke that, "Several colonies do not exist in an egalitarian framework and social equity does not abound." He was referring to the state of hidden discontent of colonies such as Virginia. It is these internal divisions and internal perceptions about internal turmoil in the American colonies which led to the creation of the grandiose American vocabulary about inequity, disorder and inhumanity in the larger world which was dutifully transmitted to the realm of the global community.

If I were a dreamy sceptic flag-wielder, then, I would delve into what catches America's attention in a foremost manner. So, I present the sceptic's version of the American Dream, maybe, an American Dream-2.0. That happens to be the question of Gun Violence including gunrunners such as Martin Rice and others at Ferguson, North Carolina and Baltimore. They 'opened up' before the audiences and let loose a"performance frenzy" in the name of mental instability and manic behavior all culminating into unbridled crime. But before they could be curtailed, hundreds of lives were lost. This has never been the American Dream despite the often reported incidents of gunrunning and homicide violence in the nation's domestic firmament.

Gun culture has given a torrid time to the evangelical zeal in United States. Though it might appear trite and bordering on to the historical and the normative, the theme of gunrunning with the attendant travesty of the Police action and behaviour has raised a lot of alarm in the American civil society, campus groups, the media players and the so-called cantankerous international community. The American toehold in public imagination requires more than a facelift. The wars in the Middle East and North Africa lift up the stupor over the international community as the dictum of preemptive action and imminent threat clinically disrupt the stolid swan song of the American Dream.

Gun-running is one of the staple brickbats which is being utilised to browbeat the Americans with a novae lore in 'negativity' and 'manicheastic portrayals' which has unassumingly become everybody's pet peeve. No society can be polemically sacrosanct and every nation-state is bedevilled with the firestorms of sociological controversies and fabrications–exaggerations of the worst degree. The viscerally attuned imagery of homeless bearded men sleeping disconsolately over plastic wraps and the staple scenario of Black middle-aged mothers scurrying around in one-bedroom houses to prepare breakfast for the four children, too, remains embedded as an imagery when an astute questioning of the American dream is in the political offing. Gunrunning and the attendant gun violence too foists itself as the same categorisation in the realm of stymieing the critically posited American pie.

In the context of gun-running, lobbying plays a significant role in charting out the trajectory of law, order and security in the nation. The lawyers since the last few decades have played a significant role in spawning a legal front against the scourge of cancer, other diseases, environment, energy and finally gun-related violence. The incidents of Waco in Texas, the far reaches of the Sinaloa drug cartel in the sand-kissed twilight zones of United States and Mexico, along with the American enforcement agents named as 'The Fast and Furious agents' have been the prime protagonists of the debate for a while. The practice of letting the guns 'walk' and then following the investigative trail in the badlands of Chicago have led to a few fiascos which have questioned the strategy of the enforcement instruments in the United States. Sportspersons and Hollywood stars such as Charlton Heston go all the way with the gun lobby in the United States. The anti-gun grouping arranged for finances and solicited the support of law firms spread all across the nation in order to create a legal and civil societal case against the gun lobby, nationally. This earned them the love of the maelstrom and more than engaging accolades throughout the global public sphere. The activism at one point of time won important legal battles and created a much needed awareness amongst the citizenry.

Chicago stood out as the battle station for the entire gamut of law enforcement agencies, wherein, gun buyers were followed assiduously and the age group of the illicit buyers, the profession of the buyers and the socio-cultural set up of the owners, was studied objectively for the first time. It turned out as a result of investigations that beyond the press corps rom-coms organised by both the legal fraternities, across the legal divide, youngsters and mostly students enrolled in schools and colleges utilised the guns for weekend gaming purposes and for 'stag-get togethers'. This incendiary trend is located amidst the development of small-arms trafficking too. It is here that the question of who owns the guns at the receptacle end, becomes a poignant matter of consideration.

The idea of untrammelled dissent and rebellion against the system is elucidated beautifully in John Updike's novel, *Terrorist* which brings to the fore, the tense and cussed spiral of school life for a high-school student, Ahmad, who is sought to be mainstreamed by a guidance counsellor, Jack Levy. The restive nature of the marginalisation felt by the youth is poignantly brought forth in the engaging narrative which reflects on what has gone wrong with the American school system. It is not reflective of the 'wrongs only' but how these rough edges of the American myth can be straightened and pedicured to pack more than a punch for a concern which is both an American domestic engagement and a global issue consequent a serendipity.

It is in the spawning of these purchases in Chicago and a few other places that the psychological checks on the buyers are not required in some states. In the follow up, these guns 'walked' through to incidents which took several innocent lives and 'made coarse' the razzmatazz of the euphoric school and college zeal which amounts to an quintessential American imagery domestically and for the rest of the viewing audiences, globally. Chicago itself fought a dodgy legal battle for its sheer survival on a bankruptcy issue. This development needs to be taken into consideration as vacant parking lots and shrubbery infested vacant mansions serve as the ideal playgrounds for gun-related crime. John Ashcroft, the ex-Governor of Missouri, played a leading role in pinpointing one sporadic case, which included increasing the serving bench strength of the law enforcing officers in Missouri. This augmented the prison's capacities in the state and included tougher provisions of standards and punishment for bringing guns within the schools.

One calculation in 2014 posits that mass shootings have not increased in the United States if one goes by the FBI definition of mass shooting which amounts to the killing of four or more people at a go. Still, the law enforcement agencies are in a staple fix when they have to pinpoint the psychiatric status of a gun criminal as different states pursue different laws. While some more conveniently follow the Federal Law related to gun crime. One argument posits that there must be a clampdown on the people who were once convicted of gun violence as they might inflict further mayhem. And, the spectacularr nature of mass murders with the victims being children ought not to be the stick with which to browbeat the practice. But, even domestic violence and other general categories of gun crime need to be primarily booked. An observation which can be formulated is that, in summation, the myriad macho credentials are not the true-blue characteristics of the American strength and omniscience. Predominantly witnessed is the dexterity with which entrepreneurship and 'smart democratic and participative policy' is made and implemented in the domestic sphere in the nation.

Iconic Icons...

"Who saw the Hollywood sign First?", "Me!", "When?", "When I was five", "How Do you Know?", "My parents took me up to the servatory and they said I pointed to it". This was overheard at the Fern Dell playground in Griffith Park near the present day Hollywood.

Leo Braudy writes in the *Hollywood Sign* that there are icons by accident and icons on purpose. Leon writes,

> "Mount Rushmore and the Statue of Liberty were built to be iconic, the focus of attention and meaning. But, Big Ben and the Eiffel Tower, like the Hollywood sign, accrued meaning over the years. Before World War II, for example, the significance of Big Ben was more local. Wars and the aftermath of wars are the fertile grounds for new icons to flourish. Uncle Sam existed as an image since the nineteenth century. But, it was James Montgomery Flagg's World War I poster depicting the character's top hat, pointing finger and stern expression sign which portrayed—I want you for the US Armythat made him a nationally recognized and widely imitated icon. Similarly, the visual imagery of the mobilization effort for World War-II, the Liberty Bell, the Statue of Liberty and Uncle Sam, played even wider roles than before."[6]

Thus, in the author's view, symbolism plays an ardent and greatly communicative role in the genre of promoting the nationalist, patriotic spirit and finally, an integrative sentiment for nations, with America being no exception to the rule. The United States has always flourished on icons and symbols to communicate its prosperity and unbridled philanthropic zeal to the domestic constituents and the foreign powers, leading on to the culture of a generic and generous culture of being a perennial and Universal, Do-Gooder, Super State. Some scholars have called it the Hyper-puissance of the Super State.

Related to the myth of the Man of Steel, is the imagery of the Statue of Liberty. The Statue of Liberty has been iconically depicted in the *Superman* movies, which, are symptomatic of what the American Dream is all about and much more. The American myth gets a prominent display in a scene out of the *Superman* movie. Once upon a humid evening, Superman alights on the terrace garden of Lana Lang who is Clark Kent's (Superman's alter ago in city life) co-worker in the *Daily Planet*. Superman embraces her as part of a romantic interlude and makes her fly all around the Statue of Liberty with the twinkling stars and the lights illuminating the hundreds of skyscrapers all around the Manhattan cityscape. In another setting, a manic bodybuilder who can fly like our Man of Steel, has been created by Lex Luthor, the vile scientist. The new villain uproots the large Statue of Liberty and attempts to hurl it at the Manhattan civilians. Superman arrives on the scene and catches the hurtling Statue all the while being scorched and burnt by the heat rays being thrown by the Villain at him. Thus, the desecration of these icons amounts to a belittlement and defacing of the American Dream itself like any other nation in Asia, Africa or South America. It's a Regime of humanism and philanthropy that the author is talking about similar to the Global Regimes of counter-terror, Climate Change, migration, arms-drug trafficking and human rights. The Man of Steel, is, thus, the saviour and the defender of the American nation, its citizenry, and, the-all-encompassing myth, of the grandiloquent American Dream. In the movie, Man of Steel's musical score, the singer intones that, "It's not easy being me and I am neither a plane, a bird or a streak of light beyond a train." In the view of the author, the endearing vulnerability of the Maximalist is thus clinically brought to the fore.

The Hollywood sign atop the mountain top near the Griffith Park in Los Angeles, is another such icon which millions of people across the globe have learned to identify with the American power and the scintillating national Dream. Hollywood, since its creation in the early twentieth century, has learned to market and spawn the Dream in various forms through its innovative and imaginative content which is meant for global consumption. The sign at the base of the hill bearing the Hollywood icon bears a "No Tresspassing" message through a board which itself communicates what the City on the Hill stands for. There was health to be gained in California and as Leon Braudy writes,

> "Heavy Industry, Alcohol, potentially contaminating minorities, and crime were to be banished so that individuals and social health could reign supreme. Even the growing progressive politics of California bought into some of those fears by emphasizing the need for Eugenics, a theory of racial renewal popularized by Francis Dalton a cousin of Charles Darwin in 1883. Early Feminists like Charlotte Gilman, who wrote *Herland*, about a Utopian world without men, while living in Pasadena, as well as Jack London, who championed Neitzchean ideas, about a super race, slip back and forth across the line between what might be called positive Eugenics for improving health and general human character."[7]

Another issue related to the larger-than-life-iconography of Hollywood, which the American Dream cherishes, is the sphere of a movie reel within the characters. Real-time characters like Charlie Chaplin, Fred Astaire, Daidea Wilcox and others, were, placed to reside in large mansions which caught the fancy of the entire informed population of the American nation. These couples, first-time stars and starlets, spawned a new system of stars in movies and they were playing similar roles in their company's movies, along with the lavish mansion house and poplar-lined personal lifestyles which they enjoyed. Thus, there was a vicarious, voyeuristic and virtual reality of the silver screen which matched with the individual lives of these select brand of, "The Bold and Beautiful," which, was eulogised and popularised as part of the founding myth of an America on the rise and on the glitzy pathway to global chutzpah. Thus, the Hollywood Billboard existing upon the hill in Los Angeles emerged as part of the symbolic pantheon and iconography of the American Union and the attendant grandiloquent Dream.

Another snippet out of the glitz of the American iconography makes for important reading. Leon Braudy writes,

> "The Lightening of the Hollywood sign by 4,000 twenty watt bulbs, another crucial element in its ability to be seen at a distance, may have been influenced by the ubiquitous wooden derricks in Los Angeles, otherwise an eye sore, that had for some time been rigged out with electric lights as part of the publicity for the oil industry. Electricity and not much later, neon and searchlights were quickly becoming some of the necessities of American Advertising, especially when it came to the movies. But, the most path-breaking event, was, the lavish premiers organized by Sid Grauman at his Egyptian and Chinese Theatres which were already part of the growing "Hollywood" image as a prime entertainment center. The initial movies which ran for months at large were with Douglas Fairbanks in Robinhood in 1922, while the first film at the Chinese theater, was, Cecil B. DeMille's, King of Kings."[8]

Thus, in author's view, the Hollywood Insignia followed by the Superman, "S" insignia, were, the all important tapestry of an arty tribal and earthy symbolism, which breathed fire into the sentiment of nationalism and patriotism and percolated down the nation's pantheon of imagery as the father-figure imagerics of the nation and its attendant American Dream. Thus, kilos of aspirations typified by the hoi polloi in the American Union, were, reflected by these sugar-coated, but, stolid manifestations of the grandiloquent American Dream.

Poet and World War I veteran, Archibald MacLeish, once wrote, "The courage of the Declaration of Independence is the courage of the act of the imagination. Don't believe it? Quick, and, the date of British General Cornwallis's surrender at Yorktown. Can't Do it? But, very schoolchild knows the day we declared ourselves a free people." Dan Rather writes,

> "The American Dream was the idea that guided us through the early days of the republic. And, it was the ideal that was compromised in the drafting

> of a Constitution that, for all its strength and stirring appeals to universal law, left African Americans in Chains and women without Franchise. It is this vision that has brought millions of immigrants to a land where a better life is possible and it held the blind spot that allowed the massacre and scattering of the Native American nations that called this continent home long before any European imagined it. It demands noting here that theirs were the first American Dreams."[9]

Thus, the act of sailing across the Atlantic by the Mayflower Pilgrims was in itself a Dream vocation which was directed by a larger-than-life vision as dreamt by the European migrants working on royal grants and personal sense of self-preservation and growth. The odyssey across the seas was a Dream which came true after the crests and troughs marked by the trajectory of the American nation. The Dream came true and the American Dream-2.0 emerges as a challenge to the stolidity and the strength of the American nation.

Dan Rather, the celebrated war correspondent, whose persona and work, is itself, very much emblematic of the American Dream, has penned several stories which showcase the strength of the nation and the true and welcoming nature of the American myth and reality, which the 'Dream,' makes, very much its own. When all else fails, Americans have the right, as the last phrase of the First Amendment tells us, "to petition the Government for a redress of grievances." Dan Rather writes,

> "Tsuyako Kitashima, who later on became known as "Sox" lived through one of the greatest injustices perpetrated by the Federal Government in the twentieth century to the imprisonment of 120,000 Japanese and Japanese Americans in the early months of the United State's entry into World War II. The Japanese citizens were paraded off into separate camps and were conscripted in the US military. The families were, like the family of Kitashima "Sox", camped for a few years in the camps where the fundamental facilities of living were missing and the quarters where Sox's family was ensconced, had been a horse stable, before, it was converted into camp quarters for the Japanese citizens of American origin."[10]

Rather further writes,

> "The Japanese who had suffered due to World War II, petitioned the American White House to ameliorate the concerns of the Japanese-Americans. The White House response arrived which said that, "A monitory sum and words alone cannot restore the years or erase painful memories. Neither can they fully convey our nation's resolve to rectify the injustice and to uphold the rights of the individuals. We can never fully right the wrongs of the past, but, we can take a clear stand for justice and recognize that serious injustices were done to Japanese Americans during World War II. In enacting a law calling for restitution and offering a sincere apology,

> your fellow Americans have, in a very real sense, renewed their traditional commitment to the ideals of freedom, equality and justice. You and your family, have, our best wishes for the future."[11]

Thus, the lady, Sox-Kitashima, definitively felt bad about the treatment meted out to her family and the family had to burn off the pictures of Japan and the Japanese Emperor even to escape the wrath of the American espionage agents. Once she was given a job and she settled down to a vocation with her family, then she sort of forgot the predicament, which her family and the rest of her stock had to live through during World War II. It was American Dream-2.0 which had already been lived by the Japanese Americans.The nation glued on together and the bad visages were gradually, relegated, to the backburner. This is consonant with the American founding myth. Thomas Jefferson contends, "It is neither wealth nor splendor, but, tranquility and occupation, which give happiness." Thus, the idea and the practice of the pursuit of happiness, plays a powerful role in the resuscitation and sustenance of the national myth.

Delores Pass Kesler used a 10,000 $ loan in 1977 to found a temporary staffing agency in Jacksonville, Florida. When she retired from the Board of Directors of Sccustaff in 1997, the company she had formed through a series of mergers, had projected revenues of 2$ billion. We as observers of the American Dream and the Myth might contend that such figures are magical 'figures and unreal'. Rather writes in his compendium of stories about the Dream,

> "My Dream was never to have a million dollars or five million dollars. That was never the gluttonous dream. The money is almost—And I know someone will say this can't be true—but its almost coinciendental. Really? How is it that millions of Dollars can be called coincidental? Does that kind of wealth just happen? In some ways, the answer is, Yes. That does not discount the value of hard work, careful planning and having the right idea at the right time. Every successful business starts with these elements. But something else, call it the invisible hand, the free market, the American way, or whatever you will, sets those elements in motion and rewards renewed effort with momentum. That is how the contributions of a single person or a small group can become an unstoppable force."[12]

The twentieth and twenty-first century America is a different ball game altogether with castigations amounting the American pathway of progression despite whatever domestic pelf is displayed on the shop front. The United States is often perceived as a hegemon with an quasi-imperialistic agenda spanning the regions where it had militarily intervened ranging from regions such as Vietnam, Panama, Grenada, Nicaragua, Guatemala and now in Afghanistan, Libya, (indirect intervention) Syria (indirect intervention) and directly in the tarred land of Iraq. Operation "Iraqi Freedom and Enduring Freedom" in Iraq became the bywords for renewed American expansionism during the George W. Bush Administration. Washington was immensely criticised in the name of maintaining international peace, cooperation, and democratisation and for the avowed zeal to sustain the human rights regime in the entire ambit of the international system. In the author's view,this academic–cultural endeavour will take up the American issue since its inception from the days of the Mayflower Pact and the American Bill of Rights, till the flowering of the mentality of being on a mission to Regulate' the global polity in a philanthropic manner.

This has been perceived to be the central operating thesis of the United States of America. This has changed since the days of the post-Cold War era, post-September 11 and post-2008 economic decline times. The socio-economic impact of the American immigration policies as perceived by the international establishment and the people of foreign origin too, forms a new dimension of the US Policy. This academic work dwells upon the premise of the US Foreign Policy which was characterised by the Policy of containment, the stress on anti-Communism, Macrythism, and the general encirclement of the Warsaw Pact countries in the 'good old halcyon days' accentuated by the grand American Dream. The US foreign policy with its stance towards West Asia with a special emphasis on the coalitions with Egypt and Israel and the international criticism attributed to the selfsame policy, will too form a matter of discussion. Also, a parallel development in the context of American policy interventions in Latin America as a further extension of the containment policy, will form another section of the work. Then, meta-narratives of the order of cultural extractions, Hollywood's cinematic lore and the myth-making functions of International Politics, will constitute the 'internecine tell-tale tales' in the stream of change in the US Foreign Policy over two decades. The US inactions in Rwanda, and the non-interventions in Yugoslavia and Kosovo, too, form the transformative point in the general tenor of the US Foreign Policy tale which has earned a general iota of global brickbats. It might seem to be belittling for a nation which is used to paeans being sung for it and its myriad achievements, still, the "Other" and "the Perennial and Forever Bugbear" has to be curtailed, mastered and countered. This serves as a counter-narrative to objectify the myth and the lore of domineering which necessitates a "Yes, We can" certitude down the ages in the times of President Barack Obama. It is here that the faltering of United States as a superpower and the American realisation of multi-polarity and institutionalism, forms another significant part of the narrative.

The US Foreign Policy that has changed from the World War II years and the Cold War years of 'confrontation' to 'constructive engagement' with the world at large including India has the welcome vacationing trend for the entire international system. Then, the rise of BRICS, the much-decreased role of the

Non Aligned Movement, the rise of China as a contending power and the shift of the pivot of power from the Atlantic to the Pacific, has initiated a new phase which is ingeniously grappling with a much deliberated upon post-US world order. Also, the running theme of US counter-terror campaign after the September 11 attacks will earmark the change in the US strategic and foreign policies in the narrative. The post-US decline as perceived through the 2008 economic recession and the change in the West Asian dynamics after the Arab Spring, adroitly posits the advent of a post US international order. The rise in the might of China and its clash with India along with the American policy choices will form another facet of the work. What needs to be realized is that in a world dotted by a much perceived American Decline, a widening gap between rhetoric and reality will only lead to cynicism. The strategic and political gap can be narrowed by establishing habits of cooperation that can withstand the vicissitudes of change, whether it be of governments or priorities in a post-US international system if the world dares to embark on any.

The post-US order, as it is called by some scholars, includes the idea of the rise of Asia and hesitantly, the "peaceful rise of People's Republic of China: the now genuflecting Panda". The South Asian context too needs to be touched upon as a significant facet of the American Foreign Policy with an emphasis on India and the general territoriality of the Af-Pak region. In the changed South Asian context, the Indo-US relations have undergone a remarkable transformation during the last fifteen years. Today, there is close cooperation between the two countries on the issues of far-reaching consequences, such as the use of nuclear energy, space technology for peaceful purposes, dual-use technology, the 123 nuclear agreement, research and development cooperation, scientific cooperation, higher education exchanges and missile defence.

Along with this is the intertwined idea of China's rise and the general narrative on the Asian pivot. Along with it the American interface with theWest Asia, South America and the anti-war and humanitarian movements in the recent past, form another indispensable part of the narrative. Still, a few signposts need to be touched upon with the attendant historicity of the American developmental trajectory if a comprehensive view and a deeper understanding of the 'American situation and the Dream' can be finally flagged off.

NOTES

1. Jim Cullen, *The American Dream: A Short History of an Idea that Shaped a Nation* (Oxford University Press, 2003), p. 25.
2. Ibid., p. 95.
3. George Santayana, *Skepticism and Abnormal Faith* (New York: Scribner, 1923), p. 29.

4. A.J.P. Taylor, *Bismark: The Man and the Statesman* (New York: Vintage Books, 1967), p. 47.
5. Simon Serfaty, *A World Recast: An American Moment in a post-Western Order* (New York: Rowman and Littlefield Publishers, 2012), pp. 10-15.
6. Leon Braudy, *The Hollywood Sign: Fantasy and Reality of An American Icon* (Yale: Yale University Press, 2011), pp. 100-125.
7. Ibid., p. 19.
8. Ibid., pp. 78-79.
9. Dan Rather, *The American Dream: Stories from the Heart of Our Nation* (New York: William Morrow, 2001), pp. 12-15.
10. Ibid., pp. 28-29.
11. Ibid., pp, 36-37.
12. Ibid., p. 43.

2

The Grand and Star Spangled American Dream: A Historical Enquiry

The great American experiment developed upon a dynamic which was wedded to the narrative of adventurism, agile vigilantism and entrepreneurship. The name United States of America was such an exercise in nomenclature which never invited the wrath or the attention of the international system. It is here that the tribalism of the indigenous concerns was a notion which reflected what America was all about in the immediate days after the Mayflower journey in the early sixteenth century global system. The United States of America as we know it today, developed gradually without much fanfare in stark isolationism. Its developmental process was buttressed upon by the notion of an identificatory calculus of self-doubt. Uncle Sam,the redoubtable Uncle Sam as the earnest military supply provider of the American army was cast and recast in an odyssey of redoubtable ramifications.

The early infrastructural and material success with which the New World seethed within the context of United States, was something (the initiation of a civilisational dream) that was never considered to be premised upon a firm footing.The Calvinistic ethos of a grand civilisational self-doubt was always touched upon recurrently and repeatedly by the American founding fathers. The political mandarins, the able leaders and others, all of which has gone into the making of the United States, the grand but reliable experiment that it is. The success story of the American nation was premised upon the idea of anticolonialism and the grand adherence to the Lockean ideal of Liberalism. These can be earmarked as the founding knell of the American nation. Still, the self-doubt that the American experiment, far removed from the Security Dilemmas of a fluid politique in the Europe, can besmirch the progress attained till the early years of the American experiment. This has remained a grand doubt in the American milieu. The fear that autocracy and authoritarianism could have subsumed the prototype American civilisation exemplifying a rebellion from the staid monarchy in Great Britain, always knelt dearly on the American nation's shoulders. Also, the American founding fathers could not trust the Booms and Busts of the economic spiral in the heydays of the American experiment. Thus, a zeal to better the past performance as a nation, as a society and as an economy ruled the roost in the American lore. These issues in author's view, went on to build the grand American myth in a decade-by-decade amalgam of growth and capitalistic–mercantile production ethos.

Also, the American system revels in this self-inflicted Calvinist self-doubt, wherein the presence of self-help myths such as Superman, Avengers, etc. can be counted on entirely to extricate the nation out of trouble, whenever the circumstance calls for. Also, the nation strives for bettering its past in a race with the past in order to dwell upon a much more stable and rarified future which makes the nation don the mantle of the most powerful and influential nation-state on the face of Mother Earth. It is similar to a kind of Mothership on the global celestial and astronomical space frontiers as frontiers remain as another quintessential concern with the American dream. The pallor of gloom at the prejudiced jealousy and inferiority at the other's progress and advancement is not the trajectory tale of United States of America. On the other hand, in author's view, it is the sentiment of striving for the pinnacle and for the legendary Mount Sinai which is the guardian and abiding tale of the nation. Rhetoric and glad Bombast have always been the mainstay of the Republic since the times of the American Republic. It is here that past undoings and a want of hard work can be unmade and a novae trajectory of national strivings can become the order of the day. It is not a polemic argument but a way with the national world which kicks off the national game with verve and determination.

Cinematic constructs have a sway over national and global imagination as the author has asserted several times. In the same continuation,the imagery of the Hollywood construct *Independence Day* can be evoked in the realm of the American Dream. The much invasive and menacing Mothership tormented all the powerful nations of the world ranging from China, India, Japan, the former Soviet Union and the United States in the film's narrative. The fundamental 'right to live' as comprehended in an unimpeded manner by the Earthlings is threatened in a very up, close and a personal manner. It takes a kamikaze derelict, a Vietnam veteran who is also an alcoholic, to decimate the alien Mothership with a last suicidal dash into the womb of the alien Mothership. The American President speaking from an open cockpit of an F-16 in a hidden Nevada Desert location too exhorts the remaining sinews of earthly resistance. He implores, "We will not go down without a fight. We will not perish into the stately and gloomy night. We will gear up for the offensive. We the American boys will gather all the strength that is left in the entrails of the World Republic and we shall survive." Thus, the grand and logical, viscose rayon smooth and iconic American Inchon was never a perplexing animal. The Founding fathers along with the open culture of debate and political protest intertwined with the quintessence of the peace, stability and warmth of the hearth, was often extolled. Challenges to national security/homeland welfare and national domicile were posited as objective challenges to the nation. The leadership of the ideal charm of the politicians and thinkers, such as, Walt Whitman and inventors such as John Ford and business philanthropists such as Carnegie and Rockerfeller were signposts of an incessant, cleansing and strengthening elements of the national dream and an attendant valour.

It was a great reprieve from the stiff upper lip and sardonically royale experience of the British knights pitted against the verve, innovation and determined vocational zeal of the all-class American dreamers. The dream to own property, a respectable home and to win the winsome rights to speak out one's mind, travel across the Appalachians and bear the brunt of the oppositional elements of the greats of the order of Abraham Lincoln, remained a part of the dream. Such is the prima facie foundation which the stolid and translucent American Dream is perched upon in an international system in the twentieth and the twenty-first centuries. This has included the rise of the new state and non-state actors. The 'American Dream' still runs as a subterranean context in the larger idiom of the American foreign policy.

Jim Cullen writes in his *The American Dream*,

> "The American dream would have no Drama or mystique if it were a self evident falsehood or a scientifically demonstrable principle. Ambiguity is the very source of its mythic power, nowhere more so often than among those striving for, but, unsure whether they will reach their goals. Instead there are many American Dreams, their demand simultaneously resting on their variety and their specificity what James Truslow Adams called in the epilogue of the *Epic of America*, "that dream of a land in which life should be better and richer and fuller for every man may be fine as far as it goes, but the devil is in the details, just what does better, richer and fuller mean."[1]

Thus, in author's view, it is apparent that there are nuanced and multiplicity of rituals, myths and uncodified flights of fancy working as the well defined sectors of the American Dream. To an uninitiated soul, twenty-first century Americans might appear very haughty and fraught with the ills and fancies of a superiority complex but unlike the British stiff upper lip they seem to be boasting about a fact that theirs is a nation which is dignified, decent and the most powerful and the prescient nation state on the face of the Earth.

More Ado about the Dream

It is not that through the instrumentality of the American Dream, the myriad larger-than-life-American idioms can be equated as mere rhetoric and assumptions premised upon rhapsodical subterfuge and generic platitudes. The ideal dreamer is a vaunted lot who premised his imagination on what does not exist existentially. The American Dream, too, weaves an understanding that it is not the prerogative of the establishment singularly, which needs to be deciphered and attained. Apart from the super puissance of the American Government, the idols amongst the citizenry too have to be activated. What the scenario of the American Founding fathers reads like, is that the citizens should be highly calibered in order to manage a nation and the higher but innately subaltern notion of the American Dream.

The 'Demos' of the nation, that is, America had to be resurrected after the revolutionaries had militated against the British King primarily premised upon the notion of, "No Taxation without Representation." The Boston Tea party incident and the Townsend Acts were other signposts of the way in which America ignited from a sleeping giant to a raving and roving dynamo of growth and progression with one big heave to oust the British through the Battle of Saratoga and others in the pristine and untouched homeland, 'la terrain'. This was the conception of an ideal and proactive citizen which was well deliberated upon in the founding myth of the agile American nation, waking up to the twilight saga of greatness and global pelf.

The Greek conception of being a citizen was marred by class distinctions wherein the Spartans and the Athenians forbade the non-endowed masses to don the mantle of kings, who had to belong to the class of the Philosopher Kings. The rest of the masses had to be duty-bound denizens who would grow food, catch fish, hunt game, make pottery and fight the battles of hallejulah, death and glory. The American Republic displays disdain for the drudgery of class distinctions, wherein the American populace could own property, run for elections and participate in debates and finally even dream for the extremity of running for the Presidential Office. Thus, class distinctions could have been socially divisive, but, the all-egalitarian and the "just cause' of all-around national flatness of endowment was one of the key artefacts of the American experiment. Thus, citizenry was the all essential and god-gifted human capital which had to be tasked and harnessed in order to task the nation on the pathway of progression and enhancement. The subsequent John Doe like Global leadership filled in America's way in the continued progression of growth and development. Gordon S. Wood writes, "Frugality, temperance, industry, simplicity and all the rustic traits of a country yeoman, were the stuff that made the society strong. The virile martial qualities—the scorn of ease, the contempt of danger, the love of valor—were what made a nation great."[2] Thus, in the author's view, the American dream had to make a dream which could be realistically and tangibly dreamt and which had to become, a 'lived-in' Dream which could actually be tested and tried in the domestic firmament of the American nation. This had to become a Republic in the truest functional meaning of the term. As the Dream had to be lived on and had to yield glorious and fungible dividends in the end, so a stolid and sturdy foundation, had to be laid by the gifted and chosen founding fathers and the participating citizenry of the Republic. The American Declaration of Independence too intones rhapsodically that Life, Liberty and the Pursuit of Happiness had to be earmarked as the signposts of the way in which the Republic had to be built, cocooned and hibernated. This had to be attained before it could ready itself for the global plunge which was awaiting a great and most important of all, a capable nation on the build.

Though the American Republic was never intended to be characterised by the nom de plume of commercialism, still, becoming a nation of shopkeepers was never an authentic motive of the American experiment. In fact, Robert Horowitz writes in his work, *The Moral Foundations of the American Republic*, that, "Strong Republics would take every precaution to quell the rise of Commercialism in the city state, as Lycurgus did in the ancient times and Rousseau sought to do in Modernity. In their view, the notion of a "Commercial Republic", would have been a contradiction in terms, for Commerce was intended to undermine the manly virtues without which a republic could not survive. It was Commerce which was sought to spur the development of those petty Urban crafts that weaken and demean the citizenry, Commerce opens the Polis or nation, to alien and corrupting influences. It widens the gap between the rich and the poor, degrading the latter, while producing luxuries that enervate the former."[3] The tilt might not be towards Socialism but it had to be communicated to the global audiences as marketisation is not only an American credo now but a global credo in a manner of speaking. This was not the substratum over which the entire working edifice of the American Republic had to be premised upon.

The idea of the "Commerce" had to be equated with the germ of the "Other and the Alien" which has always been a bone of contention with the American narrative and the attendant dream. The fear of the "Other" and the "Alien" has always been a fundamental defining element of the American Dream which should not be looked down upon as any safe and secure citadel priding upon its achievements and 'pluses' not willing to share its secret with the rest of the humankind in order to render alive. Its exclusivity with all the inclusive ideals being the incidental attributes of the final American, "Form".

Apart from the names of the founding fathers such as Thomas Jefferson, Alexander Hamilton, John Jay, James Madison and the other revered lot, cinema too has played a constructive role and an explanatory role in the process of propagating the American Dream. The notion of the success of the American Republic needs further elaboration. Someone has said that if one wants to comprehend the basics of a civilisation, then, one can have a look at the dramatic constructs, music creations, literature and now the cinema of that civilization in order to reach a comprehensive and incisive understanding of the idea of that civilization.

The way a nation leads, its humdrum and specially, attuned life, and how it prides on certain parameters of excellence and moral foundations, can be conveniently deciphered out. This can be made easy through the Mainstream Cinema's depictions about the people, figures, national events, tragedies, warts of military defeats and triumphalistic wars. Thus, it needs to be laboriously underlined here that Mainstream Cinema and its instantiation can serve as the heady and informative brew of the way America has progressed till now. How It will prosper in the future and also the impact it will bear on the global affairs and strategy of International affairs, needs to be avidly highlighted.

Let us relate the dynamics of the cinematic construct named as *Independence Day* which is a Hollywood movie with the notion of the alien and the attendant xenophobic strain of the American society. In the movie, Earth and specially the American Urbania, has been destabilised and held at ransom by an Alien mothership which parks itself over the skyscape of the great American cities and national monuments. Mt. Rushmore, the White House in the US, the Taj Mahal in India and the Pyramids in Egypt, all are hobbled by the shadows of the Alien Mothership. The dark shadow of the mothership descends upon the American cities and the towns the world over. The Aliens, as it can be imagined have a superior technology but the American President played by Bill Whitmore has the gung ho and the tenacity to rally the entire world and the remaining American forces to demolish the nest in the Alien mothership.

Once, the American President comes in physical touch with the Aliens endowed with the extra-sensory perception then he earns the power to forecast what they have come for. The Alien in Area 51 has been captured by the American ace pilot, Will Smith and the Alien enters into a conversation with the President.

Alien: Release Me. Release me.

President: I know there is much we can learn from each other if we can negotiate a truce. We can find a way to co-exist. CAN there be Peace between Us?[4]

Alien: Peace. No Peace.
President: What is it that you want us to do?
Alien: Die. Die.

Thus, the American President realises the actual intent of the Aliens. The tormented and worried President contends, "I saw his thoughts. I saw what they are planning to do. They are like Locusts. They are moving from Planet to Planet, with their whole civilization. After they have consumed every natural resource, they move on. And, we are the next."[5] Thus, the American hyper-puissance and the attendant peace in the global system is stymied because of the entirety and the superior technology of the Alien civilisation and they are not ready for a truce. The various national populations have to be saved and the Regulator nation, that is, the United States of America, once again bears the burden of the Alien onslaught on the Earth. In a way, the advent of the Daesh and the Islamic State after the Taliban, the Al Qaeda during the Cold War is a well drawn out parallel with the rise of an Alien invasion remaining true to the H.G. Wells's classic, The *War of the Worlds*. In a similar strain, the staple American superhero, Superman, too originates from an alien planet, Krypton but is domesticated in the sunny Earth to such an extent that he soon emerges as the symbol of world peace, nuclear nonproliferation and global unison against similar foes as depicted in *Independence Day*.

The Man of Steel communicates to the American citizens and the leaders alike that the 4th of July "Confetti Moment" will not arise easily unless the Kryptonian archvillains who had been relegated to the Phantom Zone, are decimated. Otherwise, the land of milk and honey which had provided shelter to the Man of Steel, would itself be annihilated by the vile pyrotechnics of Zod and his dark vision. The narrative of this book does not aim to eulogise and sing paeans in the name of the Star Spangled Banner and the iconic Statue of Liberty, but objectifies the need to render an iota of, 'normalcy and this-worldliness', to the notion of the American Dream albeit. It happens with an explanation cushioned by a descriptive and commemorative national glass ceiling. Thus, the Superman imagery remains a permanent part of the American Dream like the Avengers and other supersuit-clad and lightning-fast superheroes but the dream is all about individual finesse and exceptionalism too. The American President per se or the American nation and its citizenry grapple alone with the global threats and emerge triumphant as a part of the quintessential American Dream's narrative.

Being an author from India, one can rave about our very own national tradition but with global ramifications. This is an innocent paean to the Indian dream which is not very much different than the grandiloquent American Dream and is never too self-congratulatory and rumbustious. With a 'Glint in Eyes', the author solicits the reader's attention: Let us celebrate the Freedom Parva, their style. Coz that's the way of the world in the most fair and selfless manner. We as Indian denizens can think of nothing better! We should be made to fathom out the 'unfathomable' in their twilight zones amidst jaunty daredevilry and virtuous sacrifice. The true Indian superheroes celebrate the nation and they are our true blue—the fatigue clad Supermen!

Ronald Barthes has proposed semiology as a methodology for exploring the ideological function of myths in his book, *Mythologies*. The Modern Barthes would delve into the idiom of exploitation and the staid Marxist analysis dipped in his own but creative lingua franca. The idea was that the analysis had to be postmodern with the idea of myths, stories and cultural portrayals being the key idiom of the American Dream.[6] Craig Saper calls it the Artificial Mythologies which have been judiciously utilised all along the narrative of the work. The author would not call these as Artificial Mythologies,[7] as any idea or a creative hospice which insinuates towards a novae but yet national lore and life. This has to be investigated upon and included in the seemingly exclusive strain of national myths and lore. This is what the present book honestly attempts to do.

The present work also has a lot to with the idiom of the word, "Culture". The cultural percepts are there to be made official with the American narrative in this work about the Star Spangled Banner, the American Dream and US Foreign Policy. Several complexities, complications, contradictions and juxtapositions happen to be the order of the day in a motive to comprehend the American culture and the all-encompassing American Dream. Just because, the American Dream, is replete with the contradictions of race, military aims, sexuality, identity, the militia moment and rugged individualism, it cannot be overtly negated. Every nation, be it cocooned in the Occident or the Orient, in the divisive demarcation of the North and the South, has to be understood as a reality intertwined with the Myth. This is exactly what this work attempts to do as part of its striving narrative; to wed the American myths with policy.

The nation has pulled up its socks after every successful epoch of development and a war or an international conflict or be it a crisis like-civil war, such as, the landmark and violent internal military engagement of the 1860s. The consequence is an unparalleled quest to achieve both a spiritual and a philosophical success along with the culmination of the material and tangible gains in the form of being the largest producer, largest exporter (of goods and services), largest arms provider and one of the biggest economies. In the finality, being the most powerful nation state in the face of stiff reproach from the alternate nations and an adversarial world order, is a tough ask. Thus, the nagging self-doubt presses on the American nation with an quintessential American Christian zeal to suspect the past achievements and to strive for a better and a more prosperous tomorrow.

The American Dream as it stands, now, thus, gets a rarified reflection with the progress made by the other nations in the neighbourhood and in the Far East such as the one traversed by, India and the People's Republic of China. The American lore as it stood and stands, went on to become the buttressing upon which the entire international system rested at one point of time. The rotation of the civilisations thesis contends that nations acting as practical Empires tend to pass through stages of crests and troughs in power akin to the cyclic nature of power as reflected by the rise of the Roman Empire. Other instances too follow such as the jurisdiction of the Ottoman Empire, the rise and demise of the British Empire and the French and Jerry (German-Third Reich) power and its anxious expansionist escapades. Thus, the same facet of International Relations theory with its idiom of 'recurrence' can be alluded to the advent of the American Hegemony and the counter-national efforts to contain the all-pervasive overarch of the American Empire. One can consult the historical documents in order to congeal the rudimentary matters of the American experiment. It follows that the odyssey of the British seafarers led to the landing of the voyagers in order to settle and be known as "settlers" in the new world which was to be christened as New Jersey and New York hamlets and most pertinently Virginia as a few symbolic instances.

The idea can be further expanded with the notion that, "In the name of God, Amen. We, whose names are underwritten, the loyal subjects of our dread Sovereigne Lord, King James, by the grace of God, of Great Britaine, France and Ireland king, defender of the faith, etc. having undertaken the journey."[8] The Mayflower bearing the religious edict of the voyagers from parts of Europe further informs as part of collected historical documents that, "For the glory of God, and advancement of the Christian faith, and honor of our king and country, a voyage to plant the first colony in the Northern parts of Virginia, done by these presents solemnly and mutually in the presence of God and one of another."[9]

The Cultural Context of America: Superman V/S the Loki Challenge

Thus, the messianic and religious zeal further complemented and supplemented by the commercial and entrepreneurial instinct of the voyagers led on to the final embankment of the decreed voyagers on to the new land of Milk and Honey, i.e., United States of America. This 'religious visitation' can be beatifically compared with the much awaited superpowers which could be delivered away from a European home and hearth. The journey of *Kal-El*, the prince of the imaginary Planet Krypton with the scientific aid of his scientist father, *Jor-El*,[10] in order to land safely in an inhabited land can serve as a stark parallel with the journey of these Mayflower journeymen. It happens in order to re-link the motherland with the new host land.The new Europeans inhabited and transformed the indigenous population and the resources. In the process, they embarked on a novae journey and go on to spawn and procreate a *New Worldian Dominion*[11] which goes on to metamorphose into one of the most powerful group of citizens in the history of humankind.

The American interlude in world history was initiated with the *Kal Elian* entry inside a new, undiscovered and unobserved terrain, which was amply climate-rich with opportunities for human settlement. The European settlers were the ones who embarked on a dangerous journey. They went ahead with the adventure in the East Coast of United States and arrived as aliens in the land of the Red Indians and Chenneys. The European nationals who were Irish, Swiss French,and Briton did not know the North American scenario but made it their own. The DC and Marvel Comics character might be comic bookish in nature, but as a strong cultural American motif, the character of Superman arrived from a faraway Planet, Krypton. The one and a half years old child arrived in a see through capsule and crashed at the back of the Milk van being driven by the Kents couple in Smallville, where the American superhero grew up. Thus, the alien nature of the child, Kal-El is equated by the author as being equivalent to the European and Asian settlers who migrated to America and made it their home and hearth through their labour and hard work. Thus, the Superman myth has a place in the international perspective and serves as an imaginative take on the initiation and the seeding of the civilisation in the New World. This can be symbolically and mythically alluded to as an ample reflection of the "American Dream". Thus, the people have been earmarked as Aliens who tend to familiarise the land across the Potomac and Hudson in the search of a new civilisational rush. Also with the objective of finding less competitive lands and opportunities with a lesser chance of oppression and victimisation on a sound buttressing of religion and trade. The world system still remains Eurocentric though made rather different with a new ***Proto Euro-Kryptonian strain, thus the pathway was paved for the new youngling settlers to spawn a new order in the New World.*** Much similar to the touch that Superman always retains with the vile visitors from the past, that is, Krypton, the settlers from the European land, tend to be part of the different subcultures and ethnic ties of the people of the same stock in their homelands. Similarly, the Americans battle with the British Regime as part of the American Revolution and with the Declaration of Independence in the year

1787. Similarly, the White House was torched by the people from the destroyed planet of Krypton, albeit Great Britain, still, existed as the International Hegemon in the eighteenth century.

Thus, the American settlers militated and struggled against the British incursion in the year 1815 and the American Supermen or to be more precise, the group of ***Avengers***, tend to defend their Newfoundland in the heat of a inter continental/intergalactic battles. The ramifications which are intergalactic in nature tend to bring relief to the contours of the founding myth of the United States of America. Another element associated with the US pantheon happens to be that of the American Revolution or the American War of Independence.

The American Revolution initiated a new era of freedom and liberty in the troubled terrains of the United States. Alexis De Tocqueville remarked on the theme of equality, liberty and fraternity, as it was ushered in the United States in the following manner, "I already observed that universal suffrage has been adopted in all the states of the Union. It consequently exists in communities that occupy very different positions in the social scale. I have had opportunities of observing its effects in different localities and among races of men who are nearly strangers to each other in their language, their religion, and their modes of life; in Louisiana as well as in New England, in Georgia as in Canada."[12] He further contended, "I have remarked that universal suffrage is far from producing in America either all the good or all the evil consequences which may be expected from it in Europe, and, that its effects generally differ very much from those which are attributed to it."[13] Thus, the political ethos and the attendant political debates are the ones which vibrated with alacrity in the neophyte days of America. The stark and universal political principles still retain the selfsame identity and enough impactful ramifications in the United States and even in the parallel worlds of the other twenty-first century nations and nationalities. Thus, the political travails of a burgeoning democracy were very much present in the entire foundational edifice of the United States as De Tocqueville and other scholars have observed: America being a singular case in point.

The Calvinistic self-doubt remains as an apolitical theme to be surmised upon and deliberated intensively as the thinker from France refers to the failings of Democracy and the tales of dissipations which are attached to the novae experiments in the untried and untested lands. De Tocqueville contends in relation to the spurt of Democracy in the United States—"The Democratic governments may become violent and even cruel at certain periods of extreme effervescence or of great danger, but these crises will be rare and brief."[14] He carries on in the same vein, "When I consider the petty passions of our contemporaries, the mildness of their manners, the extent of their education, the purity of their religion, the gentleness of their morality, their regular and industrious habits, and the restraint which they almost all observe in their vices no less than in their virtues, I have no fear that they will meet with tyrants in their rulers, but rather with guardians."[15] It needs to be comprehended that no nation or society can go ahead with the creation of a democratic apparatus and the liberty interlude which becomes an enduring one unless and until its leaders and political mandarins are willing to value and learn. They have to glean from the fears of despotism and its consequences on the hoi polloi in a manner which furthers the creation and establishment of a novae democratic and liberty endowed order.

De Tocqueville is also of the view that every nation which is preparing itself to embark on a democratic odyssey needs to have an elite class embued with wealth, power and influence. This class can serve as a sieve for acculturating the rest of the hoi polloi in the nation and the society at large. Still, a Democracy need not forget the condition that people in a democratic country cannot be made bereft of the ideal of private ownership of Property. It is in the sense that the citizens of the nation need to be given "a sense of worth" which would go a long way in attaching themselves with the notion of their own tangible and physical attributes. This was an essential prerequisite to sustain the people as part of a system and a constantly attendant churning as the United States moved on from a bitter war of independence and the later civil war.

The Lockean Rights Interlude

John Locke, with his stress on private property, too, went ahead with the idea of liberty, equality, pursuit of happiness and wealth as part of his renderings in his eminent work, *The Two Treatises on Government*. It is the repetitive rendering of the American elements which sustains the American dream which are much more than proud talk in author's view. The people of a democratically inclined set up ought to be given the right to change or remove a Government of the day if they are not satisfied with the idea of welfarist attributes and the functionality of the Governing seat of power. Thus, the idea of 'Recall' in a Democratic system along with the need for change in the governing denomination due to its various functional failings is aptly emphasised upon in the American political system too with the state of California being a referral example to it. Although, John Locke's property theory is undoubtedly influential, no one seems to agree on exactly what it was that he was trying to say. Many have complained about his ambiguity. Karl Wilderquist contends in one of his papers, "I am interested in Locke's property theory because it bears on the on-going philosophical debate over equality, property rights, freedom, and the legitimacy of government powers of taxation, regulation, and redistribution."[16] Thus, the above discussion stands reemphasised with the notion of worth, property and ownership, all of which lie strewn across the firmament and the tarmac of the American political system with the Glorious revolution in Great Britain finding a reflection in the running of the War of Independence in the United States. Also, the individualism argument as to the unipropulsion of an individual's rise to eminence in an entrepreneurial America with the associational materialism of wealth aggregation and sustenance of a grasping culture, remains as one of the criticised and ridiculed tenet of the American growth trajectory and development. Karl Wilderquist further discusses, "Locke clearly relies on the maximum strength proviso to justify property *when resources are abundant*; only this version fully supports his claims of no injury, entrenchment, prejudice, or cause for complaint."[17]

Locke's own theory clearly excludes some items in this outline, such as the prohibition of taxation and regulation. Although Locke might have believed that taxation required a stronger notion of consent than other legislation[18] that clearly believed either that the consent of the majority of property owners was enough[19] or that the inheritors consent to taxation when they claim their heritage.[20] The ambiguity that Locke allowed to creep into his property theory has developed into a diverse set of appropriation-based justifications for private property. This must be fully addressed by the opponents. Anything less would be incomplete. Here-in lie the twin sides of the criticism of the United States wherein the scholars and observers have commented upon the capitalist denomination and the acquisitive nature of the American socio-economic lore and myth. Still, the discussion in the American context arrives on to a contention and a new standpoint that the property owners cannot take everything for themselves. The idea of the just and enough proviso needs to be the order of the day in the context of the American and democratic acquisition.

Also, the nations tend to have a group of people who anyway go property-less in the final countdown despite the rejection of a fully individually owned notion of property.[21] Thus, the American defacement can be curtailed and ably defended by the argument that the crassly capitalist and materialistic idiom of the American experiment is not what was ideally intended by the founding fathers, revolutionary leaders and the constitution framers. Still, the metathesis changed as the industrialisation and the big business ethics of the American nation led to the heady race to circumvent all the national and societal piety in a mad cap race to the finish for the aggregation of wealth, heft and pelf. Thus, the classwise and socialist denunciation and the counter-Kennan thesis about a natural confrontation between the Communist and the Capitalist blocs did find some of its staple fare from this capitalist anointment of the United States of America in a post-big business era.

The Way the Founding Fathers referred to it All

Apart from the story of the Mayflower Pact and the attendant developments in the Revolutionary War, the renderings and the belief systems of the American founding fathers such as Thomas Jefferson, Alexander Hamilton, John Jay, etc. too laid a foundation stone in the nation's rubric. Whenever the patriotic and nationalistic spirit of the American gatherings is talked about then the turnouts reflect the kind of pantheon following which Thomas Jefferson had unto himself. Jefferson's message can be found dangling in the rooms of the editors in the global media firmament, all across the global polity. It reads in the following order, "If I were to choose an alternative between a nation without newspapers or newspapers without nations, I would readily opt for the second alternative." Thus, the idiom of liberty and freedom of faith and expression as contained as the guiding spirit of the First Amendment to the US Constitution too finds a place in the Jeffersonian thesis. Pertaining to all this, the vigilante and the militia spirit of the American Republic finds a resonance with the Jeffersonian perception and a vision for the Republic.

Jefferson was known for his freethinking nature, intent and an attendant ideological promiscuity. It is observed by commentators on Jefferson, that "Southern secessionists loved him; Northern abolitionists worshiped him; Gilded Age moguls echoed his warnings about federal power; Populists adored his advice about the evils of a banking conspiracy and the superiority of agrarian values."[22] The facet of President Jefferson being a slave-owning person came to the fore front, which would have questioned his place on Mount Rushmore. Still, the notion that he stood for national integration, societal and racial egalitarianism, runs deep in the chromosome of an American patriot and a nationalist. Jefferson ideally stood for the notion of equality, integration and the interests of the many against the elitism of the few. Thus, the rhetoric of democratisation which troubles the international actors of some denominations owes its pristine origin to the works and thoughts of Thomas Jefferson. He has also been dubbed as a "Free Floating Icon". The Hamiltonian ideal of Governmental intervention was always juxtaposed against the economic equality, freewheeling and the independent mode of progression and development in the national context. Bipartisanship which is very much the need of the hour in the American context, was echoed by the equality and the integrative strand of the Jeffersonian thought.

Also, the ideal of a political system free from the Governmental intervention was echoed by Jefferson which became a prominent plank in the days following the New Deal era after World War II. The Reaganite concept of lesser Government and personal freedoms was coterminous with the plank of President Coolidge in the 1930s where-in the practice of freedom from state intervention was re enshrined in the American dictum. Also, in a way, some observers have connoted the connection of the American economic crisis of 2008 with this economic libertarian practice which gradually became the guiding light in an age of globalisation, convergence and transnationalism. Also, the American vision was embedded with a novae freedom which had the strains of international morality and spiritual reason.

The driving American dictum reflects the same sentiment, "*We hold these truths to be sacred & undeniable, that all men are created equal & independent, that from that equal creation they derive rights inherent & inalienable, among which are the preservation of life, & liberty, & the pursuit of happiness.*"[23] Thus, the denial of state intransigence became a part of the American discourse which was somehow taken up by the alternate wayfarers in the counter-culture days of the American nation after the political, social and military crisis of the Vietnam War. Also, the debate over slavery and the story of the abolitionist and the anti-abolitionist movement were all enmeshed in this freedom-run of racial egalitarianism with the advent of Jeffrsoniaism.[24] Thus, the development which culminated with the abolition of slavery after the Civil War and the Supreme Court Judgments such as the Brown vs. Board of Judgment and the entire legacy of the Civil Rights movement were part of one interconnected narrative of liberty, equality, freedom and egalitarianism in more ways than one. It is mentioned in the Thomas Jefferson Papers that, "Jefferson sends President George Washington, his Opinion of the Constitutionality of the Bill for Establishing a National Bank. Secretary of the Treasury Hamilton was of the perception that the Constitution can spawn a national bank. Jefferson perceived Hamilton's plans for a national bank, the creation of manufactures, and other attendant financial policies as creating conditions for the aggregation of power and graft identified with the constitutionality and the system in Europe."[25] Thus, how the national institutions were to be fathomed and created themselves began the discourse on how the national system could be integratively developed.

These were a few confrontations which had shaped a nation-state. These inherent contradictions were reflected in other spheres too. In a way, the agrarian model of development and the industrial and the Eastern seaboard economics of the developed were the twin pegs around which the developmental and the political debate in United States revolved.[26] Jefferson's First Inaugural Address, the Report on Public Credit, the Kentucky Resolutions, and other attendant and related documents, led to the compiled understanding of the notion of American growth and political development.[27] These were the formative years of the American republic which generated a host of political confrontations but the specialty was that the word of the founding leaders had led to the creation of a supple though generative two party system in the republic. Judicially, too, the reference to Federal and the Provincial divide in terms of governance led to a lot of exchange of flak with Alexander Hamilton who was supporting a strong Central denomination.[28]

The Federalist papers too reflect the same schism. The national economy and issues such as national debt were prominent themes which raised the interest of the leaders and the people alike. The social disconnect and disdain between the women of the different races and the male and female slave owners was another development worth more than some significance. Thus, the schism in the founding myth in the system was circulated even in the social context in the country. Other leaders such as Hamilton too fought duels with personages like Aaron Burr, the Vice President, which has been amply recorded in the history books and related documents.

The founding fathers emphasised upon the idea of the constitutionalism and higher ideals, morals and principles. Ethics attained one of the prominent perches of the fledgling American Republic. James Madison proclaimed in the Federalist Paper 10 which happens to be reflective of the earnest expression of the American way of doing politics. He writes, "The latent causes of faction are ineradicably sown in human nature. The most common and durable of these ineradicable causes are, namely the diversity of economic interests, the regulation of these various and interfering interests forms the principal task of modern legislation and involves the spirit of party and faction in the necessary and ordinary operations of the Government."[29] Thus, the two iron globes of the construction machine too present the same function. The construction machine takes in the sludge of cement and mortar and transforms them into the finally utilisable concrete for being utilised in buildings. This metaphor of the construction of buildings has been aptly utilised by the French political scientist, who visited United States and wrote the path-breaking *Democracy in America*. The construction metaphor had to be hinged as the tussle of factions and discrepancies in the smooth functioning of the political system in United States and that out of that sludge, emerges the concrete which builds the nation that America is. Even in today's context, bipartisanship in matters significant to the health of the American political system, is taking its decisive and moral toll on the individual party ambitions in the twenty-first century.

Another guiding ambition of the American Republic happens to be, "to secure the Public and Private Goods… and at the same time to preserve the spirit and the form of the Popular Government, is then the great object to which our enquiries are directed."[30] Thus, when the United States assumes the mantle of a super state, then, it has to judiciously balance the idea of governing in the domestic sphere and the long riding vision and the 'given-to-it' responsibility of being the Global Regulator-par-excellence. Thus, in a way, the balancing out of an individualistic streak, which, is replete with greed and gluttony with philanthropic messianic zeal, had to form a part and parcel of the grandiloquent American Dream both domestically and globally. And, it is not part of a folk tale or indigenous knowledge, but, a document extant in American history. That is the American Federalist Papers which serve as the staple blueprint of Democracy in America with its sane and sage do's and don'ts for governance, law and order and foreign relations.

Purposelessness was another threat which the purveyors of the American Dream found demeaning and stultifying. Also, exclusivity and exceptionalism of the Dream too had a prominent and a pride of place in the grandiloquent American pantheon of telltale percepts. Still, the transformation of the American civilisation took place in a particular direction, wherein an observer of American affairs pithily commented, "What is good for General Motors, is also good for America." The exclusivity which is part of the American Dream is not about discrimination, if perceived objectively. Jay Gould said, "In Republican countries, I am for the Republicans and in Democratic countries, I am for the Democrats, but everywhere, I am for the Erie Railroad."[31] The political scientist commented in the same vein, "We do not need to account for a truly inclusive interest, because one does not exist".[32] The ethics of doing politics is a great element and a driving force of the idiom of governance in America.

For instance, it can be objectively observed that the contemporary work culture of the American Congressman in the Capitol Hill offices, is a gilded age sheen incarnate. As the various Congressmen, both the graying veterans and the new hounds such as Barack Obama before he was elected to the White House, have thework ethics of regularly interacting with the constituents of their seats and solving practical problems, as, they rise with their constituents. The sepia-tinted offices with green lamps burning till late evenings form the hub image of the American Congressmen's offices. They play a pro-active role in the solving of the day-to-day issues of their citizens. This professionalism, though arrived at after a lot of encumbrance despite the large size of America, speaks volumes about the success and the, 'positive-throb' of the American dream. Not another platitude but an apt elucidation of how the ethics of accountability and provincial transparency characterise the American way of doing politics. As we repeatedly refer to the mythical part of the argument about the American Dream, a nuanced noting of the sheen and the vocational cleanliness of the political vocation is a rampant presence too.

Barack Obama, the personage, before he even became a Senator, used to travel to his constituency, away from his elder daughter and a second new-born daughter and of course, the to-be-First Lady, Michelle Obama. Obama used to congregate a few people in the initial days of his senatorial campaign and ask them questions about how they perceive their national interests, ideological inclinations and what are the prominent issues in the local setting. He would meet these prominent constituents who would be either simple and Plane Jane citizens or would belong to various lobbies such as the gun lobby, the anti-tobacco lobby, the Environmental suffragettes, etc. Thus, his country inn visits would form a fundamental premise of his election campaign when he would struggle for funds and media attention.

In another instance, taken from President Obama's memoir, he would do a tightrope walking between the anti-gun and the pro-gun lobbies, as certain sections of both the fragments could be instrumental in accepting the Obama Pageant and in providing him with funds and acceptance. These livid details are all listed in President Obama's autobiography, *The Audacity of Hope*. Thus, the Dream itself came true in the case of Presidents such as Andrew Jackson, Abraham Lincoln and now Barack Hussein Obama who recently relived his 'origination moments' in Kenya where children were being named after him and buses depicted fullscape pictorials out of his life and persona. Thus, in a related fact, the Obama-juggernaut depicts the realisation of the quintessential Immigrant and Black Dreams which have made American more or less their own as part of the smooth passage of the cosmopolitan drive of the nation. The American way of doing Politics is not as simple as saying that it is a two party structure with the twin political parties being the Republicans and the Democrats. It is the multipolarity of the interest groups which grants a truly democratic and representative veneer to the American republic. The Benedict Anderson's idea of Imagined community gets a tangible and material dispensation among the sentiment of nationalism and patriotism felt and practiced by the American nation and its citizens inclined towards the deliverance of Public goods.

The immigrant experience and its successful realization with the nation's Dream stands out in the light of the migrant crisis imploding in Italy, in Lampedusa, in Calais and around the Trans-British Channel sea link. E.L. Doctrow, in his classical work, *Ragtime* has written that, "A large number of Latinos conscripted as street artists who drew portraits of passer buys for a few dollars. They lived in nearby slum like dwellings and sat together to have luncheons with the anarchist speakers. These people spoke of the ideals and the non-discriminative nature of the political system in Communist nations." The American Dream still went on unimpeded with the matrix-like network of railroads and trams spreading their network from one city to the other and which proved instrumental for the shifting populations like Houdini's magic antics as workers moved on from a riot infested town to another nearer to the Oregon

Trail. The movie construct, *Birth of A Nation*, too sheds light upon the origins of the American Dream along with the inherent conflicts which ideally should not have been part of a national lore which was envisaged such as America was. Still, it has never been a Dream gone haywire or awry as the twenty-first century resplendence of the American Electoral circus and the preponderance of the nation in the global system would reflect definitively.

Religion too has played a significant role in the American tale of progression and growth. Samuel P. Huntington, in his seminal work, *Who We Are?*, has written that with the advent of the mad cap rush for minting green the workers in the corporate world were gradually weaned away from the religiosity of the American way of life. This development is a desultory reminder of the lack of a national identity as religion here, and, Christianity, there, is the backbone of the American experience and the attendant Dream. The world of faith and the pristine mahogany pulpit, was, permitted in an unbridled manner in the country. In the crucial religiously concerned nineties, the corporate world at the behest of the American establishment initiated Sunday services at the private offices and religious sessions in the office complexes. All this happened in the light of the dwindling Sunday masses at the Sunday Churches. In another context, Thomas Jefferson has written in the context of establishing liberty in the state of Virginia.

He writes, "That to suffer the Civil Magistrate to intrude his powers into the field of opinion and to restrain the profession or the propagation of principles on supposition of their ill tendency is a dangerous fallacy, which at once destroys all religious liberty. Of Course, Judge of that tendency will make his opinions the rule of Judgement, and approve or condemn the sentiments of others only as they shall square with or differ from his own."[33] Zechariah Chaffe Jr, contends in his seminal work, *Free Speech in the United States*, "Words About Religious Liberty hold good of political and speculative Freedom, and the portrayal of human life in every form of Art."[34] Leonard Levy says, "This statement thus refers to the field of Opinion, though in context only freedom of religion is provided for and explicitly named. Yet the principles of the statement could theoretically, apply with equal vigour to speech and Press which are related and linked together with Freedom of religion in the First Amendment."[35]

The Supreme Court Case, Everson vs. Board of Education, makes the debate much clearer and brings it in bold relief. The Supreme Court held that neither the State or the Federal Government may set up a Church or pass a law aiding one Religion or Law related to religions or prefer one religion over others.[36] Thus, the centrality of religion and Christianity has not been denied in the American Republic's founding myth but the notion has made the non-state support of any religion into a secular establishment exercise. Thus, the American Dream, is, officially neutral about the official religion in the American Republic. Secularism is an American Credo, too, despite the grandiloquent clamour and hoarse cries of the nation's progressive-conservatives. In his *Notes on the State of Virginia*, Thomas Jefferson contends, "American Institutions are not built on religious truths. The Americans are not required to regard it as an enquiry, or an injury for which the law will provide a remedy-for their neighbors to say that there were twenty Gods or No God. Such Religious Opinions, neither, pick their religious pockets or break their legs as he put it in his famous formulation."[37] Thus, the grey matter construct of religious neutrality was ever present in the socio-political and legal construct of the United States. United States was always bred on Christian and Ecclesiastic ethics, but, the centrality of religion for the institutional growth and sustenance was never a part of the founding myth of the American nation and the attendant Dream. In the author's view, this is not a partisan position but a kind of way of maintaining the separation between religion and governance and politics. Several Judicial debates and jurisprudential developments have taken place in this context but America avoids a blatant partisanship premised upon religion, in the author's view.

The American Republic has been a politically, a democratically and rights-based committed nation and society. There are five American commitments which have to be taken cognisance of, wherein the scholars and especially the political scientists have pointed at the largesse of liberalism and constitutionalism in the American polity. Robert Dahl has commented profusely upon the state of political signposts in the American Union. He pinpoints five political commitments which can be enumerated over here. Dahl contends, "The country follows a liberal, political and constitutional order that gave primacy to the protection of certain political and civil rights among its citizens. So profound was the acceptance of the Constitution that the great constitutional quarrels to follow were not so much over the validity of the Constitution as over its meaning, assuming its unconstitutional validity."[38] Thus, constitutionalism and the adherence to the traditional and documental legalese was the core tenet of the political founding myth of the United States of America which very much needed this framework, as, the various thirteen colonies had to be united as a single political entity.

Robert Dahl further contends in the context of the American political culture that,

> "The second historical commitment consolidated somewhere between 1800 and 1836 was to the belief that the only proper constitutional and political system for Americans is a Democracy. Although Democracy mainly meant adhering to democratic procedures in the operation of the Government, it also carried with it the notion of a larger society within which the social and economic conditions would favor the high degree of political, social and

> economic equality necessary to Democracy. Such an agrarian society already existed in United States which was dependent on pastoral farms where social and political inequalities for white males was very less prevalent."[39]

The third political commitment which meant a great deal for the American Republic was, as Dahl wrote,

> "The decisions of Presidents such as Mckinley, Taft, Harding, Coolidge, Hoover by Theodore Roosevelt's bombastic style and ineffectual policies speak loudly but do not carry much stick, only apart from the brief interlude of political economic reform during the tenure of President Wilson. With the excesses of private ownership coming to the fore with the onset of the era of economic depression, the post Coolidge and Hoover phases oversaw an initiation of the acceptance of the ideals of a Welfare State, far removed from the allegations associated with the unbridled capitalism of the American system."[40]

Thus, in the author's view, the Founding myth was in a phase of transition with the Laskian view propagated in the work, *Grammar of Politics*, holding sway as it would lead to a cementing of the capitalist and the socialist modes of growth and national progression.

After the domestic squabbles over the New Deal and the age of populism in the ending days of the nineteenth century were over the corner, then, the fifth and the final commitment to the Republic was spelt out in a larger manner. "This was the idea that a landmark American intervention in the Global context and with the European matrix had to be initiated by the Americans. The age of the great American Dream's disdain and isolationism was over which was to be tided over by the interventionist zeal of the American Union."[41] Thus, the standard debate in the realm of US foreign policy has been one between isolationism and interventionism. It is here that the twin activists of the two schools of thought deliberated and actually fought over the nature of the global policy to be adopted by the United States of America. They on the one hand stood for an America which had to play the role of a "Reluctant Dragon" which would be reserved in its ministrations with the East and the Europe. On the other hand, a global role of an International Super State with the prescient powers for the handling of global and regional conflicts was envisaged for America. Thus, the Americans were being readied in a positive mindset for a larger and more agile role in the different diplomatic conclaves and the surging hotbeds of conflict, all around the length and breadth of world polity. The American Dream with Global ambitions and 'Designs'—to use a pejorative term—had arrived on the global firmament.

Another founding myth stalwart, was, Alexander Hamilton, who, stood for the balanced mode of government led development in United States as against a development model sans the state in the views of Thomas Jefferson. P. Chernow, an observer of American affairs, contends, "Alexander Hamilton is sometimes considered the "Patron Saint" of the American School of economic philosophy that, according to one historian, dominated economic policy after 1861. He firmly supported government intervention in favor of business, after the manner of Jean-Baptiste Colbert, as early as the fall of 1781."[42] Thus, Alexander Hamilton can be construed as the supporter of an industry and business supported growth which is what United States finally endorsed with the rest of the West's growth patterns. Thus, simplistically placed, scholars such as Fareed Zakaria in their works, associated with the talk about the American decline, defined the fears of the earlier sceptics. This view was about the implosion of a fast-paced consumerist approach and the pattern of growth in an unending[43] thirst for prosperity and heft, both domestically and internationally.

The talk about the decline of the US power and influence can be visualized in the light of the civilisational ethos of the United States. The Chinese too dreamt big and mammoth and one of their seafarers before the advent of the European seafaring ways in the post-Renaissance age, used to move and sail around the South China Sea and the Indian Ocean littoral. They get into business deals with the nations such as Indonesia, Vietnam, South West Pacific islands, such as Vanuatu and Tahiti. This was much before Columbus sailed to the New World and much before Vasco da Gama sailed to the Indian subcontinent.[44]

Thus, the old world and the Asian national and regional communities went much ahead of the western civilisational benchmarks in the material sense of the term. In a way, this development along with the Confucian inclination not to attach much significance to the religious zeal and the religious ramifications of politics and society led to its congealing with the Western post-Renaissance context of a moral and principled-based approach. This approach was directed towards governance and politics in that time's context.[45] Thus, in the author's view the rise and fall of great powers has been an avowed theme of discussion and debate within the context of world politics with eminent historians talking about the norm of the advent and demise of the great and powerful empires of of Rome, Carthage, Ottoman Turks and the Napoleonic and Germanic crusades.

Thus, the American rise as an independent power is to be reckoned with the international system. It has a lot to do with its subsequent interventionist and all powerful footprints in the twentieth and the twenty-first century. Thus, the democratic, anti-colonial and entrepreneurial spirit of the American experiment, too, was part of the recurrence and repetitiveness of the events and developments in the international system. In the author's view,, such a factoid out of history, also, conjoins the repetitive nature of the international system as part of a nom de plume in world politics which has been often observed. The same pantheon of wars, conflicts, civil strife, reasons for international conflict, have been the factors identifying and earmarking benchmarks for the realisation of activity and reactivity in the international system.

The scholars and observers of international politics and world history have referred to the advent of the United States of America as a part of the rising saga of progression and developmental process in the American and the much larger international context. In the author's view, the nation that emerged as a bold entrepreneurial and liberal community, embarked into a novae role as a developing and bold, proactive creative and strong international actor. Thus, the American palimpsest was endowed with the characteristics of a variegated mélange of populations, ethnicities and different countries of origin. They after a context of migration went on to develop into a distinct and unique nation state. This edifice attached value to energy, entrepreneurship and individual vocation much in the strain of a new world order and a novae initiative.

Another significant strain in the progression of the American Republic happens to be that of the Civil War. The American civil war resonated with the idiom of a nationwide divide between the Eastern seaboard industrialists , the Yankees and the cotton growing Southern land lords, as they have been called historically. The context of the Civil war was further bracketed by the Southern American cotton growing farmers, who, were pure agrarians in the European mould of feudal agrarians. President Abraham Lincoln ensconced across the Potomac, was in the favour of the abolition of the staid practice of slavery. The Southern agrarians defied the Federal diktat and were in the favour of continuing with the practice of slavery. They were termed by the observers of the American affairs as the Abolitionists and the Eastern coastal Yankees. They were from now on referred to as anti-abolitionists. Thus, the people of the nation/new Republic were a divided lot and this ideological and thematic schism led to the initiation of a war among both the factions. The Southern states being called as the Confederate forces which were pitted against the Northern and Eastern Federal Government in Washington. Thus, this part of the trail of developments was beatifically manifested in Hollywood portrayals of the order of Gone with the Wind. The Film depicts the ochre colored trail of battles and the royalty tinged rigmarole of the cotton growing south in the lingo of Clark Cable as Rhet Butler and Vivian Leigh as the women lead.

NOTES

1. Jim Cullen, *The American Dream: A Short History of an Idea that Shaped a Nation* (Oxford University Press, 2003), pp. 10-20.

2. Gordon S Wood, *The Creation of the American Republic* (Chapel Hill: University of North Caroline Press, 1969), p. 118.
3. Robert H Horwitz, (ed.), *The Moral Foundation of the American Republic* (University Press of Virginia, 1974), pp. 136-140.
4. Cynthia Weber, *International Relations Theory: A Critical Introduction* (New York: Routledge), pp. 50-55.
5. Ibid.
6. Roland Barthes, "Myth Today" in *Mythologies*, trans. Annette Lavers, New York: Noonday Press.
7. Craig Saper, *Introduction to Artificial Mythologies*, Minneapolis; University of Minnesota Press.
8. "The Mayflower Compact", URL: http://www.ushistory.org/documents/mayflower.htm (Online: Web), accessed on August 1, 2015.
9. Ibid.
10. "Trailer: The Legend of Superman", URL: www.imdb.com/video/screenplay/vi732235033/ (Online: Web), accessed on August 1, 2013. The tale of Superman begins with a Superman one which paves the way for four other equally interesting parts which impinge upon the coming of age and the discovery of superpowers by Christopher Reeve who plays the part of Kal-El and Clark Kent in his earthly avatar in order to foil evil and the machinations of his childhood bete noir, Lex Luthor.
11. Ibid.
12. Alexis de Tocqueville, *Democracy in America* (New York: Penguin Classics, April, 2002).
13. Ibid.
14. Ibid.
15. Ibid.
16. Karl Wilderquist, "Lockean Theories of Property: Justifications for Unilateral Appropriation," *Public Reason* 2 (1), 3-26.
17. Ibid
18. Tassi Aldo (1972), "Two Notions of Consent in Locke's Second Treatise", *Locke Newsletter* 3: 26-31.
19. Bernard Ludwig (2000), Locke and Tacit and Express Consent: §§116-22 of the Second Treatise, *Locke Newsletter* 31: 147-56.
20. Ibid.
21. A.J. Simmons, *The Lockean Theory of Rights*, Princeton: Princeton University Press, 1992.
22. The Library of Congress Websource, Joseph J. Ellis, "American Sphinx: The Contradictions of Thomas Jefferson", URL: http://memory.loc.gov/ammem/collections/jefferson_papers/mtjessay1.html (Online: Web), accessed on 19 August, 2015.
23. Fawn Brodie. *Thomas Jefferson: An Intimate History* (New York: Norton, 1974. LC Call Number: E332 .B787)
24. Wintrop Jordan, *White Over Black: American Attitudes toward the Negro, 1550-1812*. Chapel Hill: University of North Carolina Press, 1968; New York: Norton, 1977. LC Call Numbers: E185.J69; E446 .J68, 1977
25. The Thomas Jefferson Papers, (1606-1827), Library of Congress, US Govt.
26. Noble E. Cunningham, "Jefferson VS Hamilton: Confrontations that Shaped Nation," Bedford's San Martin's, 2000.
27. Ibid.

28. Melvyn R. Durchslag, *State Sovereign Immunity: A Reference Guide to the United States Constitution* (2002), p. xix.
29. Federalist Paper No 10, USGPO.
30. Robert H Horwitz, *The Moral Foundations of the American Republic* (University Press of Virginia, 1975), p. 85.
31. D.W. Brogan, *Politics in America* (New York: Anchor Books, 1960), p. 222.
32. Ibid.
33. *The Papers of Thomas Jefferson,* ed. Julian P. Boyd et al (Princeton: Prineceton University Press, 1950), p. 246.
34. Zechariah Chaffe Jr, *Free Speech in the United States* (New York: Atheneum ed. 1969), p. 68.
35. Leonard W. Levy, *Legacy of Suppression: Freedom of Speech and Press* (New York: Princeton University Press, 1954).
36. Everson V. Board of Education, 330 U.S. 1, 15 (1947).
37. The Federalist Paper No 9.
38. Robert A. Dahl, "On Removing Certain Impediments to Democracy in the United States" in Robert H. Horwitz, *The Moral Foundations of the American Republic* (Charlottesville: University Press of Virginia, 1974), pp. 231-232.
39. Ibid.
40. Ibid.
41. Ibid.
42. Chernow, p. 170, citing *Continentalist* V, published April 1782, but written in fall 1781; Syrett, p. 3:77).
43. David Truman, *The Governmental Process* (New York: Knopf, 1957), p. 51.
44. Fareed Zakaria, *The Post American World* (New York: Knopf, 2009), pp. 20-40.
45. Ibid.

3

The Interwar Years and the Rise of the United States

After the advent of the Civil war, United States witnessed a great period of growth which the nation underwent through the periods of the era of Big Business along with the Progressive movement at the turn of the 19th century. Before the World wars, a sound substratum was laid for the American nation to smoothen its great power with rough edges in an age of new age mechanization and preparation for a super hero overflight over the rest of the comity of nations infested with the blocks of fascism and colonialism. Both the World Wars can be considered as significant pointers to the tale of the progression of the United States. The American role and the want of American participation at the few historically significant path-breaking points have become part of the debate. This debate is premised on whether US played a just and truly Wilsonian and idealistic role or not. The tale of the non passage of the Treaty of Versailles by the US Congress earned bad press for the United States. As the seat of the American delegate in the Paris Conference after World War I was unoccupied, the LON (League of Nations) went on with a new meaning. The scenario in the conference was called as, "the lengthening shadow of the Chair which was unoccupied by the American delegate." Thus, early on, after the annexation of Mexico and Philippines by Washington, the quest for an American supremacy was soon realised by the global comity and the "Advent of America" similar to the "Peaceful Rise" of China. This was a globally felt development which posited the United States in its own bracket.

Similarly, the Open Diplomacy ideal formulated by President Woodrow Wilson was soon rubbished by one of the earlier Presidents, that is, Theodore

Roosevelt, who did not want his nation to be embroiled in the "entangling alliances" which were stereotypically, European in nature. These initial founding developments were much intertwined with the European narrative and the rise of German power and nationalism had a far-reaching impact upon the way America managed its new found superpowers. The developments such as the failure of the League of Nations, the rise of Germany and Japan, the consequences of the American Depression and the entry of the United States in the Second World War with the beginning of the conflict between the United States and the former Soviet Union, were some of the important developments. These developments are the underpinnings of the way and the tale through which the fledgling power and influence of United States were reflected by its central positioning and its ascendance in the international system.

The international turmoil was adequately reflected by the conditionality of the world system with the advent of the functional and organisational approach. There was a conscious and sustained approach in the international system to find effective measures and mechanisms in order to combat the scourge of war and international conflict. The advent of modernity came with its associated evils and ills which were felt everywhere. One of them was the unregulated propensity and the aggressively unmitigated power and expansionist urge of the international stakeholders to vivisect the cooperative mechanisms of the global polity.

One can take a stroll down the historical lane too. In the aftermath of the Treaty of Westphalia, the world witnessed the initiation of the norm of subsequent treaties such as the post-Waterloo Congress of Vienna along with the Hague interludes in the year 1899 and 1907. All these paved the way for an initiation of a valid and functional, International Organisation. The superstructure of an international organisation to spawn a mechanism in order to circumvent the menace of conflict and war, was, being internationally and fervently searched for. The crisis of modernity had arrived, wherein the international community led by the great powers of the order of the United States, the United Kingdom, France, etc. were combating the rising might of the new upstarts. These were Kaiser Wilhelm's Germany and a neo-imperialistic Japan in the far east. Thus, in such a scenario, with the ferocious tide of industrialisation and militarisation being attempted at a superhuman scale, the war clouds were gathering over the international firmament. The danger of a true blue and all-engulfing world conflagration was looming large over the international political and strategic skyline.

It is amidst these troubled times that the United States was rising out of its slumber and perceived isolation since the 1880s and 1890s. The nation on a

Global mend was attempting to level up, shoulder to shoulder with the rest of the great powers such as the crowned monarch of the firmament, the United Kingdom. In terms of the tonnage of war ships owned, the strength of cavalries being maintained, newer soldier guns and artillery being manufactured for the defence forces, the United States had equalled, if not bettered the statistical strength of the European powers in more senses than one.

The time period between the twin World Wars was characterised by the want of any national enemy in the framework of the American Republic and its related foreign policy. The Cold War era communist threat was the rationale which was advanced in order to wage an antagonistic and a largely containment-oriented policy towards the erstwhile Soviet Union. Then, as a consequence of the dismemberment of the Soviet Union and the fall of the Berlin Wall, the American pet peeve changed Now, the Communist threat or the Reaganite era, "Evil Empire", was no longer the arch antagonist of the nation atop Mount Sinai. Instead, the threat of Islamic fundamentalism along the lines of the Clash of Civilizations dialogue became the concerted threat to the United States establishment and the homeland. Clash of civilizations, in the author's view, might be a making of an old and staid order and also an older thesis but the timeless and classic nature of the theoretical construct cannot be ignored as ignoble and arcane. The India-Israel and US triumvirate has remained as a new approach which pits two groupings of nations against each other in an eternal conflict. It does not amount to a divisive rendering of the theme but relates to a realistic perspective in the author's view.

In a vivid reference to a stereotypical construct, in the form of the Hollywood mainstream movie, *The Ghostbusters*, there was a revival of this theme of liberal institutionalism. In the narrative of the movie, three happy-go-lucky bumblers, happen to form a group with supernaturally powered handheld guns when the city of New York and the whole of Manhattan have been taken over by the Green ghosts. The ghosts have their origin from a spell placed in the New York City Museum in a painting from Cairo. The three male protagonists, with a comical persona, make the Statue of Liberty, rise out of the sea barrier and the people run helter and skelter. The whole sewage system and the roads of Manhattan have been swamped by a strange, green and greasy liquid, which is later on sprayed with the 'liberal' shoots from the oversized guns of the three heroes. The threesome incidentally run a ghost-busting unit from a run-down saloon in downtown New York.

Thus, the idiom and the publicised lore of the *Clash of Civilizations*, was advanced nearly by all the prominent observers of international politics, all across the global polity. Still, this more than the symbolical adherence to the liberal tenets and the democratisation project has been historically imbued with the American social political context and its external visage too.

Thus, the idea of harbouring a public evil as a nationally ridiculed hated bugbear and a hateworthy object, was, also alien to the American domestic and foreign policy thinking. In the days before the advent of Archduke Ferdinand's assassination, it was the norm of great power rivalry earmarked by the rise of new powers such as the United States, Japan and Germany which defined the general tenor of the twentieth century international system. Amidst all these developments and such a condition of the world polity, the American new-found confidence after the age of its industrialisation commonly referred to as "Big Business" was bound to present its own experience as a novae framework of analysis and practice for the international system. The tenure of President Woodrow Wilson along with the dream run of the American industry and business led to the surge of a new externally exuded confidence, energy and verve. As an apt instance, President Woodrow Wilson enumerated his fourteen points.

Still in the aftermath of World War I, the American surge reached a disappointing turn of events. Despite President Wilson's espousal of the League of Nations, the American delegation was conspicuous by its absence in the seat of the Council of the League. The US Congress disallowed the nation's membership in the League of Nations after the Treaty of Versailles of 1919. Thus, the domestic public and the political leadership of the American nation state could not be driven to the larger and messianic zeal of the new foreign policy thought of United States, which initiated the expansive, larger and interventionist designs of the Capitol Hill for a noble cause of world peace, stolidity and stability.

Still, President Wilson could not get the US Congress to permit the American membership into the League (LON). Also, the American absence in the various gatherings and meetings of the League's Council, have been termed interestingly as the, "lengthening shadow"[1] of the chair in the conference room which was not occupied by the United States. Thus, the American absence was a blow to the ***Internationale*** movement of cooperation, camaraderie and peacemaking in the general narrative of the international polity. This was the time that without the American presence in the League of Nations, the other member nations were to gather only to discuss the décor of the League's Council's room and the colours of its curtains.[2] Thus, the absence of United States led to a derailment in the international effort at organising a legally binding comity of nations which could serve as some kind of an efficacious hierarchy in an international system conscribed by anarchy, colonialism and pandemonium.[3]

In a way, the American leadership initiated the liberal and freedom run in the global diplomatic conundrum but when the push had to come to a shove, then, the American absence in the chief international body of the comity of nations amounted to a debilitating and self-defeating turn of events. The question loomed large that how could the international peace project be ascertained and achieved without the leverage and the leadership from the Peace Pontiff itself, that is, the United States of America. The nation of milk and honey which was welcoming the mosaic of populations from the Asian and the European continents during the time of World War II, could not be left aloof from the hard-power politics of the times. It was the time after the vanquishing of the foes such as Germany and Japan, that, the New World order could be created under conditions where Great Britain was leaving the world stage without a flourish. Fareed Zakaria has commented, "Great powers enter the world stage and make their exit with a great show of strength and noise like Divas on the international stage".[4] Thus, Great Britain had World War-I, as its stage from where it was beginning to declare its international drawdown or a retreat which could be inferred from the rise in the relative strength of powers such as the United States and other new entrants. It could have been an entry point for multiplicity but as events after the years would show, it was to become a one-nation show.

Thus, despite President Wilson's efforts, diplomacy could not witness the official entry of the United States in the scheme of things. In a way, the people went from one signpost to another before the deliberations of the League of Nations began. Also, the various other treaty mechanisms such as Locarno, Washington Naval Treaty and the Kellogg–Briand Pact, were signed as the adjuncts to the League's peacemaking and building mechanisms. They saw a late entry of America in the scheme of things.[5] The lore of disarmament was avidly and fervently rallied to by the United States establishment. Still, one of the framing and primordial debates doing the rounds was between the isolationist strain of thinking and the interventionist strain of thought and policymaking. This difference in policymaking behaviour and the attendant schism in the power corridors has always been a defining trend of the American foreign policy thought. Even the political denominations of the order of Democrats and Republicans have carried on this discourse on isolationism and interventionism in the American establishment. The Republicans with their ***'Gung-Ho Nationalism'*** and belief in the '***American grand overarch***' have a different tune to play and a separate bass to go by, much to the charging of the other nations. The Democrats believe in limiting the American involvement in foreign affairs which too can be challenged by looking into the available evidence.

Thus, the debate whether to be equated as a hegemon or not and whether to be a great power or not, was a tough choice for the Americans after World War I and had to be solved as a "***collective task***" and a structural demand of the international system. In the twenty-first century context, the American establishment has not been very positive concerning the working and the status of the International Criminal Court. The Americans have been ploughing a separate line on the Non Proliferation cause too. It is only in the post-2008 recession days that nuclear deals have been signed with nations such as India and the advent of the second nuclear age has levelled the international nuclear field with the context of international nuclear commerce being the primary driver of nuclear cooperation among the United States and its other partners. Thus, the American standpoint since the advent of Wilson and Franklin Delano Roosevelt has been such that a myopic assessment of the United States' international role cannot be the order of the day. In the author's view, they are a nation which peaked at a time period when there was a power vacuum in the international system and the mantle of being the Global super police pontiff accidently fell upon the American establishment. It was "serendipity" at its best functionality which resulted in US attaining an unintentional master pedestal in the global context.

In the author's view, the significance of the centrality of the United States in the fulcrum and the happenings of the international system need not be underplayed. The American indispensability since the interwar years has been the order of the day in the global polity with the international players expecting the United States to play key and game-changing roles in various global engagements. America too has played roles in arriving at solutions to myriad international imbroglios and conflicts. Thus, since the twentieth century, the American role playing has been perceived as a sine qua non amongst the comity of nations in order to act as the international balancer of sorts in the general ***'balance of power'*** **(BOP)** game. US now does not only balance but it regulates in the 21st century in the author's view.

In the author's view, the exceptionalism of the American rise economically, commercially, politically and militarily made evident by the turmoil in the interwar years, made it a central peg of the transforming international system. Thus, the American inescapability and exceptionalism concomitant with the changing statistics and material realities began to be emphasised upon the board of the international system.

The World War II Interlude

In tandem with the facts associated with the idea of Russian rise, the German rise and the changing equations in a volatile Europe, America too was passing through a transformative era of its own. It is always argued that the economic depression which the United States underwent led to the reconstruction of the American industrial and infrastructural base which further firmed in the form of the New Deal. World War II witnessed a massive construction effort which the United States witnessed in the fitness of things. It is contended that, "The night after Peal Harbour officials in San Francisco sounded an Air raid in response to a Phantom Japanese Air raid, the New York Mayor, La Guardia called out Security guards to police all bridges-tunnels and factories in the city. Within weeks, wartime resource mobilization set in motion developments that would transform American society. More than 5.6 million Americans enrolled in civil defense programs to do their part in strengthening the 'Home Front' as it was called".[6] Thus, one of the impacts of the great war on the American society and the political economy was that the Americans citizens were enrolled in the defence forces in large numbers. A massive and unprecedented objective and messianic effort to increase security and industrial productivity was launched in the nation. These developments had an eye to defeat the Third Reich and the Axis powers.

The Pearl Harbor attack had brought the Americans closer to the actual war theatre and the nation and its Government had to strive for initialising a war effort as the nation's West Coast was within the reach of the Japanese. The situation in the war theatre was rather worsened as the German Panzer divisions occupied France, Belgium and Holland and with the British being limited to their citadel after being defeated in Tobruk in North Africa. Thus, being neutral in the war effort seemed like a forgone possibility and a predestination of engagement in the hostilities awaited the Americans which was too a larger part of the "Serendipity" involved in the issue of American indispensability.

With the kind of wartime and industrial potential which the United States could develop, it became an international responsibility and also a homeland security issue to get involved in an international objective to militate against the Axis powers. They had reached their military and territorial acme in and outside Europe. William Chafe contends, "As industrialists geared up for levels of unprecedented productivity workers prepared to leave their homes to go where the jobs were in the nation, beginning a mass migration that would eventually lead to 20 million Americans change their county of residence during the war."[7]Apart from the brouhaha premised upon War, the industrial production and the economic growth of the American nation did pick up in the aftermath of the American decision to go beyond the Allies and directly involve themselves in the war effort in Navajo, Solomons and the rest of the Asia and South West Pacific. In the author's view, the immediate impact of the war was not to be materially and tangibly reflected in the general demographic and the city and county-scape of the United States.

One British observer, who visited the United States, mentioned, "No one fresh from London could fail to be overwhelmed by the contrast. Here, if anywhere, was normality-hundreds of miles of it and not a sight or connection to remind one that this nation was at war."[8] Still in the realm of productivity amidst this American cycle, "Between Pearl Harbor and D-Day, US Aircraft factories built nearly seventy thousand planes per year, supplying not only United States needs but those of Great Britain and Soviet Union as well. A similar transformation occurred in shipbuilding. When the war began, experts hoped at best that the shipping industry could produce one ship every six months. By the end of the war, the United States was launching a new ship every twelve days".[9] That is where the idea of serendipity of the American rise was conjoined with the grandiloquent and human American Dream.

Even, the labour union movement prospered in the United States, with the productivity leading on to a new juggernaut of pelf and wartime prosperity. A large-scale rationing took place with the items and usables such as tyres, gas, sugar, coffee along with the women's clotheslines being contained and sanctioned. It is further observed that, "The two piece bathing suit is now tied in with the war as closely as a zipperless dress and the pleatless skirt".[10]Thus, in the author's view, the domestic policymaking in the socio-economic and political firmament in the country was changed and transformed in no bounds as a manifestation of the requirements and demands being made out for United States in the international arena as a the consequences of the Japanese dismemberment of Pearl Harbour's defenses.

Thus, the Armageddon which was unleashed upon the world polity, was, tried to be subsumed by the policymaking in the economic realm by American dole-outs under the policies and programmes such as the Truman Doctrine and the Marshall Plan. The initiation of the Truman Doctrine led to the creation of a policy to help the spread of egalitarian and democratic ideals, all across the international system. The initiation of the Marshall Plan was aimed at reinvigorating the destroyed and spoilt portions of the European nations, as they had borne the brunt of Hitler's Third Reich with the military inundation. All this accompanied Hitler's receding from the continent which ended with the final fall of the capital city of Berlin.

Thus, as an associated accompaniment of this development, a great deal of unprecedented carnage and pillage lay strewn all across the length and breadth of the European continent.Nations such as France, devastated Germany and Britain along with Italy, Belgium and others required immediate aid and financial support along with humanitarian and infrastructural support. Also, the people were to be resettled as a result of the devastation caused by the World War.

Thus, in the author's view, the United States took up the mantle of international responsibility to provide the much needed aid and support to the war-ravaged nations in Europe. In the author's view, it is agreeably put to mention that the larger part of the world is now out of the Western aid basket. Thus, the twenty-first century American democratisation and liberalisation, owes its incipient origin to the elements of the Marshall Plan for the economic reconstruction and regeneration of the war-ravaged European nations. These nations witnessed a great deal of loss of human life and infrastructural pillage which had to be tided over by the responsible international actors and the international community at large.

The much-talked about Marshall Plan speech was the progenitor of the Marshall Plan with its origins in the US establishment. George Marshall appointed by the President Truman as the manager of the Marshall Plan and the European Recovery Plan was referred to as the sole person behind the gargantuan effort for restoring the economic health of a war-affected European continent. George Marshall commented, "*It is logical that the United States should do whatever it is able to do to assist in the return of normal economic health in the world, without which there can be no political stability and no assured peace.*"[11] The American Secretary of State committed the United States to consider a European recovery plan that would be developed by the Europeans and presented to the United States. Thus, was launched the Marshall Plan for which George C. Marshall was awarded the Nobel Peace Prize. Thus, the post World War-II times were symbolic of the ascension of United States of America as a philanthropic state and as a nation which had to begin a coincidental odyssey into the uncertainties of the larger international system.

NOTES

1. Inis Claude, *Swords Into Ploughshares.*
2. Ibid.
3. Kenneth Waltz, *Man, State and War: A Theoretical Analysis,* (Columbia: Columbia University Press, 2001).
4. Fareed Zakaria, *The Post American World* (New York: W.W. Norton and Company, 2009).
5. E H Carr, *The Twenty Years Crisis, 119-1939: An Introduction to the Study of international Relations* (New York: Harper Perennial, 1964).
6. William H. Chafe, *The Unfinished Journey: America since World War II* (New York: Oxford University Press, 1986), pp. 3-4.
7. Ibid.
8. Ibid.
9. Ibid., pp. 8-10.
10. Ibid., p. 11.
11. "The Marshall Plan Speech", URL: http://www.marshallfoundation.org/library/MarshallPlanSpeech.html (Online: Web), Accessed on November 19, 2013)

4

The IR Theory Take

Constructivists of the twenty-first century would call the World War eras as the "Altercasting" times of the international actors as during this new interaction amongst the older and new states, new, "learned iterative spaces" would be established in the structure of the international system. The new states would share their sovergnity with the senior cousins and thus a new collectivity with new international learning would become the hallmark of the post-World War II structure. And, in the author's view, a surging United States would serve as a new podium through which the new international actors could be diligently midwived. The Wilsonian and thus the American programme, was, thus structured not to unduly humiliate Germany and not to lower it in its own eyes, but, as the terms of the Treaty of Versailles were frameworked, it led to a utter humiliation and the severance of the national pride and what all remained of the German national character and strength. Thus, the American ideal of true freedom and equanimity could not be adequately festooned upon the post-war international system as the structures, constraints and figments of domination and division were enshrined once and for all in a largely Euro-centric system in a post-war partisan manner. The Americans turned to roost at the centre stage after a rotation of Empires had arrived.

Still, in the author's view, it was as always in the later day American interventions of the day that the twin strains of isolationism and interventionism remain the cornerstone of the debate and discussion in the US foreign policy thought. The thought pattern which had been the predominant pet peeve was that of isolationism. It was the founding refrain of the American Republic that it would stay away from the Europe-oriented entangling alliances. It was further advanced that the United States can very well recline on its Monroe Doctrine.[1]

The twin nation states of the order of Canada and Mexico were the immediate concerns of the United States beyond which the original political thought of the Americans did not go and quite naturally so.

Also, the isolation of the homeland was made complete by the presence of the Pacific Ocean to the west and the Atlantic to the east. This geostrategic situation and station effectively severed the nation from its adversaries from all possible directions, unknown frontiers and unfathomable dimensions. The nation was fortunate enough not to be pressurised by the misfortune of shared land borders and foreign islets in one's own territory. Thus, the phalanx of contiguity was never experienced by the United States which allowed it to progress on its own course of economic, industrial and military build-up in order to finally meet the old Europe and the rest with a surprise package of never experienced and unwitnessed strength, efficiency and entrepreneurship. In the author's view, the new entrant flummoxed all and sundry through its entry into World War I in 1917 and in the aftermath of Pearl Harbour in 1941. The time had arrived for a destined rezvendous with the netherworld of world politics and the debilitating and entangling alliances of the rest which the eminent founding fathers had abhorred to the greatest extent.

The FDR Era

The aura of protection was granted to the United States through these two great seas and the proud preserve of international realpolitik in the backyard of South-America. This geographical region was initially the favoured stratagem receptacle and the game garden of the American mandarins and operators of statecraft. Also, if we jump the narrative only to come back to the interwar years, Franklin Delano Roosevelt in the context of World War II commented that, "I hate war". Also, in1939, on the eve of the war, the United States had an army of 185,000 men with an annual budget of less than $ 500 million. America had no entangling alliances and no American troops were stationed in any American country. America's physical security, the sine qua non of foreign policy, seemed assured, not because of American alliances or military strength, but, because of the distance between America and any potential enemy.[2] Also, the presence of Britain and France to counter the threats of Fascism in Italy,[3] authoritarian monarchy in Japan and Nazism in Germany happened to keep the American peace-infested honeymoon last till the catastrophe of Pearl Harbour in 1941 which paved the way for the entry of the United States in World War II in the great war part deux.

World War Travails and the Collective Security Ideal: The International Organisational Approach

Coming back to our narrative in the aftermath of World War I, America's newly acquired 'one-uppance' was reflected by the role which the United States began to play as a non-member of the League of Nations. Though the United States entered into a separate treaty with the Central Powers and not the Treaty of Versailles, the American path had to converge despite the opposition of personages like Henry Cabot Lodge. It can be noted through a US source on the web that, "The United States remained officially at war until June of 1921 when President **Warren Harding** approved a joint congressional resolution proclaiming the war with the Central Powers ended, and later signed a separate peace treaty. The resolution and the treaty specified that although the United States was not a party to the Versailles Treaty, it retained all rights and advantages accorded to it under the pact's terms, excluding the League Covenant. The United States never joined the League of Nations."[4]

Still, in the crucial time period between the two wars that astounded humanity no bounds, a large number of developments took place which re-ascertained the presence of United States in the international firmament. In the author's view, Disarmament remained a core concern all through the 'national speaks' of the various countries in the aftermath of the pillage and destruction of World War I. So, the Washington Naval Conference in 1922 reiterated the international concern for a drawing up of a framework to eschew and contain armaments in all possible forms. In the author's view,it was, here, that the United States had a prescribed role for itself, as, it could act as a mediator and an arbitrator for the future firming up of arsenals by the various countries in the international firmament.

The Washington Naval Treaty was also known as the Five Powers Treaty which brought in the five signatories such as the United States of America, Japan, the United Kingdom, the French Third Republic and the Kingdom of Italy. As a background to the treaty it was a well known fact that the United Kingdom still had the most formidable and competitive navies followed by the naval strength of the United States and the Empire of Japan. United States too had laid the keels for five ferocious battleships and battle cruisers which could serve as a foundation for a future leadership role in defense-related needs and status. All the nations which later on became signatories to the Washington Naval Conference were aiming at doubling and quadrupling their military and naval strength and capabilities which was severe in its ramifications on the lines of the dreaded arms race which led to World War I.[5] This Treaty ended a long drawn out period of arms aggrandisement which was further limited by the London

Naval Treaty in 1936. A quota and a proportionate division of the arms, ships, etc. were worked out which were to be followed diligently by the individual naval players and international actors.

In the first plenary session held on November 21, 1921, the US Secretary of State, Charles Evans Hughes, presented the US proposals. Hughes provided a dramatic beginning for the conference by stating with resolve: "The way to disarm, is to disarm." The ambitious slogan received enthusiastic public endorsement and likely shortened the conference while helping to ensure that the US proposals were largely adopted. He subsequently proposed the following:

- A ten-year pause or 'holiday' in the construction of capital ships (battleships and battlecruisers), including the immediate suspension of all capital ship building.
- The scrapping of existing, or planned, capital ships so as to give a 5:5:3:1.75:1.75 ratio of tonnage between the US, Britain, Japan, France and Italy.
- Ongoing limits of both capital ship tonnage, and the tonnage of secondary vessels, with the 5:5:3 ratio.[6]

Thus, United States, played a very prominent role in the leading up to the signing of the Naval Treaty at Washington, though, Japan had some strong reservations concerning the limitation of the various proportions and weapons in accordance with the terms of the conference. Isoroku Yamamoto, the personage behind the success of the Japanese Naval machine in World War II and the implementation of Pearl Harbour, saw to it that Japan could not match up with the production advantage of United States and thus an effective advantage in terms of the naval strength was bound to remain with the Americans.[7] Thus, the Washington Naval conference led to the firming up of at least 'a moral coda' to be followed by the various players getting in the act of strengthening their naval arsenals after the debilitating experience and the much-felt consequences of World War I. Since the efforts of the Hague conferences of 1899 and 1907, limitation of armaments and disarmament became a prime concern for the international actors as the impact of a global war had already been felt by the global polity and the constituent international actors.

United States was, too, not averse to the threat of force or the actual force use leading to an international conflict. Still, the fact which needs to be realized as per the author's view, is that during the interwar years, United States was gradually building up its armaments and arsenal in order to meet up with a rearming of Germany and the Empire of Japan. Still, disarmament functions as an able instrument to peace-building which when combined with other approaches to peace such as collective security and pacific settlement to disputes, leads up to a robust model of peace building. Inis L. Claude mentions, "The case against competitive armaments is not so much that they may cause war as that they cost money and absorb resources, threatening the stability of the World's economic structure which is necessary for peaceful co existence."[8]

He further mentions through the charter of the League of Nations that, "maintenance of peace requires the reduction of national armaments".[9] The nations who went through the rigmarole of the Moscow Declaration and the Dumbarton Oaks proposals too were in the favour of the "the least diversion of resources both human and economic for the stockpiling of armaments".[10] Thus, the notion of disarmament as espoused by the post-World War I international generation went ahead with the idea of positing the condition of war and conflict as a catastrophe and a grave cause of world disorder which had to be avoided at any cost. The United States, much later in the light of the Soviet rise, too came up with its proposal of "Atoms for Peace" in the fifties to mitigate the dangers of the armaments stockpiling which will be dealt with later in the work.

Still later in the international trail of events, United States espoused the cause of the creation of the Atomic Development Authority which would include in its objectives themes such as ownership, management and research, licensing and inspection in order to fulfil its responsibility for ensuring the full exploitation of the peaceful potentialities of atomic energy. US strived for providing states with security against sudden attacks by enemies which had secretly violated the prohibition of Atomic weapons.[11] Thus, also in reference to the Baruch plan, the American position included the idea of developing a peaceful development and propagation of the Atomic Energy in the larger international context within the rubric of the idea of disarmament.[12]

Still, in the author's view, the United States has always stressed on the need to inculcate a halo of international faith and trust which will engage the opposite fence sitters with an equal responsibility to rely upon an expressed goodwill of the antagonist. In 1926, it officially expressed the view that, "Any limitation of armaments must rest primarily upon international good faith and respect for Treaties."[13] The idiom of international inspections was also proposed by a few Western nations along with the United States which was opposed by other countries such as the former Soviet Union.[14] Also, it has been suggested by Andrew Martin, that the standard American position is still very much similar to what had been suggested by the United States at the League Disarmament Conference. The rest of the American positioning in the post World War I stance, is a continuation of the same American positioning in the League Disarmament Conference.[15] The crux of the matter is that whether it be a post-League of Nations approach or the times of the United Nations in a post-Hitler epoch, the

American insistence has always been on a liberal, universalistic and international approach to peace-building and disarmament. Still, nations such as the former Soviet Union and a few others resisted it as their rancour was directed against the idea of universalism and deft internationalism which went against their policy grain. These nations believed and lived by the idiom of sovereignty which led to the firming up of the idiom of national independence and adoption of individual-oriented and country-specific approaches to peace-building and general disarmament. Thus, in the author's view, the construct of American internationalism had both its adherents and opponents in the post-World War I era. In the author's view, everything has not been observed to be 'holier than thou' with the approach of the United States of America; some 'riddles' still need to be recounted. In the author's view, no nation can be perfect when it attempts to reorder the global anomalies with prejudiced, alleged biases and antecedents. The corrective nation itself might get lampooned and criticized for the collective and a universal propagation of its Peace myth and dream.

The so-called halo and the public opinion-harnessed-legitimacy attached to the 'American double speak' also was expressed in the deliberations and the result of the Geneva Protocol of 1926. In the author's view, the American Double speak can be categorized as realistic and pragmatic manner of carrying on with Foreign Policy. The Geneva Protocol was aimed at banning bacteriological warfare and germ agents from being utilised in the battlefields of the present and the future. An European observer of international affairs, Reed Brent, contends, "The final effort towards disarmament during the first decade after 1919 was the Pact of Paris. Its most notable feature was not so much its contents as the fact that the U.S.A. was one of its signatories, thus recognizing once more her connection with and responsibility towards Europe."[16] Thus, after World War I there was this Kellogg–Briand Pact which was signed in 1928 which would renounce war as an instrument of national policy.[17] The Pact with the emphasis by the French and American Foreign Affairs and war offices was to be valued for its spirit and symbolic value. As fifteen nations gathered and were the signatories to this Pact which was signed in Paris and was thus known as the Pact of Paris, it nevertheless failed to prevent major military escalations. Also, it did not define the meaning of the term, "Aggression" and there existed no instrumentality to implement the conditions and provisions of the Pact of Paris.[18] Thus, Italy defined its invasion of Ethiopia as a "Police Action" and Manchuria was soon conquered by the Japanese Empire. In a way, the Pact reflected the Western and American concern about war being a paramount reason for the general misery and suffering of mankind.

Another five-power Disarmament Conference was launched in 1935, but, by that time the Third Reich was re-arming and the German threat had started to loom large over the smaller European nations. Thus, the European nations such as Italy and France ruled themselves out of the negotiations which were supposed to be another rendition of the 1928 Washington Treaty. In a way, it were the United States, the United Kingdom and Japan which ended up as the final negotiators but as the German threat in Europe had its other immediate ramifications, so the credit earned out of the Conference soon evaporated with the German and British game beginning in right earnest in the immediate European context as a prelude to World War II. Still, one positive outcome from these American alliance-making and interventions with a leadership quotients imbued within it all, was, the renewed American reflection of a potential for international leadership in matters of peace building, and a positive utilisation of resources. All this, thus, added to its attendant international misery and suffering. In the author's view, United States should have provided the crucial leadership during that cusp running parallel with German re-armament.

The Depressing Tale

The Economic Depression witnessed in the United States was another benchmark of the crisis of capitalism, unbridled growth and industrial progress, which had created a jewel out of an entrepreneurial United States. The economic depression ground to a near-standstill the engines and dynamos of the American growth and economic progress. This led to drastic and severe measures by the establishment in order to develop a nationwide developmental and infrastructural operations. National projects such as the Tennessee River Valley project had to be spawned in order to upgrade the American experiment in tandem with its new international stature bordering on universal power and influence. It was the economic downturn in the interwar years which led to the slight obfuscation of the grand American experiment.

It can be safely surmised that, "The Great Depression was a worldwide economic crisis that in the United States was marked by widespread unemployment, near halts in industrial production and construction, and an 89 percent decline in stock prices. It was preceded by the so-called New Era, a time of low unemployment when general prosperity masked vast disparities in income."[19]

It is further stressed that, "The start of the Depression is usually pegged to the stock market crash of 'Black Tuesday', Oct. 29, 1929, when the Dow Jones Industrial Average fell almost 23 percent and the market lost between $8 billion and $9 billion in value. But it was just one in a series of losses during a time of extreme market volatility that exposed those who had bought stocks "on margin—with borrowed money."[20] Taylor further contends, "President Herbert Hoover, a

Republican and former Commerce secretary, believed the government should monitor the economy and encourage counter-cyclical spending to ease downturns, but, not directly intervene. As the jobless population grew, he resisted calls from Congress, governors, and mayors to combat unemployment by financing public service jobs. He encouraged the creation of such jobs, but said it was up to the corpus of state and local governments to pay for them."[21] Thus, the talk about a Governmental stimulus was well discussed and deliberated upon by all the stakeholders in the American economy very much on the lines of the President Obama's stimulus package for the American economy which provided the much needed succour to the American economy in the US, post-2008 economic downturn which is commonly referred to as the mortgage crisis. Now, in 2015, the last seven and half years have witnessed a job growth rate of 5 percent where jobs have been augmented in sectors such as construction and retail to lead to a curtailment of the jobs in the Mining and Oil production centres.[22] The long line of skilled labour seekers in Media reports have begun to reflect a new found confidence in the job market with the Government too adding 14,000 jobs in months of November-December, 2015.

NOTES

1. The **Monroe Doctrine** was a policy of the United States introduced on December 2, 1823. It stated that further efforts by European nations to colonise land or interfere with states in North or South America would be viewed as acts of aggression, requiring US intervention. At the same time, the Doctrine noted that the United States would neither interfere with the existing European colonies nor meddle in the internal concerns of the European countries.
2. Stephen E. Ambrose and Douglas G. Brinkley, *Rise to Globalism: American Foreign Policy since 1938* (New York: Penguin, 1990), pp. 2-3.
3. Ibid.
4. "Woodrow Wilson: A Portrait", URL: http://www.pbs.org/wgbh/amex/wilson/portrait/wp_league.html (Online: Web), accessed on 19 October, 2014.
5. "Washington Naval Treaty", URL: https://www.princeton.edu/~achaney/tmve/wiki100k/docs/Washington_Naval_Treaty.html (Online : Web), accessed on 19 April, 2015.
6. David Evans and Mark Peattie (1997), *Kaigun: Strategy, Tactics and Technology in the Imperial Japanese Navy, 1887-1941*, Annapolis: Naval Institute Press.
7. Ibid.
8. Innis L. Claud, *Swords into Ploughshares: The Problems and the Progress of International Oraganization* (New York: Random House, 1960), p. 266.
9. Article 8, paragraph I of the Charter of the League of Nations.
10. United Nations Charter, Article 26.
11. Innis L. Claud, op. cit., pp. 274-275.
12. Ibid.
13. Sir Alfred Zimmerrn, *The American Road to World Peace* (New York: Dutton, 1953), p. 164.

14. Walters, *A History of League of Nations*, p. 366.
15. Andrew Martin, *Collective Security* (Paris: UNESCO, 1952), pp. 51-52.
16. Reed Brett, *European History, 1900-1960*, pp. 120-130.
17. Ibid.
18. Ibid.
19. Nick Taylor, "A Short History of Great Depression" (*The New York Times*, October 6, 2013).
20. Ibid.
21. Ibid.
22. *Indian Express Report*, 6 December, 2015.

5

The Origins of the Cold War: The Spawning of Confrontation

The division of the world polity was gradually attained by the separation of the nations as the nations led by United States and countries led by Soviet Union in the larger sense of the term. The attack on Pearl Harbour led to the entry of United States in the firmament of World War-II. In the author's view, with the American domestic preparation nearly complete as one of the most powerful nations, the world witnessed the surge of United States as a Great power. The epithet of being a great power never meant for the Americans to reflect a higher state of military and industrial power but to serve as a parent reservoir of power to balance the developments in order to usher in stability and balance in the international system. In the author's view, this was the kind of cusp which the American nation found itself before launching forth in the mainstream power dynamics of the world.

A *Guardian* report has summed up the international circumspection about Pearl Harbor. The report says, "December 7 marks the 67th anniversary of the Japanese attack on Pearl Harbor. Over the years, 'the day of infamy' has become a classic reference point for galvanising patriotic sentiment in America. In the wake of the September 11, 2001 terrorist attack, for example, analogies to Pearl Harbor were made frequently. But despite its central place in America's collective memory, Pearl Harbor remains little understood."[1] The report further informs,

> "There were legitimate historical reasons for Japan to feel humiliated on the eve of war. The gunboat diplomacy that resulted in the opening of Japan and unequal treaties in the mid-19th century was but a beginning. More immediately, the Great Depression and the subsequent compartmentalisation

> of the world into economic blocs also worked to the advantage of the already powerful. Coupled with the economic hardship of the interwar years were instances of racial prejudice in the US that aimed at preventing Japanese immigration. United by this long-simmering and humiliating sense of exclusion, Japanese policymakers, whatever their differences, stumbled towards the December 1 decision to go to war."[2]

Also, the rationales of all the great powers have been rather similar. It is not that this observation is being made with an ideological prism but that the animosities were brewing up with the Japanese in the context of strained hegemonic and one-sided economic relations with the United States. Also, the racial slurs of white Manichaeism played a prominent role in the decimation of the "Other" in the national myth and lore of the Japanese. The racial divide and the military threat of White domination, were, also other lesser significant but palpable reasons for both these nations witnessing the pillage in Pearl Harbor.

It was not that with the fall of the Third Reich the international system breathed a sigh of relief. Other international arch-antagonists or enemies awaited their opportunity to run riot on the global stage. If one delves into the theme of the article penned down by George F. Kennan in the *Foreign Affairs* journal, then, one can decipher the palpable urge of the United States establishment to spawn an antagonist where one did not exist on the actual international terra firma. Thus, some scholars pinpoint towards a villain creating propensity of US but the same effort can be witnessed in the machinations of the Soviet Public diplomacy too. The 'myriad bilaterals' and 'multiple trilaterals and multilaterals' which had developed in the form of the Dumbarton Oaks, Yalta, Moscow and London Preparatory Commissions on the way to create a World Organisation, were a mere blip on the international diplomatic scan. The antagonism of the former Soviet Union was writ large over the way the Kremlin deliberated with the Allies as an aftermath of the turning tide of World War II during the grand retreat of the German army across the length and breadth of the European continent.[3]

The race for who reached Berlin first after the mass capitulation of the Third Reich was nothing but an initiator of the to-be-ensued Cold War race which was soon to bedevil and darken the international skies. The way in which the Kremlin was negotiating treaties and the nature of its strategic understanding with the Allies during the run-up to the formation of the United Nations Organization, was already becoming a grim reminder of the portents of an impending Cold war conflict. This had to be very generally perennial in nature and in its ramifications.[4] The urge of the Club of Victors in the aftermath of the War was to create an International Organisation sans the drawbacks and the loopholes of the League of Nations. The Allies considered that they had done too little too late and a much firmer determination and interest had to be manifested by the international actors and the Security Council mandarins in the post-World War II scenario.[5]

Thus, in the author's view, the start up of an Uncle Sam-Soviet rivalry manifested itself in the myriad train of incidents such as the Berlin Airlift along with the 'larger-than-life' incidents of the Korean War and the Cuban Missile Crisis. Thus, the seminal piece penned down by George F. Kennan served as a massive receptacle of ideas and ideologies and policy programmes, which led to the fulsome fruition and escalation of the Cold War confrontation between the savvy American establishment and an equally stolid former Soviet Union. The arcadia being not necessarily limited to Europe but spreading on to the various dominoes all across the length and breadth of the international polity and the global system. Henry Kissigner, the then Associate director of the Department of International Affairs in Harvard University, too, raised his doubts about US being a successful Maximalist.

The issue of how and why the international actors, especially the United States, began to perceive a tangible threat in the form of the former Soviet Union, is a question of interest for the students and observers of international affairs and the American foreign policy. The article titled as, "Sources of Soviet Conduct" delved inside the ideology and the circumstances of the Soviet "Empire" which resonated with a deep distrust of the Steppelands and their political leaders.[6]

Keenan concentrated upon the notion of what Lenin had to enumerate about the fate and the dreary future of the capitalist world that had been ordained for the nations such as the United States and Great Britain. The excerpt from the paper runs as follows, "The rest may be outlined in Lenin's own words: "Unevenness of economic and political development is the inflexible law of capitalism. It follows from this that the victory of Socialism may come originally in a few capitalist countries or even in a single capitalist country. The victorious proletariat of that country, having expropriated the capitalists and having organized Socialist production at home, would rise against the remaining capitalist world, drawing to itself in the process the oppressed classes of other countries."

The Cold War shenanigans had been raised and thus the battle lines were to be drawn all across the Iron Curtain and the various other regions spread all across the international system. Thus, the inkling of the strategic and political future of the world politics as it would develop in the post-war scenario, was underlined in the piece which appeared in the *Foreign Affairs* journal. It had an inbuilt warning for the United States machinery to be aware of the larger threat which the nation faced from the might of a resurgent Soviet Union.

In another excerpt from the much read and frequently referred to piece, the threat potentiality of the former Soviet Union is manifested as a future element in the world politics. "In these circumstances it is clear that the main element of any United States policy toward the Soviet Union must be that of long-term, patient but firm and vigilant containment of Russian expansive tendencies. It is important to note, however, that such a policy has nothing to do with outward histrionics: with threats or blustering or superfluous gestures of outward 'toughness.'

While the Kremlin was basically flexible in its reaction to political realities, it was by no means unamenable to considerations of prestige. Like almost any other government, it can be placed by tactless and threatening gestures in a position where it cannot afford to yield even though this might be dictated by its sense of realism."[7] The inundation and the destruction witnessed during World War II had to be recalibrated and a new niche had to be invented for the American foreign policy. It had to be directed at a Manichaeistic portrayal of a developing international menace which was something which came as a global surprise. The world had just witnessed a war of unprecedented proportions and ramifications and the need to fill the void left by the Third Reich had to be replaced by a new enemy in the form of a cruel, obstinate and unflinching rise of the former Soviet Union. The Realist dictum was adhered to by Kennan in order to pass on his warning as a clarion call for the West against a divisive and costly attrition of a New World confrontation between competing ideologies and steadfast national interests.

Thus, the need to be vigilant towards the former Soviet Union was prescribed as a key idiom of the US foreign policy which dictated the nation's fundamental premise for three to four decades before the implosion of the former Soviet Union in the aftermath of the fall of the Berlin War in the post-state tenor of the nineties and beyond. The finality of the impending conflict between the capitalist and the communist systems was well brought out by the piece authored by a diplomat who had been stationed in the former Soviet Union as a diplomatic plenipotentiary. Thus, it was even interpreted that the collective peaceful co-existence between the twin inherently antagonist systems would go a long way in alerting the United States about the hidden and open threats posited by the onwards march of an expansive former Soviet Union. "It is clear that the United States cannot expect in the foreseeable future to enjoy political intimacy with the Soviet regime. It must continue to regard the Soviet Union as a rival, not a partner, in the political arena. It must continue to expect that Soviet policies will reflect no abstract love of peace and stability, no real faith in the possibility of a permanent happy coexistence of the Socialist and capitalist worlds, but rather a cautious, persistent pressure toward the disruption and, weakening of all rival influence and rival power." [8] Thus, the weakening of the Soviet might was too delineated as a diplomatic panacea for the United States's international health which did run true when the Soviet intransigence in the pressing international matters came to the fore with a stolid intention to stay and reside rather permanently.

There were several instances when the American policy in the post-War era was put to a severe and sincere test. The initialisation of the Cold War was witnessed largely through the playing out of the Berlin Airlift incident which witnessed the World War allies sparring over a piece of territory. The PBS portal run by the United States states a few intricacies about the Berlin blockade. It goes on to say, "The Berlin blockade and subsequent airlift proved to be a public relations bonanza for the United States in the Cold War against the Soviet Union. The American military provided humanitarian relief to Germans, whom they had recently fought on the battlefield, while the Soviets used starvation as a means to control a population."[9] Thus, the division of the people and the territory into four regions and the playing out of the crisis effectively sealed the fates of West and East Germany. The Americans had to help out the West Germans in order to avoid a complete domination of the region and the Berlin territory by the socialist bloc of the former Soviet Union and its Eastern European allies.

The tale of a Chocolate Pilot gained currency in the normal and ordinary oeuvre of the Berlin blockade incident.The people and the administration of Berlin, especially the children of Berlin, received the American funding and the dole-outs by the American citizens. One of the PBS reports says, "As a United States Air Force pilot flying supplies into Berlin during the Soviet blockade, Gail Halvorsen, conjured a special idea for lifting the spirits of children of West Berlin. He delivered packages of gum and candy by attaching them to small parachutes, and dropping them from his C-47 to the children who gathered to watch from the airfield below. The deliveries earned Halvorsen the nicknames the 'Chocolate Pilot' and 'Uncle Wiggly Wings'."[10] Thus, in the author's view, the American operationalising of the liberal and the democratizing methodology as a deft instrument of foreign policy-making made the world take notice.It was able to wield influence. The Americans led to the enabling of a worldwide movement and a momentum in order to circumvent Kennan's word from coming true regarding the rise of a Socialist world led by the former Soviet Union.The communist nation had already displayed its true intentions and veiled manoeuvres during the conferences leading up to the formation of the United Nations Organization. That was to be the prognosticated prelude to what the world was to witness through the prism of James Bond's cinematic constructs through and much after the cooling off of the heydays and the tension of the Cold War.

If one ruminates over the rubric of the Cold War confrontation, then, epic proportions were approached as time progressed. There was an International

Relations Theory referral which amounted to finding out the rationale behind the Cold War. Political scientists like to speak of "Security Dilemmas" or situations in which one state serves to make itself safer and secure but in doing so diminishes the security of one or the other state which in turn tries to repair the damage through the measures that diminish the security of the first state.[11] It may be reemphasised that one of the initial incidents reflecting the grand IR security dilemma being played out in the international context, was the Berlin Airlift incident. As part of the crucial incident, the foundation stone of the Cold War confrontation was laid out for the posterity to come. Stalin as a betenoir of the US foreign policy mandarins responded to the Marshall Plan with the instrumentality of tightening the grip of his person and the Soviet state over whatever they held in the European continent. It was the beginning of the classical Security Dilemma very much in the tradition of the Classical Game theory which draws its origin from the discipline of economics.

Stalin invited the Premier of Czechoslovakia in order to dissuade him from going ahead with the development of any conducive relationship with the United States. The United States was offering the Marshall Plan aid to the East European nation in the hope of breaking the communist coda. Thus, in a globally broadcast press conclave which took place at the Moscow Airport, the Czechoslovakian Foreign Minister was looking very depressed and found it difficult to even answer the queries of the media. A few hours ago on that day, the Soviet leaders, Stalin and Molotov, had castigated and vigorously pressurized the Czech leader into not accepting the economic aid as proposed by the United States as a reasoning to avoid the NATO-led bloc in Europe. Thus, since then the myth, lore and the practice of the Cold War chugged along derisively in the global firmament along with a few other such anecdotal references apart from the actual diplomatic confrontations.

The broken spirit of the Czech Foreign Minister, Jan Masaryk, the son of the founder of the country after World War I, reflected the capitulation of all modicums which might have made the Czechs becoming free from the instruments of the Stalinist Soviet Union. In the same vein, Joseph Broz Tito in Yugoslavia did not bend before the dictates of Cominform which made the Stalinist Soviet Union stand up and take notice. Stalin himself commented that, "I will shake my little finger and there will be no more Tito".[12] Then, as it turned out, the Yugoslavs who had not become free due to any help from the Red Army against the Germans, gravitated towards the fold of the United States which was a Yugoslav part of the Security Dilemma in a post-World War II Soviet ambitiousness in a Europe devastated by pillage and war. Thus, Yugoslavia soon gravitated towards the United States to receive aid and developmental help from the White House. All these developments soured the fundamentals of a relationship between the on the lurching Uncle Sam and the stodgy Soviet Bear.

According to John Lewis Gaddis, "Stalin overtook a less promising venture which was the blockade of Berlin. He may have hoped to force the Americans, British and the French out of their respective sectors of the divided city of Berlin taking advantage of their dependence on supply lines running through the Soviet occupation zone."[13] Such was the division and the profiling of the city of Berlin in a post-World War II scenario. Thus, the mutual distrust between both the nations embroiled them in an unending conflict without the defence forces of both the nations exchanging blows and having an alternative, eyeball-to-eyeball conflict with each other. The Western and American allies improvised an airlift for the beleaguered city and the gratitude of the city dwellers of Berlin city. The negatively propagandist portrayal of the persona of Stalin had begun with the failure of the Berlin Blockade bringing anew the Soviet leader as a "brutal and incompetent commander".[14] "Scoundrels, the old man noted defensively on a Diplomatic dispatch reporting these developments. Its all lies, he said, it is not a Blockade but a defensive measure".[15] The consequence of the Marshall Plan and the Truman doctrine was the Berlin Blockade initiated by Stalin which was promptly replicated by the US Congress in a resolution to pass the European Recovery Act. The events and the trail that followed led to the firming of a mutual security dilemma and mutual distrust which became the forerunner of more gruesomely poised incidents to follow which went on to become the legend and the lore of the mythical Cold War as it was to unfold before the world at large.

The nations like the former Soviet Union and United States withstood the rising and ebbing tides of Nazi Germany but they did not listen to the internal constituencies initially. Later on, as the fall of the Germans became a reality, the issue of lingering with the Allied alliance reached a culmination. Much after the fall of Berlin, the nations began jockeying around for maximum power and territorial influence in the post-War world. Thus, the squeamishness of the allies led to the divergence of the former Soviet Union for greater purposes and personal national interest oriented objectives which were related to national power aggrandisement. Also, the opening of the second front in the World War II days, led to the division of the European continent into spheres of influence with the fear of the Americans. They would be the future of Europe amidst such a situation. The League of Nations was founded on the principles propounded by President Woodrow Wilson who was also the progenitor of the theme and the doctrine of idealism. Also, the nations had to do something about the issue of self-determination wherein the right to breathe a free political air was also one of the avowed political objectives of the United Nations Organization. United Nations had surprisingly being established by a sheer bargaining with the 'selfish' motives of the former Soviet Union.

Also, as an immediate instance which the US policymakers had to respond to was the development that the Poles did not have any political space to carry on unfettered elections. Thus, initially the Soviet wartime and political machinery had not been averse to the fact that some of the satellite states and the liberated countries in Eastern Europe might become democracies. Still, with the instance of the Soviet influence on Poland, the Western powers realised that the mandarins in Moscow did not hesitate to make as their national policy the official and unofficial spread of Communism in the newly liberated Eastern European capitals such as Warsaw and Prague. Thus, power ambitions and the will to earn its own spheres in Europe in the form of the spoils of war after the fall of the Axis powers, led to the initiation of the rivalry between the twin Cold War adversaries. After the Berlin Blockade, the former Soviet Union was able to cross the nuclear threshold and in the year 1949, it was in the wastes of Kazakahastan that it detonated its first nuclear bomb. All the proliferation blame games, in the author's view, should not be directed at the Non Soviet West and United States as Moscow too did its Bikini Atolls test in order to balance out the Americans. The idiom of MAD (Mutually Assured Destruction) could have been behind the race to arm through nuclear arsenals.

Nuclear parity had been achieved by the former Soviet Union and thus the nations such as the United States had to retaliate strategically. The United States had to move towards a far greater nuclear force which amounted to a hydrogen bomb and what some strategists refer to as "Super Bombs." The Americans were left with the foreign policy decision to improve their conventional weapons strength and force potential and thus tide over the former Soviet Union's parity in the field of nuclear potential. Another strategic pathway could be to quickly attain the scientific and operational mastery over a bomb which would be at least many times more powerful than the nukes unleashed on Hiroshima and Nagasaki.[16] Also, the Pentagon announced in one of its declarations that the United States would stay away from 200 nuclear arsenals and would move beyond to the mantle of owning a super bomb.[17] The President advocated that the United States would opt for the larger Peace Dividend, wherein the Congressional consent had to be taken for the recovery of Europe after the devastation of the big war.[18] The End of Ideology narrative which arrived much later with the seminal article written by Francis Fukuyama was given its ratcheted up initiation with the progression of a decades-long confrontation through the instrument of the unforgiving and memorable Cold War. The Cold war engagement had far-reaching strategic, diplomatic and economic and much largely cultural repercussions for the entire world. Later on in the same continuum, the global geopolitics and economics till the fall of the Soviet Union, imploded with the advent of the regional clashes between both the Cold War confrontationists. The cooperation of the World War II days was soon transformed into a heady mutual display of confrontational anthologies in the times to come.

Another Cold War Prophecy

The Cold War 'prophecy' of George F. Kennan had run true when we keep in mind the developments all across the global firmament especially in the nation states of Korea, Cuba and Vietnam. Apart from the apparent norm of confrontation between Cold war states and satellites, there was another facet of intrigues and espionage related to the confrontation years which will be discussed later. The Cold War was initiated not as the manifestation of actual combat and warring in the battlefield, but, as policies and stratagems by the former Soviet Union and the United States of America. It is here that the allies and the client states of both the superpowers were arraigned against each other across the entire gamut of the international polity. Legends and landmarks still dot the terra firma of the United States, wherein the lore and the mythical tale of the dreary and unforgiving Cold War confrontation still lingers on in the memory and the psyche of the American citizens and the persona grata.

In the late twentieth century, a piece was published in the *Los Angeles Times* about the historicity attached to the tale of the Nike Mountain perches for defending the homeland against the clarion call of Nikita Khrushchev who cocked a snook at all diplomatic courtesy by declaring that, "We will bury you alive". The author says, "In the post-World War II military buildup, that followed the hardening of relations between the US and the Soviet Union, Americans lived with the lingering possibility of a nuclear attack. 'We will bury you', Soviet Premier Khrushchev threatened. In response, the Army established Nike missile control sites around the country, including 16 around Los Angeles to protect the city from possible invasion by Soviet planes that could carry nuclear warheads."[19] Thus, mountain bikers can witness the now dilapidated remnants of the missile sites which lie strewn all across the length and the breadth of the LA cityscape.

The report further observes that, "Computers at the mountaintop missile control site could alert the launching site—LA96L—four miles away in the Sepulveda Basin, where up to 30 Nike missiles stood ready to intercept enemy aircraft. Located in an area that remains wild even today, LA96C was fenced in to keep away the coyotes, mountain lions and deer that populate the hills. The missile control system consisted of radar instruments and a series of computers housed in buildings."[20] Thus, the logistics of an Armageddon was well thought by the Pentagon, the Department of Defense and the White House alike in case of any military or nuclear adventure initiated by the "Evil Empire" as was the nomenclature utilised by President Ronald Reagan in the fading days of the Cold War in the eighties.

David Cloud reported in the *Los Angeles Times* that, "The Pentagon's early Bird, an influential daily digest of news and opinion articles about the military that began early in the Cold War, died Friday, another victim of digital news and the government's desire to control the flow of information."[21] Thus, this particular mechanism as part of the state's propaganda mechanism was propped up in order to supply the civil narrative with the much needed information about the tricks of the Soviet Empire and the countermeasures undertaken by the United States Government to overcome the Communist threat. The Early Bird mechanism has a relevance even in the contemporary twenty-first century. David Cloud writes that, "Juicy scoop in the Early Bird could reverberate through the Pentagon's hallways, especially if it caught a senior official unawares. It could make or break a military career, and was read closely by almost everyone who wanted to know what was going on in the Defense Department and could get their name on the distribution list. That list had expanded over the years, starting in 1948, when a hand-copied compilation of news stories began circulating to top officials; to the mid-1960s, when it was known as the Yellow Bird because it was printed on yellow paper; to 1989, when it became the official daily news summary of the Pentagon's public affairs office."[22]

This Governmental mechanism died a silent death when it was discontinued as a Cold War relic in the year 2013. It was reported in a US Department of Defense release that, "Online-only publications and pay walls changed what it meant when the Early Bird republished an article. Warren said he felt that his integrity was compromised by redistributing content the department hadn't paid for. 'By driving traffic away from websites, I felt like I was doing the wrong thing.'"[23] The American magazine *USA Today* too, reported in the same vein that, "In its purest form, the Bird reflected the key issues of the day for troops and the Pentagon officials, giving them, in the parlance, 'situational awareness.' The Bird ranked articles in order from No. 1 to thirty or more stories. More often than not, form held. Developments in the wars in Iraq and Afghanistan, for example, dominated the top spots for years."[24] Thus, the Cold War relics such as the Early Bird publication had its own utility as is evident by its coverage and reportage of the American wars in Iraq and Afghanistan. Still, the Cold War stigma remained attached to it and the internal departmental politics also led to the discontinuance of the publication which had been for years an emblematic publication, source of information and a mouthpiece for the international intent of the United States. It also served as the rationale behind the US foreign policy directives and acts in the international firmament much to be utilised by the fourth estate, the public opinion-makers and the day-to-day citizenry of the country.

The dreary and shambolic Cold War became so much shrouded in mysteries and clandestine stratagems by both the confrontationists along with the palaver of secrecy and symbolism that it soon attained emblematic and symbolic proportions. Thus, several people came to the fore with interesting and myth-oriented tales about the various political actors and incidents in the post-World War II era. The incidents of the order of the Soviet-led Berlin Blockade, the Korean War, the Vietnam War and the Cuban Missile Crisis, all cemented the myth, lore and the larger and life clandestine scare and threat potential of the Cold War era. It was here that both the super states indulged in a myriad plethora of scientific, technological–diplomatic stratagems and parleys. These stratagems spawned a cult of Cold War historians and international relations observers in the global academic and journalistic context. Thus, no conflict in global history has been prolonged for so long a time with so many interesting and edge-of-the-seat developments and incidents. Such menacing incidents nearly brought the world on the tenterhookswith both the United States and the former Soviet Union exchanging angry and potentially blasting diplomatic expletives with each other at the highest levels. It was sheer fortune, fate and the sanity of a few mature political leadership, which saved the world from an Armageddon for more times than once.

In the light of the extension of our American Dream, a public diplomacy construct called as Red Sun Superman was created to serve as a rally-around-the-flag-phenomenon, in order to bring out the nature and ethos of the "evil Communist empire" in the former Soviet Union. As in the Hollywood instance, the American nation was used to the security umbrella being provided by the nation's believers by Superman who entered United States as a result of the mythical destruction of Planet Krypton. The DC Comics envisaged a reverse scenario, when the small child, Kal-El from Planet Krypton, lands in the outskirts of Moscow instead of landing with the Kent family in Smallville, as per the original lore of Superman. Instead of growing up with superpowers in the American countryside, Kal El grows up in the lush flower beds of a Moscow suburb and grows up to battle the capitalist onslaught of United States. He takes up cudgels against Wonder Woman who is a superhero from United States and ends up befriending her. Thus, the American lore was cleverly juxtaposed in a Kremlinseque scenario where the defender of the values of liberty, equality and fraternity is no more a quintessential American superhero but battles for Moscow and the communist movement. Thus, such creations were part of the public and soft power diplomacy which were initiated by both the Cold War protagonists in order to spawn a favourable environment and positive vibes about each other's policies and global posture.

NOTES

1. Eri Hotta, "Understanding Pearl Harbour", *The Guardian*, December 7, 2008.
2. Ibid.
3. Henry Kissinger, *Diplomacy* (Simon and Schuster, 1985), pp. 100-120.
4. Ibid.
5. Innis L. Claud, *Swords into Ploughshares: The Problems and the Progress of International Oraganization* (New York: Random House, 1960), pp. 45-50.
6. George F. Kennan, "The Sources of Soviet Conduct", *Foreign Affairs*, Volume 25, No. 4, July 1947.
7. Ibid.
8. Ibid.
9. "The Berlin Airlift Incident", URL: http://www.pbs.org/wgbh/amex/airlift/sfeature/press.html (Online: Web), accessed on May 19, 2015.
10. "Chocolate Pilot", URL: http://www.pbs.org/wgbh/amex/airlift/sfeature/candy.html (Online: Web), accessed on November 19, 2015.
11. Robert Jervis, *Perception and Misperception in International Politics* (Princeton: Princeton University Press, 1976), pp. 62-67.
12. Nikita S Khrushchev, *Khrushchev Remembers* (New York: Little Brown, 1970), p. 41.
13. John Lewis Gaddis, *The Cold War: A New History* (New York: Penguin Press, 2005), p. 33.
14. Op. cit., p. 34.
15. Ibid.
16. John Lewis Gaddis, *The Long War* (New York: Penguin Press, 1998), pp. 110-112,
17. Ibid., pp. 110-112.
18. Ibid.
19. Jose Cardenas, "Harking Back to Days When Nike Stood for Missile," Los Angeles Times, September 12, 1998.
20. Ibid.
21. David S. Cloud, "Pentagon Kills Early Bird Daily News Digest", *Los Angeles Times*, November 01, 2013.
22. Ibid.
23. "Era Ends On Pentagon's Early Bird News Summary," http://www.defense.gov/News/newsarticle.aspx?ID=121049 (Online: Web), accessed on 25 April, 2015.
24. Tom Vanden Brook, "Pentagon's Early Bird Gets the Axe", *USA Today*, November 01, 2013.

6

The Korean War: The Long Intrusion into the Chinese Backwaters

Among the expansive pantheon of various Cold war confrontations, the Korean incursion by America bears great significance. One cannot forget the American television serial, M.A.S.H. which essays the conflict with humorous ease bearing the military and human dynamics of the Medical centre in Korea. The Korean war led to many casualties on both the sides, that is, the United States Army and the North Koreans backed by the newly independent, People's Republic of China. Generally, the Cold war is about a tale told numerous times but the impact of the incidents makes a re-narration inevitable. The Korean War was fought, premised upon the notion of containment which had by the 1950s become one of the driving dictums of the US foreign policy in light of the consternation being felt due to the resulting tensions with the former Soviet Union. From 1910 until 1945, Korea was ruled by Japan, and when World War II ended, the US split the peninsula, with it occupying the south and the Soviets occupying the north. During the war, North Korea was supported by China and received military aid from the former Soviet Union, while South Korea was supported by the US. The Korean subcontinent was divided by the 38th parallel and the southern part was invaded by North Korea at the behest of China which was further aided by the former Soviet Union. General Douglas MacArthur, in charge of the American forces, was asked to confine his forces but he had a difference of opinion with President Truman as he was of the opinion that the receding Chinese forces must be followed across the Yalu River into the Chinese territory. But, President Truman thought otherwise. With the former Soviet Union also detonating a nuclear bomb and the Americans giving military aid to the

European nations, the battle lines were largely drawn for a greater and far flung and a much more expansive Cold War confrontation.

Historically speaking, it was placed as one of the deliberations of the Cairo Conference in 1943 that the Korean peninsula had to be liberated from the domination and usurpation by the Japanese. As an aftermath of World War II, the Asiatic international space was facing strategic jostling by the great powers including the United States and the People's Republic of China.The spate of a number of Commonwealth group of nations and other colonial possessions of the West winning their independence, was creating a counter current which soon emerged as a tidal wave in the Asiatic polity. The winds of change were blowing over and the colonised nations were becoming independent one after another in the round of decolonisation. This was sweeping across the new post colonial times. It is reported by the online portal, *National Archives*, "In 1945 America declared the 38th parallel of latitude as the line of separation between American and Soviet influence in Korea. The Russians set up a communist state in the north and the Americans established the Republic of Korea in the south. In 1950 North Korea invaded South Korea, marking the start of the 'Forgotten War'."[1] Thus, the war was soon to become a congregation point of the Allied forces as the Cold War edition of World War II. Unknown to many observers of the Korean War, even Great Britain entered the Korean entanglement soon with one of its official directives.[2] Though, the British were taciturn in becoming directly involved in the Korean War, the extension of the World War II dynamics into the Asiatic firmament soon found a reflection in the British decision to enter the Korean conflict.[3] Soon the conflict was entrenched as one of the initial standoffs between the Warsaw Pact nations and the NATO bloc led by the United States and Great Britain in the far-flung Korean Peninsula.

To deftly utilise a metaphor from the literary realm, the scenario depicted in the novella, *The Last of the Mohicans*, was soon reflected away from the Americas and Africa after a 100-odd years when the ideological and the strategic confrontation of the warring Cold War blocs of nations had become the order of the day. This was soon replicated in the Asian context with alacrity after the North Korean establishment invaded the South Korean denomination in 1951. A Hollywood film based on the *The Last of the Mohicans*, was made in the twentieth century which depicted the story of how wars had erupted between the various colonial powers with possessions all across the global polity. In a way, the characters manifested the angst and the vengeance of the myriad local inhabitants of the American settlements with the plot meandering between the antics of the stylish Hawkeye, a warrior of joint American–Indian descent. What was essayed was how he managed to win over and save the life of the defeated

British General's daughter Clara and how the tragedy of imported intercolonial wars turns a travesty out of the peace and stability in the American continent.

Thus, the colonial hangover still was very much a part and parcel of the deliberations and the developments related to the conflict in Korea. Recently ina related development in 2013, the Americans received a jolt at the hands of the North Korean Premier Kim Jong Un when a Korean war veteran was detained in North Korea.

It was reported in the German news agency release that, "US missionaries of Korean descent have a long history of getting into trouble in North Korea and have required high-profile figures such as former President Bill Clinton to secure their release."[4] It was further mentioned in the report that, "In his visit, Bae brought in what the North said were 'propaganda materials' aimed at overthrowing the state. An attempt by the US North Korean rights envoy Robert King to secure Bae's release in August was rejected by Pyongyang."[5] Thus, the Cold War conflict and the confrontationist psychology still remains undone in North Korea with its singularly dictatorial dispensation. The North Korean gung ho spirit of gunning down anything western and American with its bombast and policymaking now hardly makes anyone sit up and take notice. Still, all is not so gloomy and pessimistic about the Chinese, North Korean and the American interface. The notion of the all pervading influence of the tidal wave of globalization and interdependence in the soft and smart security paradigm, leads to the instilling of a new stratagem and tradition of cooperation between the nations. These countries have been Cold War rivals and nations having fought wars with each other.

Though our concern here is the historical antiquity of the Korean war, but as a comparative paradigm one can have a look at an important incident in 2008, too. This contemporary narrative might not be disruptive but congeals the relationship between China and United States in the context of the repatriation of POW's. Thus, in a recent development in 2008, the Chinese authorities agreed to share the details of missing American personnel with the American establishment.[6] A newspaper reported that, "China has agreed to allow access to military records that may provide information on 8,100 Americans missing from the Korean War. U.S. officials say that, at least at first, only Chinese archivists with security clearances will do document searches and turn over relevant records to U.S. analysts."[7] Also in one of the British Government documents a firm reassertion of the idea of ideological confrontation was brought to the forefront in a testimony speech delivered by President Truman upon the threat of Communist domination of the Pacific. He reiterates that, "The Communists have moved away from the strategy of direct subversion to the idea of invasion, wherein they have defied all the orders of the Security Council norms and have failed to preserve international peace and security. Also, I have ordered the Seventh Fleet to prevent any attack on Formosa which is independent and threatened by the People's Republic of China."[8]

The American-aided and independent island of Formosa, was the place, where, the nationalist Government of Koumintang, had fled to after losing out to the People's Army in 1949. This was perceived by the Americans as the initialisation of a larger domino process by the Chinese and the Soviet Government in order to scale up the communist influence in the Pacific. This had already been witnessed in the Pearl Harbor incident and the attendant decision to enter the fray in World War II. Thus, the Korean War was also a kind of an intelligent and strategic extension of the idea of communist dominoes spreadeagling all across the Pacific expanse and the Asiatic maritime space, which, till now had been an American and British preserve. It was further mentioned in the document that, "The Formosa was a different case altogether as the Nationalist Government was only the Administrator of the Territory while the attacks on the British ships were carried out with impunity by the Chinese naval agencies thus a Chinese controlled threat had become a threat to the Allied naval agency in the Pacific."[9]

Thus, the containment of the Chinese influence was jointly recognised as a key Pacific and containment question by the Allies and most significantly the Americans were becoming wary of the Chinese designs much like the twenty-first century South and East China sea dispute. The 21st century dispute includes conflict over the Scarborough shoals and the Senakakus in the contested seas. So, in a way the Chinese influence and its force projection potential in the important trade sea lanes of communication were perceived as a rationale to initiate a containment of the Chinese intent. The Korean conflict and the Chinese aid to the North Korean dispensation were enough inducements to the Americans and the wartime allies in World War II to initiate an intrusive exercise against the Chinese. Correspondence between Frederick Brown and Harry S. Truman concerning the start of the Korean engagement of the United States was also regarded as an initialising point of the Allied war effort. Frederick Brown Harris wrote to President evincing his interest and strategic and political standpoint on the Korean issue. He insisted that:

> "Synman Rhee ought to be the real, formalized and recognized leader, of the Korean nation as he had made ample sacrifices for the Korean cause and its eventual independence and freedom from the Japanese yoke. He was not accorded a place in the San Francisco Conference leading up to the formation of the United Nations which is a matter of great concern for me and my office."[10] He further went on to insist that, "The Chinese Foreign

> Minister, T.V. Soong, should be told about the Korean cause and the American interest and standpoint in the region.
>
> The nation state of Argentina with a black history has been accorded a place in the San Francisco conference while Korea having a white and untarnished record of militating against the Japanese aggression has been excluded which does not speak well for the stated and propagated standpoint of United States."[11]

Thus, the general house was divided about the policy to be adopted vis-à-vis Korea but the Chinese and the Russian intent was well founded and was also being deliberated upon by the American policymakers and the strategists. In a way, the Korean entanglement of the United States was also turning out to be a continuity in the post-war allied policy moves to contain a rising former Soviet Union. In a way, the Americans were adhering to the new-found former Soviet Union factor which was well elucidated by the Kennan article in *Foreign Affairs* which also forecasted the Soviet intentions and the need for containing an intransigent former Soviet Union for the stable future of the international system.

It was the National Security Council Paper-68 broadly titled as, "United States Objectives and Programs for National Security",which reiterated the theory of containment and the deepening of the wedge between the twin Cold War confrontationists. It was stressed that the nation's foreign and strategic tilt and the attendant policy had to be re-calibrated within the changing context of the international system. The paper drew the attention of the American policymakers towards the hostile design of the former Soviet Union along with the notion that the leading Communist nation was on the way to gaining parity in terms of the conventional arms, defence technology and nuclear potential. Thus, this was an insistence upon the national need to devise a counter offensive which would reinvigorate the West and the American politico-strategy plank in the international system. With the former Soviet Union having emerged as a potential threat. It was discussed in the paper that,[12] "The decline of the Western European powers and Japan following World War II had left the United States and the Soviet Union as the two dominant powers. It was argued that the Soviet Union was 'animated by a new fanatic faith' antithetical to that of the United States, and was driven 'to impose its absolute authority over the rest of the world'. Furthermore, they concluded that 'violent and non-violent' conflict between the United States and the Soviet Union had become endemic."

Thus, the endemic nature of the conflict which was also inevitable in nature resonated much like the Truman Doctrine and the X article penned down by George Kennan. Thus, the grandiose schism with an immense scare potential for the newly independent, developing and recently decolonised part of the world was immense. Several probable approaches were outlined by the 'Draft NSC-68' which would later become one of the guiding documents of the nation's foreign policy during the Cold War. The threat and the enemy would change in the post Cold War era by the scourge of low intensity, sub-conventional war waged by the diminutive Islamic fundamentalists. They in themselves were to become the subject mater of the GWOT (Global War on Terror). Another postulate of the NSC-68 reported that, "NSC-68 outlined a variety of possible courses of action, including a return to isolationism; war; continued diplomatic efforts to negotiate with the Soviets; or "the rapid building up of the political, economic, and military strength of the free world."[13] Thus, before the future cold war confrontations of the order of Cuban Missile Crisis, the Vietnam war and other Domino conflicts raged in the international system, the contours of what ought to be the American Foreign policy were carved out with all the debating niceties in the American policy firmament. What the larger international system was to witness was a larger threat of scattered conflicts which could one day transform into a sudden armed and nuclear confrontation.

NOTES

1. URL: http://www.nationalarchives.gov.uk/cabinetpapers/themes/korean-war.htm, (Online: Web), Accessed on 1 January, 2015.
2. Cabinet Memorandum. Formosa; Memorandum by the Minister of State. 3 July 50.
3. A. Farrar-Hockley, *The British Part in the Korean War*, 2 vols. (London: HMSO, 1995)
4. Laila Kearney, "US Korean war Veteran detained in North Korea: Son", URL: http://www.reuters.com/article/2013/11/21/us-korea-north-detention-idUSBRE9AK00P20131121 (Online: Web), Accessed on January 1, 2015.
5. Ibid.
6. "US to Get Data for MIA Search", *Los Angeles Times*, March 1, 2008.
7. Ibid.
8. 3 July, 1950, C P (50) 156, "'Formosa' Memorandum by the Minister of State", British Government Document.
9. Ibid.
10. "Correspondence Between Frederick Brown Harris and Harry S. Truman", May 8, 1945, Official File, Truman Papers.
11. Ibid.
12. US Department of State, Office of the Historian, "Milestones: 1945-1962, National Security Council Paper-68", URL: http://history.state.gov/milestones/1945-1952/NSC68, (Online: Web), Accessed on 28th November, 2014.
13. Ibid.

7

The Cuban Missile Crisis: The Near-to-Annihilation Quotient with Tipping Over the Precipice

If there is a biggest tale to be narrated about the Cold war's pantheon then no other nation and parley can get bigger and more impactful; than Cuba and its attendant missile crisis. The trend of the Cold War was a deft continuation of the scenario which had characterised the international system in the post-World War II scenario. The legendary proportions which the Cuban Missile Crisis has attained, is owed very much to the personalities and the deadly exchange of letters between the leaders of United States and Soviet Union. The world came near to a nuclear Armageddon and the conflict precipice from where the applecart of the international system could have tilted over anytime. This became part of the storytelling and anecdotal exercises in the Cold War and World History classrooms all across the academic and story telling fraternity. The Cuban Missile Crisis is understood to be a core element which is supposed to have brought the international system on the brink of a Nuclear Armageddon during the heydays of the Cold War. The murky and high exchange of letters between President Kennedy and his war room and Premier Nikita Khrushchev also went on to become part of standard Cold War research and the myth and lore which became associated with the Cold war's trail of events and face-offs between the United States-led NATO group of countries and the Warsaw Pact nations led by the former Soviet Union.

Graham Allison writes in *Foreign Affairs* that, "The main story line of the crisis is familiar. In October 1962, a U.S. spy plane caught the Soviet Union attempting to sneak nuclear-tipped missiles into Cuba, 90 miles off the United States' coast. Kennedy determined at the outset that this would not stand. After a week of secret deliberations with his most trusted advisers, he announced the discovery to the world and imposed a naval blockade on further shipments of armaments to Cuba."[1] Also, the stand-off between the United States and the former Soviet Union was a matter of great dialogue and clandestine negotiations which stemmed from the "Ex-Com" room of the White House and from where the tricky negotiations were carried out. Before going into the actual incidents which led to the unfurling of the peace flag between the White House and the Kremlin, certain leaves can be taken out from the book of the Cuban missile negotiations. In a way, the tumult could be understood and comprehended in all its entirety, only when the top most leaders were well versed with and well informed about the rationale of the happenings and were in touch with the repercussions which could flow from any strategic decision. Graham Allison further writes that, "A final lesson the crisis teaches has to do not with policy but with process. Unless the commander-in-chief has sufficient time and privacy to understand a situation, examine the evidence, explore various options, and reflect before choosing among them, poor decisions are likely. In 1962, one of the first questions Kennedy asked on being told of the missile discovery was, how long until this leaks?"[2] Thus, the secrecy element of the negotiations was the key to a peaceful and mature unfolding of the crisis which was brokered by the United Nations and the UN Secretary-General, U Thant, in a rather ingenious manner which bears the mark of successful conflict resolution.

If the Soviet intransigence would have been declared by the American Fourth Estate as a severe threat to national security and peace, then, President Kennedy would have found it immensely difficult to calibrate a response to the Soviet export of Inter Continental Missiles to Cuba ruled by Fidel Castro. The secrecy idiom was the secret of success of the negotiations which led to the resolution of the crisis without any bloodshed. As the international system at that point of time, led by the United States and the former Soviet Union, had gone nuclear, so any slight strategic miscalculation would have led to mayhem and a nuclear confrontation. The scenario would have had grave ramifications not only for both the Cold War foes but the rest of the world with catastrophic and incalculable consequences.

Graham Allison further mentions,

> "In today's Washington, Kennedy's week of secret deliberations would be regarded as a relic of a bygone era. The half-life of a hot secret is measured not even in days but in hours. Obama learned this painfully during his first year in office, when he found the administration's deliberations over its Afghanistan policy playing out in public, removing much of his flexibility

> to select or even consider unconventional options. This experience led him to demand a new national security decision-making process led by a new national security adviser. One of the fruits of the revised approach was a much more tightly controlled flow of information, made possible by an unprecedented narrowing of the inner decision-making circle."[3]

Thus, the historicity embedded in any foreign policy story needs to be respected and treated by the think tanks and the strategists as the panacea for the future. It could serve as a pointer to what all ails the pathway to peace and stability in the international system when two big stage nation state actors are involved in an imminent conflict situation. Also, one needs to be reminded that the practice and theory of International Relations happens to be that of repetitions and recurrences, wherein the new great powers emerge at the gravestones of others and a titanic clash of interests with the older and much more powerful great powers occurs. This leads to repetitiveness[4] in the international outcomes in the form of wars and rapprochements, thus, engulfing the avid IR observers in the mud of mundane research and theorising. Still, that is how forecasts and prognostications can lead to theorisations and a future of charting out of strategies and solutions for the future of a fast-changing international system.

In the related context of Cuba, the classical IR theorist, Martin Wight, paints a very gloomy and pessimistic picture of the international system. This is marred by wars, conflicts, competition and anarchy in a land which is craving for peace, stability and stolidity through the will of Immanuel Kant's 'Perpetual Peace' thesis. The idiom was that of a World Parliament and an attendant Inter-Planetary/Galactic system, which paved the way for an "altercasting" between the foes as they enter into an iterative relationship with each other. This further leads to a change or a gradual transformation in the individual character, sanity and policies of the confronting nations; here, the case being that of the United States and the former Soviet Union.

It is espoused as an argument by some IR observers that, "Is Wight here proclaiming the ultimate heresy that after all, theoretical understanding of international politics is not possible, only historical understanding is? Is he, so to speak, throwing in the sponge? No, he is not; this is not what he says and all of his work in this field is a denial of it—for while that work is steeped in history it is not itself history. Wight gives us the clue a little further on when he writes that the only kind of theoretical inquiry that is possible is 'the kind of rumination about human destiny to which we give the unsatisfactory name 'philosophy of history'."[5] Thus, the embedded historical content, ruminating argumentation and the historicity of the Cold War era can be earmarked as a guiding light for the IR academics and the American strategists to pick out significantly rational leaves from. It is one of the indelible drafts of history and myth which can be efficiently utilised for the dismemberment of myths and with an overture to facilitate better and efficient decisions in the contemporary foreign policymaking calculus.

Michael Dobbs has written beautifully about the entire gamut of incidents and events which led to the negotiations stage of the Cuban Missile Crisis. He writes in the *New York Times*, "Khrushchev's motivations in sending nuclear-tipped missiles to Cuba in the summer of 1962 have been the subject of great debate. Kennedy administration officials argued afterward that the Soviet leader acted for global strategic reasons. Prior to the missile crisis, the United States had around 3,500 nuclear warheads capable of reaching the Soviet Union, a 10-1 advantage over the Soviet Union."[6] Thus, the strategic calculus of the Cuban conflict makes for a very interesting and effective study where the balance of nukes played a significant role in the spawning of the crisis and the final denouement of the diplomatic stand-off between the United States and the former Soviet Union.

Apart from the strategic and the diplomatic angle to the Cuban imbroglio in 1962, there was a new perspective which Michael Dobbs highlighted in his work. The commentator on the Cuban imbroglio referred to the personal and personality perspective too, which had some tangible role to play in the Cuban issue. Khrushchev regarded President Kennedy as a novice in leadership and rather inexperienced to trounce and handle a superpower and its citizens. Dobbs writes, "Khrushchev also had more personal reasons for wanting to get even with Kennedy, whom he regarded as an inexperienced leader young enough to be his son. The United States had stationed medium-range Jupiter missiles in Turkey, across the Black Sea from Khrushchev's summer retreat in Sochi. Complaining that there were 'U.S. missiles aimed at my dacha', the Soviet premier thought it was 'high time America learned what it feels like to have her own land and her own people threatened'."[7] Thus, he demanded a quid pro quo from the American strategists that unless the Jupiter Missiles were not removed from Turkey the former Soviet Union, too, would not think of removing its ICBMs from the 'recalcitrant Cuban nation state'. It was a typical Summit-like negotiating positing and posturing which could have well have changed or worsened into a conflagration and an uncontrollable contagion for world peace.

Seymour Topping wrote in the *New York Times* on October 24, 1962, "The Soviet Union challenged today the right of the United States to impose a quarantine on the shipment of weapons of any type to Cuba. It asserted that the Castro regime could make whatever defense arrangements it pleased."[8] Thus, one interpretation was a strategic methodology for the Kremlin and Nikita Khrushchev to get even with the White House in the matter of clandestine negotiations. It was on October 27 that one of the rays of hope for the denouement of the conflict and the stand-off began to emerge. E.W. Kenworthy wrote on October 28, 1962 that, "President Kennedy revealed tonight that Premier Khrushchev had offered an acceptable solution for the Cuban crisis and then pulled away from it."[9] The United Nations Secretary-General U Thant too proposed a new solution with his own international organisational perspective in order to solve the imbroglio. Still, he did not initially agree to demobilise the blockade on Cuba as part of his strategic decision-making thought. He wrote that, "President Kennedy agreed today to talks between the United States and U Thant, Acting Secretary General, on whether arrangements can be made for negotiations in the Cuban crisis. The blockade of Cuba will continue."[10]

Thus, the international community was very much concerned about the outcome of the Cuban Missile Crisis's denouement which was much awaited. The IR observers and the leaders all across the international firmament were waiting for a peaceful resolution as the nuclear perspective of an imminent conflict was well understood by all and sundry in the Cold War-ordained international system. It was E.W. Kenworthy, who reported to the world on the 29th of October, that, the nuclear and missile stand-off between an aggressive United States and an equally intransigent former Soviet Union had ended. He went on to write that, "President Kennedy and Premier Khrushchev reached an apparent agreement today on a formula to end the crisis over Cuba and to begin talks on easing tensions in other areas."[11] It was a fruitful and a comprehensive denouement after the world had thought that the leaders were fearful to negotiate because of good reasons in order to resolve the Cuban Missile Crisis. Thus, a nuclear confrontation meaning misery to the citizens of the world was avoided by the sagacity and the maturity shown by the leaders at the helm of affairs in the United States and the former Soviet Union. Diplomacy held its larger sway, which happened to be meaningful and functional, during those dangerously heady times.

If one utilises the historical material available to us then several interesting and informative segments can be evolved out in the context of the Cuban political crisis. A few letters were exchanged between President Kennedy and Premier Khrushchev, which added to the initial diplomatic confusion and later on, led to the peaceful denouement of the Cuban political crisis, at the height of the Cold War. It was on October 24 that a letter was exchanged between both the leaders as the crisis developed between the two nations, about to be at loggerheads with each other.An excerpt from the letter addressed to President JFK by Premier Kruschev, can be cited here,

> "You, Mr. President, are not declaring a quarantine, but rather issuing an ultimatum, and you are threatening that if we do not obey your orders, you will then use force. Think about what you are saying! And you want to

persuade me to agree to this! What does it mean to agree to these demands? It would mean for us to conduct our relations with other countries not by reason, but by yielding to tyranny. You are not appealing to reason; you want to intimidate us. No, Mr. President, I cannot agree to this, and I think that deep inside, you will admit that I am right. I am convinced that if you were in my place you would do the same."[12]

Thus, it was both part of a personalised and a collective diplomatic correspondence that both the nations and their leaders had realised the iota of threat and the danger of escalation involved in the Cuban Blockade imposed by the United States.

The personality factor, too, played a greatly prominent role in the peaceful culmination of the Cuban Missile Crisis. It is here that the security dilemma of both the nations, namely, the United States and the former Soviet Union comes to the fore. Both the countries were kept in dark about each other's stealth and kill potential and the extent to which both the countries would go, if push came to shove. Thus, it was a dilemmatic scenario in which both the nations were uncertain about each other's store of patience and strategic action. It is here that the limits of the war room diplomacy were stretched to the maximum extent in order to not to try the potential and the patience of both the embroiled nations.

Thus, in a manner, the battle lines were not to be drawn by both the nations as the looming large threat of a nuclear confrontation was sought to be avoided by both the countries. Kremlin directly communicated it to the White House that the American request of the removal of the ICBMs from the Cuban mainland was being construed as a rude wake up call and a churlish ultimatum to an independent and sovereign entity. This would not lead to any kind of rapprochement between both the nations poised at a critical hour.

In a reply to Khrushchev's first letter on October 24, Kennedy wrote back with alacrity on October 27, 2014. The letter conveyed the American concern for institutionalising peace in the region and the efforts being undertaken by the American establishment to deny war from making an entry into the ongoing negotiations. The letter read as such,

"I have given my representatives in New York instructions that will permit them to work out this weekend—in cooperation with the Acting Secretary General and your representative—an arrangement for a permanent solution to the Cuban problem along the lines suggested in your letter of October 26th. As I read your letter, the key elements of your proposals—which seem generally acceptable as I understand them—are as follows:

1. You would agree to remove these weapons systems from Cuba under appropriate United Nations observation and supervision; and undertake,

with suitable safeguards, to halt the further introduction of such weapons systems in to Cuba.[13]

2. We on our part, would agree upon the establishment of adequate arrangements through the United Nations to ensure the carrying out and continuation of these commitments—(a) to remove promptly the quarantine measures now in effect, and (b) to give assurances against an invasion of Cuba. I am confident that other nations of the Western Hemisphere would be prepared to do likewise."[14]

Thus, in the author's view, the response which President Kennedy sent to Premier Khrushchev shaped the culmination of the Cuban tangle as a ray of hope which was to be seen in the context of the denouement of the international crisis. The world had already reached a precipice and an obstinate and intransigent directive and riposte from any of the leaders could have exacerbated the conflict. Still, the mature and level headed diplomacy and the epistolary communication that was exchanged between both the heads of states averted a confrontation of the worst kind between both the nations and in the world at large. Also, the universal concern of the day which was disarmament, was, very much reflected in another persuasive epistle which was sent by President Kennedy to Premier Khrushchev. The letter stated, "I agree with you that we must devote urgent attention to the problem of disarmament, as it relates to the whole world and also to critical areas. Perhaps now, as well step back from danger, we can together make real progress in this vital field."[15] Thus, apart from notionally and symbolically supporting the cause of disarmament and demilitarisation, President Kennedy realised the urgency and the criticality of the situation. The President made a well-meaning and impactful effort to bring back the imperilled international comity of countries from the brink of a military and nuclear catastrophe. It was definitively a throwback to the idea of "Atoms for Peace" which was coined by President Eisenhower in the heydays of the nuclear rivalry between the super monoliths of the United States and the former Soviet Union.

The Cuban Missile Crisis was a kind of diplomatic war game. The locusts of war had been gathering over the American waters since Operation Mongoose and the American raid over Cuba in the beginning of the sixties. Operation Mongoose was reviewed by the various military leaders in the American establishment. If we delve inside the official documents, then, we can find a reflection of the discussion in the American circles. Brigadier General Landsdale commented upon the intricacies, objectives and accomplishments of Operation Mongoose. He went to stress in a memorandum of his that, "It was asked for the CIA to get involved in collecting hard intelligence which would be later utilized in contacting people involved in guerilla activities in order to recruit and train the discontented groups in Cuba. It was further noted that the America aided operation fell short of a full fledged operation by the American Defense forces in order to minimize the risks."[16]

Brigadier General Lansdale further stated that,

> "Enough stress was laid on the psychological warfare capability of the American establishment. Short Wave communication was utilized in order to reach out to the majority of the Cuban Population. Still, the capability of the American psy-ops was found to be inadequate in transforming the public opinion in Cuba. The President's visit to Mexico was also arranged. It was hoped to reinvigorate the public interest in the military suppression carried out by Fidel Castro. Also, it was intended to utilize the Punta Del Este Conference which was not part of the original context and purpose of Operation Mongoose. The military suppression of hunger demonstrations at Cardenas in Cuba was also utilized to let the international observers comment upon the acts of the Fidel Castro Regime."[17]

Thus, a lot of greater international effort had been initiated by the American Government in order to create an environment to bolster the idea of Cuba being a recalcitrant nation state. In order to serve the objective of the Government, the US effort was aimed at creating a Manichaeistic portrayal of Fidel Castro. It was a common striving as part of the psychological efforts of the more potent and the powerful nation state to paint the political leader of the weaker antagonist state as the prototypical antagonist in order to belittle that nation. Thus, the satanisation of the enemy nation was definitely a part and parcel of the general Cold War narrative in order to cleanse the aggressor/potent superpower of all the blame that might come in the way of the super power and the nation which is propagated as the 'Do-Gooder' nation state. Fidel Castro received a great amount of negative coverage by the US mainstream media. The essentially pro-establishment coverage is the order of the day as far as the coverage of the antagonist political leaders of the United States is concerned. While every other country in the Western Hemisphere moved towards democracy, Cuba had remained a one-party state under Fidel Castro, who held power without free elections from 1959 until health problems forced him to step aside in 2006. One US-based media watchdog, Media Research Center, has covered the theme of Fidel Castro and his laudable achievements as posited by the US-based liberal media. In one of its reports, the Media Research Center comments that, "The most laudatory coverage of Castro and his communist revolution's 'achievements' have come when an American news network decides to visit Cuba for an in-depth examination. Invariably, the US networks granted access and the same have rewarded the communist government, with promotional coverage of both Fidel Castro and the supposed achievements of his revolution."[18] Thus, in the author's view, if one goes by the perception of the US interventions and wars being promoted by the US mainstream media, then it can be simplistically surmised that the media coverage has amounted to a cheerleading exercise for the various American war efforts including the Cuban Missile Crisis. Still, the media houses which were permitted by the Cuban regime to visit Cuba and cover it, have lauded the Castro's establishment and his revolution in Cuba.

In the author's view, America adheres to a religiously realism ordained foreign policy which might militate against the several other interests of countries and global-regional groups of nations. In the author's view, the seemingly highhandedness of United States can be understood strategically with the entrepreneurially comprehended and a pragmatic and national interest directed approach. Other great and powerful nations and Empires have too followed policies only to be castigated and confronted in the international system. US is no exception to the rule. Still, in the author's view, as the responsibility falls on the shoulders of a powerful nation let it be United States of America and not a Dictatorial and un democratic country which might not have the global alliances and the ground strength to manage conflicts and relations in an effective manner. Thus, in the author's view, Functionalism and pragmatism, which pinpoint towards an efficient and work allocation based responsibility, makes US emerge as the Chosen nation to manage the world, though in a just manner. It is not a Polemic argument but in the author's view, a rational one in order to facilitate a Great power to manage the global relations. No nation can be perfect and the national strategy at conflict management and reconstruction can go wrong and this limitation is bound to invite international opprobrium. Still, someone has to bell the cat like the United States found itself doing it during various critical junctures in current history.

To take an example from the pantheon of American history, there was no direct military attack by Spain against the United States prior to the exchange of declarations of war by the nations, and initiation of hostilities by the United States in 1898.[19] A notable event, the sinking of the U.S.S. Maine in the Havana harbour, provided an additional argument for war against Spain for those advocating it in the United States. The actual cause of the sinking of the U.S.S. Maine, even today, has not been definitively established. More recent scholarship argues that it was most likely as not due to an external attack.[20] Thus, the controversy doing the rounds about the course to be taken by the international community in the context of the discussion premised upon a preventive war, is a paramount rejoinder to the US foreign policy thought and practice. The idea had not gained much currency in the context of the Cold War, at least in the war scenarios such as the Cuban Missile Crisis, which had not been given any individual paramount significance. Legally speaking too, Section 503(e) of the National Security Act of 1947, as amended, defines covert action as "An activity or activities of the United States Government to influence political, economic or military conditions abroad, where it is intended that the role of the United States Government will not be apparent or acknowledged publicly." Thus, there are some limitations as far as the extension of the American military support abroad is concerned.

Americans have faced a variety of ideological challenges and obfuscations in the context of the historical incursions which they have made in the various nations of the international system. The notion of preemptive war has been extolled by some of the international law scholars which does have some truth. Still, if the Realist perspective is to be taken care of and if it is to be adhered to, then the idea of an unbridled and loyalist adherence to the notion of national interest and national foreign policy objectives has to fructify. Then, the idea of an expansionist and power-centric strategy in the context of the American case has to be understood and comprehended in its totality. There cannot be a singular faceted positioning concerning the argument of Pre emptive war. Since the destruction of the White House by the British, in 1815, the act and theology of "Pre emption" in war and Diplomacy became a key cornerstone of the American foreign policy. Such was the larger rationale behind American diplomacy in Cuba.

NOTES

1. Graham Allison, "The Cuban Missile Crisis at Fifty: Lessons for US Foreign Policy Today", *Foreign Affairs*, July-August, 2012.
2. Ibid.
3. Ibid.
4. Cynthia Weber, "Reading Martin Wight's "'Why is there no International Relations Theory?' As History", *Alternatives*, 23(1998), 451-469.
5. Butterfield and Wight (eds.), *Diplomatic Investigations: Essays in The Theory of International Politics* (Harvard University Press, 1996), p. 33.
6. Michael Dobbs, "Cuban Missile Crisis: 1962", *New York Times*, January 7, 2014.
7. Ibid.
8. Seymour Topping, "Moscow Replies: Warsaw Pact Nations to Step Up Preparations", *New York Times*, October 24, 1962.
9. E.W. Kenworthy, "Kennedy Replies: Urges Kremlin Stand By Initial Proposal", *New York Times*, October 28, 1962.
10. Thomas J. Hamilton, "UN Gets Reply: Secretary General too Start New Parleys", *New York Times*, October 26, 2013.
11. E.W. Kenworthy, "Capital Hopeful: Plans to End Blockade as Soon as Moscow Lives Up To the Vow", *New York Times*, October 29, 1962.
12. "Khrushchev's Letter to Kennedy", URL: http://library.thinkquest.org/11046/sitroom/letters.html (Online: Web), accessed on January 1st, 2015.
13. Ibid.
14. Ibid.
15. Ibid.

16. Brigadier General Lansdale, Office of the Secretary of Defense, Washington 25 DC, 25 July, 1962. “Review of Operation Mongoose”.
17. Ibid.
18. Rich Noyes, Research Director of MRC, “Fidel's Flatterers: The US Media's Decades of Cheering Castro's Communism”, URL: http://archive.mrc.org/SpecialReports/2007/castro/welcome.asp#Field%20Trips%20to%20Fidel%E2%80%99s%20Island%20Paradise (Online: Web), accessed on 1 April, 2015.
19. Declarations of War and Authorizations for the Use of Military Force: Historical Background and Legal Implications. CRS Report RL31133, by David M. Ackerman and Richard F. Grimmett.
20. Ibid.

8

The South American Case Study: The Many Years of Solitude

The exotic takes a toll of the International Relations observer and analyst and South America is a case in point. The Latin American case study can be perceived and analysed in the contemporary context of the 'Centre Periphery' thesis of the Third World Development theories. The various nations in the firmament of the developing world had suffered the impact of instigating a kind of new experience and academic thesis in the international system through their want and needy national traits and subaltern trails. The various nations, especially the nation states like Brazil, Argentina, Chile, Ecuador, Bolivia, etc. had served as the receptacles of the Third World movement in the international context aimed subjectively at the idea of militating against the Western and American geo-economic and cultural dominance. The vistas of international rebellion were well framed at the insistence of the felt-suffering of the South American nations, their systems and attendant populations. There is a stereotypical understanding of the thesis of the usurpation and the exploitation of the natural wealth encompassing the natural resources of the Latin American equatorial forests and the attendant embedded oil and natural gas wealth of the region. This understanding has been avidly pronounced, defined and propagated at the beck and call of the Third World mandarins.

Garcia Marquez writes beatifically in his Nobel Prize-winning work, *Hundred Years of Solitude*. He narrates the idea of a mythical village placed inside the timeless tropics of South America whose only contact with the external world is through the gypsies. The nomadic gypsies visit the mythical village annually and display their wares which they claim to have brought from the far-off lands such as India, China, South East Asian atolls and islands. The South American situation in the pre-World War II days was also very much similar to the same theme and the halo of 'magical realism' which pervades through the works of Garcia Marquez. He had prepared a symbolic manifestation of the untouched and the sequestered life in Latin America which got its first brush with the idea of the state much later. It happens with the arrival of the Government officials who invent the practice of preparing Government documents in order to ratify the individual ownership of houses in the Garcian mythical village. Thus, the untouched and the touch-me-not attribute and the characteristic of the untouched tropics, is verdantly brought forth as a narrative, which further reasserts the slights by the instruments of modernity and the state which violate and disfigure the individual though untrained efforts of the people. They had originally orchestrated the townsman-ship and house building in the mythical village.

This South American riposte has received a pedigreed response from the people all across the global firmament, especially, the United States of America. There is a perpetually geo-economically advanced and intertwined relationship between the corpus of the American power monolith and the attendant rubric of the South American popular movements. Popular movements have been initiated in the global civil societal context as part of the anti-globalisation and the anti-convergence movements which have witnessed the flowering of the Anti-Seattle conventions and consensus amongst the civil society in the global context in the 21st century. The rise of the 'V' movement as initiated and conceived by a British artist was turned into the mantle of an anti-globalisation and anti-imperialistic struggle all across the international polity and society.

The international conventions as conceived by the United Nations through the years have a direct bearing on the rationale of international trade and governance parameters. The principle of permanent sovereignty over natural resources has been well enunciated in the International Treaty Law. Jane A. Hofbauer contends in a Doctoral thesis in the University of Iceland that, "The past century has severely changed the interface of the international community. The number of States has quadrupled and the rules on statehood have found new addressees. Thus, in the post-World War II era, the period of decolonization prompted the forming of a tool which aimed at promoting social and economic development and ensuring equitable resource exploitation—the principle of permanent sovereignty over natural resources (PSNR)."[1] Thus, in the context of modernity and the subsequent post-modern thesis, several scholars have observed the advent of modern vicissitudes of development and new civilisational improvements. They have always been in conflict with the idea of the rampage and the vivisection of the indigenous ethos of the myriad primordial and pre-modern nations, regions and civilisations.

The advent of economic development that came with the Western incursions in the form of trade, investment and cultural incursions, has led to the development of awe, thankfulness leading on to suspicion and criticism of "the modern" in the indigenous societies and polities. The occurrence of a haphazard development and un-egalitarian distribution of wealth and income as an outcome of Western investment, involvement and industrialization is a common allegation which is headed the way of the Occident. In this context the idea of how diplomacy was initiated with South America can diligently be delved inside with some detail. The April 2016 visit of President Pranab Mukherjee to New Zealand was a Maori war like welcome, is a case in point though it is not directly related to the South American context but to an innately indigenous setting.

All About being a Good Neighbour

The American "Good Neighbor Policy" was spawned in the nation state of Argentina. It was here that the entire Buenos Aires, came to a standstill as the American President Franklin Delano Roosevelt visited Argentina to reinstate and re-entrench the United States in the larger region. Cultural diplomacy is an artifice which the United States' agencies such as the Voice of America and others have specialsed in since ages. Surprisingly the practice and the art of cultural diplomacy received its origins from the Latin American nation state of Argentina. Justin Heart writes in his book that,

> "The story begins at the Buenos Aires Conference in 1936 where the US State Department proposed a series of government sponsored technological and educational exchanges with the nations of Latin America. The initial stab at what policymakers called "Cultural Relations" grew out of FDR's Good Neighbor Policy which was the much ballyhooed effort to expand US influence south of the border, while scaling the sort of Big Stick interventionism so common in the past.
>
> With these exchanges, the State Department clearly aimed to use Latin America as the Laboratory for developing and honing an approach that it would eventually deploy worldwide."[2]

People such as Archibald Macleish were the initiators of the Office of War's Public Diplomacy Wing as new methodologies to propagate the American experiment were being tried everywhere. The intertwined turf wars as usual caused their damage to the final dawn of the New Diplomacy for the American State Department. In conclusion, the South American nations have served as the unabashed diplomatic backwaters for the American establishment which could be replicated globally in the larger international system. The exclusivity of the South American firmament has been one of the core refrains of US diplomacy in the 20th century and beyond.

Colombia Calls: A Latin American Interlude

Soccer might be the swan song in Latin America but the domestic situation in the light of external interventions and influences too requires a rendered analysis when Latin America comes into bold relief. Colombia remains another nation state which has been the cynosure of all eyes as far as the idea of drug cartels, drug peddling and drug trafficking is concerned. But, its not for all governmental and systemic dysfunction that Latin American nations such as Columbia call our attention. The South American nation is also home to a colourful and zestful culture with the soccer fever syndrome and the vibrant verve of the population in the nation. Who can forget the 'Yellows' of Brasilia and the white-interspersed light blues of Maradona's and Claudio Caniggia's Argentina. Now, the continental dissent raging all across the continental firmament is another reflection of the vitriol and the undercurrents which run across the region, ranging from Brazil to Venezuela. Colombia's lore has been visualised and brought to the fore by the Hollywood portrayals in a manner which sheds a dubious light on the South American nations as espousing the cause of a certain genre of characters. Thus, bringing forth the mantle of tin-pot dictators and unpopular regimes of the eighties and the nineties in the last days of the twentieth century. The idea of a new South America rising out of the quagmire of conflicts and drug wars has become the pet peeve of the present times wherein the idea of the 'Periphery' emerging out of the 'Centre' has become the order of the day.

Similarly, the idea of the nation as being the harbinger of jolly good times to all and sundry on the lines of a benevolent Superman militating against the Lex Lutherian tin-pot dictators of the South American firmament has become the call of the hour for the United States in the present-day international system. In the context of Colombia, the drug wars have been the order of the day and have degenerated into a quagmire which tends to have a belittling and nefarious impact upon the idea of Colombia and the neighbourhood nations in South and Central America. The *Global Post* reports in an editorial that though the menace of drug laundering and cocoa plantations has grown singularly beyond the nation state of Colombia, other nations such as Peru and Bolivia, have grown and developed from where the quintessential Colombian drug gangs left the business. The *Global Post* reports, "Using satellite imagery, the UN estimates the amount of land planted with coca bushes that grow the leaves and were used to make cocaine. But, even though the latest figures show Colombia's coca acreage declining to its lowest point in years, no one is celebrating. That's partly because coca farmers in Peru and Bolivia have made up much of the slack. In addition, Colombian guerrillas and criminal gangs that earn huge sums from the drug trade are expanding into lucrative new ventures, such as growing hydroponic marijuana and setting up illegal gold mining operations."[3] Thus, in the author's view, a region largely known for its colourful vibrancy, rich mineral resources and a verdant flora and fauna and tropical beauty, has witnessed its international visage being besmirched by the scourge of the 'dirty mafia wars' as international relations scholars and popular writers have learned to nomenclature them.

A United Nations Cocoa survey was released in 2013 which has taken note of the cocoa being produced the world over. Still, the red regions happen to be the South American nations such as Peru, Bolivia, Colombia and others and the methodologies adopted by the United Nations Cocoa report formulators have also come under a scanner. The actual area under the cocoa plantation and the quantum of the cocoa produce going for the illicit production of cocaine, have been questioned by South America-based analysts. The *Global Post* report reiterates that, "Measuring drug crops, however, has always been an imperfect science. Cloud cover can mar satellite imagery and obscure the results. It's also difficult to estimate how much cocaine can be produced from an acre of coca because farmers have switched to strains with higher alkaloid contents while some of their drug fields are denser than the other."[4] Thus, it has been rightly pointed out that in Colombia and other adjacent nations, the people are finding out innovative and cunning methodologies and techniques in order to get the better of the inspectors and the international snooping agencies in the field.

Apart from the drug war conundrum, it has been pinpointed that a US-Colombia trade pact was inked which has gone a long way in shedding reasonable light on the dynamics of the economics of the relationship. One can engage in an overview of the entire fundamentals and the key facts of the Trade Agreement between the two nations. Then an impetus to mitigate trade barriers and protectionism and the related schemata of trade policies comes forth as the characteristic of the trade relationship between Colombia and the United States. The Office of the United States Trade Representative reports, "Colombia's economy is the third largest in Central and South America. This comprehensive trade agreement will eliminate tariffs and other barriers to U.S. exports, expand trade between our two countries and promote economic growth for both the nations."

The text of the agreement reads, "The International Trade Commission (ITC) has estimated that the tariff reductions in the Agreement will expand exports of U.S. goods alone by more than $1.1 billion, supporting thousands of additional American jobs. The ITC also projected that the Agreement will increase U.S. GDP by $2.5 billion."[5] The text of the agreement further reads, "The Agreement will provide significant new access to Colombia's $166 billion services market, supporting increased opportunities for U.S. service providers."[6] The agreement also entails greater potentialities for the strengthening of intellectual property conditional ties along with opening of the Colombian services sector and the agriculture sector of the nation. Thus, the idea of the Robert Keohane's and Joseph Nye's Regime runs upfront, as far as the idea of international cooperation and trade potentialities are concerned. Still, the emphasis happens to be on the Western, and more poignantly, the American demand for the Third World nations to open up their markets and their structures economically in order to benefit their massive services and manufacturing export sectors. It is this segment of the trade and business arrangements which has been amply criticised by the political economists the world over. This makes the Supercop bear the brunt of its international trade and corporate endeavours.

Harking back to the drug wars, one can cite the contours of the drug-infested conflict which permeates the United States and the Mexican relationship. Involved with the Mexican relationship is the idea of immigration and the aliens settled in United States, which leads to the belittling of the general benevolent veneer of the relationship between the United States and Mexico. The Council on Foreign Relations reports, "In 2006, former Mexican President Felipe Calderón, in conjunction with the United States, launched a massive crackdown against drug trafficking organizations, escalating a conflict that would contribute to the deaths of tens of thousands of people in drug-related violence. While the United States has supplied funding and intelligence to increase Mexico's institutional capacity to address drug trafficking, its primary focus has been on strangulating the flow of drugs into the country and domestic law enforcement."[7] The Council on Foreign relations further says, "Weak judicial and police institutions, as well as proximity to the world's largest consumer economy, have made Mexico the hub of one of the world's most sophisticated drug networks. For decades, drug trafficking organizations (DTOs) used Mexico's entrenched political system to create a system-wide network of corruption that ensured distribution rights, market access, and even official government protection for drug traffickers in exchange for lucrative bribes."[8] Thus, the threat of illegal immigration inside the territory of United States, along with the idea of catching plane jane criminals who walk over from Mexico into the United States, remains a core cause of concern in the larger domestic political debates inside the American political firmament. The wastes and the ravines of New Mexico and Texas are home to the tales of the 'Amigos' as they used to traverse the length and breadth of the terrains of the southern United States in search for booty and adventure. Thus, the momentum of the drug lords has been stymied to a certain extent by the collaboration between the Drug Enforcement Office of the United States and the Mexican officials. A few of the prescient drug lords have been checked and imprisoned while crossing the border between the United States and Mexico in the recent past with a massive media coverage coming their way.

The Hollywood portrayals, too, have pithily and evocatively highlighted the mush and the human misery embalmed in the Mexican terrain as the drug dealers and Mafiosi travel back and forth inside the tangibles of the territory of a waiting-to-be-defiled-socio-politico and legal firmament of the United States. One such Hollywood construct happens to be *Scarface* which enlivens and invigorates the audience with the idea of a poverty-stricken hoi polloi traversing the dark dingy pot-holes of the upcoming industrial and soot-infested metropolis. They end up as drug dealers and drug lords, very much filling the vacuum of the Italian Goodfellas.

One movie review of the Al Pacino-starrer *Scarface* states, "Money, drugs, cars, girls, crooked cops and Colombian drug lords. Miami in the eighties with all of its excess. This is the story that brought the Drug War to the masses and drove the fear of a bunch of Scarfaces running around into the American public. Too bad the real political story of the Cuban exile crisis was lost in the shuffle. Al Pacino's depiction of the ambitious, addicted, megalomaniacal Tony Montana is and will always be a classic, man."[9] Thus, in the author's view, the depiction of the dark dreary and putrid-infested city walks and the dreary alleyways, shows the nature of the acrid sub-culture This sub culture has permeated the common man's existence in the consumerist corridors of the United States of America. There was a verve and the sunlit vibrancy of the superhero movies of the eighties and nineties in the twentieth century. It is here that the squalor and the detritus of the iconic American dream comes to the fore which is not characteristically an American plight, but, reflects a larger failure of the capitalist schemata in the international system.

Another Hollywood construct happens to be *Traffic* which reflects the poignant strains of the American Dream gone slightly sour and awry. The movie reflects the realism behind the menace of drugs as it showcases the efficient and stylish drug lords, complete with a phalanx of characters inclusive of corrupt policemen, selfish politicians and well-connected senators. One of the movie reviews provides an informative and poignant delving inside the entire context of drugs in the region; "Multiple story lines and racial overtones, this movie actually attempts to deal with specific politics and the repercussions of the U.S. 'War on Drugs'. It takes us through the entire cycle from the rural growers to foreign law enforcement to American law enforcement; then, on up to the more corrupt cops, businessmen, attorneys and politicians; and, back down to the inner-city dealers and suburban users."[10] The entire context of a drug infested and morally constrained urbania is evocatively reflected in the entire sanguine tale of hush money, illicit networking and the cumulative failure of the territorial system at large.

Another factor apart from the seemingly pessimistic and putrid details of the drug issue that persists between the United States and South America, happens to be the threat of the Chinese inroads inside the land which was once proscribed by the grand consensus of the Monroe Doctrine. The Chinese have, implemented the soft-power calculus amidst the South American nation states individually and in the region on the whole. A Study prepared by the Congressional Research Service for the Committee on Foreign Relations states that, "The aftermath of incidents of Sino-U.S. tension or confrontation—such as the case in 2001 when a Chinese fighter jet collided with a U.S. EP-3 reconnaissance plane, or the case in 2007 when the PRC suddenly denied Hong Kong port visits to a series of U.S. ships—U.S. officials have remained largely in the dark about the PRC's crisis management processes and about why and how PRC leaders reached their decisions. The number of unknown variables that still animate China's foreign policy goals and decision-making processes is simply too great."[11] The CRS report, thus, enumerates that not much panic should be gathered out of the Chinese interest in these regions. The report also informs that the regularised nature of Chinese foreign policy is still not clearly known to the American foreign and economic policymaking establishment.

The Congressional Research Service once again states, "In addition to the OAS, China has participated in several other regional organizations. Dating back to 1975, China has often sent its observers to the annual meetings of the Agency for the Prohibition of Nuclear Weapons in Latin America and the Caribbean (OPANAL), the organization set up in the aftermath of the 1967 signing of the Tlatelolco Treaty prohibiting nuclear weapons in the region. The PRC has been an observer since 1994 to the Latin American Integration Association (ALADI), a 12-member regional organization focusing on trade integration and the goal of a common market."[12] Thus, the American way of vouching for non-proliferation and disarmament is spread by the American public diplomacy since the days of the Cold War. The Chinese have upped the ante of non-proliferation of nuclear weapons and disarmament in the region which competes rather directly with the American principles, values and intent in the region on the whole.

Also, running in tandem with the mandate and the nature of the United Nations Peacekeeping initiatives the world over, the PRC has changed strategic gears. China has opened up to the international community as a philanthropist and a 'do-gooder' nation. The details of the Chinese peacekeeping overtures have been amply reported in the words of Rowan Scarborough that,

> "China has also helped support UN peacekeeping operations in the region

> through its contribution of a 'special police' peacekeeping contingent of 125 personnel as part of the United Nations Stabilization Mission in Haiti (MINUSTAH) that began in 2004. This marked Beijing's first deployment of forces ever in the Western Hemisphere. MINUSTAH's mission, which was due to expire in mid-October 20007, was extended for another year until October 2008. In 2005, China reportedly put pressure on Haiti to switch its diplomatic recognition from Taiwan to the PRC as a condition for supporting the renewal of the UN peacekeeping mission, but Haiti has retained its relations with Taiwan."[13]

The Chinese have definitively gone the Don Juan way but still the tangle in which they have been enmeshed with Taiwan speaks volumes about the idea of a single-mindedness of objective national interest that still underlies their equation with Haiti and the stand-off with Taiwan. Thus, the United States of America has to override the bottlenecks of trade imperialism along with a complicity in the drug wars and the consequential impact on immigration patterns in mainland United States. United States can go ahead with the idea of enveloping South America in the Umbrella of 'Reassurance' like it does with some of the European continent and some countries in the East Asian countries in the Far East. Africa and Latin America were the regions, where in a pre-Cold War era the Chinese had not made much inroads and were not regarded as major factors in the next-door playing ground of the Americans. Now, in author's view, the present age is spurred on by the age of globalisation, free trade, convergence and the acceptability of peace and democratisation as the panacea of all ill-gotten and retrograde political systems. The American interest collides with that of the Chinese as the Asiatic overlords are teleporting into a space, "where no man has gone before" in the real sense of the term in consonance with the espoused "Chinese Dream" by President Xi Xinping.

This can be an apt explanation for the American intent and involvement in South America. The local leaders of the continent a few decades back, can be compared to a specific beatific scenario in the *Hundred Years of Solitude*. The movie is of Hollywood origin and contends,

> "All the characters in the beginning of the movie's narrative climbed out of their scenic village and went ahead for an adventure and a search mission to meet the authorities and the state apparatus, which had reached a specific point beyond their forested tropics. But, when the motley group of adventurers reached a point near a river, they saw, that, there stood a ship which has moss and green vegetation with green creepers growing all over its hull and interior. It was difficult to explain that how such a beautiful vessel come all the way into the jungle but still that seemed to be the end of the odyssey for these journeymen. They convinced themselves that it was no great utilitarian decision to move beyond this marooned vessel and that

> if they were ever destined to meet and interact with the state officers, then they had better go back to their mythic settlement near the, "white lime stones" and wait for civilization to reach them."

Thus, a similar dilemma and a growth and development trajectory was witnessed by South America, wherein the idea of development was equated with the ills of modernity which brought in the advent of the 'Risk Society' in the entire narrative of South America.

In a similar vein, as there happens to be a sharp consonance between the Indian and the South American situation, a pictorial acquisition for this work's narrative is quite essential. For instance, the entire advent of the British rule in India and the hinterland in the country has been beautifully painted and explained away in a painting which was drawn by M.F. Hussain and the painting's title happens to be, "Appu and His Toy Train." The painting's canvas depicts a lush green pastoral land which symbolises the greenery, verdancy and the innocence-untainted myth of the 'rural'. Located above the green pasture is a railway track which has a high-speed train moving away with belching smoke. The train and the darkened and mildewed exterior of the carriages represent the advent and the intervention of the modern world—industrialisation, commercialisation into the quiet and withdrawn life of the pastoral. The pasture also bears the figures of a Bengali boy, Appu, dressed in a loungi with his saree-clad sister, Durga, as they witness the train speeding past them in awe, fear and tragic bewilderment. Both the children are watching a speeding train for the first time and they surmise it as an intrusion by the city civilisation and big industry into the innocent quietitude of their lives characterised by their singular-minded, isolationist and humdrum mortal routines. This civilised intrusion is also exacerbated diligently in the *Hundred Years of Solitude*, which posits the South American wanderlust for the pastoral and untrammelled natural veneer of the unhindered and the unexploited.

SELECAO AND ABECELESTE: AS THERE IS MORE TO THE SPORT...

Introduction

Since the advent of the lore of soccer, the yellow jerseys of the Selecao have been perennially pitted against the blue jerseys interspersed with stripes of white worn by the Abeceleste, that is, the Argentine soccer team. This happens to be part of the Periphery's dream similar to the all-pervading and sacrosanct but truly utilitarian nature of the American Dream in the author's view. The South American culture of rebellion and cultural verve can be understood to be the nom de plume of the protest and the alternate way of life in the context of the alternate options available before the international system. The Latin American resources have been a bone of contention for the Western nations, where, one theory suggests that individual national establishments in the South American context have invited the American geo-economic involvement in their resource mobilisation and resource development efforts. The influx of American funds and technology, has led to the development and an overall regeneration of the South American hemispheric nations, which have developed a cultural and ideological strutting against nations of the order of United States. US has become the de facto provider nation for the entire geopolitics and the geo-economics of the region.

One theory suggests that the region—and according to one estimate—other regions have too suffered from the American imperialist interventions if the American ministrations are to be construed as imperialistic and hegemonic by any gallant reading of the situation. The same rings true to a certain extent in the shape of the Russian engagement with the South American nations during the Cold War years. Recently in 2014, President Vladimir Putin visited and had a talk with the ailing Fidel Castro in Cuba and met the Nicaraguan Premier too.

Every process and development has its positive and negative impact in the context of a designated transition. As the economic theories suggest, the Latin American states are in a state of flux as the development paradigm has led to the creation of an internal dissension. The outcomes can be deciphered in the context of the massive infrastructural upgradation, rise in the standard of living, better cultural appreciation along with the rise in the individual national and pan-regional economic might of the region in the global context. This one idea again brings us back to the theme of the utilisation and development of natural resources. The role played by the United States cannot be underplayed in the economic and national regeneration of the entire region on the whole. Some scholars have termed it as the fight for Latin America between the People's Republic of China and the United States of America in a land and terrain beyond their homeland frontiers.

Robert Valencia writes, "The key question now is, will Latin American countries lean more towards China or the United States, or will it find a way to balance the two against each other? Right now, Latin American countries are increasingly confident thanks to burgeoning economic and political integration by way of trading blocs, and they're demanding to be treated as an equal player."[14] In the author's view, the Latin American resurgence is thus to be beholden in the ides of the regional global system and the international weight-throwing by the region's nations through blocs such as the G-20 and BRICS. The new geo-economic might and geopolitical positioning of these nations is up for grabs with the initiation of an irreversible process of globalisation and general development. Recently through the Fortaleza Declaration in July 2014, the idea of the BRICS bank worth a capital of 100 billion dollars, has been mooted which is all set to emerge as a counterpoise to the International Monetary Fund and the World Bank. The new Indian Premier, Narendra Modi, is all set to initiate a new deliberation in the context of the BRICS bank. The Indian Prime Minister Narendra Modi might not go till the extent of positing an alternate way, or a parallel developmental model and a progression trajectory still. The projection of an alternative via media can make the global order, defined by the WTO and the World Bank, become more transparent and accountable to the global polity and political economy. The Asian Development Bank too in the eyes of the American establishment has been perceived suspiciously as it is in the take off position in September, 2015.[15]

Thus, as a via-media through the BRICS bank and other related organisations can invest in the developing world and demand concessions and equitable treatment for the developing nations and the LDCs. Thus, in the author's view, Brazil's model can go ahead with the idea of a South American and Asian-led model of geo-economic progression. In the event of the 2015 elections in Argentina, Mr Macri, the Mayor of Buenos Aires, has been a votary of the centre-right wherein he is demanding a system, which is, characterised by a centralisation of power and governance and administration. He stands for an electoral plank, which, points to a mixed welfarist model of development in Argentina along with a people-centric mode of rule. Thus, he is demanding what all could not be attained and delivered by the last Argentine Prime Minister and whose political party appeared to be on the way out in the November 2015 elections.

One can equate the complete idea of the surge of Latin America with the new geo-economic processes let loose by the processes of globalization and convergence which are much contested by the Latin American geo-strategists and economists. Roberto Valencia writes, "The United States hasn't lost Latin America, and is unlikely to loose it completely. It is still the region's top trade partner. The United States has recently signed free-trade agreements with Colombia and Panama, and maintains other trade agreements with Peru, Chile, and Mexico. Central American and several Caribbean countries rely upon U.S. military cooperation in an attempt to curtail drug trade. Nevertheless, the post 9/11 years severely eroded U.S.-Latin American relations as the Bush administration focused heavily on the war on terror, often ignoring issues in Latin America."[16] The US–Chinese race, is, still tilted in the favour of the United States but the gap is narrowing down quickly. Also, the Chinese might lessen the geo-economic gap with the favours that they might win with the leftist-ruled national denominations, but, South America still remains a traditional American playground.

The idea of the dainty Latin American autonomy has been well supported by the author Robert Valencia. The independence of the indigenous nations has been well entrenched in the vortex of the regional identity in Latin America with a more assertive and confident regional scenario, which has sailed through the slew of international developments. He contends, "China and the United States are also encountering a more confident and more unified Latin America. It is a region that has sought autonomy in its own affairs by way of rising blocs such as the Community of Latin American and Caribbean States, MERCOSUR, and the Bolivarian Alliance for the Americas (ALBA), among others."[17] The threat that is being encountered by the United States is the rise of the belief amongst the Latin American nations, commensurate with their economic surge, much on the lines of the South East Asian hubs. The tag of being a benign hegemon might not be the ideal and staple sobriquet which the Americans might be content and satisfied with. As a regional parallel, the Indian standpoint in the South Asian region also bespeaks of the Indian discomfiture at the larger South Asian distrust of the Indian intentions in the region. The same rings true for the American intent in South America, though historical appendages and other happenings, serve as a rich tapestry of information which can cull out the objective truth.

Natural Resources et al

On the issue of natural resources, one theory suggests that the Latin American nations flower in their struggle for an independent utilisation of their natural resources. But, it might be a misnomer and a non sequitur argument, keeping in light the idea of the advent of convergence of trade practices and an internationalisation of investments and business amidst nations and the global corporate amalgam. It can be deciphered that UNESCO has pioneered an international convention titled as the "Convention Concerning the Protection of the World Cultural and Natural Heritage". The convention is not a new legal instrument, but, it is an old and classical testament to the idea of preservation of indigenousness and the nation's natural worth. A few of its arrangements run as follows:

> "*Noting* that the cultural heritage and the natural heritage are increasingly threatened with destruction not only by the traditional causes of decay, but also by changing social and economic conditions which aggravate the situation with even more formidable phenomena of damage or destruction,
> *Considering* that deterioration or disappearance of any item of the cultural

> or natural heritage constitutes a harmful impoverishment of the heritage of all the nations of the world."[18]
>
> "*Considering* that protection of this heritage at the national level often remains incomplete because of the scale of the resources which it requires and of the insufficient economic, scientific, and technological resources of the country where the property to be protected is situated."[19]

Thus, indigenousness might have become a fashionable term in the context of the contemporary times, but, still the conceptualisation has existed since the times of the creation of the Stockholm Convention and others. The rise of the decolonisation movement with the passage of the Decolonization Resolution in the year 1960 in the UN General Assembly, led to the idea of anti-imperialism and anti-colonialism and the surge of the Third World's suppressed nations from the yoke of the colonial rule. Thus, the idea of the consummation free world was brought in through the inclusion of the newly freed Afro-Asian nations through the Decolonization Resolution. The Convention was originally worded as the "Declaration on the Granting of Independence to Colonial Countries and Peoples". Thus, the control for the natural resources of an "endowed" region has always been a key characteristic of a nation's endeavor to leave its imprint on the global stage. United States as part of its entrepreneurial surge too reflects the acquisitive dream with an attainment of pelf through its various incursions in South America.

The Nicaraguan Case Study: A Study in Bilateral Relations

Apart from the legal spat between the United States and Nicaragua in the middle of the 1980s, the American entanglements in the South American states of Guatemala, Panama and Grenada and the response of the international community, generated a lot of mixed and amalgamated global opinion. One more American intrusion in the South American context, brought into relief the relationship and the hostile state of exchanges between United States and Nicaragua. One more intervention, it was as part of the Cold war's continuity of diplomacy and foreign policy. This time the recourse was taken by both the nations of the international legal instruments, such as the International Court of Justice. If one refers to the International Court of Justice's judgement in the context of the Nicaraguan case, then, the Court found that the United States establishment's standpoint to be contentious on a few counts. The following are the reproductions of the ICJ Judgement and opinion,

> "*Decides* that the United States of America, by failing to make known the existence and location of the mines laid by it, referred to in subparagraph (6) hereof, has acted in breach of its obligations under customary international law in this respect."[20]

"The United States of America, by producing in 1983 a manual entitled "Operaciones sicolÿÿgicas en guerra de guerrillas", and disseminating it to *contra* forces, has encouraged the commission by them of acts contrary to general principles of humanitarian law. It does not find a basis for concluding that any such acts which may have been committed are imputable to the United States of America as acts of the United States of America".[21]

"The United States of America, by the attacks on the Nicaraguan territory referred to in subparagraph (4) hereof, and by declaring a general embargo on trade with Nicaragua on 1 May 1985, has acted in breach of its obligations under Article XIX of the Treaty of Friendship, Commerce and Navigation between the Parties signed at Managua on 21 January 1956."[22] Thus, help and succor was imparted by the United States Administration to the neighbourhood of Nicaragua in order to destabilise the antagonist regime in the state of Nicaragua. It led to the case being filed against Washington by the Government of Nicaragua calling the American clandestine help through its instrumentality of CIA as an infringement of the independence, sovereignty and territorial integrity of the nation state of Nicaragua.

Also, the vilification and the dark and vile colouring of the Nicaraguan Government was also alleged by the nation's establishment. The United States questioned the jurisdiction of the International Court of Justice and refused to agree to the judgement and the opinion of the ICJ. Thus, according to one school of international lawyers, *the* United States was found to be in contravention of the accepted norm setting and the legal framework of the international law in more ways than one.

One of the most indicting sections of the Court was the act of finding truth in the laying of mines in the Nicaraguan waters in Puerto Sandino, El Bluff and Corinto. The section of the verbatim judgement runs as thus,

> "The Court examines the allegations of Nicaragua that the *mining of Nicaraguan ports or waters* was carried out by United States military personnel or persons of the nationality of Latin American countries in the pay of the United States. After examining the facts, the Court finds it established that, on a date in late 1983 or early 1984, the President of the United States authorized a United States Government agency to lay mines in Nicaraguan ports, that in early 1984 mines were laid in or close to the ports of El Bluff, Corinto and Puerto Sandino, either in Nicaraguan internal waters or in its territorial sea or both, by persons in the pay and acting on the instructions of that agency, under the supervision and with the logistic support of United States agents."[23]

Thus, the Court directly intimated the idea and the factoid of the contravention of the territorial integrity and sovereignty of the state of Nicaragua by an interventionist United States. Also, the International Court of Justice raised the question of the intelligence, military, training and logistics support provided by the United States agencies to the Contras internally in Nicaragua and also in the neighbourhood in order to maim and destabilise the domestic socio-political and economic dynamics of the region in general and Nicaragua in particular. These were some of the aforesaid and alleged objectives of United States through its intervention in Nicaragua. One of the claims of the Nicaraguan national authorities was that *the* United States was aiding and abetting the Contras in the region and in Nicaragua itself, but the American contention to the ICJ too ran on the same lines of argumentation.

Thus, the idea as espoused and allegedly communicated by *the* United States was that Nicaragua was equallyinvolved in rocking the peace boat of the neighbouring nation, Al Salvador. It could be accounted for by evidence provided by the Americans. The case as discussed in the International Court of Justice brought forth the quintessential and stereotypical international law argument that *the* United States was an interventionist state by which incursions were being carried out in the garb of humanitarian interventions. This militated against the nominally established but unenforceable ethos of the accepted international law practice and the attendant body of thesis of international law. Thomas J. Pax calls it, "ICJ's compulsory jurisdiction or Just Compulsion".[24] If one relates to the summary of the Judgement then one can refer to Pax as he writes,

> "The ICJ found that it had the jurisdiction to hear the complaint based on the compulsory jurisdiction of the court under Article 36 of its statute. While the overall vote was eleven judges in favor of compulsory jurisdiction and five opposed, two of the judges voting with the majority qualified their votes in separate opinions. One of these judges, Judge Singh, stated that he would have based the Court's jurisdiction solely on the 1956 Treaty, rather than exercising compulsory jurisdiction in this case. Judge Ruda, taking a different approach, found no independent basis of jurisdiction under Article 36(2), as did the rest of those voting in favor of compulsory jurisdiction"[25]

It can also be argued, by, going through a *New York Times* news report that, "Nevertheless, the very nature of the ICJ's work makes it impossible for the Court to accord respect to the principle of state sovereignty in its purest form. Absolute state sovereignty, in the most simple terms, would allow a state to go about its own affairs without outside interference."[26] Thus, the idea of being free from the externalities of interventionism and the free and peaceful navigation of one's nation's course seems to have been the ruling idiom of the International Court of Justice.

The Montevideo Convention has a great deal to contend and sermonise about the national jurisdiction of a nation premised upon its sweet free will. Its Articles one and seven run thus, "The state as a person of international law should possess the following qualifications: (a) a permanent population; (b) a defined territory; (c) government; and (d) capacity to enter into relations with the other states. States are juridically equal, enjoy the same rights, and have equal capacity in their exercise. The rights of each one do not depend upon the power which it possesses to assure its exercise, but upon the simple fact of its existence as a person under international law."[27] Thus, the rational equality of the states of Nicaragua and *the* United States can be conveniently extricated from the convention harking back to the hallowed pre-World War II years when the fundamentals of territoriality and the idea of sovereignty were being drawn and redrawn.

South America too lies on a developmental cusp where-in after hundreds of years of solitude, the likes of places such as Manas and Macaranazo are waking up to the tide of development and change. The *Hundred Years of Solitude* runs riot about the rise of the Urbania and the rule of written law in the ethereal and supernatural idyllic bliss of a village which relies upon the scientific wisdom of one man. It is upon the annual trysts with travelling nomads who bring in failed inventions and scientific discoveries before the city government somewhere beyond the marshes and dollops of frozen rivers sends its emissaries to colonise the village. The same rings true for the swathes of territories in the South America, where-in, development serves as the purpose of the socially depletive norms of life and sustainable patterns on the whole. The cosseted perphery thus woke up to the ideas of growth and development.

NOTES

1. Jane A. Hafbauer, *The Principle of Permanent Sovereignty Over Natural Resources and its Modern Implications* (Faculty of Law, University of Iceland, 2009).
2. Justin Hart, *Empire of Ideas: The Origins of Public Diplomacy and the Transformation of US Foreign Policy* (London: Oxford University Press, 2013), pp. 35-50.
3. John Otis, "Is Colombia Winning the Drug War?" URL: http://www.globalpost.com/dispatch/news/regions/americas/colombia/130620/colombian-coca-production-cocaine-drug-war, (Online: Web), Accessed on March 28, 2014.
4. Ibid.
5. "US Colombia Trade Agreement: Increasing American Competitiveness", Office of the United States Trade Representative, Govt of United States.
6. Ibid.
7. Council on Foreign Relations, "Backgrounder: Mexico's Drug War".
8. Ibid.
9. "Ten Best Drug Wars Movies", URL: http://www.mademan.com/mm/10-best-drug-wars-movies.html (Online: Web), Accessed on March 28, 2014.
10. Ibid
11. "China's Foreign Policy and 'Soft Power' in South America, Asia and Africa", A Study

Prepared For the Committee on Foreign Relations, US Senate, Congressional Research Service Library of Congress, April 2008.

12. Ibid.
13. Rowan Scarborough, "China Seen Averse to Haiti-Taiwan Ties; Blocks Extension of UN Mission", *Washington Times*, June 8, 2005 and "Haiti: Extending Minustah's Mandate", Latin American Caribbean and Central American Report, August 16, 2007.
14. Robert Valencia, "US and China: The Fight For Latin America", URL: http://www.worldpolicy.org/blog/2013/06/24/us-and-china-fight-latin-america (Online: Web), Accessed on May 2013.
15. *Indian Express Report*, 5 December, 2015.
16. Ibid.
17. Ibid.
18. "United Nations Convention Concerning the World Cultural and Natural Heritage", The General Conference of the United Nations Educational, Scientific and Cultural Organization meeting in Paris from 17 October to 21 November 1972, at its seventeenth session.
19. Ibid.
20. "Military and Paramilitary Activities in and against Nicaragua (Nicaragua *v.* United States of America)", URL: http://www.icj-cij.org/docket/index.php?sum=367&p1=3&p2=3&case=70&p3=5 (Online: Web), Accessed on March 28, 2015.
21. Ibid.
22. Ibid. 1.
23. Ibid.
24. Thomas J Pax, "Nicaragua VS United States in the International Court of Jystice: Compulsory Jurisdiction or Just Compulsion? *Boston College International and Comparative Law Review*, Volume 8, Issue 2, 1985.
25. Ibid.
26. "Generally Scorning the World Court", *New York Times*, January 20, 1985, at E22, col. 1-3.
27. "Montivideo Convention On the Rights and Duties of State", signed on December 26, 1933.

9

Vietnam Vitriol Taints Uncle Sam: The Questioning of the Grandiloquent American Dream

VIETNAM WAR AND ITS VERSIMILITUDINOUS VICISSITUDES

Introduction

What ailed the American dream and led to larger swathes of introspection? This question can be answered with a single word meaning a nation's name: that is, Vietnam. The war in Vietnam dealt a blow to the invincibility frame of the US which had a positive in providing the nation with an opportunity to re evolve its dream and living philosophy. *The* Vietnam War, as the public opinion makers and the attendant Fourth Estate would make us believe, was a prelude to the ides of debate and internal turmoil in the way the American dream was hewn around a specific myth and lore. Before the War, the invincibility and the superhuman capacity of the American myth and the resultant 'dream' was avowedly an American project par excellence in the context of the much larger international system. It was much before the scholars and the practitioners of foreign policy realised the schisms and the potholes in a yet unencumbered trajectory of the US policy in South East Asia. In the present tense, away from the richly contested hotbeds of Tet and My Lai, the American establishment under the aegis of President Obama, another Kennedy incarnate (at least during the campaign trails), initiated the rebalancing stratagem of the United States foreign policy establishment. The tale of the dominance of the Asiatic space and the resurgence of the Asiatic century was officially incorporated in the tell-tale trajectory of the twenty-first century, in the post-2008 recession American thought.

This development of the Asian Pivot as the nomenclature by the Obama Administration tends to clear the flak from the war-worn Kevlars of the American GIs. This, part redux of the Asian space with a stark Umbrella Reassurance to the East Asian nations such as South Korea and Japan through the nuclear aid as well, is much different. One can look at the sixties classic of a Cold War clash between the American war machine and the Chinese resurgence in the favour of the revolutionary, Ho Chi Minh, premised on a communist ordained North Vietnam. Still, a brief discussion of the thematic percept of the Asian Pivot is to be rekindled at this moot academic moment in order to better comprehend the salience of the vagaries and the rigour of the Vietnam conflict. The blood feud witnessed the battering of the world's superpower's might with all its military paraphernalia, humbled as it was by the 'sons-of-the-soil' or the Vietcong, which were struggling for their homeland against a far superior military foe. This detail brings into function as to what the "Look East" parlance is all about.

Thus, the twenty-first century resonance of the America's "Look East Policy" primarily amounts to containing the Chinese pelf in the region and deserves a relook and a narrative revisitation. The *Financial Times* writes, "It's refreshing to read *Breakout Nations*, Ruchir Sharma's book on the BRIC countries—Brazil, Russia, India, China—and the rest of the developing world. The book offers a careful view that has little truck with forecasts of the relentless Bric-led rise of the emerging world."[1] Thus, this literature frames a narrative out of an already emerged order which is all set to establish new statistical trends and attain new benchmarks in the period beyond 2015. This holds true for the future contours and ramifications for the American foreign policy think tanks, too.

The American Pivot: Back to the Future in the Context of Vietnam

The post-September 11 and the post-China rise international geo-economics is a matter of contemporary study. The issues at stake concern the future of the globe and its sustainable future. The stability of the geo-economic and the geopolitical scenario in the trans-Atlantic along with the state of the African nations, leaves the Asiatic rise as the focal point of all ends. It is here, where, all the nation's and corporate interests converge. Thus, one arrives at the significance of the American pivot in the Eastern hemisphere. Similar to what George Kennan had to write in the *Foreign Affairs*,[2] the threat perception seems to have returned to the American strategic thought. Earlier on, it was the becoming of the former Soviet Union as a nuclear power—the second one after the United States in the post-World War II scenario—which had invited the negative portrayal of the Soviet Union by the American strategic and defence machinery in order to do well in the Cold War era.

Historical facts can be utilised as the important signposts of the changing trends and inclinations. The place occupied partially by China-of-the-contemporary times, was gracefully occupied by the Russian Empire in the popular American discourse. It was the timing of the Soviet rhetoric which made the start of the Cold War a historic necessity. It can be observed, "From Moscow, Kennan watched US-Soviet relations deteriorate as World War II drew to a close, and he became increasingly vexed by the Roosevelt administration's efforts to delay a showdown in hopes of salvaging the wartime alliance. Eager to weigh in on Soviet policy, Kennan seized the opportunity provided in February 1946, when Moscow's more militaristic rhetoric and refusal to participate in the World Bank and IMF prompted State Department officials to ask Kennan to assess the motives and assumptions underlying Soviet policymaking."[3] Thus, finding new threats has become the order of the day in the global discourse as great powers need to strengthen their power, influence and their international overarch in order to sustain order and peaceful alacrity in the international system. This is one reading of the manner in which great powers dominate over the other states and the larger international system. In the author's view, the existentiality of an eternal foe is a prerequisite to the firming up of a rationale for further aggressive procurements of armaments and the attendant paraphernalia.

It is now that the Chinese can conveniently replace the 'idea of a threat' from the United States's quintessential narrative. The change of the American foreign policy stress has been well reflected in the official policy of the US Government. Vladimir Lenin has posited, "The unevenness of the capitalist development will lead to imminent collapse of the capitalist system when all the sources of production will be appropriated by the Socialist Bloc."[4] Thus, the yearning for the capitalist thought did not turn exactly true and now as the PRC itself stands on the cusp of crypto-capitalism thus leading to Kennan's warning about the Socialist threat and Lenin's forecast about the collapse of the capitalist system as a malapropism. Still, in the author's view saying that all the accepted and established definitions and formulations which began and ended with the White House seem to be changing, is a misplaced assessment. This fact has been deciphered by the United States' strategic and diplomatic community in right earnest.

The idea of the Asia Pacific has renewed the international discourse. Much similar to the theme of Archaic Globalization,[5] the preponderance of the East has resurfaced and it is here to stay in the international geopolitical and geo-economic discourse. David Northrup and others have written about the Eastern Dominance and the prosperity of the West in the context of the global exchange and barter of goods and merchandise. Northrup writes in one his works that, "About a thousand years ago, the forces drawing people closer together became more powerful than those fostering ever-increasing cultural diversity. From that beginning, this 'great convergence' has proceeded unsteadily to the globalization of the present day. The spread and decline of languages, the virtues and faults of empires, the periodization of history, and the emergence of world history as a discipline, are other factors which had a face changing influence on the older global geo-economics."[6]

The new twenty-first century understanding is not vastly different from the archaic times when the Orient was a prosperous trading region, though, not as any monolith. Thus, in the author's view, it is a harking back to the Orient.

Kenneth Liberthal writes in the *Foreign Policy*, "Obama came into office as avowedly 'the first Pacific President,' convinced that George W. Bush's administration had paid too little attention to Asian regional issues and that the United States should restore and then enhance its traditional level of engagement there. Efforts accelerated as China's Asia policy became more hard edged during 2010 and as, during 2011, the United States' military involvement in Iraq and Afghanistan significantly declined."[7] The question that arises is that does a retreating and internalising United States have the resources to match its words about the Asian Pivot with equal resources. Can understanding go beyond the containment of the PRC and chart a new path to a more comprehensive engagement with the Asian Pacific, the Far and the Near East? And can a cooperative and mutually non-combative mode of interaction be publicly realised by the White House in a changed world in the context of China and East Asia?

Such a twenty-first century comprehension of the Orient and the Asiatic space serves as a contemporary reminder of the forces. Such an interpretation was not present in the sixties and seventies during the heydays of the Cold War tryst between a capitalist United States and a communist former Soviet Union. In those days, the East Asian space was comprehended as a meagre 'Domino', which, had to be defended across the seven seas at gargantuan cost to men and machinery. This was the quintessential dictum of American foreign policy in those times in East Asia. Several characteristics reflect the Vietnamese terrain and milieu, such as a muggy marshland, amidst an insect-ridden tropical terrain. The human American element of the Vietnam War and the bravado of the communist opposition led to the consecration of a legend of valour, sacrifice and war. In the author's view, it all turned the American ethos, into a tailspin as it was made evident in the anti-war momentum and rallies in US. Such a trail of anti-war activism ravaged the confines of the American Universities and city squares amidst the rising chants of anti-war leaders and figures such as Timothy Leary and the flower children. Thus, the alternate-way-of-lifers reared their heads after the industrial baby boomer generation had industriously worked under the establishment's tutelage during the days of World War II and beyond, uncomplainingly and in a pliant manner. As it is said, it is the journalists who formulate the first rough draft of war history, so, it did happen exactly during the days of the war in the Vietnamese marshes and the chopper sorties. These images were to become emblematic of the American war effort in Vietnam.

The Historicity

Now for some dandy details of the Vietnam War and the initiation of the American involvement in the war effort. Earlier on, during the Truman days and after the unveiling of the Truman Plan in order to help the struggling indigenous people all across the length and breadth of the global polity, Ho Chi Minh, was the popular leader of the Vietnamese people militating against the French colonial rule. He had approached the American President Truman. It was for strategic help but it could not be realised as a stable relationship due to a few bottlenecks. The initial point was a starter and was meant to be the American help and aid to Ho Chi Minh in the struggle against colonialism, perpetrated by the French nation. It was only through the battle of Dien Ben Phu that the French rule in Vietnam collapsed and the subsequent long march of the captured French soldiers across the entire expanse of the Vietnamese territory led to the death and the maiming of thousands of French prisoners of war. The battle of Dien Ben Phu between the French forces and the Viet Cong (VC) went a long way for the attainment of freedom and liberty from the French colonial rule in Vietnam in the first half of the fifties. The Americans were presented with a dilemma as the French were the allies of the United States. Thus, the methodology of the Viet Cong (VC)'s moves later on during the times of President Kennedy necessitated the incursion of the American military advisors and diplomats in order to serve as the buttressing step against it in the marshy muddles of Vietnam, if the author may use a term. Some of it was soon to be defoliated and ravaged by the Agent Oranges and nerve gas. They were unleashed by the American war machinery over the sleepy yet aware population of Vietnam. The major characteristic of the battle was that it was premised upon the practice of guerrilla warfare and soon turned out to be a war of attrition and resolve. It is here that the VC had the advantage of being on the home terrain. The home advantage spun the web of happenings in Vietnam once and for all.

The VC knew the terrain much better and this was a detriment for the US intervention forces as young American GIs facing such marshy conditions fought for survival against the heady and very effective camouflaging and guerrilla tactics of the enemy. General Westmoreland who was in command of the American forces in Vietnam at one point of time, went on to state, "You never knew where these Mama sans came from all of a sudden. In the morning, the Mama san would work as an utensil cleaner, washer man and a sweeper but in the dark night the same person would disappear into the jungle and plant claymore mines for the advancing and raiding American men." Thus, it can be reiterated that the nature of warfare with the Viet Cong being the force in North Vietnam and the Americans and the South Vietnamese became the force in South Vietnam. It soon turned out to be a bedraggled fight unto survival, where the guerrilla and the jungle warfare techniques of the determined VC contingents in their greens meant disaster and trouble for the advancing American GIs and the American war-fighting equipment.

It can be contended that the war ended in 1972 with the surrender of Saigon, the capital of South Vietnam, and the Americans withdrew completely from the nation as the American war effort went negatively. The real war for the hearts and minds went on for years after the cessation of hostilities in the South East Asian region. The home turf did the trick for the VC along with the well-known fact that the South Vietnamese Government in Saigon was corrupt, authoritarian and corrugated to the hilt. The Regime could not even endear itself to the commoners in the South Vietnamese territory. Thus, in the view of some scholars, the Americans once again ended up propping up the wrong dictator like they were forced to do in some Latin American contexts as part of the strategy of containment in the larger global context. The Vietnamese engagement of *the* United States has been amply and belatedly portrayed in the American cinema.

War correspondents happened to become the virtual heroes during the war in Vietnam as war correspondents such as Walter Cronkite and Peter Arnett covered the gory battle with all its incisive and realistic details. Their coverage and portrayal gradually engendered an anti-war sentiment later solidifying as an anti-war public opinion against the American war effort in Vietnam. The body bags of young American soldiers fighting seven seas away and for a cause alien to their regular disco floors and baseball games, began landing in places such as Fort Sumpter in the homeland. The public mood and support for the war began to turn negative. As the wounded and mutilated war veterans returned homebound during the heydays of the American war, the hoi polloi in next door America began to turn against the war and the people began to turn suspicious and unsure about the rally-around-the-flag phenomenon. It is a public opinion moment which has showcased the highest quantum of public support for the American President when the nation was either passing through a crisis or it had gone to war for the avowed causes of liberty, egalitarianism, freedom of expression and intent.

Thus, the images which began to get relayed through the television screens and radio broadcasts all across the United States, were discomforting to the American citizenry. Images which were displayed all around were such as, American soldiers using deadly Zippo lighters and burning down Vietnamese hutments. Other picturisations included monks being dragged in the streets and the wounded and bloodied faces of soldiers lying on stretchers in choppers, became the point of national debate. The curse of war and the heavy casualties being met by the American forces could no longer be a matter of national security secretiveness akin to the intelligence exposes undertaken by the CIA contractor Edward Snowden in the twenty-first century many years down the line in American history. The war in Vietnam was getting bloodier with the images of the My Lai massacre and other battles being relayed back to the American drawing rooms besides their warm and homespun images of the Superbowl games.

The war had to be fought and ruthlessly won as Vietnam was coming through as a Domino which was waiting to fall into the hands of a vile communist junta backed by external actors with the strings attached to the large-than-life game of a Cold War confrontation. Thus, the Vietnam War also became a strategic necessity for the Americans and one of the last bastions of the Communist resistance in South East Asia. Also, the critics would argue that any such war effort in a far-off land, normally, serves as a place to test run the American war equipment upon unintended audience serving as guinea pigs.

Also, there was a lot of symbolism which was soon attached to the myth and lore of the American resistance in Vietnam in the face of all odds which necessitated a fight till the end, with the television feeds reaching the home audience. A hard-won victory had to become a self-fulfilling prophesy in the larger strategic context and the morality barometer of the American establishment. Thus, all in all, the Americans needed a victory with the alternate-way-of-life activism and dissent in the homestead demanding a more liberal and a just solution to domestic challenges of gender and racial discrimination. Thus, in the author's view, with the changing times, the honour of the American Dream had to be vindicated with the vanquishing of the VC in a far-off communist tropical marshland.

As mentioned earlier, the Vietnamese narrative would never have been the same and would never have attained gargantuan proportions if the American ideals would not have been questioned at the altar of nationality and grand sacrifices. In the author's view, in the aftermath of the war in Vietnam, the American dream was shaken and was vehemently challenged by the counter-war movement in United States. Hollywood was too inspired and aesthetically driven by the sobering experience for the Americans in the marshy muddles of Vietnam. The Calvinistic self-doubt, which was to serve as the repository of knowledge and the self-belief parameter of the American myth was to make a re-run in the American mindset through the Vietnam drubbing. The questioning spirit about the nearly-infallible discourse of the 'meaning and greatness of America' made an entry inside the conservative and hard-power propelled military engineering of the Pentagon and the US Departments of State and Defense. Thus, the Americans retreated inside a Vietnam Syndrome, which was created as part of the national psyche after the defeat in the war in Vietnam. The American self belief in its invincibility was shaken greatly going by the Asian reality that how can an Asian group of guerillas humble the mammonth American war machinery. It was after the vanquishing of Saddam Hussein in Iraq when the Operation Desert Storm emerged as a vindication of the American glory which had gathered a bit of dirt after America's defeat in Vietnam.

As Hollywood Perceives the War

Hollywood too played its own part in the grandiose perpetuation of the Vietnam War era and the American myth and the attendant dream. The culture with its emic and etic categorisations has an unnerving influence upon the forging of a nation's and population's personality, which was amply witnessed in the myriad cinematic constructs spawned in United States. The norm of culture gets reflected through the modicum of cinema, media and literature which further the visage and the significance of a historical staging point of a nation's past. Vietnam was no exception to the norm. For instance, Oliver Stone is a renowned Hollywood director who won over the hoi polloi with his epochal portrayals of the American experience through the years.

For instance, the movie *Platoon* displayed the power and the veracity of the American war machinery along with the blood, gore and decapitation caused due to the American war effort and the VC riposte. The imageries evoked are very incisive and heart-rending as they bring to fore the moral dilemmas faced by the American soldiers along with the tragedy and the ironies of war. Images include: the helmets fly off with heads in a phalanx of mortar explosions and soldiers in fatigues crawl from one bunker to another in a madcap surge to escape the sniping VC men amidst the sudden cold scent of death and deception. The beauty and the creak of silent tropics, is suddenly shattered in an quintessential Vietnam war biopic as the advancing American contingent suddenly runs for cover amidst the vegetation and the nearby grasslands to take up positions anew with blurs of lights lightening the tropical backdrop.

The war is unending, resolute and unforgiving as the battle rages on and one can delve into another Oliver Stone creation, *Born on the Fourth of July*, which serves as a deft reflection of the seething and writhing anti-war sentiment surging ahead in the popular narrative among the people in the United States. As a case in point, Tom Cruise, a GI Joe, is returned back to his homeland as a Vietnam War veteran when he loses both legs during an armed combat with the VC. The man returns, a dejected and a broken man, and he is jolted back into reality when his younger brother asks him all the pertinent questions regarding how could he ascribe a rationale to this war which the United States is fighting with body bags coming back after every few days as a consequence of the blood and gore of the battle? The younger brother's questions are met with patriotic and nationalistic answers as an effort to reason with him but the first jolt has been felt by the amputated war veteran. The American dream of the 'wonder years' had been rarified and dissected for all to see in a rather internalised and painful manner. The futilities and the uncomfortable paradoxes seemed to rear their ugly heads as a heady dope for an alternate re-appropriation of moral priorities.

The male protagonist, Tom Cruise, is anointed as a reluctant war hero but when he witnesses the bruises, both psychological and moral in nature, which the war has given to the US, he too travels along with another war veteran on a wheelchair on the odyssey of his life. He ends up as a star speaker in an anti-war rally as a part of the alternate-way-of-life movement in the American firmament which was churning and catapulting anew. The movie is all about a quintessential American dream gone sour and dreary in the dark shadow of the mayhem and the anarchic violence in Vietnam. A question lingers on and qualifies as a pertinent poser. The question is that is world dominance and a crusade for liberty and the demos, worth the blood and gore and perdition of the war in an alien war fought in an alien land with 'chipponkueks' who can hardly understand the American language and the way of life? This is the eternal American debate between description and derision, between interventionism-spreadeagalism and isolationism of an inward-looking United States of America. America has itself grown and thrives on a staple socio-political diet of self-doubt and an Utopian moralism and idealism. This goes all the way back to the right to do good in the line of President Woodrow Wilson's Fourteen Points, for instance. The Liberal tradition of inflicting pain on the bad characters of World Politics and assuring a stable and just international order is part of the Messianic purpose which the Americans have arrogated to themselves. In the author's view, the Americans arrogated to them selves the veneer of the Regulator and Manager nation in order to reorder the larger global system. In the author's view, the high and powerful station and the seat of power which United States found for itself was known to be associated with a directive for idealism driven regulator role for the American nation.

The idiom of 'With Great Power Comes Great Responsibility' runs to be seemingly true for the United States. It can be safely argued that United States has undergone a great deal since the transformative years of World War I. Since then, great power and greater responsibility, have been thrust upon the country as a peculiar circumstance of World Politics. The American nation and its consequent socio-political and cultural integration has faced a similar situation of natural selection. Empires have waned and ebbed, monarchies have been restored and revolutions have been curbed, but the 'Accidental nature of the American ascent' can sanguinely be underlined in the present context. Akin to a John Doe movie meet *John Doe?*" Bollywood produced a flick which was titled as, *Main Azad Hoon* which had superstar Amitabh Bachchan as the male protagonist. The narrative runs like this: The male protagonist is a quintessential wanderer and a street bumpkin placed in the urban complexes of Mumbai with a friendly sidekick, Anu Kapoor. Both of them do not have anything to eat and do not own a roof to sleep under in a state of penury and deprivation.

As an adjunct to the narrative of the Indian flick, both the stars break down a shop only to be imprisoned in a police station where they get what they had aimed for: shelter and food. Once both of them move out of the prison, they,end up as unintentional heroes of the cowered-down impoverished proletariat and the male protagonist begins to espouse the cause of the commoners. They are unemployed, poor, without home and hearth and without a means of livelihood. Soon, the two stars invigorate the political firmament and become an instrument of vitriolic social change. The American film was produced in the 1940's and served as an inspiration for the Indian one. Thus, the same circumstantial martyrdom and glorification and an attendant eulogisation of the American potentialities has occurred in the post-World War II times. All this, calls for a specially oriented stature, which has been bequeathed to the United States of America by some observers of World Politics.

The path to greatness and unbridled power has come the American way; whether they need the stature and the international role or not, is a different debating exercise all together. In the author's view, the United States has been the arbiter of international destinies and the fate of unintended and hostile authoritarian centres of powers which have been reduced to a rubble all across the international firmament. The Americans have always risen up the innovative and the entrepreneurial way. When the interventions in Korea and Vietnam have faltered, questions have been raised by the global mandarins and the IR visionaries about the rationale of America going the whole hog in the days of retrenchment and shrinkage of the Western pelf and economic might.

The self-doubt was the central sentiment in the American narrative, when President Johnson commissioned the actual war effort after the Gulf of Tonkin incident in Vietnam which was an unprovoked attack by the VC gunships on two American vessels (Turner Jay and Maddox). This was construed as an act of war by the American President and which was agreed to by the American Congress as well. President Johnson escalated the American involvement in Vietnam, which muddied the strategic and political waters for the nation in the years to come and which finally ended in an ignominious retreat for the American war effort and prestige in toto.

If one consults the American establishment's foreign policy documents, then one can delve into the idea that the Congressional assent to the war effort is a condition for commissioning any military act of the Government. The presence of the Constitutional prerogatives of the War Powers Act of 1971 and of the American President being the Commander-in-Chief of the Armed Forces is not justification enough for commissioning war and action abroad. In an address to the American Foreign Service Association in Washington in June 1965, the Secretary of Defense Dean Rusk elaborated the threat posed by North Vietnam to the region and the much larger international system. The address of Dean Rusk ran as thus, "The root of trouble in Vietnam is today just what it was in April and has been since at least 1960—a cruel and sustained attack by North Vietnam upon the people of South Vietnam. Now, as then, it is a brutal war marked by terror and sneak attack and by the killing of women and children in the night. This campaign of terror has continued throughout the Spring."[8] Thus, the North Vietnamese guerrilla campaigns as mentioned earlier in the narrative were being considered as the single and the most putative and potent threat to the Americans and the South Vietnamese in the conflict zone. The techniques employed by the VC were also referred to as cruel and beyond description. They necessitated an equally befitting reply by the American war machinery in Vietnam. Don't forget, the Mama sans was the American GI's refrain!

Also, the cultural and cinematic portrayals, in tandem with the strategic economic and political interpretations of the war in Vietnam, also led to the creation of mainstream cinematic spectacles of the order of the Rambo series which display the one-man-army visage of John Rambo as a Vietnam War veteran. He single-handedly undertakes a rescue atop a canoe somewhere in the marshlands of North Vietnam. The battle goes ahead with the constant rigmarole of sneak attacks—as mentioned by Dean Rusk—and the battle of attrition and rush.

The torture techniques which the VC inflicted upon the prisoners of war have been avidly depicted. The male protagonist, John Rambo, is captured during a daring raid on a canoe when one of the contact persons moves over to the VC side. Sylvester Stallone, starring as John Rambo, is, hung upside down through a pole and his arms and chest are torn apart with knife gashes and inside these gashes, soil leeches are inserted. The leeches suck the blood of the antagonist who is a POW. Rambo, too, is well adept at the guerrilla and sneak ways of the VC, so, he escapes away with his cache and accomplishes the mission for which he had come in the badlands of conflict in South East Asia. Though he does it the unorthodox way, the outcome of the mission is always an efficient and professional accomplishment of the objective. Thus, the torture methods adopted by the Viet Cong earned a great deal of opprobrium and detailed deliberations as part of the popular narrative of the Vietnam War. critics these days lambast the acts of interrogation at Guantanamo. A foreign policy analyst and an observer of international relations cannot simplistically skim through the media and larger cinematic portrayals of the Vietnam war or any such conflict, which featured an American presence and an American military and geo-economic involvement.

Thus, the pictures produced during the Vietnam war era and the latter-day depictions of the debate and the vagaries surrounding the war, too make for an indispensable part of any effort being undertaken to comprehend the American war rationale. The opposition's riposte and the cumulative impact upon the international system at large too can be perceived this way anew. The silent chatter of the forest insects, the weary marches by the soldiers amidst the tall grass and the sudden VC sneak attacks on the American columns, along with the American choppers swooping down in a battle scene, and evacuating the wounded and decapacitated GIs from the grassy dead-lands, still remain etched in the public and national memory. They all somehow, convolutedly add on to the notion of the grand American Dream of dominance and socio-cultural pelf and eternal entrepreneurial heft. The anathema of conflict and mayhem could not be ignored by the superpower, with all the imaginable military might in any circumstance. War is always brutal and unremitting; the Vietnam saga is also known as the dirty war of the sixties and seventies, which actually witnessed the humbling of the superpower.

War Reporting in Vietnam: Through the Lens of the Fourth Estate

One can delve inside the narrative as posited by the war correspondents, if the first draft of history has to be critically evaluated by the IR scholars and the practitioners alike. Walter Cronkite's name goes down as one of the astute observers of the war in Vietnam, who depicted the war in all its gory details. In the year 2009, he commented upon his coverage during the days of Vietnam war in the sixties. went on to say, "Tonight, back in more familiar surroundings in New York, we'd like to sum up our findings in Vietnam, an analysis that mwst be speculative, personal, subjective. Who won and who lost in the great Tet Offensive against the cities? I'm not sure. The Vietcong did not win by a knockout but neither did we. Then, with as much restraint as I could, I turned to our own leaders whose idea of negotiation seemed frozen in memories of General McArthur's encounter with the Japanese aboard the Battleship Missouri. We've been too often disappointed by the optimism of the American leaders."[9] Thus, the war in Vietnam and the conflict in the domestic realm in the American socio-political firmament, led to the commissioning of an internal turmoil in the United States of America. The rally-around-the-flag-phenomenon did reflect itself when during the initial years of the war, the casualties and the American involvement were not too many. The hoi polloi gathered around the Government of the day in order to support the American war striving in South East Asia.

The Vietnam War is also called as America's first television war. Such was the impact of the Vietnam War that the whole nation lay indebted to the war correspondents such as Walter Cronkite in the way they covered and reported America's first television war. It has been reported on the *History News Network* that, "In the remembrances of Walter Cronkite's remarkable career, none of his television reports has attracted more attention than his famous broadcast about the Tet Offensive in February 1968 in which he concluded that the Vietnam War was "mired in stalemate." In reaction, President Lyndon B. Johnson reportedly declared, "If I've lost Cronkite, I've lost middle America."[10]

Thus, the American rally-around-the-flag phenomenon required the war correspondents to report with alacrity about the justness of the war rationale of the US Government. In the author's view, the notion which can be advanced is that, the idea of war is repulsive to any citizenry howsoever patriotic and nationalistic it may be, as it means violence, death, misery, separation and the defilement of the home and hearth. The Pew Research polls have pointed out that initially the people tend to support the war effort but when the war's gory and putrefied veneer tends to trickle down to the commoners, the narrative changes. Then, a substantial amount of popular support for the war effort dwindles down. That is something of a phenomenon which came into being during the Vietnam War and even during the Persian Gulf conflicts I and II when the challenge of Iraqi reconstruction proved to be much of a task for the Americans and their 'Coalition of the Willing' in the GWOT or the Global War on Terror. Still, in the author's view, the retreat of the American troops on ground from Iraq and Afghanistan has created the rise of ISIS and general instability in the region which could have been avoided if the American and the larger western presence could have been prolonged in Iraq and Afghanistan. Still last reported in an Indian Express story,[11] the cities of Tikrit and Ramadi have been retaken by the Iraqi Government in Baghdad which also buys billions worth of weapons from United States. Thus, the American hand has to be there as the various, "Mission Creeps" have to be completed and given a localized station like in Iraq and Afghanistan in the context of reconstruction and rehabilitation. It has been observed that the incessant bombing by the UAV's by the Americans on ISIS held regions has led to the collapse of the ISIS stranglehold over places such as Al Raqqa and Fallujah. It is here that the Iraqi forces have been ably guided and facilitated by the American aerial firepower in order to get rid of the ISIS safe havens which they had captured by 2013. The tide seems to be turning in Iraq by June 2016.

A piece written by Chester Pach, Faculty of History at the University of Ohio, states President Lyndon Baines Johnson's concern about the negative and the jarring role which the pessimistic reportage about a national war can spawn amongst the commoners. Pach writes, "Johnson worried that any critical TV report would jeopardize public support for the war effort. He assumed that television, because it was a visual medium, had a powerful effect on public attitudes toward the war, although he had little, if any, evidence to sustain his belief. Even though many television reports from Vietnam emphasized U.S. military success, the president paid far more attention to stories about difficulties on the battlefield or problems with pacification. He became so convinced that television news coverage of Vietnam—America's first television war—was slanted and sensationalist that he told journalists at a dinner party in March 1967 that CBS and NBC were 'controlled by the Vietcong...'"[12]

The White House and the President were also concerned about the liberal bias in the US mainstream media portals such as CBS and NBC. Vice President Spiro T. Agnew referred to the media as the, 'Natterating Nabobs of Negativism' as they had a jeopardizing role to play in the context of national interest and the generally accepted veneer of patriotism. Thus, the fourth estate was looked down upon by the Washington's apparatus as it played to the tunes of the popular dissent and street activism. Thus, in the author's view, it harmed the larger objectives of the war effort in South East Asia. Thus, the fourth estate's role in the Vietnam War was disparaged and negated by the White House establishment in more ways than one. Some observers also termed the television coverage as being sensationalist and bordering on to Yellow Journalism, as the voyeuristic urges of the masses was being fanned by them.

Bruce Solhiem writes about the multiple trajectories of the narratives and interpretations about the war which he terms as the haunting experience for the United States psyche as a nation state in modern history. He writes, "The Vietnam War continues to haunt America's collective memory. With only the Civil War surpassing the Vietnam War in terms of national divisiveness, earlier discord continues as conflicting lessons from the Vietnam War are applied to current U.S. war policy."[13] Solheim, a US aviator and a Professor with the Department of History at the Citrus College in California, picturises the Vietnam War era at home and in South East Asia by combining the historical narrative with biographical profiles and personal reflections, allowing the story to unfold in multiple layers, as seen from all sides of the conflict through the eyes of those who were actually part of the inferno.[14]

Several landmark and tide-turning battles have been covered and analysed by the military historians.It is here that the significance of these military and strategic thresholds have been brought out pithily and evocatively. James H. Willbanks contends, "In the Tet Offensive of 1968, Viet Cong and North Vietnamese forces launched a massive countrywide attack on South Vietnam." Though the Communists failed to achieve their tactical and operational objectives, James Willbanks claims that Hanoi won a strategic victory. The offensive proved that America's progress was grossly overstated and caused many Americans and key presidential advisors to question the wisdom of prolonging combat.[15] Willbanks further asserts that the Communists laid siege to a Marine combat base, two weeks prior to the Tet Offensive—known as the Battle of Khe Sanh—to distract the United States. It is his belief that these two events are intimately linked, and in his concise and compelling history, he presents an engaging portrait of the conflicts and singles out the key problems of interpretation.[16] Thus, the landmark reached with the stalemate at Tet and the strategically diversionary techniques utilised by the VC, have been aptly decoded and analysed by the scholars and military historians alike.

In a discussion between President Lyndon Baines Johnson and his aides, the idea of an exit strategy for the Americans is discussed upon as the final part of the American entanglement in Vietnam. The war was turning out to be a costly and bloody stalemate. This state of self-resignation was to be rather different from the 'gung-ho spirit' of the early sixties, but the hollowness of the South Vietnamese Government of Deim was always a cause of disgruntlement and concern for the American establishment. Robert McNamara remarked in one of his dispatches to President Kennedy, "It seems on the face of it, absurd to think that a nation of 20 million people can be subverted by 15-20 thousand active guerrillas if the Government and the people of that country do not wish to be subverted. South Vietnam is not however a very organized society with an effective governing apparatus and a population accustomed to carrying civic responsibility. Public apathy is encouraged by the inability of most citizens to act directly as well as by the tactics of terror employed by the guerrillas throughout the countryside..."[17] Thus, the idea of self-doubt and the fancied estimates about the countryside goodwill and the might of the Diem Government in Saigon, was still being overrated by the American optimists. This notion was a rather unrealistic and skewed estimate of the war effort and the political sentiment in Vietnam.

Two contending perspectives held forth in the run up to the active American involvement in the strife and struggle in Vietnam. For instance, President Kennedy wrote to President Diem in December 1961: "The situation in your embattled country is well known to me and to the American people. We have been deeply disturbed by the assault on your country. Our indignation has mounted as the savagery of the communist programme of assassination, kidnapping and wanton violence became clear. We are prepared to help the Republic of Vietnam to protect its people and to preserve its independence. We shall promptly increase our assistance to your defense effort…"[18] Thus, this Presidential approach to the entire war effort and the augmented American involvement in Vietnam can be said to be reflective of the standard and official stance of the US establishment concerning the policy to be adopted in relation to the status of Vietnam. A war had to be fought in order to advance the ideals of truth, liberty and morality in the regional and global arena. It was to be a black and white schemata, wherein the "vile forces of evil" had to be vanquished by the "good order" of the establishment in Vietnam. The Good Force had to be awakened in the tropics of Vietnam which is a quaint reference to the 2015 Hollywood film, Star Wars: The Force Awakens!

There were other personages too who spoke about the other side of the picture. For instance, the Ambassador to India, John Kenneth Galbraith, sent a memorandum to President Kennedy saying, "We have a growing military commitment. This could expand step by step into a major, long drawn out and indecisive military involvement. We are backing a weak and on the record, ineffectual Government and a leader who as a Politician may be beyond the point of no return. There is consequent danger that we shall replace the French as the Colonial force in the area and bleed as the French did."[19] The solution to the quagmire in Vietnam was highlighted by Ambassador Galbraith as he intended to involve all the responsible nation state actors in order to let the Americans be free from labouring under such a risky responsibility in a terrain that was inhospitable, unfriendly and of which the United States did not have much knowledge.

In the same memorandum to President Kennedy, the Ambassador further said, "We shall find it useful in achieving this result if we seize any good opportunity to involve other countries and world opinion in a settlement and its guarantee. This is a useful exposure and pressure on the communist bloc countries and a useful antidote for the argument that this is a private American military adventure. We should measurably reduce our commitment to the particular present leadership of the Government of South Vietnam."[20] Thus, the seeming web of the debate and controversy over Vietnam was rather simplistic and twofold, where-in the idea of interventionism was often misinterpreted as American adventurism. In the author's view, this perception was pitted against the notion of a safe and limited isolationism in order to lessen the burden on an already overworked American war machinery. Thus, the confrontation between the American ideal of being the superhero in a perennially do-gooder avatar always triumphed over the realistic circumspection premised upon domestic limitations and international coalitional circumstances. In the author's view, one imaginary scenario can be imagined that if Superman would have existed in the real world then the American war machinery would never have had to embark upon such a costly and casualty prone war in Vietnam. In the author's view, all that would have been required is a kind of heat ray from the Man in Steel to scorch the VC insurgents into submission. Napalms and Agent Oranges were not to be utilised then and instead, the man in the red cape and his stellar powers and firepower would have been the kosher solution to the malady in Vietnam.

President Johnson gave an important address to the nation on 31 March, 1968, aimed at limiting the war in Vietnam. The address ran thus,

> "The North Vietnamese attack during the Tet Holidays failed to achieve its principal objectives. It did not collapse the elected Government of South Vietnam during the Tet Holidays and shatter the army as the communists had hoped for. But they did compel the South Vietnamese and their allies to move certain forces from the countryside into the cities. They caused widespread destruction and suffering. Their attacks and the battles that followed made refugees of half a million human beings. We are prepared to move immediately towards peace through negotiations. We are reducing substantially the present level of hostilities and we are doing so unilaterally and at once. Tonight I have ordered our Aircraft and our naval vessels to make no attacks on North Vietnam except in the area north of the militarized zone where the continuing enemybuild up directly threatens allied forward positions and where the movements of their troops and supplies are clearly related to that threat."[21]

Thus, the de-escalation of the war in Vietnam by the US establishment was a unilateral move by the Washington Government in order to extricate the American forces and interests out of the morass. They suddenly found themselves in a quagmire a few military setbacks. Perceived in another manner, the South Vietnamese denomination similar to the other prime actors in such international conflicts had to preserve its freedom on its own. The Americans highlighted the VC's effectiveness in surprise guerilla actions which were difficult to be tackled by the US Army. The surprise element and the ability to strike at will was further buttressed by the inefficiency and the negativity of President Deim in Saigon. Thus, the predestination of the Vietnam War and the circumstantial tilt of events took such a shape that victory eluded the American establishment.

Thus, apart from the military strategies employed in the American war effort in Vietnam, the idea of the tumult and the suffering faced by the Vietnamese commoners and being felt by the young American privates, was also a grave attribute of the war. People had left their friends, fun and sunny basketball environs which is what they did before joining the Army and longed to be back home. But here in Vietnam, the American GI's had to to lay down their lives in a place and for people who were far alien to their concerns and way of life. Tony Blair's statement in the year 2003 can be quoted here wherein he states the de-rigueur indispensability of the American might and stealthy presence in a speech before the American Senate in the aftermath of the "democratising" intervention in Iraq:

> "And, I know its hard on America, and in small corner of this vast nation, out in Nevada, Idaho, Berkeley, Oklahoma or in any one of these places, I have never been to but have always wanted to be there… I know out there in any one of these places there is guy attempting to get along with his life, perfectly happy, minding his own business saying to you, the political leaders of this country, "Why me? And Why us? And why America?, And the only answer is, "Because Destiny put you in place in history, in this moment in time, and the task is yours to do."[22]

Thus, the idea of greater and larger than normal responsibility being placed upon the American shoulders makes them brave and emboldened enough to strike out in the nature of a true-blue, weather-weary cowboy. It is this cowboy who has to take out his lasso every now and then in order to broker and mediate peace, stability, free markets. It was an essentiality to usher in the dream democracy in the larger world, in consonance with the ideals and characteristics of the American Dream.

Still, as formerly asserted, the cultural productions and presentations firm up the arcadia of a nation's cumulative narrative. It is here that the superhero tale of a rule-abiding greatly powered human mutant in the Metropole no longer remains the abiding idiom. In a way, the idea is that the quintessential superheroes of the order of Superman, the anti-Nazi Captain America and others are not to be the purveyors of the do-gooder spirit. In more ways than one, the new US television serial character of Jack Bauer, as, the lethal and effective homicidal policeman, has become a favourite with the American audience.

Our diminutive, Jack, does not own any superpowers and is also not a mutant from any far-off planet.

But he has Flash-Gordon like qualities of flying all genres of war planes, ships and choppers and can 'play' like a commando with human limitations. He tortures his prisoners with third degree and often crosses the line of law during the process of interrogation and confrontation with the arch antagonists. He too saves America, but in his beyond-the-anvil ways which is a more ordinary way of the humans. Thus, harking on to this do-gooder media construct, the message of the philosophy is that sometimes the super nations akin to their superheroes, have to outdo the law and the norm of the land in order to knit a victory podium for the nation and its people.

The World of War Correspondents and Vietnam

The world and the work of war correspondents has always shown a mirror to the world of war and conflict in nations all across the firmament of the international system. War correspondents have always persisted in their sanguine and daring strivings in order to transcend the boundaries of the real and the hyper real. The vortex of conflict and human perdition along with an unmitigated misery during war time, has led to the idea of war coverage in order to bring forth a value neutral and agnostic account of the mayhem and the misery of international conflict. In the context of the Vietnam War, war correspondents such as Michael Browne and David Halberstam, have covered the conflict with its gory intrinsic details. They have furthered the vitriol and the poignancy of what wars and human misery are all about despite the foreign policy and national interest-oriented interpretations and such attendant narratives. The coverage by the popular war correspondents might be critical of the American establishment but in the author's view such a criticality might be the correct balancer in Opinion for the American establishment. The Government can then mellow down its fundamentally aggressive stance and policy making and implementation in terms of the decisions to go to war in far off lands and terrains which involve a great deal of loss in lives, primarily. The Fourth Estate always acts as a catalyst and an able crucible in order to stem the tide of profound aggressive intent and action which might bedevil any leader and his or her army with a military and political objective.

As an instance, Michael Browne covered Vietnam for the Associated Press and was awarded the Pulitzer Prize for his value neutral and captivating coverage of the war in Vietnam. In one his stories, he even reported about the theatres in South Vietnam in the early 1960s when the vagaries of the Indo-China War and later on the vicissitudes of the Vietnam War, had not been amply projected before the domestic American audience. Michael Browne related in one of his dispatches, "Thao, the person designated to lead the raid against the Viet cong battalion near the town of Ben Tre, invited me to a theatrical performance and the inauguration of the new Theater complex in the city of Ben Tre. The performance and the regalia was not of the order of a Broadway inauguration and there was definitely a want of chutzpah and spectacular that one has come to associate with the Broadway. Still, the audience were very happy at the fact that the three characters with masks and glitzy local silk dresses were swearing aloud and had decided to murder an adversary."[23]

The report which Michael Browne further narrated was that, "Thao came over to me and said that he was not leaving the city of Ben Tre as he had some other work and would I like to accompany the South Vietnamese contingent to the area beyond the Mekong delta for harassing a VC battalion which had been reportedly active in the region.?"[24] Thus, the war went on in the central and north Vietnamese region with the Saigon Government going about its humdrum daily routine. Little realising that when the South Vietnamese contingents left the Mekong delta villages at 6 in the evening, the hapless villagers who had been asked by the soldiers from Saigon to support the Government had nowhere to go after the Saigon contingents had left for the night.

It was then that the VC second-rung ideologues would swoop down the same village in the night and force and coax the same villagers to be with the VC. They would recruit firm believing youth to fight alongside them in the VC battalions and other rung–II VC outfits. Then, the young activists were given the gun and the artillery to fend off against the Westerners and the South Vietnamese contingents. Thus, there was some planning in the South's Government, but the improper execution in indoctrination and support-building techniques among the masses, led to the final collapse of the South Vietnamese Government. It all happened despite the massive influx of American advisors, equipment and men in the Vietnam War during the different stages of the conflict.

Michael Browne incisively narrated the idea of the death of a VC suspect, which could all be a simple peasant running away scared from a contingent of soldiers from Saigon. The famed war correspondent reports,

> "Perhaps as an act of mercy, perhaps as sheer cruelty, one of the men picked up a heavy stake lying in the mud and rammed one end of it into the ground next to the wounded man's throat. Then, he forced the stake down the throat of the wounded man, trying to throttle the man. The man continued to move. Then, another man tried stamping on the man's throat, but, somehow the spark of life was still too strong. Finally the whole group laughed and walked back to the dykes separating the mud watered rice fields where thousands of the advanced VC contingents could have hid waiting for a sneak attack upon the soldiers from Saigon, that is, South Vietnam."[25]

The brutality of the war and the human misery attendant with the entire blood and grime can be related by another excerpt about the same wounded man who had been earlier felled by a hail of South Vietnamese bullets. The brutality of the war still does not discredit the American war effort in the author's view as a larger objective associated with the achievement of national interest obligations drove the war in Vietnam. As the women related to the wounded man attempted to wipe and heal his wound, Michael Browne could do nothing but watch the expressions on the face of the lady as the dead body of the man who was seemingly her husband, lay in her lap. Browne writes,

> "He died about ten minutes later. The woman remained seated, one hand over the husband's eye. Slowly, she looked around at the troops, and then

> she spotted me. Her eyes fixed on me in an expression that still haunts me sometimes. She was not weeping and her face showed neither grief nor fury, it was unfathomably blank. I was told by the commander not to be sentimental as that wounded man was undoubtedly a Viet Cong man as these regions had been the Viet Cong stronghold for years. This was war and not a sentimental party. However, he offered to give to the lady some money which Browne had offered after witnessing the death of the Viet Cong suspect."[26]

Thus, the acridity and the valour of the war correspondents can be rightly and inconveniently posited amid any narrative on Vietnam. The brutality of war from both the sides of the fence can be gauged and reflected upon by saner voices from among the academia, military historians, public opinion makers, statesman and international relations observers connected with the context of the Vietnam War. In the author's view, war begets misery, but for the stolid enunciation and the realisation of national and international objectives, keeping in view the perspective of the then au currant circumstances, a narrative on war needs two frames of references. An analyst has to be schizophrenic.

One frame of reference is the idea of patriotic fervour and nationalism which the nations talk of, which is also a part of the founding myth of those nations. Thus, the attendant eulogisation and the glorification of the idea of a nation and its propagated objectives, became the order of the day as the three pillars of containment, democratisation and a demo-liberal world order were proffered as the legitimate attributes of the rationale to intervene in Vietnam. The other frame is a very contrasting one, which refers to the anti-war and an 'avant grade idea' of eschewing war and violence even at the altar of a realism-ordained national interest oriented objectives. Thus, the idea of war and military contestations has a double-edged sword of additives attached to it and the same logic runs true for what all transpired in the Vietnam conflict despite the ideological claims of the Viet Cong and the internationalist standpoint of the realpolitik of the United States in South East Asia.

The Guerilla Grime in the Marshlands

David Halberstam was another war correspondent who too 'wrote the first draft of history' during the vicissitudes of the Vietnam War. It can be put that way, rather assuredly. His report in the *New York Times* says, "The Viet Cong had no illusions about the type of war they were engaged in. It was a war of revolution and they knew their own strengths and the weaknesses of the Government. The Americans thought of them as men carrying weapons but the fact was that they were most effective when they carried no weapons and wore no uniforms—at night when they indoctrinated the peasants. The misery of the people was their great ally and they knew how to play on it."[27] Thus, the scholars and the observers of the war in Vietnam led to the idea that guerilla techniques of warfare and the John Rambo-type jungle warfare stratagems were the strong points of the VC. Images and measures such as the avalanche of helicopters, communication kiosks, machine guns, armoured personnel carriers and overall a superior military hardware, were the primary pluses of the American and the South Vietnamese forces.

Thus, the war was a study in jungle warfare which finds a duplication in the context of the Latin America and other insurgencies where-in the forested terrain forms an important environ of the battlefield. Here, one can relate to another striving from across the cornucopia of cultural studies. The entire narrative includes within its ambit, the notion of cinematic portrayals of forest/jungle warfare. Here, the context of flying bullets amid the foliage of leaves, booby traps getting the better of the best hawk eyes and the 'rat–a-rat' of machine guns, gains significance. But very true to the context in Vietnam, what would a soldier trained in conventional warfare do and attempt as a life-saving device when the enemy is invisible and erupts suddenly from unknown tropics and the surrounding jungle flora?

Such was the trend of the battle in the tropics, that the GIs didn't know that what had hit them. They were sitting ducks for the invisible antagonist, who, would leave behind fallen outposts and chopped heads. The VC would attack only when they were superior in numbers and strategy. Otherwise, they would lie low and their absence did not have a much of an assurance for non-engagement as even in their inactivity they were busybodies building secret armament posts in the caves and training new recruits from amongst the youth. It was startling from the point of view of the American military advisors that these VC men had been comrades-in-arms with some of their commanders and had participated and won in the Indo-China wars against the French and much before that they were victorious against the Chinese. Thus, a great deal of successful combat experience was the forte of these highly qualified and elite VC battalions. They often hid in the killing fields of rice and threw up meaningful blows at the South Vietnamese contingents, propped up by the American military men, military advisors and equipment.

Mainstream Cinema Beckons

We are now looking at mainstream Hollywood constructs depicting warfare and jungle military attrition. Such a fearful and uncertain forest scenario is scarily and vividly caught and incisively depicted in the Hollywood construct, *Predator* which featured Arnold Schwarzenegger. The film and the male protagonist became popular amongst the global audiences due to the success of another war flick which was centered on a Latin American drug lord called as *Commando*. Once again, the forest saga finds a familiar echo of the war in Vietnam. The movie depicts an alien creature which lands in a war zone where the Americans are fighting off a long-simmering Latin American insurgency. The alien is not visible to the American commandos, who accidentally become its hapless victims as it camouflages beautifully amongst the trees and the forest flora. The battle pits American ingenuity against the technology of the alien which finds that in the culmination of the legendary scuffle that common sense, human sixth sense and ingenuity for lone survival win the day. The most battle-worthy commando, Arnold, succeeds in annihilating this creature from the skies. He finds out that the target of this monster-robot becomes invisible to it, when the targeted victim rubs mud upon his or her body. This technique serves as a successful survival technique for the male protagonist as he annihilates the Predator in the end in the aftermath of a harrowing and blood-curdling duel in the end. What comes to the fore is the idea that in jungle warfare the success comes from location training and the skill to utilise the jungle to the hilt both as a threat projection instrumentality and as an aid to hide and sneak away when the going gets tough during an operation. The VC in Vietnam were adept at this camouflaging as compared to the routinized technical and GI wizardry of the Americans.

Predator is a good Vietnam war allegory, but sings paeans of human ingenuity in the face of all odds during a lopsided balance of force in an altercation between military foes. A review on the web portal, Reel Good, points out officially that, "It's the story of a group of elite US commandos sent into the Guatemalan jungle on a top-secret assignment to rescue a US ambassador, kidnapped by a guerilla squadron. After annihilating the guerillas and completing their mission, the commandos are systematically hunted down one-by-one by a vicious extra-terrestrial who can become invisible at will."[28]

The widely read and quoted web portal further says, "Important to note that the Central American context of the location quickly dissolves after the soldiers leave their helicopter. This jungle is in fact any jungle where US men have been sent with guns and supplies, to die at the hands of an enemy that is comparatively destitute and undermanned. One of the characters even laments as such: "Same kind of moon, same kind of jungle."[29] Thus, a jungle is a jungle happens to be the mainstay of the Vietnam context as the American GIs too, attempt to help their Saigon buddies in a war which is quickly slipping out of their grasp. The battle-hardened veterans of the famed bloody Indo-China wars and their battle-hardened wits gained from the days of the French colonial rule have the same flora advantage; they are fighting for their own issues and have a so-called homeland to defend, so, they have nowhere to go if the battle goes the other way round. The knowledge of the terrain and the habitation surrounding the camouflaged battle stations makes them akin to the *Predator*'s Extra-Terrestrial, who, can become invisible at will and haunts while in absentia and comes back to hit the antagonist and the enemy is caught completely unawares. The *Predator* saga unfolds in the grasslands and the deadly rice fields of Vietnam with the same repetitiveness and sacred sanguinity amid the din of helicopters and the rat-a-rat of machine guns.

The war in Vietnam reminds one of the brutality and the dehumanising nature of the conflict where both the sides are well-entrenched inside the tarred terrain for a vicious slugfest. The apt comparison on Reel Good reports, "Dutch's famous line 'If it bleeds, we can kill it' is a chilling echo of the Vietnam orders of 'Kill anything that moves', the operational narrative that gave us incidents like the My Lai massacre—forever an ugly stain on the history of the West. This abandonment of our morals is shoved into the audience's face when the Predator slaughters another member of Dutch's team but refrains from killing the young, unarmed female that idly watches in terror. The commandos theorise that their enemy only kills armed males. For an extra-terrestrial entity that bleeds green, it follows a code that one would describe as quintessentially moral, human."[30] The same runs true for the Sylvester Stallone-starred flick, titled as *First Blood* which depicts a commando character and Vietnam war veteran who returns home thankfully in shape but finds himself completely confused and psychologically scarred in a dear run in Vietnam. The battle for him has not actually ended in Vietnam as he rubbishes the system in the American Urbania and militates against a routine-on-a-search-mission police in a state of marooned individuality. These issues have been taken up elsewhere as the chapter on American counter culture and its origins in the Book, later on in the narrative.

Thus, in a way Vietnam has more scars to offer to the American Dream rather than proffer psychological Bronze Stars and Purple Hearts to that segment of the citizenry which fought for the idealism of national honour and prestige in a far-off war. The war is often historically disparaged as a dirty war in a far off, dark and spitting rain[31] infested terrain of forested and tropical state of Vietnam. Thus, in the spitting rain American younglings long dreaming of the Aspen snow and sledges and the Las Vegas casinos and California women, drink and curse together the stolidity of their military existence in the forested parts of Vietnam. The same picturisation seemingly emanates from the visage of"the drunken skullduggery of the soldiers in an encampment somewhere in Vietnam and the movie is, Oliver Stone's *Platoon*. Thus, the commonality of the guerilla theme can be extrapolated out of the din and rustle of war in these cinematic presentations of war in the forest of which, Vietnam happens to be a quaint and accurate parallel. The war had to be won in the drawing rooms of the United

States but the Americans lost in generically in the Public sphere which manifested itself in the form of a defeat in the battlefields of Vietnam which turned into a kind of "Killing fields" for the American forces. The questioning frame is part of the plural and the dialogue part of the American Dream but sticklers for the nation and the "larger" objectives too had to be recruited. The larger idols fared well in United States war or no war and Vietnam or no Vietnam.

NOTES

1. Ruchir Sharma, *Breakout Nations: In Pursuit of Next Economic Miracles* (New York: W.W. Norton and Company, 2013), pp. 2-10.
2. George F. Kennan, "The Sources of Soviet Conduct", *Foreign Affairs*, Volume 25, No. I, July, 1947.
3. "The Only Way to Deal with Russia",*Reader's Digest*, October 1947, 25-31.
4. George F. Kennan, "The Sources of Soviet Conduct", *Foreign Affairs*, Volume 25, No. I, July, 1947.
5. David Northrup, "Globalization and the Great Convergence: Rethinking World History in the Long Term", *Journal of World History*, Volume 16, Number 3, September 2005, pp. 249-267.
6. Ibid.
7. Kenneth Liberthal, "The American Pivot to Asia: Why President Obama's Turn to the East is Easier Said than Done", *Foreign Policy*, December 21, 2011.
8. Richard B Stebbins (ed.), "Documents on American Foreign Relations 1965" (Council on Foreign Relations, Harper and Row Publishers, 1966), pp. 168-169.
9. "Parting words from Walter Cronkite: His famous Vietnam Commentary", originally aired on a special *CBS News* broadcast Feb. 27, 1968.
10. Chester Pach, "The Way It Wasn't: Cronkite and Vietnam", URL: http://hnn.us/article/ 104635 (Online: Web), Accessed on July 28, 2015.
11. *Indian Express Report*, 28 December, 2015.
12. Ibid.
13. Bruce O Solhiem, *The Vietnam War Era* (University of Nebraska Press, 2008).
14. Ibid.
15. James Willbanks, *The Tet Offensive: A Concise History* (Columbia University Press, 2008).
16. Ibid.
17. US Department of Defense, "United States-Vietnam Relations, 1945-1967" (Pentagon Papers, 12 Books, Washington, Government Printing Office, 1971) Book II.
18. PPP: John F Kennedy, 1961 (Washington: GPO, 1962), 801. Alternative Source: Senator Gravel Edition, Pentagon Papers, pp. 805-806.
19. FRUS, 1961-1963, Vol. 2 (Washington, GPO, 1990), p. 297. Alternative source: Senator Gravel Edition, Pentagon Papers, pp. 670-71.
20. Ibid.
21. PPP: Lyndon Baines Johnson 1968 (Washington, Government printing office, 1970), pp. 469-71.
22. Michael Mandelbaum, *The Case for Goliath: How America Acts As the World's Government In The 21st Century* (Public Affairs, Perseus Book Company, 2005), pp. 6-7.

23. Jon E. Lewis (ed.), "The Mammoth Book of War Correspondents: Death in the Rice Fields" (Robinson: London, 2001), pp. 465-469.
24. Ibid.
25. Ibid.
26. Ibid.
27. Jon E. Lewis (eds.), *The Mammoth Book of War Correspondents: David Halberstam: The Face of the Enemy in Vietnam* (Robinson: London, 2001), pp. 465-469.
28. "What was it Sergeant: Mcriernan's Predator and Vietnam", URL: http://www.reelgood.com.au/what-was-it-sergeant-mctiernans-predator-and-vietnam/ (Online ; Web), Accessed on April 10, 2015.
29. Ibid.
30. Ibid.
31. The term 'spiting rain' was developed by the French Colonialists in Vietnam and the larger Indo China where-in a sticky dew surrounded the atmosphere and made wet the entire environment and droplets of water fell down without rain fall impacting a said spot in the forest. The term became synonymous for death, despair and dissipation of life and all hope during a long drawn out war in the region.

10

US Foreign Policy and West Asia: The Oriental Escapade

Introduction

Pandit Jawaharlal Nehru, the Indian Prime Minister, had, contended in the hallowed years of India's independence movement, that India is a centrally located nation state which lies at a significant geographical and a geostrategic cusp. It connects South East Asia with the Southern Asian region to the east and further serves as a bridge between East Asia and West Asia. Thus, the West Asia configures in the strategic and political fulcrum of theory and praxis in the realm of international relations and World Politics. The Americans on the other hand were fortunate to have the twin natural safeguards of the order of the Atlantic and the Pacific, which kept them safe and disconnected from the European turmoil of the continental political legerdemain and the hustle and bustle of the rise and fall of empires in the Orient. Thus, they had the best of both the worlds and only had to contend with the friendly near neighbourhood of Canada and Mexico and the harmless Caribbean. These immediate neighbors kept the United States ensconced within the rubric of stolidity and assurance of unhampered and uninterrupted growth and consolidating patterns of development. When the time came during the World Wars, the United States emerged out of its cocoon in order to catapult itself upon the Nazism and Fascism-threatened world stage. The American advent was as if the historical processes had configured the advent of United States of America.'

A region such as the West Asia did not have the luxury and the strategic fortune of remaining disconnected from the myriad near-neighbourhood in order to buy time for the development of its pelf, geo-economic and geopolitical might in the immediate region and the far abroad. Apart from the cosseted contiguity of the region, the ever-present colonial legacy and the ever extension of the British, French and later on the American influence dominated West Asia. Through Empire-oriented narratives and non-Empire-oriented structures of the United States, the West Asian nations had always had to subsist with a subordinated and a borrowed influence. The grandeur and the middle-age pelf of the Ottoman Empire and the Persian Empire in the much earlier epochs, was also different in nature. Who can forget the battle between the Persian Empire of Xerxes and the three hundred Spartans, as the Greeks in a united striving fought for the survival of their civilisation in the aftermath of the Battle of Thermopylae. Thus, the invaders and the interventions had their field day and later on with the ending days of the nineteenth century and the World War years in the twentieth century. The West Asia's geopolitics developed as a faint echo of and a replica of the Continental Europe in the twentieth century. Also, the idea of shadow boxing by the European nations was a familiar narrative akin to the cross-sectioned squaring off and cartelising of the African continent. In the context of Xerxes, the quintessential depiction in the movie *300* portrayed the Persian Emperor as a bisexual and a cross-dressing King who wore ornaments like the women in Persia. The ambiguity of the stature of Xerxes was a cinematic metaphor to depict the vile and the treacherous nature of the Persian overlord who also boasted of some dark flings with the supernatural in the narrative of the film. Also, the darker side of the Orient and the West Asia is further depicted by the conversation which ensues between the Spartan King, Leonidas and Xerxes. When the initial thrust of the Persian slingers has been blunted by the brave Spartans, then, at that point of time, Xerxes arrives in his white shimmering chariot out of a canopy of dark cliffs and dark oceans to ask for the surrender of the Spartans. The Spartan King reprimands him with the words that he is a brave person with fidelity towards his nation and people. He will perish in the battle rather than perish as a slave to an alien power. The Spartan King contends haughtily that, "Let the Persians make the environment dark and dingy with arrows and vile spells but the Spartans will fight on till the last breath and will not capitulate to this darkness which subsumes the sea coast now." Thus, the metaphor of the dark and dingy in the Movie, 300 Spartans reflects the standard vision of the region wherein it is often portrayed that the people, rulers and the culture is staid, and has an iota of banal vileness about it. This depiction may be regarded as degenerated but that was how the Europeans perceived and further propagated the myth about the Orientals.

West Asia was no different in its own individual way as externalities have remained as the key ordaining factor in the geopolitical run up to the state of the region since at least the last hundred years. Thus, the idea of the son-of-the-soil phenomenon and the region's momentum has attained a new face with the idea of the Arab Spring which has festooned changes and a grand socio-economic and political metamorphosis of the region. The populations in nations ranging from Tunisia, Egypt, Morocco and Yemen and even cosseted states such as Saudi Arabia have been feeling the heat of the momentum.

People have revolted and rebelled against the restrictive monarchies and secular democracies, all across the political firmament of the region. The external actors such as the United States have extended a qualified and diplomacy-induced stance in the region where it is said that lip service has been paid to the sustenance of the ideals of liberty, equality and democracy. Though a singular and blanket response is too much of a task as different regional states have separate and well-delineated socio-political and economic conditions which required graded and separate responses in the larger sense of the term.

The Raison d'Etre of the Oil Factor

The region has remained mired first in the throes of Arab nationalism which was largely propelled by the idea of anti-colonialism and also the race to carve out zones premised upon the oil factor too. The discovery of oil as the black gold of the region, initiated the entry of Western oil firms such as British Gas, European firms and American oil interests in the region which involved strategic deals with the individual monarchies and regimes of the day. In fact, the enigma of oil has affected Palestine's thorny issue of self-determination and various wars such as the Iran–Iraq war and the Persian Gulf conflicts I and II which have involved the Americans, whether military or diplomatic, in one way or the other. In the author's view, oil begets war and it also begets the onerous task of conflict resolution in the region which should have been taken up by the United States in a more engaged and fervent manner living true to its Regulator role playing as part of IR speak. Thus, external influence, the oil factor and the strategic presence of nations bordering the maritime trade routes in the Persian Gulf are some of the factors which have led to the surmounting significance and the all-pervading tussle over turfs in the region.

The Yom Kippur war of the year 1973 ran true to the prognostications of the idea of an oil-ordained apocalypse. It was during the Yom Kippur war that some West Asian states had interrupted the supply of natural gas and oil resources to nations such as the United States and Netherlands. This development led to cars queuing up in the Western urban complexes and nearly brought the industrial complexes to a halt. Thus, the various nations chose to appease the regional oil-producing nations and the OPEC in exchange for granting an observer status to the Palestinian Liberation Organization in lieu of the reinstatement of oil supplies.

Thus, West Asia also opened up a new Pandora's box which led the beleaguered and now-testy Americans to opt for and develop an alternate and other-than-Arab sources of natural gas and oil. Shale gas in the United States and alternate sources in states in Latin America such as Venezuela and the Caspian Sea resources in the erstwhile Soviet Union became the new jostling grounds for the Occident and United States. These developments included nation states such as the United States and Germany opting for wind and solar power for about 78% of their energy needs.

Thus, oil has always existed as a geo-economic and geostrategic factor in the run up to power and influence in the region. Also, the unending and the unremitting nature of the balancing of power and diplomacy over the status and the future of Israel and Palestine has been another facet of the troubled group of nations in the region. The Americans have a specific viewpoint. The rise of Iran and Iraq as recalcitrant nation state actors in the region riding on the allegations of being state sponsors of global terrorism (linkages to the Al Qaeda) and the idea of being nuclear weapons proliferators, too, militates against the counter-terrorism and counter-proliferation planks of the American foreign policy. These are the founding pillars of the nation's tilt since the beginning of the post-Cold War era. When proverbial impoverishment is being talked about, the name of Africa comes to the fore and when oil politics and Saharan tales and the Shiekhdoms are the pet peeve during a discussion, then it is the West Asian lore which comes to the fore. Its colour and verve, come to the fore along with the cultural imagery of the white-skinned and slightly built and lean Lawrence of Arabia whose belongingness and sacrifice to the region and its lore has been beatifically depicted in the cinematic portrayals through the Hollywood construct in David Lean's, *Lawrence of Arabia.*

As Hollywood Perceives the Issue and the 'Gaza Troubles'

The Hollywood construct, *Lawrence of Arabia*, was very much a topical and historical biopic in every sense of the term. It depicted the Arab revolt and the advent of Arab nationalism. A prominent history web portal states, "The revolt, one of the most dramatic episodes of the 20th century, was a seminal moment in the history of the modern Middle East, the touchstone of all future regional conflicts. Advised by liaison officer T.E. Lawrence—"Lawrence of Arabia"—Arab troops would play a vital role in the Allied victory over the Ottoman Empire in World War I."[1] The web portal further states that clandestine warfare and the failure of nation-building in alien lands which remains the bane of Western interventions till day, marred any positive developments in the Arab land and further added to the misfortune of the region and its attendant actors. The author adds, "The Arab Revolt of 1916–1918 also saw the development of guerrilla tactics and strategies of modern desert warfare. And the political intrigues surrounding the revolt and its aftermath were as significant as the fighting, for Great Britain and France's myopic attempts at nation building planted the seeds of the troubles."[2]

The issue led to the diversionary techniques against the traditional and withering Ottoman Empire. The British incited a rebellion in the areas ruled by the Ottoman Turks other than Cairo in order to contain the Ottoman Empire. The antagonism was further exacerbated by the Turkification of the countries in the Ottoman Empire and the alignment of the Ottoman Empire with the Germans and the other Central Powers. Also, the British promised to liberate the erstwhile nations of the order of Israel, Palestine, Syria, Lebanon, etc. in order to stem the tide of the Germans while the region and the larger international system was on the verge of World War I. Thus, the Arab-Anglo détente was utilised to a successful extent in order to militate against the German-led coalition. This led to the further delineation and diversification of the entire region led by the so-called torrent and tradition of colonial, imperial rule and tradition.

Still, it was this interventionism by the Western powers which led to the spawning of a tradition of conflict and vitiation of a liberal, liveable and peaceful narrative in the region. It can be surmised as the part of a general understanding of the region's ethos or a want of it that one blogger states, "West Asia has always been an area of conflict from biblical times—state against state, religion against religion, tribe against tribe, and even clan against clan within tribes. It will always be that way. It's a way of life that we Westerners can't understand. It seems to us to be crude and uncivilized—and we keep trying to 'fix' it. Since the Crusades, our interferences have only been met with resistance and never-ending hate." This is a quintessential view which is reminiscent of the idea of the White man's burden. Still, the Americans need to go beyond their Camp Davids and other Summits in order to arrive at a tangibly achieved Road Map to peace in West Asia, especially after the passage of the UNSC resolution by the Security Council in December, 2015. The role of the United Nations interlocutor is carved out and the person is Staffan Misruta who needs to solve the tangle of Syria and the Global community needs to know that what is to be done with Bashar Al Assad and the Syrian Government. The strategic confusion has been exacerbated with the Russians bombing the Assad's rebels and the Americans targetting the ISIS in the mainland of Iraq. The, Saudi Arabian and the Iranian rivalry too has been the bane of peace in places such as Lebanon and Yemen on the lines of an intra religious divide. Still, the passage of the UNSC resolution holds more than a ray of hope for the situation in West Asia with a proper American support and legalese aid.

On the contrary, crass pessimism about a vibrant and kaleidoscopic civilisation is uncalled for as there exists the cradle of life and survival amidst the tales and rigour of Arab life. The resilience of the local population and the will to survive and thrive amidst 'a scanty and desertified context' with a want of the regular flora, fauna and water makes life difficult and challenging. The will to live became the will to power through the ages of conflict and it is this unfortunate facet which has become the central pillar of investigation and research in the region. The cultural perception and the critical tendency of enumeration and analysis, also, forms a staple and prominent element of the idea of conflict analysis in the context of the Israel–Palestine and the Israel–Arab conflagration since the last few decades. Also, the idea of how the region's hegemonic dimensions and the coverage of the conflict has developed through the years is also a question and a poser worthy of research and elaboration.

The historical details of the order of the Balfour Declaration, the Naqba war, the legacy perpetuated by Ben Gurion and Goldemeyer along with the details such as the Gallilie war and the Suez Canal crisis, saw the need for an American intervention. These are all old pedestals which need to be considered with an innate understanding. New and contemporary dimensions of the order of the Shia–Sunni divide, the rise of the Islamic State in Syria and Levant along with the Iran factor in Syria and the Kurdish angle with the current Turkic policies, are developments which need to be given a greater amount of significance for any reading of West Asia. The dominant reading of the conflict and the doomed resistance frame of the Arab–Israeli conflict, can be further understood by delving inside the idea of an effort to decode oppositionality. Tamar Leibis writes in his academic work, "Having shown that the Media framings of the conflict construct an "Us and Them theme" in which the other side is dehumanized, depersonalized and sometimes demonized. Does it follow that the Television viewers and the newspaper readers follow the hegemony through the same frame of reference? The obvious answer is that if the viewers' view of the conflict is mediated by Television they should see the conflict through an even more tightly framed steel frame than do the journalists."[3] The idea of the manufactured frame of analysis can be equated with the idiom of manufactured consent as the idea of feeding the audience through a well-delineated source of information and selective content becomes the mode of operation of the media/ fourth estate. In the author's view, sometimes the media are found to be hand and glove with the military and the industry complex as enumerated by the novel perception of President Dwight Eisenhower. This American President called the manufactured consent of media portrayals as being a structured product of the grand MIM or the 'Military Media and Industry complex' which not only exists in the United States, but, can be witnessed as a functional reality in the larger frame of reference anywhere in the world.

Tamar Leibes further contends, "To say that the Israeli Press represents the Arab Israeli conflict from where 'we' stand is a redundant exercise. We have learnt that any report on reality expresses the reporter's point of view and conflict makes it physically and psychologically difficult to look towards the other side."[4] The argument which is being made out is that culture ordains the way and the manner in which a conflict gets selectively portrayed. In the author's view, this might be a simplistic explanation as the culture is a difficult-to-define entity which has an inalienable and inseparable impact on any of its socio-political and economic constituents.

The Israel–Palestine turmoil has every now and then erupted in spates of violence in the recent past. It was in 2008, 2012 and in June 2014 that the Hamas militants operating in the contiguous Gaza strip attacked the Israeli cities of Tel Aviv with rockets and inflicted violence upon the Israeli state through the clandestine and underground tunnels running under the border. The Israelis led by Prime Minister Benjamin Netanyahu blame the Hamas for attacking the civilians in Israel and for seeking the outrageous condition of demilitarising and ending all efforts of Israeli civilian settlement as a part of the Jewish nation's foreign and regional policy. Thus, in the months of June–July 2014, about 1,000 Palestinians perished along with 30-odd casualties on the Israeli side. The point is that Qatar and Turkey to a certain extent bankroll the Hamas efforts in Palestine and Hamas has an uncomfortable truce with the other non-terror outfit of Mahmoud Abbas's Fatah which is premised on the West Bank. The Muslim Brotherhood during the times of Mohammad Morsi in Cairo was a strong supporter of Hamas but since the times of Al Sisi in Cairo, after the removal of Morsi, the Egyptians have emerged as the strong critics of Hamas with Saudi Arabia, too, following suit. In the ending days of 2015, Jerusalem has once again become the cynosure of all eyes as the Palestinians stabbing the Israeli soldiers has been avidly reported by the international media. In the author's view, these violent developments have led to the development of a further crisis like situation which had been earlier exacerbated by the Israeli take on Iran's nuclearisation along with the Israeli policy of constructing settlements in the contested territories. The Israel Arab conflict has become a festering wound in the peacenik efforts of great powers and the involved regional actors. The pariah status which Israel suffered with too can be reflected in the late and delayed Indian political decision to accord recognition to the Israel as a sovereign country in the first half of the nineties.

The American standpoint was portrayed by the Secretary of State, John Kerry, who leveraged for supporting a solution to the 2014 'Gaza trouble'; Cairo being his staging point to negotiate a truce between Israel and Hamas. The American line is also amply explained by the conceptualisation of a new 'Marshall Plan' for Gaza. This plan would be sponsored by the regional bankrollers and the West and would be worth a quantum of 50 billion dollars.[5] The American eye for this Marshall plan redux would be to enhance the infrastructure, educational and health services in the beleaguered Gaza. Thus, the American establishment too remains intrinsically engaged with the larger trouble in the region with the aim of concretising the sustenance of multitudes of ceasefires in the bedevilled region.

Apart from being a geopolitical and a geostrategic flashpoint with the great powers playing regional roles, the Gaza crisis in 2014 seemed to turn out into a grave humanitarian crisis too. Thus, the United Nations acted likewise. The CNN reported, "With more than 1,000 people killed in the Israel-Hamas conflict, the U.N. Security Council held an emergency meeting in New York early Monday and announced 'strong support ... for an immediate and unconditional humanitarian cease-fire' in Gaza. The cease-fire would allow for the delivery of 'urgently needed assistance.'"[6] Thus, the essential role brokered by the United Nations with the shuttle diplomacy of John Kerry was bolstered by a deft and proactive action by the organisation. But, it was widely witnessed in the context of the Gaza crisis of 2014 that the United Nations Security Council acted after more than three harrowing weeks had passed in Gaza and many had already suffered the plight of the Israeli tanks and the Hamas rockets. Still, media reports confirmed the rut that had set in Gaza, with the brewing up of another humanitarian crisis after Syria and Iraq's Shia–Sunni conflict in 2014.

Thus, American culture with its phenomenon of the CNN effect and the conservative and the pro-establishment coverage of the US interventions in Iraq and Palestine are part of a de rigueur, normal and an unescapable narrative. This line of thinking is domestically and internationally-systemically ordained. Thus, the narrative as espoused by the US mainstream media is not something hegemonic, but, very much a part and parcel of the global geo-economic and geo-cultural narrative. This permeates through the nook and cranny of the international system and the attendant public opinion outcomes. Tamar further asserts, "This is all about soft hegemony. This consolidation of our point of view may be effectively demonstrated by the effective press coverage of the first and second Intifada, the Palestinian uprising. During the first weeks of the Intifada, reporters interviewed Palestinian victims in order to place forward their point of view on Israeli and Western Television News."[7] The author further says, "As clashes between the protesters and the authorities went on, 'they' disappeared from the media scape leaving behind only a threatening mass of stone pelting protesters., faces obliterated behind their Kafias. This was not a policy decision but an ongoing process in which the various constraints that operate in the routines of covering conflict, conspired to construct a hegemonic and dichotomous picture. As clashes on the streets continued, Palestinians in the streets became less accessible to the reporters and the correspondents, travel to the 'territories' became difficult. An alien and a foreign four wheeler, could, be smashed and 'their' witnesses would be reluctant to talk to an Israeli reporter even if someone got there".[8]

In 2015, as a related development, the Israel–Palestine conflict quagmire goes ahead in an unabated manner. Intolerance remains the order of the day in the Israeli and the Palestinian societies. Barring aside the external factors, the issue of settlements in the country is the single most important bone of contention after the idea of the separation of the urban complex of the city of Jerusalem. The idea of both the Jews and Arab citizens being the victimised and strangulated populations since the larger times is another poignant pet peeve about the conflict. Intolerance of the acts of extremism is a notion which is being paraded about in Tel Aviv as the mid-2015 incidents of violence during a gay parade and the killing of a Palestinian baby happen to be the onerous acts in the present context in 2015.

Al Jazzera reports, "Thousands have protested in Israel against the killing of a Palestinian baby in a firebomb attack and last week's stabbing during Jerusalem's Gay Pride parade. Israeli Prime Minister Benjamin Netanyahu offered strong words of condemnation. Speaking after a cabinet meeting on Sunday, he pledged zero tolerance for what he called 'all kinds of extremism'." Thus, these acts of stifling whatever tentative steps at understanding and reconciliation have been attempted, tend to mar and harm the attempts at normalcy in the strife-torn region. Still, the antagonism, which is being attempted to be heaped at Prime Minister, Netanyahu is that creating and spreading terror through other terror attacks such as the menacing arson attack at Gaza can become a part of policy. This goes a long way into advancing the stratagem of expanding the settlements in the Gaza Strip and the West Bank.

The question which is being prominently raised in the global firmament is that, is the United States disengaging from the Israel–Palestine conflict. A weak Palestinian leader and an undeterred Israeli leader have been able to further foment the Palestinian question. It is no more a matter of self-determination that the Americans going by Wilson's fourteen points can award rights to the Palestinians. The coopting of Turkey has not been complete in the aftermath of the rise of the ISIS in the region. The Turks have been supported by the NATO consensus, but, they have not been able to be just and egalitarian towards the question of the Kurds. The Turks have been ambiguous to the notion of Five Star Jihad[9] and have reneged on the agreement with the Turkey-based PKK and Ocalan and gone on to devastate the Kurdish settlements in the war-torn region. Five Star Jihad refers to a recent phenomenon that some of the young and indoctrinated European citizens are made to join the movement of Islamic fundamentalism. These groups of youth as they hail from an elitist European background, are, referred to as Five Star Jihadees who then enter the fray perpetuated by the ISIS in the regions of Syria, Iraq and Turkey. Once they do not get the divine satisfaction out of terror acts they get disillusioned and return back to their countries of origin such as UK, France and Netherlands. Harking back to the mainland region, Uri Savir writes in *US News* that, "The May 14 Camp David Summit between President Barack Obama and leaders of the Gulf counties was only a partial success. Saudi Arabia's King Salman bin Abdul-Aziz Al Saud stayed away, as the US president was not ready to negotiate a defense pact that would protect the Gulf against Iranian ambitions. Obama did, however, assure his interlocutors from the Gulf that the United States' prime goal was preventing Iran from developing nuclear weapons and that his administration will continue to strengthen Gulf security and interests."[10] Thus, the Obama Administration is also externalising the Palestine issue which is being equated with the Iran factor and the larger interest of the Gulf Cooperation Council and its constituent countries. The various nations in the GCC have had an age-old complaint and grievance against the United States' divide and rule overtures, domineering intent and related policy in the immediate Persian Gulf. The recent overtures of the Obama Administration in mid-2015, are meant to assuage the same concerns of the countries in the GCC so that the alien and xenophobic veneer of United States is reduced considerably.

President Obama has seemingly ushered in the new disengagement doctrine in 2015. The days when the Americans would use force as the first resort are bypassed now and instead "Force Majore" happens to be the policy dictum of the last resort. No longer will the Americans militarily intervene but slapping sanctions and economic strangulation might still be the preferred strategy in the strife-torn Israel–Palestine scenario. The *US News* reports, "This policy doctrine means bad news for the Middle East, Arabs and Israelis alike. The days when one could ask for US support and then burn American flags in mass demonstrations are over. So are the days when one could count on secret US military intervention and then condemn it. West Asia mired in religious, political and ethnical conflicts, is in the eyes of Washington more of a hopeless case than a strategic asset."[11] Thus, the oil factor, too, has ceased to be the guiding light of the American foreign policy in the region. The Israeli and the Palestinian issue is being left aside by the US, as also by the larger international community. As the land might witness another intifada or another round of Israeli settlements in the contested territories, then the various nations including the US might have a re-think on this festering wound in the region. In 2015, the negotiation is going on as the Iran talks seem to be the new saving grace of Western and Uncle Sam's diplomacy. The author is here referring to the Iran and the West talks on the issue of Nuclear non proliferation about the denuclearisation of the state of Iran. The West Asian scenario and the related talk of Diplomacy is now marked by the idea of the Iran and Western Diplomacy which has an indelible impact upon the regional politics in West Asia. In the author's view, the Israel-Palestine theme has taken a backseat in the larger context of peace and Democracy in West Asia in a post-Arab Spring world and in the light of Iran's mainstreaming.

Thus, the frame of reference of the coverage, was decidedly selective, but, the idea of conflict promotion through an institutional lens also gained ground in the process of the selection of the covered incidents and the nature and tenor of the interviews selected for the conflict coverage. In a way, the consent and consensus were being prepared in the way the various audiences and the complexes wanted to view and receive them. The internalisation of the conflict through the fourth estate was bound to pass through the Western and American prismatic structures.

The Iraqi and Syrian Scars in the Region

Linked to the idiom of the Arab Israeli conflict is the idea of the other West Asian nations, such as Iraq and Iran, along with the nation state of Syria which is mired in a thankless conflict in the present times till 2016 running. Since the last few decades, the struggle for political and strategic one-upmanship in the region has led to the states struggling amongst themselves. The routinised rituals of others such as the United States and Soviet Union in 2015 taking sides, which further complicate the situation in West Asia still as a Schizophrenic reading, nations such as US have to play a redeeming role. The countries such as the United States were very close to the state of Iraq under Saddam Hussein while the change in regime in Iran in 1979 had soured the pitch between Iran and Washington. In the author's view, the culminating days of 2015, Vladimir Putin's manoeuvre to militarily aid Bashar-Al-Assad's Regime in Syria, has increased the complex nature of the conflict in Syria with different factions of militia being supported by different countries in a bid to neutralise the rising tide of ISIS. This, in the author's view, is the kernel of the problem in West Asia with the Syrian problem becoming the cynosure of all eyes with the Russian entry in the regional conflict.

Going backwards in time, the long-drawn out Iran–Iraq war, too, witnessed some of the worst casualties of men and equipment for a period of more than eight long years. The twin antagonists were locked in a fight to the finish with one of the objectives being to claim the dominant strategic perch over the region. At that point of time, Saddam Hussein was in the good books of Washington. Still, the autocratic ambitions and the expansiveness of the Baghdad Regime led to the Iraqi invasion of Kuwait, the oil state in the region. This imperial overarching of the Iraqi state led to the America-led coalition of the willing including several Western states to evict Saddam Hussein's forces out of Kuwait after a short war in the Mesopotamian wastes.

Thus, the long-drawn-out tradition of conflict was initiated between the United States and Iraq, wherein Saddam Hussein was faced with the allegations of aiding global terrorism along with the Al Qaeda affiliates. Another allegation which could not be proved was the clandestine Iraqi programme of developing the weapons of mass destruction in order to dominate the oil riches of the region. This allegation immediately provided the United States with the rationale to go to war with Iraq in March 2003, which finally resulted in the capture and the execution of Saddam Hussein with all the melodrama befitting the 'ides' of international politics.

Alongside the Iraqi dragnet, Iran too was found to be developing nuclear weapons and the Europeans states along with Russia are still negotiating with Iran in order to tame its nuclear energy programme. In July 2015, JCPOA-II was inked between the European and Chinese, P-Five plus One nations, and Iran which has heralded an ending of all sanctions over Iran in exchange for it closing its nuclear defence programme and opening up its nuclear energy facilities and nuke reactors for the standard IAEA inspections. All this has happened in mid-2015 which goes down well as one of the extended foreign policy achievements of President Barack Obama. Also, sanctions had been slapped on Iran by the United States, which had hobbled the economy of the country. Iran since 2014 led a delimited and a constrained existence. Thus, the American intransigence against the 'Great Satan' in American phraseology continues unabated though diplomatically for now but the whole process is interspersed with the threat of sanctions and armed retaliation as well. Israel has seemingly jumped on to the bandwagon, wherein it has left no opportunity unturned to threaten Iran with missile retaliation. Thus, the region remains mired in a state of discord, mutual hostility and shadow of war but it has become less now. Even the Israeli voices in the American policymaking lobby and in the region were being given a short shrift in the favour of the formulations of the nuclear cooperation agreement between Iran and the Western nations in mid-2015.

In fact, Prime Minister Netanyahu commented upon Iran's intentions in his UN General Assembly address. He drew a picture in the hall and drew a red line which referred to the enrichment of the nuclear fuel by Iran which could lead to the future production of nuclear weapons. He also called it the line of tolerance for the Israeli nation state. 'The thin red line argument' of Benjamin Netanyahu ricocheted all across the regional and the international firmament. The Israeli national daily, *Haaretz*, reported in an April 2013 news report "Prime Minister Benjamin Netanyahu attracted world attention when he drew an actual red line on an image of a bomb at the United Nations last September. His speech suggested that the issue should be relegated until this spring, the point at which Iran would ostensibly have accumulated one bomb's worth of 20 percent enriched uranium, and could then dash within 30-40 days from reactor-grade to weapons-grade fuel if it chose to 'break-out'."[12] In the author's view, this approach of hyper-aggressiveness has not gone down well with the larger international opinion and it remains one of the strivings of the Obama Presidency to tame the interests of its ally, Israel, in order to usher in some sense of normalcy in the region. With the spectre of Israeli settlements still looming large over the region, it remains a tough and uphill manoeuvre on the part of Washington to rein in the Israeli rhetoric and its intent.

Syria is also headed towards another quagmire in the region, wherein the idea of President Bashar Al-Assad being pitted against the rebels which have now come to include members of the Al Qaeda, remains a sore point for the peace negotiators in the region. The United States of America is vouching for the Syrian opposition while the Russians traditionally have been aligned with the Assad Regime in Damascus. They have been traditional Cold War allies. The idea of the spread of weapons of mass destruction has too taken root in the region in the context of Syria, as a team of weapons inspectors has been allowed to search out chemical weapons in Syria which have already caused an alarming quantum of collateral damage in the besieged nation state of Syria.

The conflict in Syria has opened up old chasms between the United States and Russia as both the ex-Cold War rivals are arraigned in the opposite camps in the context of the conflict in Syria. In the author's view, the new equation can be equated to a new Cold war. Recently in January 2014, a new war of words ensued between the twin superpowers. It was reported in the US national daily *Washington Post* that, "A senior Obama administration official lashed out at Russia over Syria on Friday night, saying the country can't expect to host a "happy Olympics" at the same time it is supporting the "brutal" regime of Syrian President Bashar al-Assad. They can't have it both ways," the senior official said of the Russians."[13] An official in the Obama Administration asserted, "They can't say they're in favour of negotiations in Geneva and a transitional governing body with full executive authority and humanitarian access and have a happy Olympics, and then be part and parcel of supporting this regime as it kills people in the most brutal way."[14] The Geneva negotiations premised with the objective of solving the conflict in Syria has witnessed several confrontations within the international negotiators with the Russians and the Americans finding themselves on the opposite side of the field more often than not.

Thus, the conflict can also be perceived in the light of a Cold War-like situation which developed in the Ukraine standoff. Here, the American

Government supported the new political dispensation in Kiev and Moscow paraded its demographic interests in the southern and eastern regions in Ukraine which led to John Kerry and Sergey Lavrov, Russia's Foreign Minister holding a slew of negotiations over the besieged state of Ukraine which is an erstwhile Soviet Union state. Also, the annexation of Crimea by Russia emerged as another sore point in the bilateral relations which is somewhere echoing the idea of the international dissensions which the Syrian conflict has already witnessed. In 2015, a pact has been signed between the South Ukrainian rebels backed by Moscow with the Kiev dispensation reflecting all the readiness for an end in violence in the region which is directly impacting the larger equations in Central Asia and West Asia. In the beginning of 2015, cities such as Donetsk and others in South Ukraine became the hotbed of conflict between the rebels and Kiev and after much ado and violence, with the aid of American and European intervention, a ceasefire was arrived at which has been unfortunately breached once by the twin conflicting sides. 2015 has witnessed innumerable rounds of recriminations and mud-slinging both in the global bodies and during regional diplomatic jamborees. For the present, an uneasy peace prevails in the conflict which has been equated by some scholars as the "New Cold War" sans the traditional threats and the satellite nations.

The Council for Foreign Relations too has an idea about its response to the Syrian conflict. The objectives of the US mandarins in Syria are very clearly delineated through its Council For Relations statements and releases. One of the releases states, "The goals of U.S. policy should be to end the violence, bring down the Assad regime, and lay the bases for a stable democratic system with protection for the Alawite, Kurdish, and Christian minorities. It is a tall order. The Obama administration has already abandoned the goal of regime reform, and rightly so: there is no basis in Assad regime behavior for sustaining a belief that he could lead a transition to democracy."[15] Thus, the idea of the American "Reassurance" has led to the nation reaching a brink as regards important decisions in the far-off international conflicts. In the context of Syria, the standard process would have been the idea of regime change in Syria followed by the practice of nation-building and reconstruction. As the present day American strivings reflect in conflict zones such as Afghanistan and Iraq, the idea of nation-building sounds too costly and expansive a pathway to be adhered to. In the author's view, the Americans also want the conflict to end and intend to move away as soon as possible which leaves the populations of such regions in a dirty quagmire involving grave humanitarian tragedies. In the author's view, US need not bring in new boots on ground in these conflict zones but it ought to stay for the entire length of the reconstructive and rebuilding efforts.

Still, evidence reflects that the United States has always been involved in the internal dynamics of Syria with the ethnic equation too playing a role in the entire idiom of the conflict. In the CFR release, it is advised to the Obama administration that, "The United States' first goal should be to isolate the Assad family and its closest cronies from the rest of the Alawite community, which largely has not shared in the riches Assad has dispensed to close supporters. While all Alawites fear vengeance against their entire community should Assad fall, there are varying degrees of loyalty to the Assads. The United States should continue to press the many groups now opposing the regime to present a united face."[16] The entire ambit of the American involvement harks back to the days of Assad's father, where, too the White House had more than a mere involvement and a major stake in the happenings in the Syrian nation state. Thus, the historical linkages with Syria as a modern state in West Asia had strong ramifications as a West-friendly regime in the region which has amply characterised the US–Syria bilateral relationship. The Americans had been following the idea that it should be marketed to the sections of the Alawite sect which Assad also belongs to. The regime in Damascus is bound to fall and they should follow the larger interest of their sect and the Syrian nation and thus abandon the Bashar Al-Assad regime.

A Congressional Research Service Report informs, "The humanitarian and regional security crises emanating from Syria now appear to be beyond the power of any single actor, including the United States, to contain or fully address. Large numbers of Syrian refugees, the growth of powerful armed extremist groups in Syria, and the assertive involvement of Iran, Turkey, and Sunni Arab governments in Syria's civil war are all negatively affecting the regional security environment in the Middle East."[17] Thus, the humanitarian tragedy which has evolved across the region has led to an international hue and cry over the state of Syrian commoners. They have sought refuge in neighbouring states, such as Iran and Turkey. The conundrum of refugees continues unabated in Syria which has led to the idea that now even the United Nations, its agencies and the United States, are finding it difficult to subsume the stream of people crossing international borders in the region.

Difference of opinion remains embedded in the entire negotiation process led by the United States and Russia as the opposition to the Damascus regime remains unsure. It is not known as to how to engage the Assad Government and how to eke out the technical engagements and the details of the proposed Transitional Government. The same issue holds true in the entire context of the United States–Russia stand-off. A Congressional Research Service release reports, "With internationally supervised disarmament proceeding, U.S. diplomatic efforts seek to set terms and conditions for negotiation to end the fighting and establish a transitional governing body as called for by a communiqué agreed to in Geneva in June 2012, which was further endorsed in Resolution 2118. Opposition forces remain divided over the questions of whether and under what conditions to participate in negotiations with the Assad government."[18] Thus, all the pillars of international security such as disarmament, non-proliferation, regional security and international governance emerge as the path-finding issues in the conflict in Syria. The super-actors struggle to carve out a peace solution in Syria and the related terrain.

Thus, taking in view the idioms prevalent in Syria, Iran, Iraq and the Arab–Israeli conflict, the Americans have always played a pivotal role in the realm of regional security in West Asia. Still, the accusation and the allegation which seems to be gaining ground in the international firmament is that the United States is disavowing its global over-arch and is drawing down its role in the region much to the cost of peace and stability in the region. A report which appeared in the *Guardian* speaks of the same international concern, "The signs of alleged American fecklessness are everywhere: withdrawal from Afghanistan, which followed the ignominious departure from Iraq; negotiations with the mullahs in Iran rather than bombs over Tehran; an aimless and hollow pivot to Asia that is failing to deter a rising China; a newly assertive Russia seizing territory without consequence; cuts in defence spending while al-Qaida franchises pop up across the Middle East and perhaps the worst of all sins—failure to stop the bloodletting in Syria. It's a policy that Niall Ferguson calls 'one of the great fiascos of post-World War Two American foreign policy'." To reiterate a theme, which has already been done up by the likes of Michael Mandlebaum and Niall Ferguson, the US policy can do with an iota of rethinking and re examination. One can carve out the argument that the isolationist inclination in the US policy towards the West Asia is being rekindled. The interventionist urge in the face of grave humanitarian tragedies needs to be delved into with a secondary outlook. In the author's view, the charge being labelled at the United States that it is withdrawing from its global responsibilities should have some substance, which it does.

The American ethos of furthering the American dream across frontiers and its attempt at new strivings where no man has gone before, needs to be remembered and reconsidered by the American strategic thinkers. In an age wherein, the Chinese are also harbouring objectives of "world domination" and for an Oriental hegemony on their own personalised terms, mere economic hardship ought not to be a debilitating factor in the entire corpus of the American strategic thought. In the author's view, the recent Chinese victory march organized in the second half of 2015, which was the celebration of victory over Japan, was, festooned upon the visiting leaders of the international community. The Chinese insistence on developing a blue water Navy along with developing a slew of Stealth fighters reflects the largely militarist facet of the "Chinese Dream".

The Five Star Jihad: The Rise of ISIS (Levant Unsettled)

The notion of Five Star Jihad has been seldom discussed in the Asian space and intelligentsia. In the aftermath of the instability and Islamic leadership vacuum in Iraq and the Syrian neighbourhood, the ISIS emerged as the regional threat to peace under the leadership of Al Baghdadi. He declared an independent Caliphate in Iraq and Syria in the areas which it was able to wrest from the Iraqi Shiite rule in Baghdad. The quaint and differentiating quality about the phenomenon about the rise of ISIS is that for the first time the temporal and other-worldly rationale of a terrorist organisation was changed into the territory governing idea of any terrorist organization. In the author's view, tangibility reflects one of the initial efforts by a terrorist organization to grab and hold on to a territory. Thus, it's a new found tangibility about a terrorist organization. The ISIS generally communicates in its communications that they are establishing a caliphate—a separate universal kingdom akin to the Middle Ages, where the Taliban-like religious and ethical norms would rule the roost inculcating a terror environment among the hoi polloi. It is the general philosophy of the Daesh. The rise of terror groups with invincibility issues have been seen in the rise of Al Qaeda, but the rise of a terror nation on the lines of the definition of the "Rogue Nation" by the Americans has now become a dreaded reality to be contented with.

For instance, the cyber reach of the ISIS is phenomenal. Recruits have been attracted from the disgruntled and misguided souls from the developed nations such as France and the United Kingdom. The stirrings of the migrants and volunteers for ISIS being found in United States have also been exposed. The travel plans for these western Jihadis are very well organised and mapped globally. They have to travel to the border towns near Turkey and Syria where most of them are escorted to the border towns such as Al-Raqqa, wherein the new recruits are given refreshing stays for brief periods. They are then transported to the battle zones in Syria and mostly to Iraq, wherein they are indoctrinated and some of the weaker ones are engaged in teaching, training and establishment tasks. While the tougher and warrior-like neophytes are sent ahead for war training and weapon acclimatisation.[19]

The various nations and the United Nations, too, have woken up to the challenge and the unprecedented nature of the threat posed by the rampaging and brutal ISIS. The terror group has become synonymous with the myriad public videos featuring the beheadings, humiliation and the water-boarding of Western reporters, journalists and the Shiite counterparts.

A fundamentalist vacuum was created in Iraq after the death of Saddam Hussein in Iraq in December 2003. For a few months, the American Coalition

Provisional Authority was established and it nurtured Iraq till the first elections under the stewardship of John Bremmer and his innumerable flights over yellow and sandy urban complexes in Girmaniya, Al Hashima, Al Kut and Baghdad beyond the comfort of the Green Zone in Central Baghdad. He settled a few questions but people in Iraq soon realised that though they were free to speak their mind now after the demise of the Baath party, the deplorable conditions of the schools, hospitals and the national and provincial infrastructure was much worse as compared to what had been available to the citizens in the days of Saddam Hussein's rule.[20]

Dexter Filkins, a renowned *New York Times* war correspondent has produced an unsettling account of the war in Iraq and the conditions which paved the way for the surge of forces such as the ISIS and the related mayhem in the land lying between the Tigris and Euphrates.[21] The *New York Times* bestseller, *The Forever War* mentions, "The personage of Nathan Sassaman was much respected in the Iraqi mission. He was accorded the most respect that can be accorded to a soldier and a Colonel. When he encountered violence and shelling at his forces in the Green zone then he would make his soldiers talk to the people and physically push the insurgents in the nearby Tigris river. The same fate awaited the insurgents who eluded the curfews imposed in Baghdad and instead of involving them in a fire-fight, he, would undertake them for partial water-boarding. He even faced an enquiry from Pentagon and later on went on to lead his life as a busy body civilian."[22] Still, in the author's view, what the American forces and contractors did in Iraq and to its people was out of compulsion to usher in stability and a non-violent culture of governance in the country. The American war effort attempted to reconstruct and resettle the torn Iraqi land. But, the ethnic fissures and the conflicting undercurrents remained embedded like the US embedded war correspondents, only to re-emerge in the form of the rise of the ISIS.

Literary and real life evidence has provided a reel-life quality to the war in Iraq and what the nation is facing now after the withdrawal of the American forces from Iraq. The depictions of conflict and human misery have been so rampant in the American Public sphere that it has attained a metaphorical reality of its own. Has it all resulted in the rise of the ISIS? Chris Kylis writes in his autobiography *American Sniper*, "In one of my operations, with the Irish GROMS in Fallujah, we ransacked a house in the street. As we entered the basement after blowing off the door-lock, we witnessed a stack of open intestines, stacked up elbows and legs along with other cadaver lying beside the dark wall. Also, chains and signs of occupants who would have been hung on the stirrups in this dungeon were also available."[23]

A section of the Public Opinion believes that United States and the Western world incubated the ISIS in the first place and it happens to be a kind of Boomrang redux which they seem to be facing now. Seumas Milne writes in the *Guardian* that, "For the past year, US, British and other western forces have been back in Iraq, supposedly in the cause of destroying the hyper-sectarian terror group Islamic State (formerly known as al-Qaida in Iraq). This was after ISIS overran huge chunks of Iraqi and Syrian territory and proclaimed a self-styled Islamic caliphate. The campaign isn't going well. Last month, ISIS rolled into the Iraqi city of Ramadi, while on the other side of the now nonexistent border its forces conquered the Syrian town of Palmyra. Al-Qaida's official franchise, the Nusra Front, has also been making gains in Syria."[24]

Thus, the ISIS has been able to market its universal and Ummah image and lore while being wedded to the territoriality of an Islamic state which sets it apart from the rest of the fundamentalist outfits in the region and the larger Globe. Their terrorists have become globe trotters with the instance on the Paris attacks in December, 2015 and the related London subway stabbings. The cowboyish lore which exemplifies the frontier spirit of the United States finds a distinct echo in the dystopian world of the ISIS and Al Qaeda. It is all similar to the idea of a dystopian world and an attendant post-war scenario where all habitation and vestiges of human civilisation have been terminated. In the Hollywood construct *Mad Max*, the raging fury of the male protagonist, Mel Gibson, is symptomatic of the American Marines and Seals, which, seek to find redemption after the demise of Saddam Hussein. But, nobody expected the ISIS to surface as a strong foe in the badlands of Iraq and Syria.

Mad Max's narrative is originally about a policeman who seeks revenge through homicide after his spouse has been killed in a vendetta mission by some outlaws—highway goons on bikes and clad in leather attires. He survives a world war—in fact, a nuclear conflagration—which makes the survivors create medieval fortress-like habitations for themselves which are buzzing with the vintage world-war, open-bodied four wheelers and open Chinooks. This mystic, dark, venal and dystopian world is similar to the reality which persists in Iraq and the Mesopotamian wastes of Mosul, Ramadi and Tikrit and Palymra, where the ISIS has stymied every vestige of civilisation. This post-Saddam world is symbolised by the rise of a recalcitrant ISIS, which is riding the tide in Iraq and Syria in order to provide for a new habiliment for the war-ravaged Tigris and Euphrates Delta.

The yellow cake houses of the dusty Iraqi terrain are no more home to the simpleton, easily decoded insurgents as the Marines, Irish GROMS and Seals called them. But a neo-world make-over has been attempted in the same ravenous wastes, as if no humans subsisted in these loyalty-changing-badlands. It can be pithily pointed out that the phoenix-like strength and versatility of the fundamentalist insurgents akin to a changing amoeba can be attributed to the fence-changing ethnic loyalties of the insurgents. This was amply reflected in Afghanistan during the civil war in the way thousands of Taliban soldiers crossed over to the Northern Alliance in order to escape death at the hands of the insurgents of Abdul Rashid Dostum and others who themselves had changed flanks several times in order to survive and make some moolah.

One can finally take a look at the innate philosophy of the hydra-headed ISIS. The dystopian world which has been mentioned earlier on, is similar to the idea of the rise of the ISIS. The US national daily, *The Atlantic* reports, "The Islamic State, also, known as the Islamic State of Iraq and al-Sham (ISIS), follows a distinctive variety of Islam whose beliefs about the path to the Day of Judgment matter to its strategy, and can help the West know its enemy and predict its behavior. Its rise to power is less like the triumph of the Muslim Brotherhood in Egypt (a group whose leaders the Islamic State considers apostates) than like the realization of a dystopian alternate reality in which David Koresh or Jim Jones survived to wield absolute power over not just a few hundred people, but some 8 million."[25] Thus, the anarchic statehood is one attribute which is the core character of the terrorist organisation which seeks superiority and leadership under the West Asian and the global sun. President Obama, too, failed to comprehend the strength and the futuristic threat of ISIS as he lightly wrote it off as "Un Islamic" and as "Al Qaeda's team". This might have led to a misreading of the strategy to be adopted against this rising terror outfit in West Asia.

Thus, the anathema of violence and perdition and an unending saga of attrition has unfortunately become the staple description of West Asia. The region is besmirched in regional conflict with external actors overlording conflict resolution which speaks volumes about the state of 'political poverty and maturity' in the region. Still, pragmatically speaking, nations such as the United States can play a vital role in conflict resolution in the region with their global network of alliances and coalitions. Lastly, David Fromkin paints a beatific picture of the West Asia, when he unearths the ethereal beauty of the place. He writes, "The daughter of the British Prime Minister with her friends lay on her back in the grasslands amidst the ruins in the island. The ship carrying the British Prime Minister and Winston Churchill was docked near this ruined structure overgrown with trees and vegetation. In the evening twilight, all the women talked about a new era dawning on the region as new forces and developments were all set to leave a mark on West Asia."[26] One can expect that amid the vitriol of conflict, political and ethnic skulduggery and the impact of insurgency, the region may awake to a new dawn. The population of the region also faces flitting changes in political leadership and an all pervading security dilemma which permeates through and through in the region's countries. The iota of hope which emerged through the Arab Spring soon dissipated away with the rise of the military juntas as an aftermath of the "rising". Then, the present American predicament in the light of rise of terrorism and insurgency can be cited as the immediate challenges which have acted as a spanner in the works of the American and domestic efforts at stabilising the tides of instability in West Asia.

NOTES

1. Orein Brown, "Creating Chaos": Lawrence of Arabia and the 1916 Arab Revolt", URL: http://www.historynet.com/creating-chaos-lawrence-of-arabia-and-the-1916-arab-revolt.htm (Online: Web), Accessed on April 1, 2015.
2. Ibid.
3. Tamar Libies, *Reporting the Arab Israeli Conflict: How Hegemony Works* (London: Routledge, 1998), pp. 80-81.
4. Ibid.
5. "Trouble in Gaza", CNN international edition, URL: http://edition.cnn.com/ (Online: Web), Accessed on May 19, 2015.
6. Karl Penhaul, Raplh Ellis, Hally Yan, "UN Security Council Calls For Immediate Ceasefire in Gaza" (Online: Web), URL: http://edition.cnn.com/2014/07/28/world/meast/mideast-crisis/index.html?hpt=hp_t1, Accessed on May 28, 2015.
7. Ibid.
8. Ibid.
9. Five Star Jihad refers to the development that a group of young people involved in rebellious activities and anti Government manuvres who are swayed by the online and off line propaganda spawned by the terror web portals and ideologues of terrorist groups such as ISIS.
10. Uri Savir, "Is the US Disengaging from the Israel Palestine Conflict?" URL: http://www.usnews.com/news/articles/2015/06/01/is-the-us-disengaging-from-the-israeli-palestinian-conflict (Online: Web), Accessed on August 1, 2015.
11. Ibid.
12. Gabrielle Tudin, David Makovsky, "The Thin Red Line: Is Iran Outmanoeuvring Israel and United States?" *Haaretz*, 24 April, 2013.
13. Zachary Goldfarb, "US Official Takes Russia To Task For its Role in Syrian Conflict", *Washington Post*, 16 February, 2014.
14. Ibid.
15. Elliot Abrams, "American Options in Syria", Policy Innovation Memorandum No.8, URL: http://www.cfr.org/syria/american-options-syria/p26226 (Online: Web), Accessed on April 1, 2014.
16. Ibid.
17. Congressional Research Service, 7-5700; Christopher M. Blanchard, "Armed Conflict in Syria: Overview and US Response" January 15, 2014.
18. Ibid.
19. Economist Writer, "Five Star Jihad," *Indian Express*, February, 2015.
20. Dexter Filkins, *The Forever War* (New York: Penguin Random House, 2010), pp.110-125.

21. Ibid.
22. Ibid. 1.
23. Chris Kyles, *American Sniper* (New York: Penguin Random House, 2015), pp. 110-125.
24. Ibid.
25. Graeme Wood, "What ISIS Really Wants", *The Atlantic*, March, 2015.
26. David Fromkin, "A Peace to End all Peace: The Fall of the Ottoman Empire and the Creation of the Modern Middle East" (Holt Paperbacks, 2009).

11

The Alternate Way of Leading Life and Doing Politics in the Super Bowl: When the Ball was in their Court

Introduction

Since the days of Vietnam War, the Calvinistic self-doubt began to have a creeping impact upon the national ethos in United States. The social, psycho-political and geo-cultural influence of the counter-culture in the United States was having its own influence. Gordon S. Wood, too, writing in his work, says, "The Idea of America reflected that the founding and the sustaining myth of United States had a great amount of intellect and intellectualism embedded into it." He wrote that the, "American revolution can be considered as an intellectual movement. If the origins of the American revolution lay not in the usual passions and interests of men, then, where did it lie?"[1]

The success in the World War and the initiation of the space race which involved the placing of the first human in space along with the heady, inspirational days of President John F. Kennedy, led to another set of days. These times were the adversarial times of the Cold War which necessitated a national purpose and more than an ordinary messianic zeal, in order to circumvent the advances made in the military, scientific and technological prescience by the former Soviet Union.

All was well, but the singular decision of the nation to intervene in a far-off Oriental land where war veterans of a few revolutionary struggles were ensconced with an astute political leader, led to a cumulative questioning of the American intent globally and domestically. The quintessential parameters of the 'American experiment' were riled upon and questioned by the civil society and the youthful verve of the college and university students along with the fuzzy vistas of the flower children and the likes of Timothy Leary. This quixotic group questioned the veritable bedlam of the stable state order and the accepted norms of life and politicking.

The mainstream cultural discourse of the United States is a veritable amalgamation of all kitsch and ethnic, linguistic and racial admixtures. The mainstream ethos as propounded by the founding fathers of the nation and the larger than life and influential Presidents or the heady executive, has left an indelible imprint upon the socio-cultural matrix of the country. The nation with a global oeuvre and an internationalist vocation, has had to undergo an inbuilt and inherent catharsis and an attempted purge of the quintessential lacunae of the American socio-political system. The challenges to the American mainstream narrative emanated from the anti-war movement of the 1960s which converged with the counter-culture movement and the cult of the 'hippies' of that age. The tumultuous times were imbued with a questioning spirit but what all was being rejected and questioned, also happened in the garb of a bohemian socio-cultural matrix. This was further buttressed by the idea of charting untraveled trajectories and initiating new social norms earmarked by freedom in the sense of a libertarian matrix, loaded with an anti-establishment message.

New genres of music, dance and ethnic performing arts and literature along with the depictions in alternate media and the Black press were the trail-blazing icons of this new momentum. This new American revolution in author's view, gained ground as the eternal critique in the aftermath of the American drubbing and debacle in Vietnam. The humiliation delivered to the state's doorstep by a determined flock of guerrillas succeeded in fomenting fissures amongst the mainstream narrative of the American Dream. The notion of a 'non-empirish empire' which had till now ratcheted up the patriot verve and the 'Rally Around the Flag' phenomenon during crisis and war times, was, being avidly questioned by the combined group of University students, hippies, war correspondents (reporting American military failure and the returning body bags from Vietnam) and the opposition's civil society communities and politicians.

Thus, the stable and cemented American citadel, atop Mount Sinai, was being questioned fervently and diligently by the commoners in those times. It was here that doubts about the invincibility of the American military and economic spectacle were being raised in the public sphere for the first time. Also, it is here in the words of Thomas Bailley that the great connect between the domestic scenario and the international and global positioning of the American visage was reflected vividly for the first time in the American narrative. The 'Grand Strategy' was being questioned and the doctrine of containment which had brought grief to the American hearth, and home also became part of the general construct of domestic criticism. In the author's view, the entire gamut of criticism was aimed against the seemingly well-oiled and greased state machinery in Washington, and now the turbulence of the sixties was being echoed through the length and breadth of the American firmament. It was the sixties counter-culture which counted for all and sundry.

Musical sensations of the age of the sixties, such as the Beatles adorned with rag-tag and loose habiliments, along with an unkempt visage and long hair, became the emblems of youthful rebellion in the country. A young student writes in one of the prominent journals being published in the US, "Throughout the 1960s, the Beatles exerted enormous influence not only as a critically acclaimed and commercially successful band, but also in the realm of social and cultural change. A number of factors facilitated the Beatles' rise to success, including the model of 1950s rock n' roll culture, their Liverpudlian roots, and a collective synergy as well as a unique ability to adapt and evolve with their era."[2]

With the past miseries of the Depression and devastating war fresh in the collective mind, the ensuing economic boom and cornucopia of wealth were being cherished all the more. Robust with confidence, the flush of prosperity and the thrill of victory, the American economic boom came to be measured in terms of the number of births in an unparalleled baby boom. In the growing age of consumerism, the middle class flourished in "rows of well-to-do houses with lawns and television sets in each living room with everybody looking at the same thing". As the Puritan Utopia of a "city upon a hill" found its culmination in suburban conformity, it seemed as though the promise of opportunity in the land of plenty at long last was coming true."[3] Thus, it resonated with the idea of the city on Mount Sinai which permeated the triumphalism of the American experiment as the land of milk and honey. The preponderance, pelf and prosperity, guided by the ides of unbridled individualism along with the freedom of the spirit-idea, were being reflected in the success of America.

De Groot too wrote pithily and accurately about the influence which the verve of counter culture had on the mainstream American discourse. He writes, "A second important result of their upbringing in the economically depressed city was the Beatles' identification with working class, proletarian roots, a sentiment which was attractive to the increasingly discontent members of American youth culture. In a sense, the Beatles were the "first working-class heroes", in that the band was the first to make rock –n' roll respectable by winning over 'the class snob, the intellectual snob and the music snob'".[4] Thus, the Kennan's X Article in the late forties which had warned the American establishment about the dangers of the rise of a single minded communism too was reflected in the Beatles' charm which worked for the working class and the so-called proletariats of the sub class in the United States. The larger-than-life and international persona of the music groups resonated with the lowermost and the young sections of the American population, where-in the staidness and the universally accepted and preached official nature of day-to-day routinised existence was being rejected en masse in the American society. Also, there were a few back-to-nature movements, gaining ground in large numbers and variety. The free-for-all gatherings of cocaine-smattered heads and scarves along with the legs rising and falling to the din of smoke-filled fields with the background drums, seemed to become the new anthem of the country. This was not the pristine American Dream which the Founding fathers had fought and striven for, though revolutions with their passions and interests have been comprehended as the attributes of change and activism.[5]

Author Steve Turner, too, writes echoing the same message, "Above all, it communicated a sense of infinite possibilities. There was nothing one could know that was not known. There was nowhere one could be that was not where one was meant to be." Timothy Leary, an LSD advocate, advised the generation that, "Close your eyes and listen to the sermon from Liverpool. Learn that it's the oldest message of love and peace and laughter, and trust in God and don't worry".[6] The message of the universality of love had an instant attraction for the American pupils and it seldom mattered that the sermon of culture emanated from the conservative British portals. Theoretically, the Victorian norms of the American way in the white-awash-fifties, was being questioned and the wonder years of the age, were being given a short shrift by the anti-war and anti-society activists of art, culture, music and the performing arts.

There was no loud theatricality to the momentum but a practical youthfulness which was soon to be reflected in the political firmament too not as a mere fad for free libertarianism but as a movement. This envisioned the age of questioning and reformist change in the socio-cultural and political milieu of the United States. This is another way in which the counter-culture movement can be approached by the scholars and the reviewers of the United States's affairs. It was the political 'correctness' of the fifties which was being questioned and repulsed by the disenfranchised lot. The tumult was also a revolution for change within the ethics and the bounds of the "idea of Americanness" which had a distinct Yankee flavour to it all. The movement did get overboard at times but it never became 'Un-American'. This is an argument which is often missed by the observers and writers of American affairs. After all, the beauty and the success of the American Dream relied heavily on the practice of dialectics and argumentation with the perverse, the humane and all other possible strains of thoughts and lifestyles in the arc of the United States's public discourse.

The American Cinemascope and the Angst

What all these questions were all about can be beautifully narrated once a person views a few episodes of the American TV serial, the *Wonder Years* which, in the author's view, forms a perfect and official testimony to the politically correct stability and prosperity of the 'Middle Kingdom' America. It is here, in these mediocre environs, that a hardworking father goes to work and comes home with roses for his wife and burgers for his children. The elder teenage son and daughter are getting influenced by the counter-culture attires and the anti-war narrative on the streets and on the TV screens. The women wear the flower-patterned kitchen aprons and serve tea with steel kettles which foam and with the bright yellow warmth of the homestead while being comfortably ensconced in the suburban middle kingdom in the United States.

People and audiences, still listen silently and respectfully to the narration in the background as Apollo 11 lands on the moon and the idiom of, "One stride for me, is the one big leap for the humankind" rules the roost. The JFK age seethes with patriotism and new hope for the country's future, where, every citizen gets shocked at JFK's assassination in Dallas. Then the Vietnam war footage on the TV screens showcasing the American GIs shooting with Zippo lighters, brings to fore the mental and attitudinal change, in the American denizens. It is all a visual motif but it holds true for the age-wise story of American history and all that matters to be an American. Thus, the drawing room stability and the warmth of the sixties, was, in for a change and a rude cultural shock.

The concept of the baby-boomer generation, too, crept up as a consequence of the military success of United States in World War II, with the war veterans returning from the front and becoming engaged in vast industrial production which initiated the consumption of goods. The age of prosperity had begun and so had the age of the baby-boomer generation; "Whenever someone mentions the **baby boom generation**, several images from the 1960s immediately come to mind: civil rights marches, anti-war demonstrations, political assassinations, student sit-ins and riots, rock music, sexual freedom, fashion trends, cynicism about government, and much, much more."[7] In author's view, the idea of being the agent for socio-political change was never a socialist idiom, but was entirely included in the regular narrative of the American Dream and the attendant ethos. The nation learned a lot from the anti-race movement with judgements such as the Brown VS the Board of education, guiding the changed narrative of the sixties, as part of the civil rights movement. All these imageries and the domestic restiveness reflect the societal situation in US during those times.

The idea of racial discrimination, emerged in the mainstream tale of the United States after the sit-ins and Martin Luther King's, "I Have a Dream Speech" which was later on made part of the legal jurisprudence of the national scenario. The picture of a small girl of schoolgoing age, peering across the glass window and witnessing her troubled father having a heated discussion with the Principal of the school and his emerging out of the office in a tense state of mind, would remain etched in the memory of any regular American Studies' student. The idea of the segregation of the white and black schools was a divisive issue in the American social narrative, which, has been commented upon and written about vastly. "Segregation of white and Black coloured children in the public schools of a State solely on the basis of race, pursuant to state laws permitting or requiring such segregation, denies to Negro children the equal protection of the laws guaranteed by the Fourteenth Amendment—even though the physical facilities and other "tangible" factors of white and Negro schools may be equal."[8] Thus, in the author's view, school segregation was an issue which was regarded universally as a divisive issue, which created a fault line across the entire edifice of the American society and polity and the divide still resonates till today.

The idea of slavery had been another such facet, which divided the country and is largely considered as a cause for the civil war in the 1860s. The legislation abolishing slavery in the year 1865 which was termed as the Thirteenth Amendment and the Fourteenth Amendment, promulgated in the year 1868, accorded good conditions for the freed slaves and ran true to the conditionalities of equal protection by law and the realisation of the due process of law. Finally the Fifth Amendment strengthened the lives of the freed slaves by disallowing any state to deny the right to vote to them. All this came into being before the Brown VS Board of education case, which is the issue in contention here.

According to a PBS excerpt, the judgement also led to the reinstatement of the lore of equality in the truest sense of the term as it overruled the statement in the Plessey VS Ferguson ruling: "After reviewing psychological studies showing black girls in segregated schools had low racial self-esteem, the Court concluded that separating children on the basis of race creates dangerous inferiority complexes that may adversely affect black children's ability to learn. The Court concluded that even if the tangible facilities were equal between the black and white schools, racial segregation in schools is 'inherently unequal' and is thus always unconstitutional. At least in the context of public schools, Plessy v. Ferguson was overruled. In the Brown II case decided a year later, the Court ordered the states to integrate their schools with all deliberate speed."[9] Thus, the justification of ideals such as equality and egalitarianism was embedded deep inside the judicial mitochondria and the DNA of the American psyche, if not socially. In the author's view, the Americans if perceived through the lens of the precepts of their Founding fathers, dwelt at large upon a new phase of social-political change wherein the rebellion fomented by the alternate-way-of-lifers was the fountainhead from which the grasping ideal of metamorphosis emerged. The tirade against racial discrimination soon became an avowed cause celebre amongst the masses and the popular sit-ins and the movement against events such as 'busing' became the order of the day. The idea that dissensions must be dealt with legally and officially by the state gained ground and it seemed as if the old practice of 'lynching' was being met with a vengeful vendetta which was mostly peaceful in nature and intent. In the author's view, social divisions and race based discrimination was rampant in the US but the fact that the Black movement was accepted and gradually internalised as the Governmental policy and the legislative idiom pinpoints towards an innately plural ethos of the land. The hiccups remained but the American state was made to make efforts towards institutionalising 'equity' which remains a fundamental tenet of the American declaration of Independence.

This cultural context was best depicted by the Hollywood movie, *Mississippi Burning*. The narrative of the American biopic dealt with the idea of a sun-tanned sheriff in a small sleepy town coming to terms with the societal cleavages inside the town over which he had presided as the guardian. The Sheriff rebels against the White domination and he monitors a few cases of White gangsters maiming a few Blacks and the narrative is symptomatic of the Southern sentiment. The Blacks had been turned into a tormented and discriminated lot in the country, whose declaration of independence gets sacredly initiated with the idiom that, "All men are born equal and seek freedom of life, liberty and happiness under the aegis of the New American Republic." Thus, the counter-culture movement emanated from the stolid and sagacious suggestions of the founding fathers, wherein the ideal of liberty and universal equality was grounded in the legal phonetics of the republic. The ingrained ethos when stymied by adumbrations in the post-World War II narrative soon reverted back to the founding myth of the republic and a great nation in the making premised upon the egalitarian entrepreneurship and ingenious innovation of the country. In the author's view, the taint of discrimination remained in the republic but ideationally the preachings of the US Constitution and the Declaration of Independence said otherwise. It was the questioning of institutionalised discrimination which bore the beauty and the dialectic nature of the American Governing structures which the author intends to bring out.

The extension of these alternate yet mainstream counter-currents in the American system was the movement against the war which was being rapaciously waged in Vietnam. The war was to be won in an alien territory, amidst armed humans with the wit and valour of seasoned revolutionaries. Thus, the question that was being raised before the establishment was that in the hallowed idealist traditions of the country, was it fair and reasonable to send young men and women in a far-off land only to be sacrificed for the betterment of foreign people. This did not have much of an affinity with the mainland America? Some pertinent poser! To what use, a military victory will be placed, if the war was won and the VC humbled in its own backyard? Was it worth the lives of young Americans who could have been gainfully employed in the hardworking domesticity of the United States and grown corn, built dams and taught the younger lot all in a grand effort to uplift the standards in the country? All these domestic activities could have led to the ideal of development and growth of a nation facing stiff Cold War challenges from a stout and astutely determined adversary.

On the contrary, the American war effort was not to be sullied by going against it. Still, if one delves into the chronicles of history, the surge of the effective and loud anti-war movement did not originate from the idea of the Vietnam War. It was much before—in the build up to World War II—the personages in the American public who could voice their concerns, favoured a de-escalation and a non-involvement of the nation in the war. Justus Doenecke said, "Yet, during all this time, major segments of the American public hoped that the United States would not enter this new world war. While most sympathized with the Allied cause, they did not deem the survival of either Britain or China worth the risk of American involvement. In fact, they argued conversely-that full-scale participation in the war would help destroy whatever global balance remained and would ruin the internal fabric of American society."[10] Thus, in the author's view, the forecast held that if the military–industrial complex was to be understood as an essential element of the US policy then it would lead to untold loss of lives which might not be acceptable to the American public.

The global ramifications of this trend would be deleterious for the economy and the strategic posturing of the United States in the forthcoming decades as such a policy would precipitate a nexus-like linkage and symbiotic exchanges with forces inimical to the notion of the progression of peace and stability. The geo-economics of a weapons bazaar, wars serving as testing grounds for new and untried weaponry and the propping up of strange dictators and ungainly regimes, were to soon lead to the fading away of the American halo of being the philanthropist and the do-gooder nation state. This scholarly 'internationale narrative' was very much 'Un-American'; but, still had some weight attached to itself. Thus, the commercial and the industrial overarching of the country's apparatus had a deleterious impact, which also ran contrary to the ethics and values of the country's founding myth.

Justus Doenecke further asserts in the run up to World War II that, "Many anti-interventionists, particularly in Congress, opposed the continual supplying of aviation gasoline and scrap iron to Japan, both on the grounds that such an activity violated the spirit of the neutrality acts. Also, Japan's conduct in China had been barbarous. Without American supplies, Japan's war effort could not continue."[11] Thus, the arduous task of confronting strong military foes was realised by the lobby of the anti-interventionists even during the intervening days in the period between the two world wars. This isolationism has always been a vocal minority in the American public discourse. The sixties negation of the global wars very much owes its origin to the ideas propounded during the later thirties in the country while Europe was hurtling towards a war of randomised and mammoth proportions.

The historian Manfred Jonas has attempted to provide a just rationale to the idiom of isolationism in the US foreign policy which ran aground after confronting the dominant inclination of interventionism in the US establishment. In a summary of Jonas's book, one can decipher the footprints of history:

> "Other scholars of the topic—including Wayne S. Cole, Selig Adler and Robert Divine—crafted works focusing on specific organizations or about legislative battles whether the United States should join the war in Europe. Jonas's book takes a decidedly different track by examining the thoughts and underlying assumptions of American isolationism. The author rejects the obstructionist label so many applied to the individuals and groups that opposed United States entry into the war[12]... Rather, men such as William Borah, Gerald Nye, Norman Thomas, and Charles Beard regularly engaged in debates and issues with an international focus. None supported the sorts of extreme closed-door policies practiced in Japan and China during the nineteenth century. What they did support was an America that would and could control its own foreign policy by staying out of potentially damaging foreign entanglements. Isolationism of the 1930s, argues Jonas, was the heir of two guiding principles first articulated in the earliest days of the American Republic: unilateralism in foreign affairs and the avoidance of war as a primary means of foreign policy."[13]

Thus, originally, in author's view, the United States of America was not far removed from the idea of pacifism in a few strains of its founding and practiced national ideology. In the author's view, the war-mongering epithet and predilection which has been attributed to the mandarins of the US foreign policy has never been its guiding leitmotif. War has never been the American clarion call but Patriotism and the continuity of the triplet of God, Country and Family has always been one. If one delves into the core thesis of President Woodrow Wilson's Fourteen Points, then the idea of "Open covenants openly arrived at"[14] comes to the fore. Here, the navigational freedoms and freedom to international trade, commerce and cooperation, formed the founding element of the early twentieth century principles of the US foreign policy.

It was the Wilsonian progressivism which formed the leitmotif of his years as the President of the country. The other side of the coin is what interested the young protesters and revellers of the anti-war counter culture tradition. They raised posers to the 'understood understanding of those such as the questioning of the credentials of Presidents such as Woodrow Wilson, all of which make for an interesting and funny reading. An excerpt follows, "Wilson embraced the Democratic Party with its unbending support of white supremacy, segregation, and lynch law. The first Southern president since the Civil War, Wilson not only gave the pro-Klan Birth of a Nation a White House screening, he imposed Jim Crow policy in the District of Columbia and blocked a Japanese effort to include a declaration on racial equality in the League of Nations charter."[15] Thus, the idea of promoting war was never an American prerogative and standard policy. But, further involvement in an alien war and in a far-off land, whose civilisational and practical interests were strange to the immediate security concerns of the homeland, were some issues which were raised by the anti-war and the counter-culture movement and other alternate strains of thought and action. In the author's view, some of the official declarations and statements can be attributed to the idea of racial discrimination and segregation in United States. But, the challenges faced by immigrants and black population in United States can be attributed to be part of the political journey as any nation has to traverse the trail towards political sanity and maturity. The Americans being no exception to the rule. In the author's view, US was developing towards an egalitarian ethos and praxis which did encounter its own challenges and obstructions.

Symbolism in the Counter-Culture Tirade

Founding myths and symbols occupy the seat of central lore in the living history of nations. Nations have always required and felt the need to rally the citizens and the positive energy of the collectivity in order to initiate an internal cleansing and for fending off external challenges. The US is no exception to this phenomenon. There were ample symbols which were evocatively utilised for the attainment of prominence by the anti-war protest. Also, as it is being reiterated, the United States along with its European counterparts has a vibrant history of pacifism. One can account for Aristophanes as the progenitor of the idea of anti-war sentiment and pacifism. Aristophanes has written about the futility of war in favour of a scenario of cooperation and human security. The futility of war for women as their men serve in far off military assignments is poignantly brought out by Aristophanes in his Comedies. This has been brilliantly brought out by Vassiliki Kotini in his paper in Comparative Politics.[16] Kotini argues that the trauma generated by war causes a instability in the nation and for that he cites the instance of Athenian involvement in the Peloponnesian war between the

Athenians and the Spartans. The grime of war also gets reflected in the degeneration of literary genres as it is represented by the narrative and character portrayals of the Comic hero.[17] Still, in the author's view, though everyone revolts against the issue of war, but, there remains a fascination with the American war apparatus somewhere which leads the IR scholars, media personages and military historians not to focus upon the fabric and the mantle of pacifism in the US narrative.

The Port Hutton statement gleaned from a student gathering in the American political firmament listed the reasons as to why the university fraternity in the country was opposing the war. The statement cannot be said to be reflective of the mood of the nation but it does shed some light upon the idea of the annulment and the rejection of the American Dream, as, it was being attempted by a section of the masses and their leaders. The statement runs as follows, "There is definitely an iota of radicalism involved in the idea of protest as students converge together to protest against the people who make decisions over which even senior citizens have no control. Also, the students reject the opposition of communism as a pernicious doctrine. It was wrong on the part of the American establishment to deal with the Universities and colleges as the receptacles and hotbed of communism and by protesting against the accepted principles. The student fraternity felt equal with the senior citizens of the country."[18]

Also, it was being emphasised that can an organisation which is prevented from assembling peacefully in an university or a college premises, be called illegal and as provoking public disturbances, only because it can cause such an activity?[19] Thus, the college authorities who were sympathetic to the cause of the anti-war congregations were caught in a dilemma as to whether the authorities had been right in deriding the right of assemblage in the campuses and the general public sphere. An avalanche of student protesters used to converge upon the premises in the campuses and write in the university magazines and create collages and graffiti in order to tear asunder the rationale of the dirty war as the Vietnam War as it was being popularly termed by the people all across the international and the domestic firmament.

Finally, in the year 1975, the President of the *Racquet* magazine in the Washington State University, laid the anti-war movement to rest in the month of April as the last American soldier left Vietnam for their homeland. "I do not understand what Vietnam was all about, It cost America 55, 000 lives and was a military and political debacle for the country. There is not much to be said which has not been said in the last 20 years and the two decades. Not being a student of Political Science, I cannot say, who did the correct thing and who did the wrong thing. Not many experts of Political Science can be sure about it. We failed in Vietnam because we failed to take note of the differences between the Asian and the American values."[20] In the author's view, this statement brings forth the human predicament where the sensitive intellectual and a sane and aware citizen is non-plussed by the confrontation which gets germinated between the pacifists and the aggressive war supports. Can the dilemma be presented as the riding narrative of the nation, is a million dollar question. Thus, what the student movement did was to posit the very true-blue American nature of the anti-war movement in the sense that the difference between the American daredevilry and love of supreme technology and equipment was pitted against the idea of Oriental values of silent orthodoxy, avid determination and stolid determinism. So the principles of the anti-war movement, were never anti-American in nature, as per the standard intellectual argument, but, reeked with the idiom of what the United States was not at all about. In the author's view, democratic consensus has been a striving with extreme freedom being accorded to divergent discourses. After all, plurality has been a guiding and abiding founding ideal in United States of America.

Harking back to history, the political justification of President Lyndon Baines Johnson depended upon the decision that he would take in the context of the Vietnam War. The people and voters hoped that President Johnson would withdraw the American contingents in Vietnam. The escalation in 1965 pinpointed to a completely different and adversarial direction, which laid the foundation of the anti-war protest all across the length and breadth of the American firmament.

It was not that President Johnson was a warmonger. A White House Aides Files states, "From beginning to end, President Johnson tried to steer America down what he conceived to be a middle course of involvement in Vietnam. Claiming an inherited national commitment, the President sought to maintain an anti-Communist regime in Saigon at the same time as he shunted aside his advisers' encouragement either to carry the war beyond Vietnam or to undertake military de-escalation and early peace negotiations. Inevitably, the President's course produced domestic discontent."[21] Thus, in the midst of strategic confusion and for the want of a real-time analysis, the domestic dissent could not be quelled by the establishment. The idea of carrying the war beyond Vietnam, was also mulled over by the military advisors to the President. The anti-communist tilt of the entire exercise led to the mediocritisation of the American stance which turned the Administration's response into a kind of McCarthyism of the fifties. But, in the author's view, it was never a witch-hunt as the student protests brought the anti-war movement into the mainstream of the American discourse.

There was a great iota of symbolism attached to the anti-war protest. One can cite the traditional symbolic value of a Pablo Picasso creation, which has rendered war in any format as a menace to be tackled globally. His celeberated painting *Guernica* emerged as a classic anti-war symbol during the tumultuous times of the Vietnam War. The painting is provided with a background of news print which is where Picasso admittedly first heard of the massacre in the town of Guernica in the Basque country.

Also, the picture of a raging bull goading a human along with the severed hand of a soldier bearing the religious symbols reflected the sacrifice of the commoners against the regime of General Franco. As an attendant fact, a lady figure looms large over the canvas, signifying hope in the entire genocidal happening, as the town's population gets mowed down by the barrage of the German Stukas and bombers which swooped down upon the people in swarms after swarms. Also, there is a glowing bulb inside the room in the masterpiece which relates to the Basque term, *bombila* which meant bomb in the local language. This depiction in the *Guernica* has been utilised by anti-war and anti proliferation protesters all across the world.

Thus, the people learned the art of protest through a deft and skilful utilisation of art and literature. Pablo Picasso remarked about his masterpiece in a very matter of fact manner, "This bull is a bull and this horse is a horse... If you give a meaning to certain things in my paintings it may be very true, but it is not my idea to give this meaning. What ideas and conclusions you have got I obtained too, but instinctively, unconsciously. I make the painting for the painting. I paint the objects for what they are."[22] Thus, in the author's view, the scholars evinced the view that Picasso had personal and cultural reasons which inspired him to paint this masterpiece. The bullring which is depicted in the canvas is very much symptomatic of the entire cultural motifs of Spain since years. The Bull is regarded as a symbol of virtue, principles along with being a curious amalgam of both masculinity and feminity.

There have been lesser interpretations of the Picasso masterpiece. People have not been exactly disparaging but the phenomenal approach often attached to the painting has been belittled by analysts and commentators by relating the work to the personalized idiom of Picasso. "Picasso's smartest decision in "Guernica," a consummate feat of pictorial intelligence, was to limit its palette to black-and-white. He thereby forged his chief handicap into a thematic weapon, inferring that war is no time for indulgence and, by evoking the look of a newspaper, factored in the modern experience of comprehending catastrophe (and of inflicting it) at a distance. Proto-Pop, the trope anticipates the use of grainy tabloid photos in Andy Warhol's "Disaster" series. Other aspects of the work are less persuasive."[23]

The anti-war movement as posited in a much more specific American milieu had its own symbolic elements which soon took the shape of a larger social movement in the age of anti-racial discrimination totems doing the rounds in the sixties. Ron Kovic became a human symbol of anti-war activism and the legendary protester lives on beyond the activism of the Vietnam War. It is reported in the *New York Times* that, "In 1968, during his second tour of duty in Vietnam, a bullet tore through his spinal column. He returned home a paraplegic, paralyzed from the waist down, emotionally as well as physically shattered. That was the beginning of a long, painful spiritual rehabilitation that coincided with his political radicalization."[24] Thus, the regular war-veteran tale reminds one of the Hollywood flick, *Born on the Fourth of July*.

The *New York Times* further wrote in the same movie review, "No other Vietnam movie has so mercilessly evoked the casual, careless horrors of the paraplegic's therapy, or what it means to depend on catheters for urination, or the knowledge that sexual identity is henceforth virtually theoretical. One of the film's problems is that it becomes increasingly generalized as it attempts to dramatize Mr. Kovic's transformation from a wide-eyed Yankee Doodle boy to an antiwar activist."[25] In the author's view, the war as an event was initiated by television as the Vietnam War was the first instance of a fully televised war. It had the making of an epic as it involved the notion of the patriotic spirit or the futility of the sacrifice by the American soldiers who were young, fresh-faced and freckled boys. Some of them actually came to the badlands of war in a mood searching for some excitement and adventure. The war had other signposts to achieve, which made martyrs out of common, next-door boys. This might be one pessimistic and negative manner in which the mayhem of the war could be looked into but it was this one-off sentiment which became another rallying around the flag phenomenon in the American context. This philosophy bespoke of a very American concern—the cry for justice and liberty.

The Vietnam memorial is another fulcrum for the anti-war activism globally. The entire edifice is built with a V-shape which has granite walls. It was President Carter, who gained popularity with the idea of sanctioning the building of the V memorial in Washington. The way in which the architecture of the memorial has been calibrated is 'an eternal paean in the making'. It has been written by an author that, "Is there anyone who has ever visited this memorial without being deeply moved? I sincerely doubt it, just as I doubt that 100 years from now, when the conflicting passion of this war have faded almost beyond recall, visitors to the memorial will not be profoundly affected by the experience."[26] Similar to the symbolic value of the Japanese shrines signifying Japanese sacrifices in World War II, the V Memorial has been anointed to the hilt, where-in, the stolidity and the toiling internal dissent in the country has been concretised and canonised. Some Cheer for the American Dream!

Timothy Leary, too, emerged as a psychedelic guru during the anti-war Vietnam movement and the Hare Ram Hare Krishna Movement during the heydays of American counter culture, too gained grounds in the youthful imagination. He was a Harvard Professor, who had his psychedelic moment when he went on to refer to LSD which was legal, then, to his Harvard students. It has been reported in a piece in the Guardian that, "In 1962 Leary took LSD and reportedly had "the most shattering experience of his life". This new, purely synthetic drug seemed to reveal previously hidden realities and he wanted to share his discoveries with the world. Yet his own world began falling apart. Having claimed he had given LSD (which was then legal) to hundreds of Harvard students, he, was eventually sacked for not turning up to teach classes."[27] Thus, it was over the odyssey to search for hidden realities, that Timothy Leary was called as the "Most Dangerous Man in United States"[28] by President Nixon. It was also some positives that Timothy Leary dabbled in when he researched on and practiced with the medicinal qualities of LSD and involved himself with a programme to reform prisoners in a local prison house. Thus, it was not only about a dreamy Leary with universal audiences, who knew about it, but the idiom of being an academic and a reformer, which played a prominent role in the gestation period of the solidification of his persona in the American counter-culture norm. The Vietnam memory and the attendant social ferment, had a role to play somewhere in the larger idiom of the sixties' counter-culture which was espoused by the likes of Timothy Leary. The gory descriptions of war-torn landscapes and the scarred populations have always highlighted the self-doubt of the believers in the American Dream that are all wars in the name of higher ideals, worth it? In the author's view, another poser comes to the foreground that can we as civilised human beings let the burning imagery of the World Trade Centre, Twin Towers, exist as the symbols of a capitulated humanity and civilisation? No Dreamer will agree with this scorching and revolting imagery and the related interpretation, art or no art!

It can be further surmised in the words of Sonja K. Foss that, "The Vietnam memory should not be summarized as a point of war between 'Us VS them', where-in, the idea should not be made ordinary and mundane as a confrontation between America and the rest. Instead the lack of stark dissimilarities between people all across the global polity and the American citizens specifically, is a stark reality. This avowedly negates the sheer confrontationist nature of anti war activism."[29] Thus, ambiguity could be utilised as a shroud through which the ides of clear-cut confrontation could be avoided, as there are just wars, too. These are being fought and have to be fought with the Vietnam War being a different case study altogether. Jane Fonda, the Hollywood star, paid service to the popularity of the anti-war activism during the ides of the Vietnam War.

Sarah King comments in her thesis that, "Jane Fonda's early activism was characterized by frequent protests against the war, speeches at antiwar rallies, college campuses, and involvement with the organization of 'Vietnam Veterans Against the War'. In 1971, Jane Fonda organized an antiwar troupe, FTA, which performed antiwar songs and sketches to active-duty servicemen in America and Southeast Asia. Fonda's notorious trip to North Vietnam is examined in detail, as are her comments in 1973 regarding American POWs. Negative reaction to Fonda's activism is examined, and the myth of "Hanoi Jane" is traced from its wartime origins through its post war evolution."[30] In the author's view, the idea of Hanoi Jane is an interesting case study. Thus, similarly in the aftermath of the Iraq war, porn magnates and several Hollywood stars developed a 'creative - collective-commune' to publicly oppose the war on terror being waged in Iraq which is part of the same trail as Vietnam. Hollywood, generally and incorrectly perceived as the progenitor of war and violence fed by US, has itself rallied behind the anti-war voices in several instances. The popular *Hollywood Reporter*, talks about the popular anti-war and the anti-establishment film maker that, "Perhaps the best-known protest came from **Michael Moore**, who used his acceptance speech at the 2003 Oscars, just days after the invasion, to declare, "We live in a time where we have a man sending us to war for fictitious reasons. (Whether it's the fictitious duct tape or the fictitious orange alerts, we are against this war, Mr. Bush.) Shame on you, Mr. Bush, shame on you." He was booed and played off the stage, but undaunted; his next documentary, *Fahrenheit 9/11*, explored and condemned the case for war."[31] There is a long list of film personalities who opposed the war highlighting the power, brute force, money and the hegemonic and oil dimensions of the war in Iraq, calling it as an invasion and not an American war. The Hollywood reporter further reports, "In appearances overseas, other movie stars spoke out. At an awards ceremony in London, **Dustin Hoffman** said, "This war is about what most wars are about: hegemony, money, power and oil," while at the film festival in Berlin, **Richard Gere** urged, "We have to say 'stop,' there's no reason for a war. At the moment, Hussein is not threatening anybody"."[32] Thus, there emerges a natural consonance between the public visage enjoyed by these two stars and the actual activist role being essayed by them in real life out of their popular reel life portrayals.

The idea of Hanoi Jane is well thought over ridicule and disparaging nomenclature, which has been labelled at the Hollywood star, Jane Fonda, as she allegedly visited Hanoi and played an extensively visible role in the anti-Vietnam War protest movement. In a web excerpt, it was mentioned, "Jane Fonda, on the other hand, chose to be a traitor, and went to Hanoi, wore their uniform, propagandized for the communists, and urged American soldiers to desert. As we were being tortured, and some of the POWs murdered, she called us liars. After her heroes, the North Vietnamese communists, took over South Vietnam, they systematically murdered 80,000 South Vietnamese political prisoners."[33] The above written text also highlights the torture faced by the American POWs in the throes of dark cells in Vietnam after the withdrawal of the American forces from the Vietnamese terrain. The utilisation of Hollywood figures gave good benefits and dividends to the anti-war movement. Still, in the author's view, Hollywood predominantly remains a mainstream media apparatus and that too signifying the core commercial interests but another reading of the phenomenon of Hollywood would say that its depictions primarily do national service by propagating the myth and lore of the American dream.

In such a scenario, what remains to be analysed is the notion that how can the lives out of the 'Rich and Famous' catalogues and picture-perfect artists, be made one with the proletarian masses on the erupting streets and the hippy ethos of the American anti-war effort. This remains a mystery to be solved in the true adventurist strain of the grandee American Dream. Another pertinent poser! Still, too much of a critical posturing does nothing but besmirches what nations stand to gain out of a democratic and nationalistic consensus. In the author's view, nations have become great and have been lauded globally due to their steadfastedness which might not gel with the global causes and concerns at some point of time.

The conspiracy theories, too, played a significant role in the spawning of counter-culture methodologies and traditions. For an instance, the Japanese attack on Pearl Harbor was also tinged with a conspiracy theory. It was reported by alternate observers of American foreign policy that American commanders intentionally decided to reduce the strength of fighter planes, anti-aircraft guns and warring vessels from the dug-outs in the harbour and the port. Thus, it reduced remarkably the capacity of the American contingent at the harbour to successfully engage the Japanese marauding air strikes and led to their grave humiliation and tame surrender. Thus, the spin doctors of these conspiracy theories tend to reinforce the counter-narratives in the American discourse and tend to cast shadows upon the mainstream narrative of patriotism, sacrifice and create a sense of disenchantment with the mainstream tale of America among the hoi polloi. Not a pertinent poser but rather obvious an effort! In the author's view, this cannot be equated with a revolution but is a striving to belittle the American ethos and what all it stands for.

Thus, these factoids of history tend to destabilise the normalcy associated with the idea of the American Dream and reduce faith in the system in general.

It has been reported in a web portal dealing with American affairs that, "There is an abundance of scientific and forensic evidence to support alternative theories, yet the BBC and other mainstream news corporations have continued to dismiss this information as conspiracy theory."[34] Thus, going by the issue of conspiracy theories against the American Government, the Japanese knew about the attack definitely and the Americans too had an inkling about it. They were searching for an excuse to enter militarily and directly into World War II. The allied think tanks had realised that the German onslaught in the European theatre was also going strong by the middle of 1942 and the same was the case with the fighting in the former Soviet Union. The American help and military machinery, was being acutely missed in the entire context of the war. In the author's view, these conspiracy theories have not proven convincingly and the American decision to militarily enter World War II was prompted by the American military debacle at Pearl Harbour. The American entry into the war and the US aided landings at Normandy led to the turning of the tide of the war in the favour of the Allies.

All these reasons necessitated an American involvement in the Allied war effort, as Washington just could not sit idle and let the Third Reich destroy the Allied war machinery. It was upon the outcome of this war that the destiny of Europe and the larger world hinged. This conspiracy theory might be straight out of the 'theatre of absurd' and one amongst the Vaudeville creations, as how could a nation sacrifice its prestige and the lives of thousands of its military personnel in order to gain a rationale for initiating action against the Axis powers. The United States hardly required a national tragedy and an act of humiliation to enter the war. Instead, following the reasoning of the pre-emptive war doctrine, an imminent threat and mere threat of invasion, was enough to initiate a response to incubate the threat before it could actually materialise. Article 51 of the UN Charter too uses the same logic.[35]

The September 11 terrorist attack which became the American cause for the, 'Global War on Terror', has been misinterpreted by certain observers such as Robert Fisk, and the likes of academics such as Lynn Margulis. They contend that the September 11 attacks too have been engendered with American connivance in order to serve as an excuse to fight a Global war against Al Qaeda and other Islamic terror outfits. It has also been allegedly referred to as the 'New Pearl Harbor' which quaintly categorises it as a staple counter-culture narrative which is reminiscent of the anti-war protest of the Vietnam war. Eric Walberg writes in the *Al-Ahram* national daily that, "Another recent convert, University of Massachusetts Geoscience Professor Lynn Margulis referred to 9/11 as "this new false-flag operation, which has been used to justify the wars in Afghanistan and Iraq as well as unprecedented assaults on research, education, and civil liberties", and credited, *The New Pearl Harbor,* by David Ray Griffin "which provides overwhelming evidence that the official story is contradictory, incomplete, and unbelievable."[36] Thus, it has been posited by these alternate narratives that akin to the Pearl Harbour incident, the WTC bombings were also a fake call and a dummy incident in order to deliver a plausible excuse at the doorstep of the American establishment and the neoconservatives along with the actors in the PNAC (Project For New American Century). This was engineered in order to initiate an intervention in Afghanistan in order to inundate Al Qaeda in its home turf and its own back yard.

During the investigations, observers and conspiracy theorists such as David Ray Griffin have contended that the 9/11 Commission report included information collected by the CIA, which was once again based upon interviews and sessions with the Al Qaeda operatives such as Khalid Sheikh Mohammad (KSM). In one of the interrogations, it has been posited in the 9/11 Commission Report that, "*Bin Ladin ... finally decided to give the green light for the 9/11 operation sometime in late 1998 or early 1999.... Bin Ladin also soon selected four individuals to serve as suicide operatives.... Atta—whom Bin Ladin chose to lead the group—met with Bin Ladin several times to receive additional instructions, including a preliminary list of approved targets: the World Trade Center, the Pentagon, and the U.S. Capitol.*"[37] *Thus, the idea of the degree of authenticity of the Report and its evidence has been raised by these Alternate-way-of-lifers which are not part of the American context as the anti-war protesters during the Vietnam war definitely were. In the author's view, these conspiracy theories have an Un-American origin and cannot be equated with the anti-war and counter culture movement in United States which the nation experienced during its various cusps of history as part of its growth story.*

Ray Griffin has come out with a startling observation which is shocking for the formalised comprehension of the entire episode of September 11 catastrophe, as any proud American would like to remember the incident as a terror incident aimed against the American homeland. "Osama Bin Laden has been dead for many years. In the present essay, I have shown that, there is not even any good evidence for the claim that bin Laden was responsible for the 9/11 attacks. Accordingly, insofar as the justification for the continuation of the Af-Pak war, is based on the fact that bin Laden in the region both before and after the 9/11 attacks, that justification would seem to be doubly baseless." Thus, this shielding of Osama bin Laden with evidence which might not be too authentic cannot cast aspersions on the American rationale for undertaking the GWOT. Bin Laden or No Bin Laden, any nation had to retaliate against the enemy nation or any other non state actor which had violated its peace and tranquillity. Earlier on, when an American Department of State official, visited New Delhi in the early nineties then she cast aspersions on the intent of the Indian Government. She did not believe in the complicity of the Pakistan's involvement in the terror incidents in the Indian state of Jammu and Kashmir. It was only when the USS Cole was attacked and the American Embassies were attacked in Kenya and Tanzania, that, the Americans became aware about the real threat of terrorism through "failed states" such as the Islamic Republic of Pakistan. The terror boomerang had hit right where it was not originally supposed to have hit.

In the same manner, as an adjunct to the trajectory of conspiracy theories, it can be surmised that the Gulf of Tonkin incident in Vietnam was being referred to as the idea as to why the United States of America escalated its presence there. Still, the incident points out that two American vessels were fired upon by VC boats. But the conspiracy theorists present a rather imaginative perspective in the entire tale of the Gulf of Tonkin. David Aronowitch writes, "When a co-worker told him that he believed Neil Armstrong's 1969 moon walk actually took place on a Hollywood soundstage, journalist David Aaronovitch was appalled. Aaronovitch had seen the moon landing on TV when he was a kid, and he couldn't believe anyone would think it was a hoax."[38] Thus, some of the landmark moments of American history have been lampooned and pooh-poohed as constructs out of a Hollywood set with the American landing on the moon being a significant pointer to the same debunking and debilitating trend. The same journalist further writes, "The conspiracists work hard to give their written evidence the veneer of scholarship. The approach has been described as death by footnote. Accompanying the exposition of the theory is a dense mass of detailed and often undifferentiated information, but laid out as an academic text. Often the theory is also supported by quotations from non-conspiracist sources that almost invariably turn out to be misleading and selective."[39] Thus, the genre of the conspiracy theorists has been charged with that of belonging to perennial sceptics seething with angst and disenchantment with a proper system and being experts in the art of make-believe. Also, the way they go about collecting their evidence, makes one wonder at the authenticity of their sources and the ingenuity of their imaginativeness, along with raising the poser of academic credibility at their scandalous exposes.

Though, if one takes a literary perception of the entire genre of counter-culture conspiracy theory, then, one can refer to the idea of how a war can be conveniently constructed in order to divert the attention of the domestic audience from the local failures of the government of the day. In the author's view, this view does come at a grave cost to the ideals, principles and the credentials of a steadfast and self-loving nation with United States of America being no exception to the entire discussion. In the movie, *Wag the Dog*, an artificial war is created in Albania by an avid and talented Hollywood director. All being shot on a Hollywood set in order to divert the public attention away from a political scandal involving a woman and the American President. In the election scandal, the incumbent American President seems to be involved with a woman which is popularised in order to defame the incumbent. The entire narrative of the flick makes for an avid and careful viewing where the sham nature of the television has spawned off a conflict in a far-off land and how it becomes the saviour for a beleaguered American President.

The film involves interesting exchanges between the actors which makes for symbolic reading of the entire narrative of the movie. The President's Assistant Conrad Brean (in this case Robert De Niro) who moves around harmlessly in a crumpled hat and a worn-out overcoat, goes ahead with contacting Stanley Motts, who, is a renowned movie producer. He tells the entire motive to Stanley and Stanley agrees to film the fake war in order to distract the public away from the accusation of a sexual misconduct by a fire-fly girl on the incumbent President.[40]

When the war has been cannily invented by Stanley Motts, he cries in exasperation, that it is not CIA's war, but is his artefact; "Stanley: The CIA cannot end the war as they are not producing the war. Conrad Brean contends, "The war's over guys." Stanley retorts back exasperated, "No!" Conrad: Its all over. I saw it on the Television. Stanley retorts back: No, the war isn't over till I say its over. This is my picture. This is not the CIA's picture."[41] Still, Stanley insists on a Part Deux to the tale of the Albanian war. Though, the Albanian war ends in a victory for the Americans, a soldier is invented by Stanley in order to be given a hero's welcome as he returns to the homeland.[42] Stanley utilises his creativity to introduce another twist to the tale, wherein he delves into the inside story of the American POW in which he adds to the story that the soldier had raped a lady which adds a new angle to the entire *Wag The Dog* tale. The tale is actually a picture in order to save the sagging electoral fortunes of a beleaguered American President who is also an incumbent. Thus, the myth of the American Dream is deftly perpetuated through the movie through the artifice created by Stanley Motts, whose character is played vividly by Dustin Hoffman. The American myth and lore has lived on even after the virility and the floral Hawaiian tenor of the counter-culture movement because of the sole reason that it was all about the idea of being an American and being imbued with the non-Empirish Americanness.

The author is describing a just and egalitarian ethos of life, along with societal and political contours which characterise a way of thought which can be attributed to the myth and lore of hallowed nationalism. United States of America was an ordinary nation till the turn of the nineteenth century. Before the British Empire gave away to American preponderance in the entire international system, America was building its own innate and inner strength and geo-economic capacities.

The rest of the European firmament was involved in its own power games, BOP legerdemains and colonial races. It was United States of America which was preparing internally with its consonant industrialization and the advent of the Big business era. The ending of slavery as an aftermath of the 1864 Civil War and the rise of the Populist movement in order to curb the nepotism and graft in the executive, firmed up the national resolve of the American population and the political executive. Especially, there is an innate stress as part of the American myth making on the all important significance of human life and the significance about the rights of the general and ordinary citizenry. This plural and individual character of the American narrative makes up the format of the definition of being a "true blue American". The idea of being an American is about how a nation sticks to a realistic foreign policy with concurrent improvement in the positions of equity domestically, in order to attain the status of a Super State. These form a part of the insight on being an important regulator nation which is premised upon the ideals of the French Revolution, too. The conjoined liberal narrative thus attained, in the author's view, stresses upon the egalitarian and a Government invested governance of domestic relations and the Foreign Policy. The Counter culture movement acts as a question mark upon where the American progression to power and comfort went wrong. Its a reminder, and a reality check on the perceived excesses of the American establishment which emerges as a stark and positive reminder of the fact that 'Plurality' and 'Dissent' are no more seditious and a crime but form part of the mainstream narrative of the American nation.

The American citizen or the image of the great American nation bears a close resemblance to the idea of the, "Ubermensch" or the super being which militates against all that is ideationally unjust and non liberal. This super being much in the sense of an American super hero emerges in the societal-political landscape of a nation to improve and uplift the lot of the common citizenry. Thus, the organic image of a nation such as United States of America is equated with the chosen nation which any given but powerful nation is. United States of America and its inhabitants become this super visage which is part of the American Dream of intellectualism, gravity, global responsibility, entrepreneurial and individual grit.

NOTES

1. Gordon S Wood, "The Idea of America: Reflections on the Birth of the United States" (New York: Penguin books, 2011), pp. 20-35
2. Jessica Corry, "The Beatles and the Counter Culture" (TCNJ Journal of Student Scholarship, Volume 12, April, 2010, pp. 1-10.
3. Todd, Gitlin, "The Sixties: Years of Hope, Days of Rag," New York: Bantam Books, 1987.

4. Gerard de Groot, *The Sixties Unplugged: A Kaleidoscope History of a Disorderly Decade* (Cambridge: Harvard University Press, 2008).
5. Gordon S. Wood, "The Idea of America: Reflections and the Birth of the United States, (New York: Penguin Books), pp. 20-40
6. Steve Turner, *The Gospel According to the Beatles* (Louisville: Westminster John Knox Press, 2006).
7. "The Baby Boom Generation: The Wonder Years", URL: http://www.dailykos.com/story/2010/12/19/930054/-The-Baby-Boom-Generation-Part-I-of-III-The-Wonder-Years# (Online: Web), Accessed on 1 April, 2015.
8. "Brown vs Board of Education of Topeka", URL: http://www.law.cornell.edu/supremecourt/text/347/483 (Online: Web), Accessed on 1 April, 2014
9. "Landmark Cases: Brown VS Board of education Topeaka", URL: http://www.pbs.org/wnet/supremecourt/rights/landmark_brown.html (Online: Web), accessed on 1 April, 2015
10. Justus D Doenecke, "Explaining the Anti War Movement: 1939-1941: The Next Assignment", *The Journal of Liberation Studies*, Volume VIII, No. 1, Winter 1986.
11. Ibid.
12. Manfred Jonas, *Isolationism in America 1935-1941* (Imprint Publications, 1989).
13. Ibid.
14. H.W. Brands, *Woodrow Wilson* (Barnes and Nobles, 2003).
15. Ibid.
16. Vassiliki Kotini, "Aristophanes Response to the Peloponnesian War and the Defeat of the Comic Hero," Journal of Comparative Politics, No. 30, (2010), pp. 134-149
17. Ibid
18. Harold Taylor, "Students Without Teachers" (New York: McGraw-Hill Book Company, 1969), p.39.
19. *The Racquet*, Wisconsin State University-La Crosse, 17 March 1967, p. 2.
20. *The Racquet*, Wisconsin State University-La Crosse, 10 April 1975, p. 12.
21. William Lutchternberg (ed.), "Research Collections in American Politics: Microfilms from Major Archival and Manuscript Collections: The Johnson Administration's Response to Anti-Vietnam War Actvism", Lexis Nexis, Lyndon Baines Johnson Library.
22. "Questions of Meaning", URL:http://www.pbs.org/treasuresoftheworld/a_nav/guernica_nav/gnav_level_1/5meaning_guerfrm.html (Online: Web), Accessed on 1 July, 2015
23. Peter Schedadhl, "Spanish Lessons: Picasso in Madrid," *New Yorker*, 19 June, 2006
24. Vincent Canby, "How An All American Boy Went To War and Lost His Faith", *New York Times*, April 14, 2014.
25. Ibid.
26. B. Forgey, "The Statue and the Wall", *Washington Post*, p. 8.
27. Sue Blackmore, "Will Timothy Leary's Paper's Turn us on to LSD", *Guardian*, 18 June, 2011.
28. Ibid.
29. Sonja Foss, "Ambiguity as Persuasion: The Vietnam Veterans Memorial", URL: http://www.sonjafoss.com/html/Foss2.pdf (Online : Web), Accessed on 10 April, 2015.
30. Sarah King, "Jane Fonda's Anti War Activism and the Myth of Hanoi Jane", Thesis of University of Waterloo, Ontario, Canada, 2011.
31. Jordan Zakarin, "How Hollywood Fought against the Iraq War", URL: http://www.hollywoodreporter.com/news/iraq-war-anniversary-hollywoods-anti-429697 (Online: Web), accessed on August 1, 2015.

32. Ibid.
33. "Hanoi Jane Rumours Blend Fact and Fiction", URL: http://urbanlegends.about.com/od/janefonda/a/hanoi_jane.htm (Online: Web), Accessed on 10 April, 2015.
34. "9/11 and the British Broadcasting Conspiracy", URL: http://topdocumentaryfilms.com/911-and-the-bbc/ (Online: Web), Accessed on 10 April, 2014.
35. UN Charter, Article 51, UN Documents.
36. Eric Walberg, "9/11 For Dummies", *Al Ahram*, 6-12 September 2007.
37. The 9/11 Commission Report: Final Report of the National Commission on Terrorist Attacks upon the United States, authorized edition (New York: W.W. Norton, 2004), 149, 155, 166; henceforth 9/11CR.
38. David Aoronovitch, "Debunking Conspiracy Theories in Voodoo Histories"(Online : Web), URL: http://www.npr.org/templates/story/story.php?storyId=123127032, Accessed on 1 April, 2014.
39. Ibid.
40. Cynthia Weber, "International Relations Theory: A Critical Introduction: Is Anarchy what States Make of it?" (London: Rutledge), pp. 64-70).
41. Ibid., 70.
42. Ibid., 71.

12

The Telling Triad of the Iran Hostage Crisis, Nuclear Iran and the US-Iran Relations'

Introduction

The chapter will specifically deal with the Iran hostage crisis in the year 1979, the Iranian Revolution and its general impact on the US–Iran relationship till present. The Reaganite notion of the "Evil Empire" will be dealt with here along with the new strain in the Cold War before the final fall of the Iron Curtain. The theme of Iran's nuclear expansionism and the issue of Western sanctions till 2013 also call for a narrative. Much before the Iranian Revolution, the United States was an ally of the Shah of Iran who had left the country after the Revolution. The secularists lost the political battle in Iran and everything which had a Western hue and shade was castigated and marginalised in the nation's discourse.

Iran has been declared as a recalcitrant nation state by the working and functioning of the general dynamics of the United States's foreign policy. The US foreign policy makers and implementers, have since long stood for intrusions which are political in nature and tenor, with an emphasis being on Regime change as a chief objective. President Ronald Reagan initiated the 'new' Cold War, wherein the states of Iran and Iraq fitted in. They both fought an eight-year-long bloody war over territory in the region and with the political mindset of propelling their nations over West Asia, as they both had strategic and political interests in the region.

Thus, the idea of Iran emerging as the intransigent nation state is made simpler and clear after the Iran hostage crisis, when the American embassy in Tehran was taken over by the Iranian students. The idea of the United States was branded as the "Great Satan" and was recorded by the international community with aplomb as the Islamists and the Iranian students stormed into the corridors of the American Embassy holding the American occupants hostage for a perilous period of 255 days. Despite the botched military attempt by the United States to liberate the Americans and the efforts of President Jimmy Carter, the American hostages could not be released. This also had negative repercussions for Carter's second Presidential campaign, where-in, he lost to the Republican designate, Ronald Reagan. Reagan was also a second-rung Hollywood star, thus ushering in a new era of Iran–US estranged relationship—or maybe no diplomatic exchanges at all—at least at an overt level.

Iran has since then been targeted as a rogue nation state and a sponsor of disturbances in the Middle East. Nation states such as Iran, Iraq, Libya and North Korea have been accorded the sobriquet of being the recalcitrant nation states and rogue states by the US. The Americans have always believed in the significance of dominating the oil alleys of the region and the seaways such as the Persian Gulf and Babel-Mandeb, as a maritime asset. But unlike the Asia Pacific scenario, where no other nation can control the seaways effectively, in the West Asia, Iran has a commendable capability of controlling the maritime ways adjacent to the nation. Thus, Iran naturally emerged as a strategic nation and power to be contended within the larger context of the region as the United States too has interests in the natural wealth and the seafaring routes. The American interest lies in the fact that nations in the region ought to be prevented from becoming the focal points of Anti-Americanism, which can further sour the turf for the regional ambitions and the stakes of United States and maybe global stability. In the author's view, US has been avidly following a strategic policy in order to counter the negative depictions about its people and institutions which entail not letting a region become a hotbed of criticism for United States.

The Iran hostage crisis, has since the last few decades, been calibrated as one of the acts of terrorism against the carte blanche which the United States had enjoyed in West Asia. A PBS release provides an illuminating overview of the US involvement in Iran, where-in the United States played Reza Shah Pahlavi against the pro-Soviet Prime Minister, Mohammad Mossadegh. The release states, "Till 1953, the United States mostly stayed on the sidelines, advocating for an independent Iran under the leadership of the young king, Reza Shah Pahlavi. But that year, fearing that charismatic Prime Minister Mohammed Mossadegh might be moving Iran closer to Moscow, the CIA directed an operation to oust him and consolidate power under the Shah.[1]...Carter seemed to have a hard time deciding whether to heed the advice of his aggressive national security advisor, Zbigniew Brzezinski, who wanted to encourage the Shah to brutally suppress the revolution. His more cautious State Department, which suggested

Carter to reach out to opposition elements in order to smoothen the transition to a new government."[2] Thus, it has been deliberated upon that President Carter lost out on Iran, as he was not able to decide upon a tangible and winning strategy in relation to the state of Iran. Thus, the Iranian Revolution led by dissenters created a difficult choice for the American establishment, as the oil as always was a telling factor in serving the interests of the US foreign policy in the larger context of the region.

The Iran Hostage Crisis et al

Public opinion-makers and the larger fourth estate can serve as an ideal service provider to document the complete idea of an international strategic–political development. The Iran hostage crisis is an appropriate instance of the argument and the observation. The Cable News Network (CNN) provides a list of historical facts, concerning the Iranian hostage crisis. It is significant to comprehend the fundamental chronology of the Iran hostage crisis if the larger-than-life strategic impact of the climactic event has to be understood and underlined in all its seething ramifications. The CNN report provides an illuminating insight into the events which unfolded during those eventful and heady times that transformed the region and in a way initiated the unending spiral of Anti-Americanism amidst the global polity.

The CNN has reported,

> "**November 4, 1979:** Iranian students demonstrating outside of the U.S. embassy in Tehran storm the embassy and take 90 people hostage including 66 Americans. The students demand the extradition of the Shah from the United States. Ayatollah Khomeini issues a statement of support for the students' actions. **November 5, 1979:** The Iranian government cancels military treaties with the U.S. and the Soviet Union, treaties that would permit U.S. or Soviet military intervention. **November 6, 1979:** Premier Mehdi Bazargan and his government resign, leaving Ayatollah Khomeini and the Revolutionary Council in power."[3]

Thus, the idea of the Iran hostage crisis gets an ample coverage, as to when what happened in the context of the storming of the American Embassy in Tehran. After the coming to power of Ayatollah Khomeini in Tehran, he began to be considered as the religious head of the state of Iran along with glowing ambitions to emerge as the doyen of an Islamic age in the region. In a way, later on before the complete release of all the hostages to United States, the grand Khomeini demanded the unfreezing of all Iranian assets in United States along with the return of the Shah's wealth. All Iranian diplomats were coerced into leaving the United States and Iran was sanctimoniously sanctioned. Thus, the bottlenecks in forging healthy and friendly ties with Iran were spawned right after the denouement of the hostage crisis and the further regime of Western sanctions under the ambit of containing Iran and preventing it from attaining a potent nuclear power potential.

Decades later, the Iran hostage crisis still continues to haunt the US–Iran relationship. In the year 2014, the then Iranian Ambassador to the United Nations had been denied a visa to the United States where the UN body is housed. In a news report it is mentioned, "Responding to a groundswell of domestic pressure, the Obama administration has denied a visa to Iran's new UN ambassador, Hamid Aboutalebi. The White House decision goes against normal diplomatic protocol, raising questions about Washington's ability to unilaterally veto another country's choice of representation at the world body."[4] Thus, it was reiterated by President Obama that spying and espionage under the cover of diplomacy are other irritants in any 'bilateral relation', so, they must be stymied before they raise their ugly head.The domestic public opinion in the context of the US–Iran relations remains a poignant factor in the larger context. Thus, in a way the legacy of the hostage event is a landmark, even if perceived in the firming of the cordial relations between both the nations. Thus, the decline in bonhomie, camaraderie and mutual understanding became a routine affair, rather than a one-off incident, in the larger rubric of the 'US-Iran bilateral relation after the denouement of the Iran hostage crisis.'

Internationally too, the Iran hostage crisis has been appended as a part of the international law narrative debates. Iran and the United States did involve themselves in an agreement which was decidedly a kind of quid pro quo in the entire matrix of the incident. Iran released 52 hostages held in Iran and in return the United States decided to transfer to an escrow account in the Bank of England an amount of almost 8 billion dollars worth of Iranian assets held in the United States and in the related branches of the American banks.[5] Article 27 of the Vienna Convention of the Law of Treaties states that a nation cannot utilise the argument that its municipal law does not allow the implementation of an internationally agreed upon agreement between two sovereign nation states.[6] One Iranian misrepresentation came to the fore that the hostages were not maltreated by Iran in Tehran while the opposite was found to be the case and whether the Americans were aware of this misrepresentation by the Iranians is unknown in terms of the process of their entering into agreement with Iran.[7]

The International Court of Justice was also approached in the aftermath of the Iranian hostage crisis. In a landmark judgment, the Court decided, "Iran has violated and is still violating obligations owed by it to the United States; (2) that these violations engage Iran's responsibility; (3) that the Government of Iran must immediately release the United States nationals held as hostages and place the premises of the Embassy in the hands of the protecting power; (4) that no member of the United States diplomatic or consular staff may be kept in Iran to be subjected to any form of judicial proceedings or to participate in them as a witness; (5) that Iran is under an obligation to make reparation for the injury caused to the United States, and (6) that the form and amount of such reparation, failing agreement between the parties, shall be settled by the Court."[8] Thus, the Court necessitated the idea that the state of Iran was found to be in a state of fault as a result of its hostage-taking act and thus criminal liability was heaped on Tehran. Also, Iran did not respond to the allegations as a proper respondent, thus, delimiting its role in the final judgement and along with that it questioned the right of the International Court of Justice to tackle the case filed through a Memorial by the United States Government. It is reported in the events that led to the final judgement that, "Iran took no part in the proceedings. It neither filed pleadings nor was represented at the hearing, and no submissions were therefore presented on its behalf. Its position was however defined in two letters addressed to the Court by its Minister for Foreign Affairs on 9 December 1979 and16 March 1980 respectively. In these, the Minister maintained *inter alia* that the Court could not and should not take cognizance of the case."[9]

The Contemporary Context

Even now, the shadow of the Iran hostage crisis tends to cast an impact upon the relations which are already not in the right direction after Iran's nuclear ambitions were meant to be contained by the United States and the rest of the nuclear haves. It was reported in a news piece in *Euro News* that, "Iran asked the United Nations on Tuesday to demand that the United States grant a visa to Tehran's proposed new U.N. envoy, while Washington stood firm on its decision to deny entry to Hamid Abutalebi over his suspected links to hostage-takers. The United States has said it would not grant a visa to Abutalebi because of his connection to the 1979-1981 Tehran hostage crisis."[10] Thus, in the author's view, the historical and dead skeletons, have promptly fallen out of the closet and the shadow of the 1979 incident still has a negative impact upon the fate of the relationship between the United States and Iran in the larger context of the nuclear issue. Talks are still continuing between Iran and the European nations and America to re-order the nuclear ambitions of Iran which saw the passage of the joint agreement in the form of the JCPOA (Joint Comprehensive Plan of Action) and the final reaching of the agreement between the P-plus-5 nations and Iran through JCPOA-II in mid-2015. Thus, the estrangement over the nuclear ambitions of Iran have been amicably solved which allows for the IAEA and Western inspections of Iran's nuclear installations. While the US on the other hand has agreed to scale back all the economic and political sanctions on Iran in mid-2015. Still, a debilitating rider remains in place which contends that the Iran–US nuclear deal is contingent on its passage by the US Congress. Israel and the Jewish lobby, too, exist as problems in the entire negotiating exercise. Israel has every now and then thwarted attempts at, rapprochement between the United States and Iran. The various nations in the United Nations have been privy to the rigmarole of the American sanctions over a nuclear Iran but the denouement has been peaceful in mid-2015.

The US foreign policy has been amply criticised with the weapon that the American establishment is very selective concerning the act of interventions in its external dimensions in far-off locales and strategically significant stations. One criticism remains that the US has always been taken to the task as it interferes with the domestic context of any state which is in a dilapidated state of affairs as the aftermath of a conflict. The idea of impinging upon another's sovereignty is often utilized as a perennial accusation against the Reluctant Empire. The decision not to go for a direct military engagement with states such as Iran and North Korea, seems selective, but, it is a decision directed by realism, as, it refers to the retaliatory potential of a nation state. It means that weaker foes are easily attacked militarily while the stronger ones can be left alone and can be differently tackled. This debate and international law schism, is very well recorded all across the academic firmament of International politics and International law. The entire issue is that United States has been blamed for interfering in the domestic affairs of some of the nations which sometimes militates against the sovereign concerns of those receptacle nations. Iraq and Vietnam are instances which have been cited by the critics of the US foreign policy. Going by the tenets of a national interest oriented foreign policy and the doctrine of Hans Morgenthau's 'Realism,' sustaining a dominant, humane and a powerful positioning for the home nation is always a priority which is what United States does naturally to maintain its global preponderance.

Andrew Roberts writes in the *Wall Street Journal* that, "It goes back earlier than Israel's successful pre-emptive attacks on Iraq's Osirak nuclear reactor in 1981 (not to mention other pre-emptive Israeli attacks like the one on the Syrian nuclear program in 2007). It even predates Israel's 1967 pre-emption of massed Arab armies, a move that saved the Jewish state. History is replete with examples when pre-emption was successful, as well as occasions when, because pre-emption wasn't employed, catastrophe struck."[11] Thus calculating risks is a significant instrument of a nation's security concerns and if an imminent threat to the national security is palpable then the nations sometimes amass armies for going to war. Even Napoleon was pre-empted by the British Royal Navy in order to sink the amassing of the battle fleet in the seas. In the battle of seas near Copenhagen, the Danes were preempted by the mortar guns and the rocket fire guns of the British Royal Navy. Even, Jeremy Black mentions that, "John Lewis Gaddis a prominent Historian with links to the British Government saw a precedent in the Burning of Washington in 1814 claiming that it was a surprise attack which led to an emphasis on preemption as a means to ensure security."[12] Thus, the British royal Navy and the Americans had been preempting each other in places such as Canada, Newark and York. In the author's view, the all pervading British threat was one of the prime reasons why the American establishment later on engaged itself with a Preemptive doctrine in military interventions and foreign policy.

The realm of international law has a definite idea about the notion of pre-emptive war. One can delve into the United Nations Charter's Article 51, if the debate in the realm of international law has to be properly understood; "Nothing in the present Charter shall impair the inherent right of individual or collective self-defence if an armed attack occurs against a Member of the United Nations, until the Security Council, has taken measures necessary to maintain international peace and security. Measures taken by Members in the exercise of this right of self-defence, shall be immediately reported to the Security Council and shall not in any way affect the authority and responsibility of the Security Council under the present Charter to take at any time such action as it deems necessary in order to maintain or restore international peace and security."[13] The entire spectrum of the debate has been divided into the twin groups of Restrictionists and Counter-Restrictionists. The former contend that unless an actual armed attack has been noted and a nation has been materially victimised, a pre-emptive war is illegal. The opposite ilk states that even when a nation state can foresee a war and a threat to its security and stability, then pre-emptive military acts can be indulged in self-defence. Thus, these two options emerge as contesting and antagonist perspectives, which have been the cynosure of all eyes in the realm of observers analysing the subsequent US interventions.

Thus, Iran in the present context, has been spared under the rubric of the restrictionists or is it a selective strategic and military decision by the Defense Department and the White House in the tradition of a national interest-oriented policy? And, even if it is, there is no harm in it as failed nation states tend to have the destructive potential of debilitating the apple cart of peace and stolidity in any national and regional context. Thus, Iran has been saved because of the realpolitik of the international system in the context of rapidly aggressive nations such as Israel in the neighbourhood. As the nations cannot be perennial and difficult-to-find-fault-with entities, the self-interest-oriented behaviour of the states is something which gets reflected in the reticence and recalcitrance of the United States too in the context of its Iran policy.

Iran is a state, which is replete since the historically significant last few decades, with the element of leadership and the potential to be an eminent player in the regional and the international context. There has been all the talk and the stereotypical narrative about the norm of either Pakistan or Iran becoming the leader of the Islamic World with the acquisition of the Nuclear Bomb though in two different contexts for two different nations. Still, Iran has always been a front runner in this regional pursuit of power. Benjamin Netanyahu in his riveting speech in the United Nations General Assembly went ahead with the notion of the international community especially the West waiting for Iran as a recalcitrant nation state crossing the threshold of the 20% limit. The 20% limit[14] is the threshold after which the Iranian nuclear enrichment of uranium will cross criticality and thus enable its nuclear establishment to manufacture a nuclear warhead which gives it deterrence over an antagonist—Israel. The rest of the Gulf Cooperation Council countries, some of which are supported by the United States and the rest of the West too will feel the Iran's strength then. The Israeli Premier referred to the red line as the point of departure beyond which the state of Israel will be bound by its national interest to invoke aggression against the state of Iran.[15] The speech was very emphatic in its nature and its tenor generally reflected the intent to aggress upon Iran's nuclear intransigence.

The Intertwined Stereotypes

It is a principle well utilised by scholars and observers of international politics, that if the need arises to comprehend the schemata of the foreign relations of a state then an innate understanding of the internal and domestic security and the internal socio-political milieu, needs to be a scholarly calling, too. Thus, the politics of modern Iran can be a staple theme for discussions and deliberations within its domestic confines. As an Islamic Republic, Iran from 1979 to 2000, perceived and broadcasted its Islamic system as the ideal model for the West Asian region. Even after the upheavals in the Arab West Asia, Iran's leaders chose to project their domestic political model as the panacea for all the ills of the Muslim world which was worthy of emulation.[16] Khomeini took for himself the role of an international spokesperson for the entire Muslim World and as a kind of a spiritual leader for the entire swathe of Muslims all across the length and breadth of the international polity.[17] He championed the cause of Bosnian Muslims, those in Somalia and Lebanon along with the grave Palestinian question. He stressed that the final appearance of Palestine on the world map was an "Islamic matter" and supporting the international and regional causes were efforts to circumvent and counter the influence of the United States and Israel in the region and beyond in the terms of the larger global system.[18]

The United States and Israel to a certain extent hold five myths as the constituents of their foreign policy myths. They being,: The world is populated by nation states. The East-West power struggle is the most important event in world politics. All other political relationships can be ranked in terms of it.[19] It is this second myth which reflects the general fear psychosis and the political disdain, for, all things and principles Iranian in terms of the responses by Israel and United States in the context of the Nuclear Armageddon strived in by Iran. This, shakes the Western applecart of Nuclear ownership. Myths refer to the age old and traditional belief system of the various nations which have become embedded in the socio-cultural ethos of the political systems and the Governmental systems of these countries. US and Iran are also home to some such belief systems going by their different political systems and political and development trajectories.

The Iranian myths are much different than American myths. The Iran's hoi-polloi contended that the level of materialism had taken over the nations' civil life. Iran is essentially a spiritual civilization and its the spiritual candour of the local populace which could be managed only through a recourse to the spiritual and religious tenets of an Islamic prescription.[20]Thus, the Islamic revolution tended to serve as a bulwark according to which the Iran's foreign policy was remodeled. Arch antagonists such as United States and Israel modeled their foreign policy responses upon the espousal of the nuclear issues by the Iran's establishment in the tenures of Rafsanjani and Ahmadinejad. The *Guardian* did a study on what would happen if the Israelis nuked Iran, and came out with a few observations. The ex-spies of Israel as part of an Israeli think tank mulled over the idea of what would happen; after an Israeli strike over Iran, the Hizbollah would erupt in a rebellion with neighbors such as the state of Israel.[21] One American simulation predicted that such a scenario could lead to a larger regional war which could have been worsened by a Syrian involvement too had it not been embroiled in a long-stretching civil war. The sanctions too have brought in a new perception, where-in the inner strength of the Iranian economy has been made fragile by them.

Additionally, the pressure from the Iranian electorate has been for improving the economic performance, advancing the human rights record, registering palpable progress in terms of political freedom, etc. Thus, the impact of the sanctions has largely been on domestic issues and has not been a call on the government to alter the nuclear policy or to amend its conduct of international relations. As for the United States, the continued threat[22] of launching a military strike on Iranian sovereign territory lacks any legal sanctity. The legality of the American penchant for pre-emptive use of force is also present in a slender manner. One assessment is that 'there is no self-appointed right to attack another state because of fear that the state is making plans or developing weapons usable in a hypothetical campaign'.[23]

There is no need to stress upon the historic divide between the states of Iran and Israel though the American factor in the entire fulcrum of the relationship, has been a changing and fluctuating one depending upon the commensurately transforming strategic, political and ideological underpinnings of the regimes in Tehran. In the recent spate of political developments, apart from the Iranian standpoint on Palestinian self-determination, the issue of Israel and Iran bombing each other's nuclear installations has been the bone of contention and everybody's pet peeve. The Israeli newspapers have often reported on and analysed the notion of what iota of damage can occur to the Israeli installations in the event of an Iranian attack. A former Revolutionary Guard commander has contended in *The Times of Israel* that, "Around 10,000 Israelies would perish if Israel attacked Iran."[24] Hassan Nasrallah, the Hezbollah leader, too contended likewise in tandem with the general Iranian political refrain, "Israel goes to war with Iran, his group would fire rockets at Israel and "transform the lives of millions of Zionists in occupied Palestine to a real hell." Nasrallah said the attacks would result in tens of thousands of Israeli fatalities.[25] The Iranian contention is very simplistic in the sense that it asserts that the state of Israel will reach a point of no return. Thus, Iran, Hamas and Hezbollah predict a *fin de siècle* and a 'doomsday' for Jerusalem in the event of an Israeli incursion into Lebanon or Iran.

The fulcrum of the Iran and Israel transactions rests with the all-pervading and incisive role which can be played by the United States. Still, if one analyses the foreign policy positioning and the strategic perch in the region, then President Obama will not make much of an intrusion and did not evince much interest in the Israeli factor in West Asia. The Palestinian locus standi changed for the better in the United Nations officially in the ending days of 2012. Such a development could have been generated due to the Iranian intransigence which threatens to destabilise the US–Israel relations in the larger context of the situation. The news portal *National Post* reports, "In a highly unusual rebuff to a close ally, the White House said on Tuesday that President Barack Obama would not meet Israeli Prime Minister Benjamin Netanyahu during a U.S. visit later this month, as tensions escalated over how to deal with Iran's nuclear program."[26] The American President, too, denied a meeting with Benjamin Netanyahu on no clear pretext, which has definitely soured the relationship between the two nations despite their historical and coalitional proximity.

Also, the Israeli establishment has been too averse to the American standpoint on the region with special reference to Iran's position in the context of its nuclear ambitions. "The World says to Israel to Wait and Israel tells the World, till when and why".[27] These were the words of Benjamin Netanyahu when he declared that the United States has forfeited the right to intervene on the behalf of Israel as President Obama has not agreed to the "Red Line" warning which Netanyahu mentioned in his UN General Assembly Speech.[28] Thus, the rigmarole of diplomacy between Israel and the United States of America has led to a schism being created between the two nations as President Obama came out with an intention to mend fences with the Arab world in general, in order to stem the slide of the great power in an age vitiated by the streak of Anti-Americanism.

The Lighter Side of the Conundrum

A rather contentious joke would reflect the way the diplomats function and the present one showcases the clash of civilisations theme which is still generally part of the larger narrative of the idea of diplomacy between the United States and Iran. The joke runs something like this, "An Arab diplomat visiting the US for the first time was being wined and dined by the State Department. The Grand Emir was unused to the salt in American foods (frenchfries, cheeses, salami, anchovies etc.) and was constantly sending his manservant Abdul to fetch him a glass of water. Time and again, Abdul would scamper off and return with a glass of water, but then came the time when he returned empty-handed." Abdul, you son of an ugly camel, where is my water? demanded the Grand Emir. "A thousand pardons, O Illustrious One," stammered an exasperated Abdul, "white man sit on well."[29] Thus, diplomats have a role to play in mitigating and pre-empting conflicts but what might happen if the cultural and the civilisational ramifications of the negotiating nations are present at the contrasting ends of the negotiating VIBGYOR? Thus, the state of affairs between the twin sides as depicted in the popular portrayals, too, play a significant role in the firming up of communication gaps between the negotiating sides. The differences of the order of culture and society and national character, are often used to make a nation and its people more superior and domineering and as part of bilateral or multilateral exchanges between the nations.

The Hollywood construct *Argo* reflects the sentiment behind the real goings-on behind the contours of the happenings in the Iran hostage crisis. The excessive tension and the melodrama of the situation, the terror-stricken American consular staff along with the manner in which the hostages were mistreated and the Embassy was vandalised and turned into a garrison with the students, is all depicted with finesse and class. The movie construct of the Iran hostage crisis brings to fore the politicking, the distraught American response and the general response of the international community in all its gory detail. *Argo* is a stark reminder of the harsh reality of the state of Iran–US relations. Joseph Sarkisian writes in *Policymic* that, "The film tells the true story of how the CIA helped six U.S. State Department consular affairs employees escape Tehran under the all-seeing eye of the Revolutionary Guard during what was arguably the worst period of hostility between Iran and the U.S. in history[30]...But the transition to Islamic theocracy was not a welcome one to some. Under the Shah's rule, questioning the regime may have landed you in prison, but Iran was a much more secular nation. To many, the Islamic revolution came as shock and awe, depending on whom you ask of course! But, under the Shah, Iran's economy was better than it is now, struggling under the death grip of Western sanctions due to its controversial nuclear program and all around aggressive attitude."[31]Thus, there is lot more than Ben Affleck's good looks that the movie Argo extols, as it brings out the narrative of the tense nature of the relationship between Iran and the United States along with the idea of how the Central Intelligence Agency can be effective if it is provided with all the manoeuvring room and strategic space in any operation, which is definitely an American-oriented approach.

The questions of accuracy, too, have arisen out of the depiction of the Iranian narrative during the Iran hostage crisis.D. Parvaz, a journalist in *Al Jazeera*, writes about the general visage of the nation state of Iran in the western media, "To say that Iran's image has taken a sound drubbing in the Western media is an understatement—it's all *nuclear this, human rights that.* To read the headlines, you'd think the entire country is made up of nothing but prisons and suspicious nuclear facilities. Iran has no art galleries, universities, playgrounds filled with kids. Just enraged hijabbed and bearded (yikes) hordes, shouting in...what's that phlegm-based language?... looking for a fight."[32] Thus, there seems to an iota of negative portrayal involved in the general discourse of Iran's portrayal in the Western public opinion. The idea of terrorism, terror-mongering and unbounded dark aggression gets a manifestation in the general argument about Iran. It is something which is easily and conveniently lapped up by the public and the opinion makers in the domestic discourse in the United States. The art of vilification in the West is a stark reminder of the Cold War mentality which gets to resurface in the entire narrative of relations with Iran. There has to be a perennial bugbear, a perpetual foe which needs to be lambasted, castigated and, if possible, ridiculed at the altar of national interest. This demeanour is not specific to the United States only but it happens to be the case with any nation intent on identifying a traditional and quintessential foe and adversary and for survival.

In another Hollywood construct titled as *Not Without my Daughter* there is another standardisation of the Iranian nation and the national character. D Parvaz further writes, "The makers of *Not Without My Daughter* seemed to not mind working without a fact checker, blithely painting Iran as a nation of fanatic misogynists. Hell, if we're not cinematically rendered as baby-eating cave-dwellers, we're doing all right. A tribe of savages with facial piercings with claw-handed executioners to do our bidding?"[33] Thus, the rabidity of the portrayal is astutely detested in Iran and it tends to do no good for the future of a positive public opinion about the "Great Satan"—United States—which is the sobriquet which some of the official press utilises about America. The American public diplomacy efforts all tend to take the international attention away from the global opprobrium which the US establishment has been able to generate for itself as a fall-out of a few international interventions.

Still, efforts and diplomatic strivings have been underfoot in order to spawn a betterment and steadying of the bilateral relationship between the two estranged powers. For instance, public diplomacy has been ardently utilised to patch up the relationship despite the nuclear intransigence of Iran as perceived through the American viewpoint. Also, the people have been attuned to the American education system since the last three decades in Iran despite the state of the bedraggled relationship between the two nation states. As an instance, the United States has put in place a Virtual Embassy for Tehran. It is here that the Iranian students can attain all kinds of information about the educational opportunities in the United States, which is definitely part and parcel of the norm and practice of cultural diplomacy in the larger sense of the term.

The content and the nature of the Virtual Embassy of Iran can be deliberated upon in some detail as it envisions the renewed American striving to concretise a new visage for the United States as a nation and what it stands for vis-à-vis the American Dream. The effort is an e-diplomatic striving, to circumvent the allegations and the vitriol embedded in the well-developed and an all-enveloping streak of Anti-Americanism. The content of the web envoy involves newspapers, life in general, political economy and other details about Iranian Americans which might be of some interest to the Iranians staying in the United States. The attempt is to target the youth of the state of Iran in order to stymie the wave of Anti-Americanism in the global context with a sharp focus being on Iran. Also, observers have pointed out that an introduction to the 'noble and ideal American way of life' is also being attempted in the virtual portal.A separate section has been devoted to the Hollywood productions in order to posit a liberal and a friendly visage of the United States of America. Thus, the genie of Anti-Americanism, is sought to be tackled by the American diplomatic effort utilising the impact of 'New-Age diplomacy' for winning the battle of hearts and minds of the Iranian youth. Soft Power galore!

Certain 'expose' kind of news is also portrayed in the Virtual Embassy, which sheds light on the difficulties being faced by the commoners in Iran as a result of the American sanctions, which can be read with the caveat that the difficulties being faced by the Iranian citizens. This is a consequence of the obstinate and recalcitrant attitude of the regime in place in Iran. Frud Behzan writes in one of the reports in the Iranian Virtual Embassy that, "Iranians have gone online to vent their frustration at the government after it slashed state subsidies on gasoline, a move that has seen the price at the pump skyrocket by up to 75 percent. The dramatic price hikes, which took effect at midnight on April 25, are expected to test President Hassan Rohani's support among a population fed up with stubborn inflation, rising costs, and high unemployment[34]... The government has defended its decision, saying the subsidy slash aims to release government money for production and infrastructural projects in order to improve efficiency and bolster the economy. Iran first began cutting energy and food subsidies under former President Mahmud Ahmadinejad in 2010 to help the ailing economy as it faced increased international pressures over its disputed nuclear program. Some Iranians, however, have called on Rohani's government to be given time to change the country's economic fortunes. One of them, Raha Karemi, posted on Facebook: 'Give him more time'."[35] Thus, much before the Western sanctions were imposed upon the Iranians, the Iranian Government even through the times of Ahmedinejad, had reduced allocations for the subsidies in the sphere of gasoline, in order to beef up the infrastructure and other sectors of Iran's economy. Still, people seem to be sympathetic to the new government as they feel that Rouhani needs to be allocated space and time for the implementation of his electoral promises. He seems to be a reformist and a liberal voice, in the entire context of the relationship between Tehran and Washington and that is where a fig leaf might work.

Hassan Rouhani, the new Iranian Prime Minister, after Ahmadinejad, might be facing a tough time at the saddle of power after he became the Premier in Iran. The Government is facing a paucity of funds due to the sanctions imposed by the West and that development is having a cascading influence upon the state of economy in Iran and on the austerity measures. These have been initiated by Hassan Rouhani. These were already in place, during the times of Ahmadinejad and are taking their toll upon the common Iranians. *Dawn* recently reported that, "The 455,000-rial ($14) monthly handout scheme, initiated in December 2010 by Rouhani's predecessor Mahmoud Ahmadinejad, is part of broader economic reforms aimed at overhauling the country's massive subsidy system. The reform—which phases out parts of remaining subsidies on energy, utility bills and basic food costs—is forecast in this year's budget to save the cash-starved government $18 billion."[36] Thus, the issue of subsidies, in the light of the international sanctions, has had a far-reaching impact upon the functionality of the political economy and the interests and the ratings of the Hassan Rouhani leaving the Iranian citizens reeling under the impact of sanctions. *The Economist* reported in 2013 that there have been food shortages and 'chicken riots' in the city of Tehran and other major Iranian cities when the Government sellers and distributors went among the people to sell chicken supplies to the people.[37] This was an indictment of the West's position on the issue of Iran's nuclear intransigence which is having an impact upon the standard of life for the commoners in Iran which some sticklers for panic have equated with the start of a humanitarian crisis in Iran.

A *Dawn* report also pithily surmises upon the dilemma being faced by the Iranian Government under Rouhani: "Self-declared moderate Rouhani was elected last summer, beating conservative rivals after vowing to fix the economy, seek improved relations with the West and promote greater freedoms. Much of his election campaign was waged across reformist platforms as well as social media where he retains strong support from the upper and middle classes."[38] The decision to refuse direct aid in tandem with the nationalistic sentiment of being a proud and steadfast nation, has also seemed to rebound back on the Rouhani's political fortunes in Iran. As the nation's nuclear negotiators further engage with the Western diplomats, in order to make them lift the economic sanctions, Prime Minister Rouhani, faces an uphill task for the restoration of national, political and moral sanity in Iran.

Let us see how the Americans perceive the Rouhani regime and the change which he astutely promised to bring about in the nuclear stand-off with the West and the United States of America. Steven Ditto of the Washington Institute, "surveys Rouhani's vast output over the past thirty years, assessing its implications for policymakers as they evaluate potential Iranian overtures on the nuclear issue and other matters. Thus far, the new president's engagement with the international community and his prospects of instituting limited domestic reform show some promise. Yet given his background as an ideologue, he may view such moves as a way of reinforcing the authority of a system that has continually failed the Iranian people since 1979." Rouhani has a background as a Persian writer and is known for his comparatively liberal frame of thought but on the other hand he has also been an ideologue. The big question is that can he make the Iranian nation state emerge from the macabre round up of the hostage crisis of the year 1979 and seek a better deal with the West? Still, the extremism and the tardiness as showcased by the steady and the unstinting nuclear rhetoric of Ahmadinejad, has been relegated to the back-burner to a great extent.

The Carnegie Endowment of Peace has too delved into the question that can Rouhani change Iran? For the better or for the worse? In an interesting and insightful take on the state of Iran and United States relations, Ramin Jahanbegloo, Nazila Fathi, and Mehdi Khalaji offered their perspectives on recent developments in a televised deliberation. The issues which were on the table for deliberations were, "In his first two months in office, Iranian President Hassan Rouhani has freed political prisoners, sent conciliatory tweets, and broken a thirty-four-year-old taboo by speaking with US President Barack Obama. Is Tehran seeking a tactical nuclear compromise or even contemplating a fundamental strategic shift? How would a détente with America affect Iran's internal political and societal dynamics?"[39] The themes in the context of the US Iran relations which were discussed, were that Iran is attempting to conceptualise a new idiom of a peacenik Iran, which will eschew the nuclear weapons option or the nuclear negotiations, will transform into a new strategic shift which is being planned by Iran. These developments will go into furthering the diplomatic and political rift with the United States. Also, the question which is of key significance to the entire Iranian nuclear Armageddon, is the idea that what will be the domestic spillover of the negotiations which are being undertaken with the Western negotiators. More specifically with the European Union diplomatists too playing a role in the diplomacy how can Iran make the West understand about its strategic intent?[40]

The ilk of counter proliferators such as Richard Einhorn, stand for the traditional opposition of the nuclear have-nots. This lobby states that the United States should enter into negotiations for subsequent nuclear cooperation agreement with nations such as India only when these countries give a pledge through the signing of the NPT and CTBT. Only then they will not go nuclear and will not conduct nuclear weapons tests and will utilise their nuclear powers for peaceful options only. Thus, this brings us right back to the word which I have been utilising, which is, "Nuclear Intransigence" of nation states such as Iran and North Korea, which due to the strategic, regional and geo-economic consequences, get a different treatment, than the 'interventions,' which were meted out to countries such as Iraq and Afghanistan.

Thus, the nuclear question is the contemporary case in point which exists as a spoiler in the bilateral relationship, between Iran and the United States. Iran, in light of a Cinematic portrayal, is associated with the aggressive and the rasping Emperor Xerxes who prided on predating upon the 300 Spartans thus envisioning the narrative of the "Clash of Civilizations" when we are subsisting in a fast amalgamating world and an altercasting' international system. It is in such a collaborative effort that the security dilemmas and the non porous walls of a Prisoner's Dilemma, seem to have become a thing of the past. Even now, in the author's view, antagonists, such as Iran and United States, can cooperate and subsist in an international system, which is not as of now, directed by the United States of America alone in a grand unipolar quality and its dreamer like quintessence-chutzpah. In the author's view, the Clash of civilizations, theme, seems to be the overarching theme which circumscribes the US-Iran relationship which mars the larger ambit of West Asia and Iran.

In 2015, the central idea behind the US policy with Iran is to prevent Iran from acquiring a nuclear weapon. The nuclear agreement is an improvement over the JCPOA reached in November 2013 and the Lausanne agreement reached in April 2015. JCPOA refers to the Joint Comprehensive Plan of Action to ensure that Iran's nuclear program will be exclusively peaceful. JCPOA intended to provide Iran with phased sanctions relief upon verification that Iran has implemented key nuclear commitments. The official White House release states, "This deal stands on the foundation of the Joint Plan of Action (JPOA), achieved in November of 2013, and the framework for this Joint Comprehensive Plan of Action (JCPOA), announced in Lausanne on April 2, 2015 that set the requirements for the deal with the P5+1 and Iran, alongside the European Union announced today."[41]

The present deal reached between Iran and the US and other nations effectively closes the uranium pathway which was hitherto open for Iran before the inking of the historic deal. Much before the deal was signed and in the heydays of the negotiations, much before Ahmadinejad made his acrid rhetoric public Iran had made a couple of advances to the US to patch up a solution in 2003 and later, too. Iran had made a case for friendship a couple of times but President Obama did not reciprocate being under pressure of the domestic constituencies. Iran is now completely out of the nuclear power loop as a result of the JPOA-2. The White House portal succinctly reports, "Iran would need two key elements to construct a uranium bomb: tens of thousands of centrifuges and enough highly enriched uranium to produce enough material to construct a uranium bomb. There are currently two uranium enrichment facilities in the country: the Natanz facility and the Fordow facility. But thanks to this nuclear deal, Iran must reduce its stockpile of uranium by 98%, and will keep its level of uranium enrichment at 3.67%— significantly below the enrichment level needed to create a bomb. Iran also needs tens of thousands of centrifuges to create highly enriched uranium for a bomb[42]...Right now, Iran has nearly 20,000 centrifuges between their Natanz and Fordow facilities. But under this deal, Iran must reduce its centrifuges to 6,104 for the next ten years. No enrichment will be allowed at the Fordow facility at all, and the only centrifuges Iran will be allowed to use are their oldest and least efficient models."[43] Thus, the deal effectively negates the nuclear power and weapons capacities of Tehran. In a way, in the author's view, a stable quotient has been reached in the region with the sanctions being rolled back by the United States.

It is a well-known fact that the US and Europe had imposed debilitating sanctions on Tehran with this diplomatic approach reaping benefits in mid-2015 when Iran capitulated under international diplomatic pressure. *USA Today* reports, "The United States, the European Union and the U.N. Security Council imposed sanctions on Iran to pressure it to stop its nuclear program. These include restrictions on trade, and the seizure in foreign bank accounts of $150 billion of Iranian oil revenue."[44] The **United States** wanted sanctions to remain in place until Iran implements the deal, with a 'snap back' mechanism to reimpose them if it cheats. It said weapons embargoes and sanctions targeting Iran's ballistic missile program and support for terrorism would remain. **Iran** wanted all sanctions removed immediately when the deal goes into effect. The result was that the relief of sanctions will only start when Tehran has met the commitments of this nuclear agreement, including the removal and destruction of the Arak nuclear reactor core, and shipping uranium stockpiles abroad. Then sanctions relief will begin in stages and a U.N. weapons embargo will remain in place for five years."[45] Thus, President Obama has informed his countrymen that the deal guarantees that Iran cannot develop nuclear weapons. Still, what needs to be understood is that in the context of Iraq, Shia Iran has ably supported the Shia regime in Baghdad as part of a larger understanding between it and the United States. The myriad Iranian outfits have infiltrated Iraq in a much prolonged battle against the Daesh. In the author's view, the Iranian support for the Palestinian issue through the support for Hamas and Hizbollah is still an obstruction to the relationship but the various permutations and combinations will peter down to a stable truce between the West, Washington and Tehran, as the outcome of the eighteen-days negotiations, over the nuclear status of Iran. In the author's view, the clash of civilizations frame will become an element of a turbulent past as the twin arch antagonists have reached a stage of conflict resolution through summitry and stay poised for a larger regional rapprochement. In author's view, the future augurs well for Iran and United States as the current churning in the West Asia will make both the arch antagonist nations to converge at least notionally in order to stabilize the situation in West Asia.

The First Proposal and the Current History

In a way, several overtures were made by Iran's establishment way back in 2003 but the Bush regime did not reciprocate and neither did President Obama's Government. Trita Parsi writes, "Tim Guldimann arrived in Washington in early May 2003. As the Swiss Ambassador to Tehran, he served as the caretaker of American interests in Iran because United States did not have an embassy there. Then, Saddam Hussein had been recently defeated in Iraq. Hundreds of thousands of US troops were now deployed on Iran's eastern and western flank. Tehran, could, very well have been the target."[46] All this, served as the background to the Iran's proposal to Washington to solve the perpetually divisive and fractious tug of war imposed, by the West and the United Nations. Trita Parsi further writes, "Iran in a surprising turn of events accepted the Beirut Declaration of the Arab League which recognized and normalized relations with the Jewish State. In return, Israel would agree to a withdrawal from all occupied territories and accept a fully independent Palestinian state. Iran agreed to recognize the two state solution. In return, the Iranians wanted members of Mujahideen-e-Khalq Organization (MEK), US designated terrorist organization in Iraq, handed over to them in return of Al Qaeda operatives which the Iranian authorities had captured. Also, the Iranians demanded a lifting of all sanctions on their nation and its economy."[47] Thus, despite the Satanization and the vilification which the twin nations indulge-in, against each other, the Iranians were the first on official records to do more than send a feeler to the Americans in order to initiate a diplomatic proposal. JCPOA-I and JCPOA-II came much later in the recent past. Though Iran has been criticized by the Americans but the American scholar Trita Parsi has written that Iran made an early friendly overture in 2003 which was not treated handsomely by Washington. All the arguments which the author advances in the Book's narartive, are, not meant for defending the American position so the author has included the criticism part, too, where the American standpoint cannot be blithely defended.

The Americans rejected this first overture on the part of Tehran. Trita Parsi further writes that, "But, merely rejecting the proposal was not enough. The hardliners in the Bush administration wanted to add insult to injury. Instead of simply turning down the Iranian offer, the Bush Administration decided to castigate the Swiss for having delivered the proposal in the first place. Only a few days after its delivery, Washington rebuked Gulimann and the Swiss government for having overstepped their diplomatic mandate. The message to Tehran was clear—not only would the Bush Administration refuse Iran the courtesy of a reply, it would punish those who sought to convey messages between the two countries."[48] The Iran–US estrangement has been a perpetual blood feud which has gone on for more than three decades. The various nations have been witness to the conflict which is no more a phenomenon but an institution in itself. The estrangement makes life much more difficult for the Politicians and the bureaucrats in Washington as, US might find reaching and brokering a two nation solution in the Israeli-Palistinian feud and annihilate Al Qaeda and now the Islamic State/Daesh in the West Asia. The nom de plume of the conflict is also about the well pronounced leadership role in the region and Iran can no longer be counted out of the regional conflicts and the battle against Daesh, with its intertwined Shitte linkages with both the state and non state actors. In the author's view, the success of the recently inked nuclear agreement with the

United States might stick or not but the centrality of the Iran factor and the attached American role in the region remain as the twin signposts of diplomacy in the region. With the ISIS emerging as the new state and terror actor in the region, United States and Soviet Union are on the verge of collaborating to counter the threat of Daesh. The same can be surmised as a forecast that keeping in view the rational approach of President Obama in the region with US carving out its conditions of behaviour on Israel, Iran and US can eschew their traditional mutual hatred and suspicion.

One can gauge that how the trends of the Iran and the "Other" confrontation have developed down to a much mellower shade. Iran's President, Hassan Rouhani in December 2015 contended that "The Islamic people all around the Globe and the Moslem nations in West Asia need to be more rational. They ought to castigate the activities of the Islamic State in Iraq, Syria and the world over. The people ought to be realise that it is our duty to correct the image of Islam in the world Public Opinion. Did we ever think that instead of enemies an albeit small group from the Islamic world using the language of Islam would present it as the religion of killing, violence and injustice?"[49]

It can be said that now a modernising Iran under the leadership of Hassan Rouhani does not perceive any strength in the argument of the conservatives and the Ultra conservatives led by Ahmadinejad. The Iranians also do not foresee any political and strategic gains in keeping their nation as an insular security state. Iran no longer perceives any gains by competition with Saudi Arabia based on religion in places such as Yemen, Lebanon and the Allawite regions in Syria. Though Iran supports the Shiite movements all across the West Asian firmament, the fervour of a religious zealot is not the characteristic of the Iran's diplomacy. Similarly, the reformists credo of aligning with Russia, Turkey Iraq and most importantly United States of America, happens to be the much followed strain of thought in a modernizing Iran which bodes well for West Asia.

NOTES

1. "The Iranian Hostage Crisis", URL: http://www.pbs.org/wgbh/americanexperience/features/general-article/carter-hostage-crisis/ (Online: Web), Accessed on April 10, 2014
2. Ibid.
3. "Iran Hostage Crisis: Fast Facts", URl: http://edition.cnn.com/2013/09/15/world/meast/iran-hostage-crisis-fast-facts/ (Online: Web), Accessed on 10 April, 2014.
4. "Decades Later Iran Hostage Crisis Still Haunts US Iranian Relations", URL: http://www.dw.de/decades-later-hostage-crisis-still-haunts-us-iranian-relations/a-17574943, (Online: Web), Accessed on April 19, 2014.
5. Gerald T Mclaughlin, Ludwick A Tacklaff, "The Iran Hostage Agreements: A Legal Analysis", *Fordham International Law Journal*, Volume 4, Number 2, 1980-81.
6. Ibid.

7. Ibid. 1.
8. United States Diplomatic and Consular Staff in Tehran (United States of America VS Iran) URL: http://www.icj-cij.org/docket/index.php?sum=334&p1=3&p2=3&case=64&p3=5 (Online: Web), Accessed on 19 June, 2015.
9. Ibid.
10. "Iran Asks UN to act on US Ban on New Ambassador", URL: http://www.euronews.com/newswires/2463684-iran-protests-at-un-committee-on-envoy-ban-as-us-stands-ground/ (Online; Web), Accessed on June 19, 2015.
11. Andrew Roberts, "The Case for Pre-emptive War: From Goliath to the Dardenelles," *Wall Street Journal,* 30 April, 2013.
12. Jeremy Black, "The War of 1812 in the Age of Napolean," (University of Oklahoma Press, 2014)
13. United Nations Charter, "Chapter VII: Action with Reference to Threats To the Peace, Breaches of the Peace and Acts of Aggression", URL: http://www.un.org/en/documents/charter/chapter7.shtml (Online: Web), Accessed on May 19, 2015.
14. "The Iranian Red Line", *Indian Express,* 26th November, 2012.
15. Ibid.
16. Shaul Bakhash, "Iran's Foreign Policy Under The Islamic Republic, 1979-200", (L. Brown (Ed.), Diplomacy in the Middle East: The International Relations of Regional and Outside powers," London: I.B. Tauris, 2001, pp. 247-58.
17. Ibid.
18. Ibid 1.
19. William O. Beeman, "Double Demons: Cultural Impedance in US-Iranian Understanding", (Iranian Journal of International Affairs, 2-3) (1990): 319-34.
20. Ibid.
21. "What would happen if Israel bombed Iran's Nuclear Plants", URL: http://www.guardian.co.uk/world/shortcuts/2012/nov/04/israel-bombed-iran-nuclear-plants (Online: Web), Accessed on 10 December, 2012.
22. Including the threat of nuclear attack on Iran ("all options are on the table").
23. Mary Ellen O'Connell, "The Myth of Preemptive Self-Defense", *The American Society of International Law Task Force on Terrorism,* (August 2002).
24. Ilian Ben Zion, "10,000 will Die if Israel Attacks Iran, Says Former Revolutionary Guard Commander", *The Times of Israel,* October 8, 2012.
25. Ibid.
26. Reuters, "Tensions Over Iraq Strike Hit Boiling Point and Threaten to Put US Israeli Relations into Crisis", URL: http://news.nationalpost.com/2012/09/11/tensions-over-iran-strike-hit-boiling-point-threaten-to-throw-u-s-israeli-relations-into-crisis/, (Online: Web), Accessed on 19 June, 2015.
27. See *National Post,* 12 September, 2012.
28. Ibid.
29. "Jokes Buddha", URL: http://www.jokebuddha.com/joke/An_Arab_diplomat_visiting_1#ixzz29wFsEYC3 (Online: Web), Accessed on April 1, 2014.
30. "Ben Affleck New Movie Argo is a harsh reminder of Iran-US Relations", URL: http://www.policymic.com/articles/16415/ben-affleck-new-movie-argo-is-a-harsh-reminder-of-us-iran-relations (Online: Web), Accessed on April 19, 2015.
31. Ibid.

32. "Why Iran wants US to Argo Itself", URL: http://www.huffingtonpost.com/d-parvaz/why-iran-wants-hollywood-_b_3018416.html (Online: Web), Accessed on 1 April, 2015.
33. Ibid.
34. Frud Behzan, "Iranians Go Online to Vent Anger After Cut in Gasoline Subsidies," URL: http://www.rferl.org/content/iranians-go-online-to-vent-anger-after-cut-in-gasoline-subsidies-/25362703.html (Online: Web), Accessed on 19 June, 2015.
35. Ibid.
36. Mohammad Davari, "Iranian's Rouhani's First Political Defeat", *Dawn*, 26 April, 2014.
37. See *The Economist*, June, 2014.
38. Same as 35.
39. Carnegie Endowment For Peace, Televised Discussion, "Can Rouhani Change Iran?" October 11, 2013.
40. Ibid.
41. "The Historic Deal that will Prevent Iran from Acquiring a Nuclear Weapon", URL: https://www.whitehouse.gov/issues/foreign-policy/iran-deal (Online: Web), Accessed on June, 2015.
42. Ibid.
43. Ibid. 1.
44. Oren Dorell, "Iran Nuclear Deal: What Each Side Won and Lost", *USA Today*, July, 14, 2015.
45. Ibid.
46. Trita Parsi," A Single Roll of the Dice: Obama's Diplomacy with Iran," (Yale University Press, 2012), p. 1.
47. Ibid., pp. 2-3.
48. Ibid., p. 5.
49. *Indian Express Report*, December 28, 2015.

13

The New Winds of Change: Post-Cold War American Foreign Policy

Introduction

> "*Born into a New age, we are, witnessing the crass vicissitudes of past rivalries being thrown away into the heap and rubble of History.*"
>
> —**Author of this Book**

The United States Foreign Policy has followed a quintessential trajectory in its chequered odyssey since the last few decades. The framework which underpins it can be conveniently divided into four time frames: the Cold War era, the post-Cold War era and the post-September 11 era along with the post-economic recession in the contemporary times.

These lines should also remain and it is already a summary of the thing. Thus, for the Americans, the end of the Cold War was a phenomenal victory with long ranging positives, where-in the contours of the international system were transformed for ever. The perennial American bugbear of the Soviet Union had collapsed and a new threat had to be tackled which soon developed in the form of the amorphous and amorous threat of global terror fuelled by an extremist and fundamentalist wing of 'insurgents'.

Thus, one of the primordial concerns of the post-Cold War US policy has been the "GWOT", the Global War on Terror.

All the details of the GWOT (Global War on Terror) as advanced by the 2002 National Security Strategy of United States, came to the fore with the idea of countering the global extent of the terror outfit, Al Qaeda. The bombings of

USS Cole and the American embassy in Tanzania woke up the American establishment as to the cascading and the boomeranging impact of the menace of the Global terror apparatus which had the possibility of turning nuclear. There were concerns raised in the decade of the nineties that certain non state actors could attain access to the discarded and insecure nuclear weapons of the erstwhile Soviet Union.

Thus, with the advent of the idiom of convergence, globalization and economic interdependence, United States, was invited to occupy the international saddle as a reluctant power. After the fall of the Soviet influence, the inter state low intensity conflicts along with ethnic cleavages all across the international firmament, came up in the system. A power vacuum was created by the collapse of Soviet Union which had to see a replacement in certain regions of the world. With the United States fresh from its success from the war in Iraq, US appeared as an amenable power to lead the global struggles. In the author's view, it was a historical coincidence which the Americans found themselves to be involved in.

Numerous academics have written about the unipolarity in world politics where, the paucity of a balancing out of United States has been repeatedly pointed out and the question has been partially answered by the rise of China as a replacement for the former Soviet Union though in a more of a competitive–accommodative framework. Christopher Layne writes "The conventional wisdom among U.S. grand strategists is that U.S. hegemony is exceptional—that the United States need not worry about other states engaging in counter hegemonic balancing against it. The case for U.S. hegemonic exceptionalism, however, is weak. Contrary to the predictions of Waltzian balance of power theorists, no new great powers have emerged since the end of the Cold War to restore equilibrium to the balance of power by engaging in hard balancing against the United States—that is, at least, not yet. This has led primacists to conclude that there has been no balancing against the United States."[1] In the current context, the new-found and the "New World Order" dominance of United States has been challenged by the rising multipolarity of the global comity of nations. The rise of multiple centres of powers including the Asia-Pacific and China have bedevilled the singularity of an omniscient United States of America.

The US should have realised the logic of "With Great power comes great responsibility". It is here that the United States intervenes to restore hope, order and tranquillity. US has since been engaged in its role as a balancer nation.

The Last Man Walking

Francis Fukuyama coined the phrase, the "End of History and the Last Man". He dwelt upon the capitulation of Communism. He also wrote about the rise to ascendancy of the norm and the way of life of liberal democracy. The battle had been won over by the United States and the arch-rival, the former Soviet Union, had been disabled, but newer challenges were soon in the offing. Francis Fukuyama asserts in his work that, "As I have mentioned before that Karl Marx has the idea that there would be the rule of proletariat and that would be the end of the history, but, there rose another idea these days. It is the idea of liberal democracy. The world order was transforming towards democracy and communism had collapsed to a great extent. The world is moving towards what we in the West, consider decent and humane political institutions—that is, Liberal democracy."[2] This view had raised a great deal of controversy and debate in the academia and amongst the sphere of International Relations scholars and observers. Later on, Francis Fukuyama too commented upon the new post-cold war challenges of fundamentalism, terrorism, religious and ethnic codes and challenges pertaining to politics in the post-Cold War era which have earned him critical acclaim. Thus, the de rigueur narrative of the post-Cold War era, has, been written anew by him.[3]

All in all, the collapse of Communism along with that of the Berlin Wall led to the development of a new ethos in which involved the long standing strategy of containment. No eternal foe, existed as the Great 'Soviet' Bear as the American conservatives called the Soviet Union and no longer did Soviet Union exist as a physical and a standing tangible threat. The people learned that the Iron Curtain had symbolically fallen and the initiation of liberal democracy had taken place in an American-led international system. Thus, the idea of American preponderance through the futuristic instrumentality of American unipolarity, became the driving idiom and the order of the day. Thus, the tides of international politics had changed with the advent of a Liberal Democratic order in the aftermath of the fall of the Soviet Empire.

Francis Fukuyama writes, "In watching the flow of events over the past decade or so, it is hard to avoid the feeling that something very fundamental has happened in world history. The past year has seen a flood of articles commemorating the end of the Cold War, and the fact that 'peace' seems to be breaking out in many regions of the world. Most of these analyses lack any larger conceptual framework for distinguishing between what is essential and what is contingent or accidental in world history, and are predictably superficial."[4] Thus, in the author's view, Fukuyama insisted upon the centrality of a 'real' theoretical framework which could lead to the development of a new theoretical re-look and an international relations paradigm. Peace-building, too, came into prominence in the realm of the new-found international realities in the structure of the international system with tall claims being made about the advent of a new era in the global system and conflict resolution.

Fukuyama further wrote, "What we may be witnessing is not just the end of the Cold War, or the passing of a particular period of post-war history, but the end of history as such: that is, the end point of mankind's ideological evolution and the universalization of Western liberal democracy as the final form of human government."[5] Thus, in the author's view, the ideological significance of the fall of the Soviet Union too earmarks a significant standpoint in the entire rubric of the discussion. In the author's perception, the event signified the full-blown ascendance of liberal democracy with the internationalist role of United States coming to the fore in all its trail-blazing sheen and glitter with the age-old messianic zeal assuming a full frontal charge and significance in the global geo-security dynamics.

Fukuyama says, "The end of history will be a very sad time. The struggle for recognition, the willingness to risk one's life for a purely abstract goal, the worldwide ideological struggle that called forth daring, courage, imagination, and idealism, will be replaced by economic calculation, the endless solving of technical problems, environmental concerns, and the satisfaction of sophisticated consumer demands. In the post historical period there will be neither art nor philosophy, just the perpetual care taking of the museum of human history. I can feel in myself, and see in others around me, a powerful nostalgia for the time when history existed. Such nostalgia, in fact, will continue to fuel competition and conflict even in the post historical world for some time to come. Even though I recognize its inevitability, I have the most ambivalent feelings for the civilization that has been created in Europe since 1945, with its north Atlantic and Asian offshoots. Perhaps this very prospect of centuries of boredom at the end of history will serve to get history started once again."[6] The scholars will refer to the development of the end of a grand narrative, where the established nature of the historicity of the international system will wither away and the development of the paradigm of multipolarity will take its place and bloom further. As has been witnessed, in the author's view, the rising importance of the Conference of Parties climate change negotiations, is an apt reminder that what Fukuyama had forecasted, has already happened. The COP-21 consensus between nations arrived at including the responsibility of the developed world to train the developing nations in Climate change mitigation, adaptation and funding mechanisms, has seen the efflorescence of the new post ideological times. The same post cold war consensus emanates in the form of the consensus to tackle terrorism with an urgent need to define it in 2015 after a spate of terror attacks in 2015.

The post-Cold War era has witnessed the development that post nation ethnicities too have reared their heads. The idioms of self determination and separatism, have come to the fore, along with a localized and unsynchronized narrative of spatially located conflict zones of the world. The narrative also includes new developments in the post-Cold War era, where-in, the idea of the decreased regularity of large scale and full-fledged conflicts will usher in a peaceful condition in the international system. In the author's view, a globalisation-ordained and 'non-state-centri-territoriality' will evolve in the post cold war world, with ethnic concerns coming to global prominence.

Jan Lodal argues, "With the end of the Cold War, most Americans stopped thinking about Nuclear weapons. They assumed that such weapons were now of little use and that Washington would soon sensibly wrap up any problems in the nuclear arena."[7] Still, with the fall of the Soviet Union, the United States realised the reduced but still potent conditionality of Russia. At the core of Lodal's vision lies a reaffirmation of deterrence rather than defence as the central principle of US nuclear strategy. Lodal notes that the United States in a reduced high-wire European context can reduce the number and girth of the land-based intercontinental missiles and base its deterrence strategy on a second-strike capability of roughly a thousand highly survivable weapons based on bombers and in submarines.[8] The idea of a national reduction of the ICBMs has been well documented and the necessity of the sustenance of only the surgical and tactical weapons is one idea which is now being stressed upon by observers and scholars alike in the United States.

The China factor too has to be diligently factored vis-à-vis the US foreign policy's fundamental moorings in the twenty-first century. Robert Jervis says, "The Chinese threat has to be justified not as a menace of a tangible variety such as that posed to the United States during the Cold war era but rather from the American commitment to Taiwan, which is a matter of choice rather than necessity. NATO'S expansion and its European commitments have hardly been required by traditional conceptions of security. In designing a post cold war nuclear strategy, one must be concerned by asking not only what nuclear weapons can do, but what the United States can do."[9] Thus, a new paradigm in the post-Cold War era was that of 'Splitist international relations', where-in, the localised conflicts were drummed up and America marched on to newer engagements in the European context and elsewhere in the decades of the nineties and the twenty-first century.

Richard Hass too proposes that, "It has been several years, since the end of the Cold War and still there is no name for the present era, much less a US foreign policy to replace the obsolete doctrine of containment. The book titled as *The Reluctant Sheriff* fills that void. It can be discussed as the first work to delve inside the global dynamics of the post cold war era in the then changed ramifications of the entire global system[10]... In the author's view, new approach termed as 'Regulation' can be earmarked for US Foreign Policy, where-in, United States could work to promote order in an unruly world. Americans can contest the idea of isolationism and maintain spending on defence, intelligence, foreign aid and diplomacy at current levels."

Thus, the American Overarch as a benign hegemon was what the Doctor ordered for the day, which, in a way, was not an imposition, but, the need of the hour. During the same decade of the nineties, the United Nations too was too on a rebuild, so the American idea had to be reformulated and recalibrated in the various regions of the international system. The fundamentals of the peace-building and peace-making mechanisms were being redone through the efforts of the interested and pro-active United Nations Secretary-Generals such as Kofi Annan.

Tudor Onea states, "Strategists assumed the United States would practice a restrained foreign hand by the modicum of the sparing use of force, multilateral diplomacy and a reduction of military commitments abroad. However, the Sheriff nation opted for the reverse course of action, where-in, it marked its actions by assertiveness, foreign interventions and unilateral action."[11] The internally felt need to maintain the global pontiff's role and the avatar as a world leader had to persist with the interventions undertaken by the United States of America. Thus, emerged, an American-led global move, against the idea of Islamic fundamentalism and the various fissiparous non-state actors in the decade of the nineties. The American ideal of manifest destiny still reverberated as the key idiom of the entire post-Cold War era. It unfolded with the denouement of Iraq's incursion into the principality of Kuwait, the sanction regime imposed upon Saddam Hussein along with the various incidents and conflicts in Central Europe. The idiom of Manifest Destiny is another US foreign policy percept which made a dainty comeback in the post-Cold War times despite the talk abounding about the withdrawal of the American Overarch and power. It is not that it is only the modernist tenets of liberal democracy, marketisation and democratisation which led to the persistence of the American interventionist zeal. All of it is already enmeshed in the founding myth of the American Republic which has been avidly reinstated in the fulcrum of the nation's myth and lore. John L. Súllivan writes, "America is destined for better deeds. It is our unparalleled glory that we have no reminiscences of battle fields, but in defence of humanity, of the oppressed of all nations, of the rights of conscience, the rights of personal enfranchisement. Our annals describe no scenes of horrid carnage, where men were led on by hundreds of thousands to slay one another, dupes and victims to emperors, kings, nobles, demons in the human form called heroes. We have had patriots to defend our homes, our liberties, but no aspirants to crowns or thrones; nor have the American people ever suffered themselves to be led on by wicked ambition to depopulate the land, to spread desolation far and wide, that a human being might be placed on a seat of supremacy."[12] Thus, the anointed nature of the American nation as the 'select' county, which became great not due to a singular motif of religious sanction and Fore Majore,[13] but, also due to the entrepreneurship and the hard-working ethos of a market nation with its own localised ideals of community and nationhood, remains deeply embalmed in the America's national make-up. This very much defines the grandiloquent American Dream on a crest of world civilization.

Sullivan further writes, "The far-reaching, the boundless future, will be the era of American greatness. In its magnificent domain of space and time, the nation of many nations is destined to manifest to mankind the excellence of divine principles; to establish on earth the noblest temple ever dedicated to the worship of the Most High—the Sacred and the True. Its floor shall be a hemisphere its roof the firmament of the star-studded heavens, and its congregation an Union of many Republics, comprising hundreds of happy millions, calling, owning no man master, but governed by God's natural and moral law of equality, the law of brotherhood of 'peace and good will amongst men'."[14] All in all, on second thoughts, the construct of religion still echoed largely in the American myth but the idea of 'Universalis Civitas' loomed large over the skyline of the fast-industrialising nation. The 'truism of being true' to the concerns of mankind and higher intangible ideals, still resonated through the terrain of the American Dream. The issues of ethics, morality and international goodwill, were still the founding stone of the nation as it was rebuilding and recasting it in the name of assuming greater global roles for the future in a world. The future world needed an International actor which could act as a modulator and a benign benefactor for the rest of the international system. The American Dream maintains that United States is a special nation which might be realistically contested, but going by a nationalistic and patriotic popular assumption, US goes by the idea of being a human actor on the international stage. The nation is imbued with the literature and cultural depictions of being just and responsible which might be a tough objective to be attained by any nation on a pathway to development in the middle of the intervening global developments.

The sobriquet of being an 'arm-twisting and sabre rattling nation' does not do justice to a nation founded on higher morals and ethics, which choose to stay away from the entangling alliances of the European context. US had to do otherwise when a confused United Nations and other great powers were not in a position to deliver the global goods. In the author's view, the founding fathers of the United States maintain that the nation worked for the larger humanity and thus, entered the need for interventions though besmirched with the rationale of "Realist" and national interest oriented international system, which US too is a part of. The American nation has been regularly ridiculed, lampooned and criticised for helping besieged nations which are either failed or are failing. The world suffers from a want of helping nations and leaders which is a role which responsible nations such as US can take up in the light of the low intensity conflicts and sovereignty struggles enveloping parts of the international system.

Frederick C. Cuny writes in one his reports for PBS, "Perhaps more important, there will be opportunities to make fundamental changes in the international humanitarian architecture. Major flaws in the United Nations system can be corrected, new organizations can be created to reach groups of victims who heretofore have been untouchable, and the larger powers can focus their energies on trying to stem the growing tide of human rights abuses, separatist wars, and ethnic conflicts that have proliferated in recent years."[15] New challenges had cropped up in the international system, with neo-liberalism has come to the fore as the new mantra for the contemporary times. The United Nations, as the foremost international organisation, was being thoroughly tested in the times to come since the decade of the nineties. The European crises exploded one after another with NATO and the Western European nations being called upon to perform the duty of global balancers and regional fire fighters with United States coming to the fore in the role of the "benign" hegemon. It was deftly working as a nation being called to carry on the dirty and flak inviting task of humanitarian tasks in the form of its 'interventions and intrusions' which were unfortunately ridiculed and criticised in the global comity of nations.

Frederick Cuny further writes, "The use of Western troops to create a safe haven to permit the repatriation of the Kurdish refugees and the willingness of the US to forcibly impose restraints on the Iraqi government to prevent it from killing its own people, demonstrated what could be done when all the necessary pre-requisites converge. Even as Operation Provide Comfort ended, there were calls for similar military-civilian interventions in Yugoslavia, the Caucasus, and Somalia." It was an interesting and challenging epoch in the fundamentals of the international structure of power relations and expected responsibilities of the great powers. The United States had not emerged out of the Vietnam syndrome which posited that America had been politically and strategically humbled militarily at the hands of a determined but a primordial foe, which had resulted in ferocious criticism in the domestic sphere. Also, the idea arose that after the American victory in the Persian Gulf War I in connection with Iraq and Kuwait, the nation's confident spirit made a quick comeback with the one sided defeat of Saddam Hussein in Iraq. After the Vietnam war, United States suffered from a lack of credibility about its power and might, which the American military victory in Iraq changed to a great extent. The syndrome has been often mentioned in the annals of American contemporary history which points towards a questioning of the American foreign policy decisions. The victory in Iraq in 1991 made the American establishment emerge out of the defeat in Vietnam which also coincided with the collapse of Soviet Union. In the author's view, these developments then reascertained the American self belief of intervening and changing external outcomes. This fanned the spirits of the American strategic thought which now mulled over the thought of extending in the conflict zones in the European and other immediate regional contexts. Incidentally, the Balkans erupted and the American standpoint of "humanitarian" interventions was vindicated handsomely.

Marvin Kalb writes in a Brookings Institution report that, "It is the belief, born of brutal experience during the Vietnam War, that never again will the United States gradually tiptoe into questionable wars without a clearcut objective, overwhelming military force, an endgame strategy and, most important, the support of Congress and the American people. In today's world of terrorist threat and guerrilla war, the Vietnam syndrome means, if nothing else, a fundamental reluctance to commit American military power anywhere in the world, unless it is absolutely necessary to protect the national interests of the country."[16] The immense measures of the Vietnam War were not enough to demystify and curb the Viet Cong in North Vietnam during those heady times in American history. But, the propensity to indulge in far-off lands, placing young American men and women at risk with an added burden on the state exchequer was severely criticised in the global firmament. The strategic, military and political zeal of the American interventions was questioned and the American outlandish spirit went into a slumber and with the setbacks such as the Iran contra affair and the Iran hostage crisis. As a result, the American self-confidence was at its lowest ebb after the debacle in South East Asia. The New World Order speech in the aftermath of Operation Desert Storm initiated a new era of renewed vigour and a re-invention of the American cowboy spirit in the decade of the nineties in the context of phased-out older foes and the emergence of newer ones. Thus, the bad press and the negativism abounding in the domestic firmament in United States soon dissipated as the "besieged" nation achieved a new set of priorities and objectives, in tandem with its objectives of democratisation and do-gooder spirit. One view holds that, the American Dream is about philanthropy and the do-gooder spirit of Kevin Costner's, "Robin hood: The Prince of Thieves." US, in the post cold war scenario too intends to imitate and falls in the same larger helpful and extricator framework, which enters conflicts in alien contexts. The objective being to bring back normalcy and peace in the strife torn zones in the third and first worlds. In the author's view, US has the internal strength, the military and the economic strength to manage the unstable and strife torn regions and countries of the world. The only rider is that if the suffering nations can be taken into political confidence and assured of the honesty of the American intention then the American overarch can be justified to the fullest extent.

A change was witnessed in the American grand strategy. Jeremi Suri mentions, "In December 1988, the leaders of the United States and the Soviet Union flew into the city amidst great fanfare and anticipation. President Ronald Reagan, President-elect George H.W. Bush, and Soviet Premier Mikhail Gorbachev met on Governors Island, off the southern tip of Manhattan. They were to celebrate how they had, through unprecedented arms reduction agreements and credible personal commitments to cooperation, built what Reagan called "a strong foundation for the future."[17] Thus, arms reduction served as a prelude to the military success in Operation Desert Storm which was validated by the leaders of both the superpowers. The new epoch came into being with the 'New World Order' speech by President Bush Senior after vanquishing President Bush. Both the nations made strides towards redesigning their bilateral security architecture through an agreement to reduce their nuclear arsenals.

The new world order was expected to be presided over by the United States and the world was supposed to become a less dangerous place with a dwindling away of conflicts but that didn't take place in the aftermath of the fall of the Communist dominion in Soviet Union. In the author's view, though the American strategic clash was with the Communist dispensation, but the abiding ideals of the American Dream had the innate strength in them to support the American interventions abroad going by the founding ideals of liberty, freedom and egalitarianism. President Bush Sr. in his address to the world spoke in the context of his decision to intervene in an invaded Kuwait that, "Standing up for our principle is an American tradition. As it has so many times before, it may take time and tremendous effort, but most of all, it will take unity of purpose. As I've witnessed throughout my life in both war and peace, America has never wavered when her purpose is driven by principle. And in this August day, at home and abroad, I know she will do no less. Thank you, and God bless the United States of America."[18] Thus, it was a direct justification for the ushering in of a new world order, where-in the idea of the significance of Saudi Arabia and the rest of the Persian Gulf was brought to the fore by the American President. It was mentioned that the American allies should be protected with the sanction of the United Nations and the rest of the global comity of nations.

The American Grand Strategy

The American grand strategy was inaugurated with a sternness of purpose with no fanfare attending it. The battle had to be taken to the tyrants and the dictators where-in a global guarantee of peace and tranquillity had to be imposed upon the international firmament. It was in effect a "New World Order" which was to be counted upon as a new bulwark for the American strategy in the region and the larger world. The American President added that "We are more dependent upon imported oil and are even more vulnerable to Iraqi threats. We succeeded in the struggle for freedom in Europe because we and our allies remain stalwarts. Keeping the peace in the Middle East will require no less. We're beginning a new era. This new era can be full of promise, an age of freedom, a time of peace for all peoples. But if history teaches us anything, it is that we must resist aggression or it will destroy our freedoms. Appeasement does not work."[19]

Thus, the need for a unified striving for an attainment of the global peace dividend, was reinstated, as the American grand strategy, where-in, the Global coalition had to be gathered together akin to the world wars when few obdurate forces had attempted to snatch away a victory from the forces of peace and liberal democracy. The same stint had to be redone in the West Asia, as the region was host to a vast and much needed reservoir of natural resources and most important, the "Black Gold" and a Yom Kippur-like stalemate could not be envisaged by the Americans and the rest of the West. Thus, all this necessitated a combined effort of gargantuan proportions with the lead falling into the able hands of a much vilified but able bodied international actor of the order of United States of America. In the author's view, the American positioning has always been a deft amalgamation of the national interest oriented outlook and an idealist zeal in various international situations. A nation which has emerged out of Colonial usurpation and had fought its way through a Revolution amounting to an armed revolt, can have the intrinsic values and ethics to impart to a troubled but "willing world". In the realm of foreign policy making, realism and self interest always have a significant position in decision making while the driving ideals of a nation also run parallel and get reflected in the rigmarole of global events, including wars, insurgencies, revolts and humanitarian crises. In the author's view, nations commit mistakes and can be blinded by excesses of power and global leverage and the strains of predestination enter their official vocabularies, but great and successful nations have to play significant roles in mankind's destiny.

Apart from the change in the arms control regime of the post-Cold War era between the two superpowers, a change was attempted within the rubric of the National Security Strategy of United States, too. In the quintessential tenor of the post-World War II and the Cold War era, too much of an importance was given to the military and intelligence apparatus of the United States, which began to be questioned. Carnes Lord writes, "Not long ago the fiftieth anniversary of the National Security Council came and went with little public notice and President Bill Clinton despite his commitment to reinvent the Government and to refurbish the National security agenda has shown little change in institutionalising change in this sector of governance."[20] Thus, change in the National Security architecture was a prominent voice which was aired in the aftermath of the Cold War era.

George Foster asserts, "We must seek a fuller integration of civil military, domestic-international, national supranational, government industry, air land sea and routine emergency structures and processes that now exist. Implicit in the suggestion is the proposition that the time honored term "Coordination" is inadequate to describe the central function performed by inter departmental institutions such as the NSC and NEC. Fuller integration within and across departments can be seen as a particular imperative in our post cold war era of the so-called emergencies involving more tasks, more agencies and more international actors than in the past."[21] Thus, the multiplicity of actors and the multiple claims of a large number of agencies became the sine qua non of the post-Cold War international system.

The United States realised that the instrument of invading and attacking a recalcitrant nation state actor led to other responsibilities and complexities such as national reconstruction and nation building. As an instance, "As a candidate for American Presidency, George W. Bush repeatedly criticized the Clinton Administration for its attempts at nation building. Within a few months of the attacks on the United States, however, the Bush Administration was openly acknowledging that its campaign to topple Taliban in Afghanistan would have to be accompanied by a serious effort to create a viable Afghan Government to be accompanied by a serious effort to create a viable Afghan Government and rebuild this war torn nation. Nation building it seems is not such a bad idea after all."[22]

Other concerns such as the global negotiations on Climate Change, the deliberations on the International Criminal Court and the American intransigence towards the Anti Landmines Treaty, too characterised the US difficulties in the post-Cold War era. But the re-emergence of Pakistan as a frontline state in an effort to combat the Al Qaeda and the Taliban in the besieged nation state of Afghanistan, too, characterized the new credentials of the US foreign policy. The American reluctance to share the lion's share of the burden in training, financing and equipping the developing countries in order to reduce Green House Emissions along with the idea of sharing the burden of carbon fixing, too, were significant facets of an unwanted American withdrawal and a strategic reticence to entangle in the new issues of international polity.

Finally, before the talk of the American decline and the American withdrawal became the order of the day, September 11 changed the way in which the Americans had carried on their foreign policy. Stephen M. Walt writes, "The business as usual approach of US Foreign Policy vanished on 11 September.

Instead of education reforms and tax cuts, the war on terrorism dominated the administration's agenda. The September 11 attacks were quickly traced to Al-Qaeda, whose leaders had been operating all across the global system from the nation state of Afghanistan."[23] Thus, the cost of American ambitions, had, become too high even for the most powerful and the most resourceful nation state of the international system. Thus, changes were attempted in the realm of imparting a seriousness and sincerity to the nation's foreign policy. The nation had to stop being cocooned inside its labyrinthine superstructure of an all overwhelming nuclear deterrent, along with the oceanic moats, while newer alliances and combinations, were engendered in the context of the foreign policy objectives. More had to be attempted to attract the talented personnel to join the Government service and foreign cultures had to be respected anew with the emergence of the multiple centres of power.

The United States, all in all, during the decade of the nineties, involved itself into the vortex of global polity through several actions and foreign policy decisions. It expanded the core alliances created during the Cold War era and fought a brief but intense war to subvert the expansionist proclivities of Iraq. The United States sought to make Iraq comply with the UN weapons inspection regime through a combination of economic sanctions and coercive bombings. It intervened in the civil conflicts in Haiti, Somalia, Bosnia and Kosovo and fiercely attempted to broker a peace arrangement between Israel and Palestine and strived to foster a liberal market economy through the creation of the World Trade Organization and the spawning of the North American Free Trade Association. Thus, its not all about the fall of the Soviet Union and that of the Berlin wall and the success of Operation Desert Storm, but the post-modern conditionalities of climate change, disarmament and crimes and all in all, the crimes against humanity and genocides, too, engaged the US foreign policy mandarins in an eventful, tide-changing and a yet much more complex post-Cold War era. We do not intentionally delve into the post-September 11 and a post-recession world as the ambit of a post-Cold War era would be stretched a wee-bit too long.

NOTES

1. Christopher Layne, "The Unipolar Illusion Revisited: The Coming End of the United State's Unipolar Moment", *International Security*, Fall 2006, Vol. 31, pp. 7-41.
2. Francis Fukuyama, "The End of History and the Last Man" (New York: Free Press, 2006).
3. Ibid.
4. Francis Fukuyama, "The End of History and the Last Man?" *National Interest*, Summer, 1989
5. Ibid.
6. Ibid. 1.

7. Charles Kupchan, *The End of American Era: US Foreign Policy after the Cold War* (New York: Barnes and Nobles, 2002).
8. Ibid. 1.
9. Robert Jervis, "Weapons Without Purpose? Nuclear Strategy in the Post Cold War Era, Foreign Affairs," Council on Foreign Relations, July, August, 2001
10. Richard N Hass, "The Reluctant Sheriff: United States After the Cold War", June 1988, Council on Foreign Relations,
11. Tudor Onea, *US Foreign Policy in the Post Cold War Era: Restraint Versus Assertiveness* (New York: Palgrave Macmillan, 2013).
12. John N.O. Sullivan, "The Great Nation of Futurity", *The United States Democratic Review*, Volume 6, Issue 23, pp. 426-430.
13. Force Majore is a Political Science concept which points at the use of crass power and military might by nations and leaders in order to fulfill the aims and objectives of national interest.
14. Ibid
15. Frederick C. Cuny, "Humanitarian Assistance in Post Cold War Era", URL: http://www.pbs.org/wgbh/pages/frontline/shows/cuny/laptop/coldwar.html (Online: Web), Accessed on March 1, 2015.
16. Marvin Kalb, "Its Called the Vietnam Syndrome, and Its Back", URL: http://www.brookings.edu/blogs/up-front/posts/2013/01/22-obama-foreign-policy-kalb (Online: Web), Accessed on 10 April, 2015
17. Jeremi Suri, "The Promise and the American Grand Strategy after the Cold War", URL: http://www.fpri.org/articles/2010/03/promise-and-failure-american-grand-strategy-after-cold-war (Online: Web), Accessed on May 1, 2015.
18. President George H.W. Bush, "Address on Iraq's Invasion of Kuwait August 8, 1990", URL: http://millercenter.org/scripps/archive/speeches/detail/5529 (Online: Web), Accessed on April 1, 2014.
19. Ibid,
20. Carnes Lord, "NSC reform for the Post Cold War Era," in "*Foreign Policies of the Major Powers: Politics and Diplomacy since World War II*", edited by Pauline Eadie and Llyod Pettiford (New Delhi: Viva Books, 2013), p. 339.
21. Douglas E. Lute, *Improving National Security Capacity to Respond to Complex Emergencies: The US Experience* (New York: Carnegie Commission on Preventing Deadly Conflict, 1998).
22. Stephen M. Walt, "Beyond Bin Laden: Reshaping US Foreign Policy" in *Foreign Policies of the Major Powers: Politics and Diplomacy since World War II*, edited by Pauline Eadie and Llyod Pettiford (New Delhi: Viva Books, 2013), p. 374.
23. Ibid., p. 368.

14

The Iraq and Afghanistan Conundrum: The American Standpoint is Different

Introduction

Emilo Paculi filmed a Youtube movie, titled as *Hollywood War*. The Internet movie showcases the bravado tenor of the American war efforts, the cow boyish spirit and the dominion trend of the United States, at its best and brightest sparkle. The narrative begins with a rousing speech by the American General Patton, who, is a much decorated US military legend and is a part of the nation's myth and patriotic lore. The background is served by a huge twenty-feet high and thirty-feet wide star-spangled banner, which reflects in the background and the General roars on. He says, "America never as a nation decorated losers and specially the ones who laugh after losing. We hate to lose and there has never been a war where the nation has lost. We like to be winners and victors and we love to battle it out and to be in the thick of war." This oration sets the stage for comprehending the soul of the American myth as the most powerful nation state loves to dominate and win wars and the ones which it becomes embroiled in. This is also what the American Dream is all about, that is, super puissance in the global sphere.

This is not to be concluded as a hypothesis, that, United States is a war mongering nation state, which has a genetic inclination for vanquishing all kinds of foes, in all kinds of far off lands. The Star Track lingo of, "Where No Man has gone before", need not be misread and misinterpreted as a tale of United States establishments and war rooms being the epicentre of war mongering and unnecessary military action over unsuspecting inferior foes. Realism ordains domination, but, it has always been undercut and buttressed by a rationale of great power responsibility and the global veneer of being a responsible nation state. The nation has been circumstanced with an additional global burden to regulate and involve itself in causes of Global governance and "forced-on policing" of the international system. In the author's view, *If they are not there, then, who will do the dirty work of maintaining order and pelf and managing Justice rendering? Anarchy and global pandemonium, is the natural consequence of an American disinterest.*

The entire discussion on American interventions in Iraq, can, be divided into three time periods: the American role in the Iran–Iraq war during the eighties and the Persian Gulf Wars I and II in 1991 and 2003. Thus, the American involvement in Iraq is part of the larger framework of United States foreign policy in West Asia. The American support and supplies to Saddam Hussein in his battle against Iran was the initial cornerstone of the intervention and the American interest which was very much served by thus balancing the Iranian claim to Islamic dominion in West Asia. Thus, the support for Iraq was initiated by the United States as a kind of containment of the dictatorial Regime in the region by propping up Iraq as a powerful and aggressive claimant to the seat of pelf and as the leader of the nations in the Islamic world. The theme of the American engagement in Iran has already been dealt with in one of the preceding sections of the work. The onus of this segment would lie with the American involvement in Iraq in both the Gulf Wars which had far reaching consequences for the rest of the international system and the coalition of actors. The trick being not to negate the American wars in Iraq as a bland and direct tool to usurp the Oil resources in Iraq but it is rather important to station the American interventions as an instrument of global responsibility and as part of a larger zeal of liberal democratization in the global polity. This is an issue which stands much randomized and ridiculed by alternative opinion makers in the realm of international affairs and elsewhere. The debate about Iraq being important for the Americans only because of Oil, is a rather simplistic and too much of a scientific and rational reading of the situation. Though, materially directed, the usurpation of West Asia by a Dictatorial Regime would have served to defeat the purpose of a Democratic space in the region. Also, the threat which a tyrannical ruler posed to the peace in the region is another reason why Oil should not be intellectually advanced as the sole and imminently understandable, visible raison D etre for the war in Iraq.

The Mesopotamian Morass: Iraq Challenged

Dexter Filkins in his national bestseller, the *Forever War,* has written an evocative, first-hand account of the war in Iraq, much before the emergence of Daesh in the land. The descriptions make for a poignant and illuminating illustration of the grime and the dusty specks of a bloody war. For an instance, the battle of Fallujah in November 2004 meant the end of insurgency in the terrain in and around the town, which was besieged by terror outfits. The following is an excerpt from the book: "The Marines were pressed flat on a rooftop when the dialogue began to unfold. The minarets were flashing by the lights of airstrikes and rockets were sailing on trails of sparks. First came the voices from the minarets over the American thunder[1]... The Americans are here. The Holy War! The Holy War! Get up and fight for the city of Mosques. These voices bellowed from the loudspeakers of the minarets where the insurgents thought that they would be untouched as they were fighting from a religious place."[2] Thus, the battle was getting trickier and trickier with the idea of minarets being the shelters for the insurgents. The Marines in their free time listened to a loud rendition of the Australian band, AC/DC and its song, *Hell Bells* which intoned the songs of Satan and the grand and dark evil personified. The Marines used to enjoy the tintinnabulation of the church bells as part of the background score of the AC/ DC number.

Thus, we reach the idea of the American Dream which propelled Church going, sporty boys, to leave their girlfriends and sunny schools in order to serve their country which was also a respected vocation for them like national duty. Its not a plane jane democratization mission but the salvo is the one of the "Good and Acceptable" which is being lobbed at, "the Bad and the desecrated" which might be misunderstood due to the personalized comprehension of the American Dream. That ought to make the domesticated American Dream much more acceptable and universal in nature! The only exception to the rule is that the order of God, Country and family changes but the continuum exemplified by the triad remains indelibly etched in the nation's psyche. The nation does not domineer nor thus it run amuck like a dragon captured in a closed Victorian house. The nation balances out the strength of Good over the bad and the ugly! Its all very evident and true in the context of Iraq and the sacrifices of the American forces delivering the goods through its vastly inexperienced but talented and dedicated GI's. Not quite Polemic as yet and nor even the mysterious homilics! Esotcric it might be.

An eyewitness and a much celebrated account of Iraq war can be cited here which has wide-ranging ramifications for the art of war and for living it up, the American way. It is once again very much about the grandiloquent American Dream as asserted before in the book's narrative. Chris Kyle, a decorated sniper who participated with glory in the Iraq war, too, writes an evocative account on the war in Iraq. He writes in the introduction to his Book, American Sniper, "They love to call me as a bad ass, abad ol' boy and a sniper for the SEALS. In the end, my story is not about killing enemies only or fighting evil. Its also about being a man and being true to one's love and one's hatred in personal relationships."[3] The notion that only bad characters join the army as they can kill with impunity, is a misdeed in thought and writing as smart soldiers and officers are required to defend the nation, its assets and finally the all significant homeland. Chris Kyle argues and confesses candidly that, "You shoot an enemy once and when he comes into your visor, you get nervous as the feeling you get is that why to kill another human. But, once you have killed a few, you understand that you are doing it for your countrymen."[4]

Chris Kyle, the celebrated American sniper further relates about a rescue act he did which was normally unwarranted of a sniper working for the Marines, GROMS and the Seals. He writes, "The insurgents began focussing their fire on me. I tucked my MK-11 under my arm and fired back as I ran. The semi automatic is a great, versatile weapon, but in this particular situation, its twenty round magazine seemed awfully small. I blew through one mag, popped the release, slammed in a second and kept firing. At some point, as I ran to the lying Marine, one insurgent threw a frag. The grenade exploded somewhere nearby. Pieces of wall peppered my side, from my butt cheek down to my knee. By some lucky chance, my pistol took the biggest fragment. It was sheer luck or else there might have been a hole in my leg. My butt was sore for a while, but it continues to work well for the while."[5]

The global scepticism and criticism of the American policy in Iraq can be delved into with some of the views of the observers of international affairs. It has been contended by Paul R. Pillar that, "The most extraordinary aspect of George W. Bush's administration's launching of a war in March 2003 was the absence of any apparent procedure for determining whether that the war was a good idea. There was not a poor policy process or an incomplete one or a biased one, there was no policy process. Investigative reporters down the years have found no meetings, no policy papers, no debate in the White House situation room, or anything else that addressed that whether the war in Iraq was in the US interests or not as an input to a Presidential decision on whether to invade or not."[6] Thus, the opinion of one segment of the global observers was that the United States did not have a clear war rationale for entering into both the Persian Gulf Wars. In the second Gulf War, which was launched in March 19, 2003, the war rationale as advanced by White House was that Saddam Hussein was sheltering Al Qaeda which included their diminutive leader Osama bin Laden and that Iraq was linked to the sponsoring machine of global terrorism through Al Qaeda and the Weapons of Mass Destruction (WMD).

Also, another allegation which was utilised by the White House war room was that Iraq was on its way to the creation of a stockpile of weapons of mass destruction in the chemical, biological and nuclear mould. The Iraqi excesses amounted to genocidal proportions in Northern Iraq populated by Kurds, where in towns such as Halabja, scores of sleeping Kurdish villages were decimated with their entire populations. Thus, the human rights record of the Saddam Hussein regime was also a cause of concern for the Western community including the United States which after the September 11 attacks on the World Trade Towers was concerned about its homeland security. The American alarm had reached a calamitous proportion as the enemies had attacked the heart of the American system in a suicidal yet effective enunciation of their cause celebre. Soon, the September 11 attacks acquired a Pearl Harbor-like pedestal in the itinerary of American reverses in the gamut of American military, political and cultural history.

The critics were out to hound the American juggernaut in Iraq and the attendant Mesopotamian wastes. The Deputy Secretary of State, Richard Armitage, when asked after leaving office whether the process for making war on Iraq war was warped replied, "There was never any policy to break by Condi Rice or anyone else. There never was one from the start, Bush didn't want one, for whatever reason."[7] Still, the contrary school of thought represented by the personages of the order of Dick Cheney, Donald Rumsfeld and Richard Pearle, reflected a contradictory subset of the American foreign policy thought, which was much more in the mould of the neoconservative strategic school of thought. For instance, since the terrorist attacks on the USS Cole and the American embassy in Tanzania, till the Boston marathon bomb attack in 2013, the PNAC or the Project on New American Century, ruled the roost in the State Department. In this connection, even the doves in the policymaking process were not able to make a dent in the entire rubric of the US policy in Iraq in both the Gulf wars. The chairman of the Senate Foreign Relations Committee, Richard Lugar, went ahead to order a rethink on the US decision to enter Iraq and augment the strength of the combat forces in the nation. The bipartisanship was still being reflected by some older and traditional segments of the American Senate as a fresh whiff of air in the larger American legislative firmament, which is now in the 21st century prone to lewd partisanship.

The Project on New American Century, is a much deliberated subject matter which makes for a brief reference for the comprehension of the US Policy in Iraq. The PNAC can be elucidated through one of the sources; "Established in the spring of 1997 and funded largely by the energy and arms industries, the *Project for the New American Century* was founded as the neoconservative think tank whose stated goal was to usher in a 'new American century'. Having won the Cold War and no military threat to speak of, this group of ideologues created a blueprint for the future whose agenda was to capitalize upon our surplus of military forces and funds and forcing American hegemony and corporate privatization throughout the world."[8]

In their statement of principles PNAC ideologues outline a fourfold agenda:

1. Increase an already enormous military budget at the expense of domestic social programs.
2. Toppling of regimes resistant to our corporate interests.
3. Forcing democracy at the barrel of a gun in regions that have no history of the democratic process.[9]
4. Replacing the UN's role of preserving and extending international order.[10]

Thus, this was not the official policy of the Bush establishment but its persistence was interpreted by some of the international affairs observers as the real backbone of the US policy in Iraq and West Asia. Thus, the idea was that the United States cobbled up a coalition of the willing in the first case study in 1990, when Iraq invaded Kuwait to oust the royalty there. The United States with a United Nations sanction intervened in Kuwait and liberated the oil royalty from Saddam Hussein's clutches. Then, the international community exercised a slew of sanctions upon the Baghdad regime in the form of trade and oil blockades and no-fly zones in order to soften up the adversarial opposition of Iraq. Israel too supported the American line of thinking in this context. The weapons inspectors of the International Atomic Energy (IAEA) led by Mohammad Al Baradei and Scott Ritter soon gave "a near-to-clean-chit" to Iraq's WMD programme, which it was believed, had been surreptitiously shifted to Syria during the heydays of the conflict. Thus, the entire set of developments led to the scenario that the US had to bring about a regime change in order to a initiate a post-Saddam Hussein and nation-building and reconstruction process through the receptacle of itself and the rest of the Western allies. Still, the debate about the efficacy of the White House's war rationale was severely questioned by the US mainstream media and the global opinion-makers alike. An avid anti-war movement on the lines of the Vietnam War protests developed in the US (though on a much lesser scale as compared to the sixties' counter-culture movement).

Also, the intervening years for the population in Iraq was one of suffering and misery like Iran later on, as elaborate sanctions had been heaped upon the nation. Iraq was dilly dallying in its decisions to give a free hand to the weapons inspectors and the larger American interests. Sanctions definitely had a debilitating impact upon the way of life in Iraq that needs to form part and parcel of an academic discussion. The *New York Times* has reported, utilising the United Nations sources, that child deaths were recorded as a result of the West-sponsored sanctions. The *New York Times* reports, "As many as 576,000 Iraqi children may have died since the end of the Persian Gulf war because of economic sanctions imposed by the Security Council, according to two scientists who surveyed the country for the Food and Agriculture Organization. The study also found steeply rising malnutrition among the young, suggesting that more children will be at risk in the coming years. The results of the survey appeared too in the *Lancet,* the journal of the British Medical Association."[11] Cases of malnutrition and stunting of growth of children were reported by the population in Iraq, when the blame was diverted the way of American sanctions. The *New York Times* report further adds, "The percentage of Iraqi children affected by 'wasting', or emaciation requiring urgent attention, rose to 12 percent in 1995, from 3 percent in 1991, and it was reported, adding that these figures are extraordinarily high, similar to those found in Malagasy and Myanmar. Several United Nations agencies, including F.A.O. and UNICEF, have expressed concern about the damage being done to Iraqis, especially children, by United Nations economic sanctions."[12] Thus, sections from the international organisations groups falling under the ambit of the United Nations and other allied agencies mouthed these concerns about the emaciated and 'suffering' children in Iraq after Persian Gulf War-I. The American viewpoint had a different pronouncement up its sleeves, which can also be enumerated as the American defence of the sanctions despite the humanitarian complaints of some segments of the international opinion. The rationale of crime and punishment, can be regarded as one of the reasons d'etre of the entire exercise of the sanctions being imposed upon Iraq. In the author's view, war is one retribution which can be used for treating recalcitrant nations. Tangible and material military measures lead to misery and perdition for populations and also result in a great deal of collateral damage. If collateral damage which is much pointed out by the global community, has to be minimized, a non military instrument of containment has to be utilized. This can be the economic sanctions which at least do not cause material and dehumanized damage and casualties to the enemy state. Thus, one can arrive at the efficacy of plane jane sanctions instead of supplying boots on grounds in alien lands. The strategy amounts to "smart diplomacy" with least global fuss.

Professor Lucas has mentioned in defence of the American sanctions, "In the first place, if Saddam had been allowed to get away with one iota of his aggression towards Kuwait, it would have been only the first step to his domination of the Gulf region, and perhaps the Middle East more broadly. One should note that if he had got his hands on Kuwaiti oil and Saudi oil, in addition to what Iraq had, he would have controlled no less than 40% of the world's oil reserves. The reasons for Desert Storm being called off when it was were equally compelling. The United Nations mandate for the campaign was confined to expelling the Iraqis from Kuwait. To continue the march to Baghdad would certainly not have guaranteed that Saddam was overthrown, and even if he had been, it then would have probably involved us (the Americans and the British) sitting in Baghdad trying to govern the ungovernable."[13] Thus, one may attempt and escape the exigencies of the the all important oil factor". Still, the centrality of the reasoning was that United States attempted to contain the growing might of Saddam Hussein and the sceptre that the dictator might usurp the nationality of Saudi Arabia along with a major chunk of the oil resources, emerge as primary factors in the discussion on the efficacy or the non-efficacy of sanctions on Iraq. The counter-view about the non-efficacy and the deleterious ramifications of the sanctions on the Mesopotamian nation too can be brought about in bold relief. It can be mentioned that sanctions had a debilitating and negative influence on the economy and the general wellbeing of the people in Iraq, which, is an unfortunate corollary of any conflict resulting in "Collateral Damage".

Professor Lucas in the same document cited above, referred to the sanctions in Iraq. He says, "The political use of sanctions is important, but made specific criticisms both of the Oil-for-Food programme's failure to incorporate an evaluation component and of interference by the US in rectifying that failure. He distinguished between short- and long-term assets, citing the damage done to the latter—especially in the provision of clean water, reliable electricity, and literacy through primary education—by the Gulf War and the sanctions regimes."[14] The humanitarian portents of the economy hurting, education styming and health stultifying nature of the sanctions, has been brought out in the above written and detailed account. To scholars and audiences following the contemporary trends, the idea of a post-nuclear and post-Geneva talks—Iran suffering from debilitating sanctions without having fought an overt war with United States, too, serves as a reflection of how recalcitrant nations suffer from the sceptre of such impositions.

How the US mainstream and alternate media reciprocated to the American action in Iraq also makes for an interesting case study. One can delve into the coverage by the US national dailies such as the *New York Times* and *Washington Post* along with the electronic media such as the Cable News Network (CNN) and Fox Television. They initially portrayed both the conflicts as being of great importance to the national interest and the patriotic relevance of the nation. The idea of a pre-emption of the threat and a military response, which was initiated as a response to a future threat to the homeland, was also dissected by the media in the United States.

The 'American Rally Around the Flag Phenomenon' was referred to as the ideal reasoning why the American population should too support the American interest and the executive decision to go to war with Iraq. It was initially observed by public opinion watchdogs such as the Pew Research Organisation that in the initial months of the war effort, around 70% of the American citizens were able supporters of the war effort. As the American body bags started coming back to the homeland, the public support for the war dissipated and soon the entire

American nation was engulfed in a nation-wide debate about the war's efficacy or its non-essentiality among other larger burdens of the American nation. Was the American decision to intervene in Iraq to be considered as a continuity in the larger grand strategy of the nation? Or was it a discrepancy in the tenor of the scepticism of anti-war voices in the nation and the commentators in the media? These are a few questions which need to be pondered over by the various IR observers and scholars alike.

The Storytelling and the Anecdotal Side

Several stories such as the one where-in Iraqi soldiers entered a Kuwaiti Hospital in a paediatric ward and smashed the incubators, where premature babies were being tendered care, have become part of the manicheastic portrayal of Saddam Hussein which might not be so manicheastic after all. Also, the incidents as reported by Peter Arnett, where-in a milk factory for the kids was bombed as a military target, were some of the issues which served as a severe indictment of the Saddam Hussein regime. In the 2003 edition of the war termed as 'Iraqi Freedom', the idea of war was taken to the hilt by the mainstream news portals where the eulogisation and the canonisation of Private Jessica Lynch took place. It was an incident when a female American soldier, Jessica Lynch, was caught in a fire fight while her armoured personnel carrier was entering Baghdad city and the entire country was treated to a patriotic hero story.

It was reported that she emerged out of the burning vehicle and fired shots till she was mowed down and taken to a hospital. The authenticity of the account cannot be traced, but, it did win scoring points for the American war effort where courage and sacrifice were to be extolled and the bravery of the ordinary American GI, was to be celebrated as a young 'Rookie' who was fighting treacherous foes in an alien land. Thus, the mainstream media provided the patriotic frame for a clear and dignified war effort which was being fought for larger-than-life-ideals. In more ways than one, the historic appeal of stodgy and determined war correspondents as an endangered species was brought to the forefront in the entire gamut of the war coverage in Iraq.

Another "specific," which emerged was that during the 1991 conflict war correspondents from the media did not escort the troops to the battle stations but were limited to the 'Press Pools' which were to be given daily reports at the military Press Centre at Doha. In the 2003 war effort, the concept of embedded journalists was initiated which included the official policy that journalists covering the war would be 'embedded' with the travelling and in-action troops with a view to enlighten the audiences. This was how the real picture of the war, unfolded live in front of the television cameras, crews and the satellite phones in the battle zone. In a way, the idea of the immediacy of the conflict and its first draft as prepared by the media chroniclers of war, was, presented before the audience. For some, the war turned out to be a spectacle of sorts akin to a super-bowl game being played out in an American arcadia with the viewers witnessing several scenarios. The vision of a bomb being loaded in the turret of an American bomber along with the scenario of the bomb disappearing in the mass of the sky and then exploding with a target being blown to smithereens, became the quintessential pictures of the superiority-frame of the military and technological might of the United States. In the author's view, these representations of the war effort and individual 'stand outs' are routinely amplified in the public sphere to rev up positive frames for the national war effort. If the Americans did it, then it was in the ordinary frame of events in the larger continumm of war efforts and in the process of advancing the raison d'etres of the national interest.

Thus, the 'Patriotic spirit frame' of the Americans, was re-ignited during the run up to both the Persian Gulf wars, where, Iraq was posited as the aggressor. Thus, the idea of America was once again proudly festooned upon the nation and the global community amid the hullabaloo preceding the American military interventions in Iraq. John Simpson was the ideal instance of how during the Western Press pools gathered near the battlefields and reported the war, as it was reported to them through the Coalition's war releases. Also, John Simpson writes that, "In the darkness of the lobby angry hands grabbed us and pushed us downstairs into the shelter. The smell of frightened people in a confined space was already starting to take over. Anthony held the camera over his head to get past the sobbing women who ran against us in the corridor. Children cried. Then the lights went out and there was more screaming until the emergency power took over. Most of the western journalists were hanging around the bomb shelter. I was surprised to see one of the journalists there: he had a reputation for courage and independence but now he was looking at the waves of sheltered commoners with frightened red eyes. This would be the first high tech war in history."[15]

Outside the bomb shelters in Baghdad, the aerial fight between the ravaging American bombers and the gradually receding anti-aircraft guns went on unabated. Thus, in a way the whole idea of the war in Iraq in 1990 did not start with a traditional trench warfare variety and a-bayonets-raised conventional military conflict. The confrontation started with a aerial 'shock and awe' campaign in the Baghdad skies, where-in, the battle for the aerial supremacy was decided on the first day of the war itself. The American F-16s grounded the obsolete Soviet-made MiGs into complete submission which was an easy and expected outcome of the first aerial skirmish between the air forces of both the nations.

Another imagery which became a poignant reminder of the dangerous tradition of the Iraq war, was, the grainy picture beams and the shaky pictures of a tracer-lit sky which was astoundingly beatific as the American warplanes raided the Iraqi capital at will from the nearby bases. The war in the skies had already been won. One can hark back to the CNN feeds as the war reporter, George Bernard Shaw, steadied the camera with his own hands and spoke excitedly as the star-lit sky could be seen in the background during an American aerial raid. Such was the instantaneous nature of that form of warfare which took place over the nation state of Iraq and laid the foundation of an unimpeded American incursion into the Iraq-occupied Kuwait. The print media was too not far behind in a candid coverage of Iraq war.

Thomas Friedman wrote in the *New York Times* that, "I say this possible Iraq war is partly about oil because it is impossible to explain the Bush team's behaviour otherwise. Why are they going after Saddam Hussein with the 82nd Airborne and North Korea with diplomatic kid gloves—when North Korea already has nuclear weapons, the missiles to deliver them, a record of selling dangerous weapons to anyone with cash, 100,000 U.S. troops in its missile range and a leader who is even more cruel to his own people than Saddam?"[16] Thus, the quintessential question was raised by protestors arriving in Humvee loads and in SUVs across the traffic on the roads and across the terrain in the United States. The criticism was always around the issues of what moral purpose would be served by the American military action in Iraq. It could lead to human losses and a great burden on the national exchequer. These were some of the other factors, which, were indicated by the mainstream media to a lesser degree and by the alternate media to a much greater extent in a far blatant and blunt form of a vituperative attack on the American establishment on the efficacy of the national rationale to go to war with Iraq. It was over a cause, which was comprehended by the American establishment as being close to the larger purposes of US power and its selfsame immediate well-being.

Soon after both the Iraq wars were made part and parcel of antiquated history, the American effort instituted the idea of nation-building and national reconstruction in Iraq after the second Iraq War as part of the democratising mission of the global power. The larger purpose was to re-engineer some semblance of normalcy in an ethnically divided nation which was soon to witness elections and it was Nouri al-Maliki who became the Prime Minister of a war-ravaged and politically challenged nation. It was much after actual military action halted and the tempo was being only disturbed by suicide attacks and terror incidents aimed at the American facilities in Iraq. Another target was the well protected Green Zone, in central Baghdad, where the American headquarters were located. Soon, a special seat of a Special Inspector General for Iraqi

Reconstruction was instituted by United States Government which was to mandatorily submit quarterly and annual Reports to the US Congress about the American progress in Iraq.

In one such report by the SIGIR, it was stressed that, "Over the next 20 months, a series of events will alter the dynamics of bilateral relations between the United States and the Government of Iraq (GOI): a new government will take the reins of power in Baghdad and conduct Iraq's first nationwide census in a generation; the United States Forces-Iraq (USF-I) will see a change in leadership, and a new commander will oversee the conclusion of the U.S. military's advise-and-assist mission; a new Chief of Mission at U.S. Embassy-Baghdad will be responsible for the evolving U.S. diplomatic presence in Iraq; and—in December 2011—the last U.S. troops will withdraw from Iraq, 8 years after deposing the totalitarian regime of Saddam Hussein."[17] The roadmap for the American withdrawal from the besieged nation state of Iraq and the political transition of leadership in Baghdad along with the idea of restoring peace, stability and order in the hinterland in Iraq, were thus the prominent themes of the Special Inspector General's Reports. This sheds light on the idea of the larger American concern of restoration of normalcy in Iraq after two American intrusions. It is here that the Iraqi security and police forces had to be trained, sustained and made to survive as independent entities of some significance in the light of the ethnic and religious insurgency raging in the country. It all occurred after the ouster of Saddam Hussein. Thus, in a way the quarterly upkeep of records of sorts was attempted by the US establishment, when the nation began to move away from the critically dangerous years of 2006–2007. This had witnessed an unprecedented spurt in insurgency and violence in Iraq which finally led to the augmentation of American forces under the Bushism of 'Surge'. The names of cities such as Mosul, Kirkuk, Rufayat, Baquba, Muqtadiya and Ramadi now with the advent of the Daesh and the Islamic State, happen to be more than mere names. It can be said that the conflict has transformed from being a conflict between United States and Iraqi insurgents to an internal war or a civil war where-in, ethnic cleavages mean doom and perdition for all and sundry in Iraq. After the American surge, the American effort in Iraq was directed towards reconstruction of Iraq which pinpointed at the upkeep of its health, education and infrastructure facilities. But, the advent of the Shia-Sunni strife and the inability of the Shia Regime to stop the advancement of Daesh, has led to the belittlement of the American objective in Iraq. In the author's view, the American withdrawal from Iraq was rather too early as the national military and Police facilities had not been adequately developed in Iraq to combat the insurgency alone in an individual capacity. The Brookings Report of 2012 termed as the Iraq Index, serves the purpose of dissecting the US tale and the conflict in Iraq.

The Brookings report goes on to assert, "The civilian casualties in Iraq ranged to the maximum figure of around 4,000 in 2007 which was the worst affected year and went down to a few hundreds in 2011 and 2012. The GDP estimates too improved in Iraq from a paltry figure of 13.6 billion USD in 2003 to a healthy quantum of 128.1 billion USD in 2012. Thus, the year of first warring contact was a much impoverished nation while when the talk of Americans leaving Iraq was affot then it was to be vacated in a much better conditionality. The estimated members of Al Qaeda were to vary between 800-1000 in numbers."[18] So, in a way such eminent think tanks and public policy research centres have done wonderful work in indexing and collecting critical data on Iraq war. It is here that the myriad variables such as casualties of civilians in Iraq, casualties of Iraqi Police and security forces and casualties of Americans, can be gleaned. It is here that the employment figures of Iraqi Youth, the state of national Gross Domestic Product in Iraq from peaceful times to insurgency ridden times, too can be derived. Other indicators too have been analysed by the highly renowned centres of research institutes working in the realm of world politics in the United States.

Thus, a kind of an analysis premised upon human and comprehensive security, has been creatively and quantitatively attempted by Brookings. This pattern provides a rare and insightful picture of the state of the nation in Iraq with an eye for the need of response for the larger Iraqi Policy. As of now efforts are on to add self-sufficiency to the strategic stew in Iraq in all its imaginable aspects.

The Contemporary Context of Iraq and the American Angle in the Quandary

Iraq faces a new challenge with the passage of the American forces from its land. The American withdrawal took place in December 2011 and since then and from much before that the administration of Nouri al-Maliki has not fared well in Iraq. The Shiite–Sunni divide and the intransigence of the Kurdish nationalism in northern Iraq, has led to a disgruntlement and disaffection setting amidst the Sunni groups in the country. The general refrain in the nation is that, the Sunnis have been short shrifled in the Government positions in Baghdad though the Vice Prime Minister belonged to the Sunni group. He himself has aired his opinions since the initiation of the Sunni upsurge in Iraq since May 2014.

In an unprecedented development, the Sunni groups led by the ISIS (Islamic State of Syria and Levant) have taken over several Iraqi cities which also happen to be housed by oil wells and refineries and thus form a significant section of the Iraqi oil revenue. In a way, when the ISIS insurgents attacked the cities such as Mosul held by the Baghdad Government of Al-Maliki then the Iraqi forces which have been trained and equipped by the American forces fled these battle stations without much of a struggle. The tame surrender of the Iraqi forces in these cities remains a development mired in mystery and bewilderment for the rest of the world. The Americans have been debating anew about the need to send more, 'boots on ground' as a riposte to the ISIS surge. The core American policy happens to be that of no-more-of-a-military engagement in Iraq though the logistics and the strategic advisors are to still remain. Thus, the Americans have been taken by surprise but the Obama Administration has been pressurizing the Iraqi Premier to go ahead with a true coalition-building, where, all people and interests get a representation in the governance of the country.

Soon the Shia volunteers all cross the region gathered around a clarion call to fight off the Sunni surge in Iraq with the Iraqi Prime Minister, who is a Shia, leading the Shia riposte against the Sunni and the ISIS surge across the country. In the ISIS-controlled regions in Iraq, the militant group which is an offshoot of Al Qaeda has given forceful strictures against women and others. A *Guardian* report states, "Islamic State (ISIS), the al-Qaida offshoot that seized large swathes of northern Iraq last month, has warned women in the city of Mosul to wear full-face veils or risk severe punishment. The Sunni insurgents, who have declared a caliphate in parts of Iraq and Syria and have threatened to march on Baghdad, also listed guidelines on how veils and clothes should be worn, part of a campaign to violently impose their radical brand of Islam."[19] Also, one of the reasons for the quagmire in Iraq can be analysed in the form of a policy paralysis which has ailed Iraq since the nation-wide elections in April, 2014 when sectarian divisions became exacerbated. In July 2014, the Iraqi Parliament elected a Kurdish President, in order to bolster the coalition-building exercise and thus enable the joint Iraqi coalition to tackle the insurgents. This has also been a running demand from Washington, the United Nations and the international community. According to a BBC report, the ISIS are also targeting the Shia-religious shrines and heritage sites such as in Palymra in Iraq. Recently, the London people made an attempt to re build a gateway which had been destroyed in the destruction of the city of Palymra.[20]

Also, the *Economist* and the Indian national daily, the *Indian Express*, have reported in mid-2015, about the fallout of the ISIS devastation in 2015. With the takeover of Ramadi and the historic city of Palmyra, the Daesh intends to erase off the older historical legacy of the country that is Iraq. The globally renowned colonnade in Palmyra was razed to the ground in 2015 and comparisons are now being made to the Taliban who razed the Bamiyan Buddha structures to the ground in Afghanistan. Also, the videographed images of water-boarded and executed Western correspondents and soldiers wearing orange jump suits are an avid example of attempting to do a 'Guantanamo' on the American contractors and the Western interests in Iraq and Syria.

A BBC report says, "Historically speaking, the 2014 crisis can also be traced back to the days of Prophet Mohammed and the issue of the successorship of the caliphate since the days of Karbala. Still, as the American withdrawal loomed large, the Nouri-Al-Malilki Regime could have attempted a more inclusive governing architecture which could have stymied the disaffection among the larger groups and clans." The days of Saddam's intransigence and his endeavors in Kuwait might be a thing of the past decade, but the turmoil and instability which ensued 11 years after his capture in a hell hole in Iraq pinpoints towards the need of a nation building approach and a reconstruction oriented policy to be implemented by Washington.

Richard Lugar who is known as the 'Statesman of the Senate' was on the Senate Foreign Relations Committee when President Bush Jr announced the surge or an augmentation in the American forces in Iraq by 21,000 on the ground. Lugar commented, "The international community, will take notice of our staying power in Iraq and Afghanistan. If we are to help in transition into a secure Democracy, we will be able to bolster our ability to attract allies in the war against terrorism. Our commitment to Afghanistan is also a demonstration of how we will approach post conflict Iraq. American credibility is on the line in these situations and we must understand that failure to follow through could have extremely negative consequences on the war on terror."[21] Thus, the overwhelming credibility of the American posture and its consequence in foreign policy, which is championed by the Pentagon, is a relic of the past. What is required is the stabilising potential of the world's sole surviving superpower which more or less amounts to nation-building and reconstruction in strife-torn and fundamentalist/ Daesh-infested, Iraq and a terrorism infested Afghanistan. What happens after the evacuation of the evil and the tyrants and how the local populations benefit with the won peace, is a significant testing barometer of how much successful the American interventions have been in Iraq and Afghanistan.

The substratum of the current conflict in 2014 was also realised way back in 2007 by Lugar, who was a Republican Senator from Indiana. John T. Shaw writes, "He acknowledged that the surge coupled with the key policy shifts by Sunni and Shiite leaders helped lessen the volatility in Iraq. But he worried that the necessary political reconciliation was still not occurring. And he was frustrated that America's Diplomatic resources were not unleashed in the region to bring together the many affected parties. He was not much enthusiastic about the Status of Forces Agreement in 2008 which was signed in order to facilitate the withdrawal of the American combat troops from Iraq."[22] Still, similar to the strain of bipartisanship in the US Senate in the decades of the 1970s and 1980s, Richard Durbin, the Democrat Senator rose up from his seat and congratulated Lugar on his attempt to question the Bush policy of 'surge' in Iraq. Thus, Richard Lugar and other Republicans have voiced their concern and public scepticism, about the US policy in Iraq, echoing the bipartisanship and non-party line voting patterns in Committees in the days of yore. Carl Levin, another chief Democrat, who was the Chairman of the Senate Armed Forces Committee, commented upon Kugar's bipartisan approach that, "I am encouraged by what he said and it just adds to the momentum of change. Hopefully, he will take some very specific steps to implement what his words mean. They are powerful words."[23] It is the selfsame bipartisanship which was required of the Iraqi Prime Minister which was a precondition for the American support to the Iraqi Government. The failure of the Shiite Government—if it can be called so—to provide a full spectrum of representation to all people and ethnic groups, has been a shortcoming of the Government in Baghdad. This has let the nation slide into the vicious vortex of ethnic and religious conflict characterised by the rise of the Islamic State in Iraq and in the neighbouring Syria. Observers of the region and the commentators, engaged in covering the American involvement in Iraq, have written about the shortfall of the governance dividend for the complete vibgyor of denizens in Iraq since and before the withdrawal of the American combat troops from the country.

The issue of the optimum American withdrawal or a strategic redeployment were discussed threadbare in the various lengthy and incisive Senate Foreign relations Committee debates. In a Congressional transcript, Richard Lugar aired his trepidation. He argued, "The pace and the intensity of American regional Diplomacy related to Iraq has failed to match the urgency and magnitude of the problem. We still lack a formulae with which to engage Iraq's neighbors on a constant basis. We are allowing conditions in which miscalculations can thrive."[24] The Iranian stance on the Iraqi crisis in 2014 is a case in point which needs to be delved into with some analysis. Iran offered a hand at solving the problem with the Americans and the Americans, too, at one point of time attempted to mend the fence in line with the argument of a Shitte unity in the region. Now, with the inking of the J CPOA nuclear deal with Tehran, the United States is well placed to ease the sanctions on Iran in exchange for the curtailment in its nuclear ambitions as is evident through the Lausanne Agreement in 2015 and the July 2015 JPOA-II agreement reached with the West and Tehran. Thus, going by the achievement of the signing of the nuclear agreement by President Obama with Iran, it should not be read as giving a clean slate to Tehran to finance and encourage terror in the region as Republican Senators such as Leonard Lance and Ted Cruz pointed out in mid-2015.[25]

The great unravelling of the US Iran enmity included the idea that Iran and

United States need to work together in Iraq in 2014. Iran too wants to avoid a full frontal confrontation with the ISIS though Damascus has already bombed Iraq against the ISIS and it is Assad in Syria who wants to involve the region in a full-blown ethnic war akin to his own nation, according to one observation and analysis. *Haaretz* has reported that, "The Syrian Air Force strike in Iraq on Wednesday, which killed 57 civilians, was a clear indication of Assad's intentions. He wants to prove to the West, and especially to the United States, that he is the only leader who can take action against the extremists. Unlike the West, he is not bound by political restrictions, since Iran and Iraq hope to crush ISIS, and unlike Assad, they do not want to get into, or cause, an ethnic war. Iran sent several small units into Iraq, but will avoid a head-on war against the Sunni population."[26] Also, Iran's involvement with the United States in the Iraq crisis might not be a full-fledged one as it is viewed by a section of observers and strategic experts. Syria might attempt to ignite the situation and the American war room, but the United States and the Western coalition, along with the regional allies, might not be interested in fanning the fires beyond Iraq as part of the "new delimitation mindset" of the American establishment.

The Afghanistan Conflict: The Badlands of Yore

When one refers to the theme of the Iraq wars, then, the other dust-bowl conflict being fought in the neighbourhood in Afghanistan, too, can be delved into with attendant importance. The United States has been involved in Afghanistan since the Cold War years, but things came to a passé when it supported the various ethnic groups in the country to oust the Soviet-supported Najibullah government.Later on, the Americans had to battle the Islamic fundamentalist group known as the Taliban which usurped power in 1996 and then the Al Qaeda attacked the World Trade Towers, the symbol of American military and financial might. Then, the United States led by an aggressive President Bush initiated the GWOT (Global War on Terror) which came to be initiated in Afghanistan, as its first international hot spot. The Taliban were ousted by the Americans but Afghanistan remained mired in a guerrilla-type civil war, with vast swathes of territory being still controlled by the dreaded Taliban with ethnic loyalties changing fast between the Northern Alliance and Taliban.[27]

The nearness and proximity of Pakistan with the Afghan land has lent the region a complex balance of power equation altogether. As the nation hobbles on from one political obstacle to another, the significance of Pakistan being the frontline state in the American South Asian plan, has invited grave criticism. As a correlation, Islamabad keeps India unengaged in this vital nation and receives military equipment and weaponry from the United States in return for mitigating conflict in the region. Still, FATA—in particular—serves as an ideal breeding ground for terrorists and insurgents, which spew venom and perdition in the entire nearby region including India. Thus, instead of serving to mitigate regional and cross-border terror, Pakistan acts as a sponsor of international terrorism, which includes the free-run being given to Al Qaeda and now Taliban in its territory.

Also, the Navy Seal raid in the Pakistani city of Abottabad led to the death of the Al Qaeda supremo, Osama bin Laden, which highlights the twilight zone trajectory and the amorphous nature of boundary and politics in the region. This has gained new importance as Afghanistan has been included as a member of the SAARC (South Asian Association of Regional Cooperation). In a way, the region was rightly titled as the "most dangerous place on the globe" which President Obama referred to as Af-Pak. Currently, the quagmire of civil war with the inclusion of the NATO forces, seems to be at the centre-stage with the American establishment mulling over an exit strategy for its forces leaving behind a self sustaining Afghan national security force and a rehabilitated governance mechanism in place in Afghanistan. Thus, the post-2014 turn of US policy in the besieged and challenged nation is of immense significance for its welfare and the future stability.

The Af-Pak region, as a whole, has wide-ranging ramifications for the nations of the region, such as India which yearns for a larger role in the conflict mitigation. This assumes increased significance as the Indian relations with the United States have been on an upswing and India too contributes astutely in the sectors of health, education, capacity building and infrastructure in a strife torn Afghanistan.

The source of trouble can be observed with the stereotypical client-state policy of Pakistan. Steve Cole writes in the *Ghost Wars* that, "When the CIA team visited the turbulent region of Pakistan sponsored military training camps where fighters were being trained for confronting the Taliban in the nineties, it so occurred that quick makeshift training camps were erected days before the arrival of the CIA inspectors. They came looking for evidence. The evidence was that the American funds were being utilized for the actual establishment and the sustenance of the camps in western Pakistan."[28] It is also mentioned in the narrative that initially only a few training camps were set up in Pakistan for utilising the Mujahideen in Afghanistan, while the rest of the US funds were being diverted clandestinely by the Inter Service Intelligence (ISI) to be utilised for being diverted to India and the state of Kashmir and other activity grounds for insurgents.

This amounted to a breach of bilateral security contract and limited the viability of Pakistan as a true blue frontline nation state in the context of the 'second Afghan war.' The redundancy of the "first Afghan war" was already exposed with the retreat of the Soviet forces from Afghanistan. Thus, a surreptitious role was played by a frontline agent such as Pakistan which played with the Taliban and with its extremist ideology. This impacts the strategic health of India, too, as now it has to deal with a "failed state" in its north-west and an unpredictable and menacing geopolitical and economic giant in the northern sector, that is, China. Thus, Pakistan's utility as an utilitarian hand diminishes, with the nation plunging in a state of political instability and insecurity. All this, adds to the rising tide and the strategic and political importance of India as a strategic South Asian bulwark aiding United States in its grand strategy in Afghanistan. India too attains regionally strategic significance with a decrease in the America-Pakistan cooperation in Af-Pak.

With the advent of Prime Minister Narendra Modi in New Delhi, the various South Asian nations including Afghanistan, have, been made part of the near-neighborhood girdle of South Asia, which has unfurled itself as the pivot theme of India's Foreign Policy. In his inaugural ceremony itself, PM Modi invited the heads of state to India in order to initiate a new beginning in bilateral relations, relations with Pakistan and relations with neighbors such as Nepal and Bhutan; all with an eye to improve the idea of regionalism in South Asia. This, "Innovative Diplomacy" also tends to improve, the credibility and the efficacy of SAARC, as, the flagship regional organisation in South Asia.[29] Also, India has initiated the new paradigm of 'Connect Central Asia' which includes the various 'Opportunistans'[30] along with Afghanistan. In a way, there are several Indian efforts afoot in order to develop and reconstruct Afghanistan and India with the support of United States, has earned a toehold inside the nation's reconstruction effort and national administrative capacity building. Still, Pakistan has emerged as the new diplomatic interlocutor which has paved the way for Taliban agreeing for peace negotiations with the Kabul regime led by Ashraf Ghani after his electoral victory. Still, the appointment of Mullah Mansour as the head of the Taliban has ushered in a new moderation in the style of functioning of Taliban which can be further exploited by Washington and Islamabad in the post-2015 reconciliation scenario. Mullah Mansour has extended the moderate form of Taliban, which, has expressed interest in carrying on negotiations with the Kabul denomination and is willing to take the strategic help of all the facilitating states.

Containment of Taliban, in Kabul and the ushering in of a post Taliban governance mechanism, are the core strains of the larger American strategy in Afghanistan. Kenneth Katzman writes, "Afghan security forces have led security responsibility throughout the country, and the United States and its partner countries are reducing military involvement in Afghanistan. The current international security mission terminates at the end of 2014 and is expected to transition to a smaller mission consisting mostly of training the Afghanistan

National Security Forces (ANSF). A "residual force" that will remain in Afghanistan after 2014 is likely to consist of about 12,000 U.S. and NATO trainers and mentors, of which about two-thirds would be U.S. forces, plus about 3,000 mostly U.S. counterterrorism forces."[31] Thus, some observers have contended that since the United States is living in an age of domestic and global economic recession, its myriad global engagements of the defense variant, involving the incurring of expenditure, have been folded up to a certain extent. Still, after the despondency from 2008-2014, the 2015 scenario has witnessed an "***American rebuild***" in the economic sphere, which, can have a transformative impact on the American foreign policy in South Asia as far as the degree of engagement in far off nations and regions, is concerned.

A fact can be considered that the task of nation building, has been initiated and supported since a decade in Afghanistan. All this is a part of the Washington's Truman plan for conflict zones after the battle has receded into the background. The time is considered to be opportune for the nation state of Afghanistan, to resurrect on its own after more than a foundation of reconstruction and rebuilding has taken place with a larger Western—NATO and American—aid and succour. In a way, the American drawdown was largely eminent after the security situation had stabilized. Apart from external threats and great power involvement in Afghanistan, several internal problems too bedevil Kabul, such as the scourge of arms and drug running.

The Congressional Research Service Report released in 2014 further enunciates that, "All of the insurgent groups in Afghanistan benefit, at least in part, from narcotics trafficking. However, the adverse effects are not limited to funding insurgents; the trafficking also undermines rule of law within government ranks. At the same time, narcotics trafficking is an area on which there has been progress in recent years, although some question whether progress is sustainable. Fifteen of Afghanistan's 34 provinces are considered "poppy free" by the U.N. Office on Drugs and Crime as of the end of 2013."[32] Thus, governance in Afghanistan is directly related to the parallel economy of the weapons bazaar and the practice of drug trafficking, as, Afghanistan happens to be one of the three triangles of drug trade apart from the other known hubs in South America and South East Asia. The insurgents and other pro-government ethnic groups are equally financed by the drug money and the impact of the illicit trade percolates down to the commoners in the country. Also, governance in Afghanistan is too looking up as the nation is seeking global and South Asian expertise in training Provincial governors and officials in nations such as India and other places. India is considered to be far advanced in its pursuit of best practices in good governance.

Along with the need for a localised governance, the quest for a rule of law is another prime concern in Kabul. Corruption along with the rent-seeking functionality of the new institutions, brought the US supported Hamid Karzai Government under the scanner till 2010. Stephen Biddle contends in a Policy Innovation Memorandum in the Council for Foreign Relations paper that, "Afghan governance is now shaped by a series of powerful patron-client networks designed to provide political top cover for corruption that enriches the network at the citizenry's expense. President Hamid Karzai depends on the networks' leadership to deliver political support; in exchange, he empowers them with critical appointments, protects them from prosecution, and allows them to prey on the public. The result is a government of informal political deal making rather than rule-based administration by publicly accountable institutions."[33] Also, the idiom of good governance resonates with the liberal and the larger security providers of the West wherein international administrative assistance has been provided and happens to be the cornerstone of reforms and normalisation efforts in Afghanistan. Regarding this, there is a consonance in policy between the United States and NATO.

The United States continues to support a broad-based and bipartisan government in Kabul, despite the relations falling to an all-time low when Washington attempted a rapprochement with Taliban in a foreign location in the Middle East, that is, Qatar (Doha). Both the nations have recently inked a decade-long agreement, which, is very comprehensive and inclusive in its nature and ambit. It can be quoted from a US State Department, Fact sheet that, "On May 2, 2012, the United States and Afghanistan signed the *Enduring Strategic Partnership Agreement between the Islamic Republic of Afghanistan and the United States of America*, a 10-year strategic partnership agreement (SPA) that demonstrates the United States' enduring commitment to strengthen Afghanistan's sovereignty, stability, and prosperity and continue cooperation to defeat al-Qaeda and its affiliates."[34] Thus, the future of Afghanistan lies in a self-sufficient nature of the Afghan state which will be supported from the outside by the United States which departs militarily but intends to indirectly serve the Afghan people. Differences such as how to diplomatically engage with the Taliban have surfaced in the recent past with the Americans attempting a separate solution to the conflict with the involvement of other state actors such as Pakistan.

There is enough documentation that provides an ample evidence about the comprehensive nature of the bilateral relationship between Afghanistan and the United States. A few of the framework cooperative arrangements include themes such as a "Trade and Investment Framework Agreement" with the United States in 2004.There is no Bilateral Taxation Treaty between the United States and Afghanistan. The United States and others in the international community currently support Afghanistan with a broad array of assistance programs including private sector growth, capacity-building for government institutions, support to improve the professionalism of the security forces, programmes to support civil society and respect for human rights, counter-narcotic programmes, infrastructure projects, special support for the advancement of Afghan women and girls, and humanitarian relief."[35]

There have been allegations on the West concerning the state of affairs in Afghanistan. NATO's personalising the war in Afghanistan and the attachment of a Western orientation in the war, is part of crystal clear politics which has led the North Atlantic Treaty Organization to re-orient its role and mandate in Afghanistan. A *New York Times* report says, "The shrinking ambitions for the postwar mission reflect fears that the United States Congress and European parliaments might cancel their financial commitments—amounting to more than $4 billion a year, the largest single military assistance program in the world—unless American and NATO troops are positioned at Afghan military and police headquarters to oversee how the money is spent in a country known for rampant corruption."[36] The vast nature of the NATO-led mission in Afghanistan has also attracted domestic criticism. The financial implications of the aid being rendered to the nation and the actual accountability being practiced in the Afghan firmament were issues that were raised by the West including the agencies in United States, which led to a redrawing of the NATO role in Afghanistan. Thus, NATO itself vouched for an increasingly minimalistic role for itself and the allied nations such as the United States, which, reflect the twin trends of the global impact of economic recession and the general isolationist strain of the West. Also,regions in the form of Asia-Pacific, Far East and Africa, also need attention for geopolitical and geo-economic gains and for the purpose of forging the much needed partnerships in other strife torn, unstable and economically challenged third world nations. As already, the international system is passing through a difficult learning curve with the non state actors, globalisation, ethnic self-determination and revanchist trends raising their heads in the different subsets and contexts.

It may be safely surmised that the United States state machinery which evolved after a World War II victory and consolidated as a Cold War fighting machine, has risen to face new global threats in the form of piracy in the African seas and the rise of Taliban in Afghanistan. With the rise in the Asia-centric discourse in the realm of international affairs, the American interest was being drawn across the Pacific by factors such as the rise of China. Then, came the Russian conflict with Georgia and the annexation of Crimea along with the American–Russian conflict in Libya and Syria, which have tended to prevent a reorientation of the American policy in the global system. The comity of nation states in the European steppes and the boulevards of the continent along with the sun scorched mountains of Afghanistan, seem to be an interconnected 'new mass connectivity' as the land routes of arms transfers run through these tracks. All these developments necessitate a new continental approach for Afghanistan. The resurgence of Afghanistan in the region with its strategic significance, is there to be seen which all along the the British times has acted as a buffer state and has been a punching bag in global and regional strategic war games. The state of Afghanistan was barely free in any sense that it lay geographically between the great power rivalries as part of the great game in history.

In 2015, the nation state of Afghanistan swings between blood and hope which might serve as a popular slogan for an Republican Party Bumper sticker or the US elections to be held in 2016. The American policy in a post-Karzai era is very clear. A Brookings report says, "The Taliban and its affiliated insurgent groups, such as the Haqqani Network and Hezb-e-Islami, are still deeply entrenched. New international jihadi groups, such as the Islamic State of Iraq and Syria (ISIS), may also be trying to establish themselves in Afghanistan. An atmosphere of uncertainty regarding ongoing difficult security, political, and economic transitions has pervaded Afghanistan since the beginning of 2013."[37] Thus, in the post-2015 scenario, United States intends to rely upon the regional nations such as Pakistan and China, which have made repeated efforts recently to resolve the conflict in Afghanistan. As the US has moved out of the nation as part of an agreement with Kabul, the author, like many others, still believes that the chances that Afghanistan might slide away into another era of anarchy, is one possibility. The ANA (Afghan National Army) and the police force are still underprepared to take on the efficiency of operation and the dreaded surprise of the insurgents. The self-sufficiency which the Asian scholars refer to, is a state of affairs which cannot be attained in the near future as the origins of a national force and stolid governing structures cannot be overlaid and serve as a global buttressing. The Americans too need to include the strategic help of major actors in the region such as Pakistan which have an intertwined role to play in the post-2015 scenario in Afghanistan, as, is made evident by regional diplomatic efforts such as the Heart of Afghanistan conferences to be held in Pakistan in 2015 and beyond. Iraq in the neighbourhood seems to be on a mend as the ISIS have been ousted from the cities of Tikrit and Ramadi which serves as a stark reminder that Iraq might be on the verge of being liberated from the clutches of ISIS by making the group deprived of its precious funding for primordial governance and war making. In conclusion, Afghanistan, has emerged as a crucible through which the peace and stability ethos in the international system and South Asia should shine through with the practice of dialogue and diplomacy making inroads into a culture of conflict and clashes.

NOTES

1. Dexter Filkins, *The Forever War* (New York: Vintage Books, 2009), pp. 1-15.
2. Ibid.
3. Chris Kyle, *American Sniper* (New York: Harper Collins, 2012), pp. 1-10.
4. Ibid.
5. Ibid., 1.
6. Paul R. Pillar, *Intelligence and US Foreign Policy: Iraq, 9/11 and Misguided Reform* (Columbia: Columbia University Press, 2014) p. 13.
7. Ron Suskind, *The One Percent Doctrine: Deep Inside America's pursuit of its Enemies Since 9/11* (New York: Simon and Schuster, 2006), p. 225.
8. "Project for the New American Century: All About Them", URL; http://www.bibliotecapleyades.net/sociopolitica/sociopol_PNAC01.htm (Online: Web), Accessed on May 1, 2015.
9. Ibid.
10. Ibid. 1.
11. Barbara Crosette, "Iraq Sanctions Kill Children: U N Reports", *New York Times*, December 1, 1995.
12. Ibid.
13. "Sanctions on Iraq: Background, Consequences and Strategies", Campaign Against Sanctions on Iraq, United Kingdom, 2000), pp. 24-26.
14. Ibid.
15. Jon E. Lewis, *The Mammoth Book ofWar Correspondents* (London: Constable and Robinson, 2001), pp.580-585.
16. Thomas L Friedman, "A War For Oil", *New York Times*, January 5, 2003.
17. "Special Inspector General For Iraq Reconstruction (SIGIR), April 30, 2011 Quarterly report to US Congress", URL: http://www.globalsecurity.org/military/library/report/sigir/sigir-report-2011-04.htm (Online: Web), Accessed on May 19, 2014.
18. Michael E. O'Hanlon, Ian Livingston, "Iraq Index: Tracking Variables of Reconstruction and Security in Iraq", February 2012, Brookings Institution Publication.
19. Reuters in Baghdad, "Iraq: ISIS Warns Women to wear full veil or face Punishment", *The Guardian*, 25 July, 2014.
20. Indian Express Report, December, 2015
21. John T. Shaw, "Richard Lugar: Statesman of the Senate: Crafting Foreign Policy from Capitol Hill" (Indiana: Indiana University Press, 2014), pp. 110-115.
22. Ibid.
23. Jeff Zelney, "Key Senator Splits with Bush Over Iraq Policy", *New York Times*, June 26, 2007.
24. Senate Foreign Relations Committee Transcript, September 11, 2007.
25. The *Economist*; "The Politics of the Deal with Iran", *Indian Express*, August 11, 2015.
26. Zavi Barel, "Iraq Crisis pushing Obama towards Alliance with Syria and Iran", *Haaretz*, June 29, 2014.
27. Dexter Filkins, *The Forever War* (New York: Penguin Random House, 2009), pp. 140-160.
28. Steve Cole, *The Ghost Wars: The Secret History of CIA, Afghanistan, Bin Laden from the Soviet Union to September 10, 2001* (India: Penguin Books, 2008), pp. 5-20.
29. C. Rajamohan, *Modi's World* (New Delhi: Harper Collins, 2015), pp. 1-10.

30. Ibid.
31. Congressional Research Service, 7-5700 RL 30588, CRS Report, Kenneth Katzman, "Afghanistan Post Taliban Governance, Security and US Policy", April 9, 2014.
32. Ibid.
33. Stephen Biddle, "Salvaging Governance Reform in Afghanistan", Policy Innovation Memorandum No 16, URL: http://www.cfr.org/afghanistan/salvaging-governance-reform-afghanistan/p27778?cid=ppc-Google-grant-afghanistan_pim_biddle&gclid=CN6S5pf6tL4CFVgIvAodYq0AQg (Online: Web), Accessed on August 10, 2015.
34. US Department of State, Diplomacy in Action, "US Relations with Afghanistan: Bureau of South and Central Affairs", Fact Sheet, September 25, 2013.
35. Ibid.
36. Thom Shanker, "NATO Reduces Scope of its Afghanistan Plans", *The New York Times*, October 27, 2013.
37. Vanda Felbab Brown, "Blood and Hope in Afghanistan: A June 2015 Update,"URL:http://www.brookings.edu/research/papers/2015/05/26-isis-taliban-afghanistan-felbabbrown (Online: Web), Accessed on August 10, 2015

15

The Ramifications of Economic Recession: The Pre and Post Downturn Story

Introduction

The argument and a detailed account about economic recession is an amalgamated narrative which has done well in countries such as India but afar in the third world nations such as Brazil and China, unbridled capitalism has emerged as the instrument of progress and development though with growth caveats. The left wing parties in Brazil criticize the capitalist pathway of growth and in China capitalism is not verbally accepted by the establishment as the instrument of their nation's growth. In the United States, the story is all about a buoyant celebration of market-led development and the gluttonous tenets of individual consumerism. In the author's view, the political tenet of development and doing politics might be venerable in United States, but the manner in which entrepreneurship has transformed into unmitigated capitalism, is what has placed the nation and its dream into a quandary. At one point of time, entrepreneurship was a holy cow in the American firmament which is now akin to a gargantuan behemoth gone berserk in the conundrum. The twin trends and their deft admixture have been the staple characteristic of many societies and economic systems being adapted by myriad nations. Still, in the author's view, what happened in America in the post-2008 scenario did not do much to sour the grandiloquent American Dream.

In line with the idea of development, Milton Friedman writes about the state of development and urban growth of Bethseda in United States. For instance, Friedman's cousin was returning from the metro rail station in Bethseda and narrated the scenario that the entire accelerator in the metro station is not functioning. The civic authorities had been approached six months ago but they had not undertaken the repair of the accelerator resulting in hundreds of people getting jammed in the railway station hallways. Does this resonate well with the grandiloquent American Dream? The Chinese Olympics and the Maglevs in the PRC have given way to the break-neck rise of the Chinese nation. Does this augur well for a nation, recovering from the supreme crisis? Is the Betheseda incident symptomatic of a national infrastructural rot or is the story an instance of beating the dead donkey a bit too much? The Obama Stimulus and his various confabulations with the corporate world would lead to a few answers.

Let us look at the Indian narrative in 2015 in the same context. In the regimen under Prime Minister Narendra Modi the entire bulwark of India's development is premised upon the development of infrastructure through increasing rail-road connectivity, transport and communication enhancement and improvement in freight transport throughout the length and breadth of the nation. The target according to some sources is that around 80 billion dollars would be invited in the infrastructure sector through the aid of foreign nations out of which a wide catch has already been assured through China during PM Modi's visit there in 2015.

China too has gone the way of inviting foreign capital in order to resuscitate the nascent rural and semi-urban norms of living as they have existed there. In a post-modern China, the urban staff quarters for local political leaders and Government officials, gardens, green spaces, schools and other official spaces have been replaced by an influx of malls, economic process zones, highway networks, flyovers and height-seeking flyovers.

Rajiv Bahl, a prominent entrepreneur and the owner of the TV 18 network in India, writes in his work, "Shanghai was a reflection of national resolve seldom seen in India and that too never in cities such as New Delhi and Mumbai. While Manhattan's skyline evolved over more than a century, it took nearly a decade for the construction of 4,000 skyscrapers which was double the number of skyscrapers in New York, the Big Apple. But, Mackinsey calls it China's only truly modernizing city. Shanghai now attracts over a quarter of foreign investment coming from abroad. Its stock exchange does 87 percent of the country's stock trading."[1] The urban sprawl accompanied by the era of big business in United States was brought into force in a fast urbanizing and modernizing United States at the turn of the twentieth century through the California's gold rush, the gambling racket in Las Vegas and the Hollywood den near Los Angeles. The Big Business era refers to the spurt in industrialization and modernization along with urbanization as part of the general turn of the century's progress and development in United States. It was the turn-of-the-century parable of development which made United States create a solid brass for its future edge over the rest of the nations. In the author's view, this resonates with the American tenet and value of a cherished speciality and pride in the nation, amounting to serendipity.

Scholars have pointed out that the cult of uncontrolled capitalism and consumerism has been the major cause of the economic downturn which the American state has witnessed despite its visible grandiose sheen and material aplomb. Marshall McLuhan is an American scholar and philosopher and he has contended that the grasping nature of individuals is the single major characteristic of the modern times, which, involves the idea of arguments such as women being treated as objects of desire and vilification. He also sheds light on the idiom that people have utilised the new inventions such as telephones, cars, etc., as the signifiers of progress and advancement in the modern times. McLuhan also brings forth the idea of communication as a reflector of growth and convenience in the present-day world in his work, *Understanding Media*. This is part of the quintessential American narrative.

Marshall McLuhan writes, "The basic rapidity of communication through electric media echoes the speed of the senses. Through media such as the telephone, television and more recently the personal computer and the 'Internet', we are increasingly linked together across the globe and this has enabled us to connect with people at the other side of the world as quickly as it takes us to contact and converse with those who inhabit the same physical space (i.e. the people that live in the same village). We can now hear and see events that take place thousands of miles away in a matter of seconds, often quicker than we hear of events in our own villages or even families, and McLuhan argues that it is the speed of these electronic media that allow us to act and react to global issues at the same speed as normal face to face verbal communication."[2] Thus, the virtual reality has come to play a significant role in the way progression is measured these days especially in the context of the American system of geo-economics. Telephones and cars serve as extensions of the human ear and legs which make communication faster and better and make people save valuable time and much-needed energy. McLuhan thus pinpoints the recent technological advancements as the new medium of progress and development in a capitalism-ordained world. Its also not as if, a socialist and a mixed economic matrix of economic exchanges would serve as a panacea for the American nation in a post-2008 scenario.

In a paper in *American Economic Review*, it is stated that, "The dynamics of house prices, sales, construction, and population growth in response to city-specific income shocks are characterized for 106 US cities. A dynamic model of search in the housing market in which construction, the entry of buyers, house prices, and sales are determined in equilibrium is then developed. The theory generates dynamics qualitatively consistent with the observations and a version calibrated to match key features of the US housing market offers a substantial quantitative improvement over models without search. In particular, variation in the time it takes to sell induces transaction prices to exhibit serially correlated growth."[3] The mortgage housing system had led to the economic slippage in United States, which had to be later on tided over by the Obama Presidency. An attempt is made to bring out the general dynamics of the housing system and the mortgage system, which was reflective of its own characteristic equanimity. The bubble and the surrounding matrix did burst later with the larger networks of the investment market and banking holding sway over the middle class mortgage purchases. This precipitated the economic crisis in the United States.

The *International Socialist Review* too said, "The US economy is currently experiencing its worst crisis since the Great Depression. The crisis started in the home mortgage market, especially the market for so-called "subprime" mortgages, and is now spreading beyond subprime to prime mortgages, commercial real estate, corporate junk bonds, and other forms of debt. Total losses of U.S. banks could reach as high as one-third of the total bank capital. The crisis has led to a sharp reduction in bank lending, which in turn has caused a severe recession in the U.S. economy."[4] Thus, Fred Moseley contends likewise that the dubious and uncontrolled role of bank lending led to the initiation of the economic crisis in United States, which also initiated the crisis of other forms of debt and corporate junk bonds and the banks. Thereby, the American economy incurred unprecedented and phenomenal losses which resulted in one of the gravest economic crisis America had witnessed since the times of the Great Economic Depression in the pre-war decade of the tumultuous thirties.

Fred Moseley further writes, "The most important cause of the subpar performance of the U.S. economy in recent decades is a very significant decline in the rate of profit for the economy as a whole. From 1950 to the mid-1970s, the rate of profit in the U.S. economy declined almost 50 percent, from around 22 to around 12 percent. This significant decline in the rate of profit appears to have been a part of a general worldwide trend during this period, affecting all capitalist nations."[5] Thus, the impending economic imbroglio had been in the offing as a peculiar characteristic of the capitalist system in general. The industries and the corporates in most of the Occident had begun experiencing the decline in the steady stream in profit in their turnovers which remained hidden due to other positive indicators.

Unemployment has been one of the significant attributes of the economic stagnation in United States since 2007. The inability of the US policymakers, to bring back the work force has been one of the major signifiers of what all ails the American economy. Neil Irwin writes in the *Washington Post* that, "The United State's long-term economic potential has been diminished by the fact that policymakers have not done more to put people back to work quickly. Our national economic potential is now a whopping 7 percent below where it was heading at the pre-2007 trajectory."[6] Thus, the economy has not been properly injected with job-inducing policies according to this particular view, with a larger impact on the potential and the sturdiness of the American economy in the long run. As the eligible youth cannot find work in consonance with their wherewithal, the purchasing power of a specific section of the population too suffers which leads to the idea of a large section of eligible people not being able to contribute to the national economy and its stolid output and innate strengths. This is a universal phenomenon and it ran true for the case study of the American downturn, too.

The *Washington Post* write-up further states that, "There is a tendency to think of a nation's "aggregate supply," or potential output, as something that exists outside the realm of influence by short-term economic policy. The economic potential, after all, comes from the education of its people, the richness of its land, the quality of its machines—all things that a central banker can't do much of anything to influence. In other words, supply is "exogenous" to a policymaker's economic model. But that may turn on its head in circumstances like the present."[7] Thus, the rationale posits that the fundamentals of the economy get roiled then there is little role which the banking practice and trade can play for the general health and the supply and demand relation in the economic system. That is what exactly happened in the American system. The small and micro changes were made the influential factor in the larger economic showing of the American economy. Also, other soft power domestic indicators, such as the state of the health, education and infrastructure in the nation also tend to converge in order to contribute towards a larger understanding of the general upkeep of the house. It is not only all-too apparent economic indicators and fiscal pointers of hard nut economics, which present a general comprehension of the nation's political economy. Several socio-political indicators too play a discernible role in the impact which they have upon the economy. This factor was not so well pronounced in the case of United States as the role of the "disenfranschised Rebel" was not much impactful in the general decline in the economy in United States. The role of deprivation being felt by a section of population in United States is too a factor which goes into defining the difficulties being faced by United States in the realm of economics and the state of popular well being of the not-so-well off section of the American population. The magnet stickers on a gargantuan refrigerator along with a panelled photograph of Martin Luther King, stand testimony to the challenges which a family faces in a fast infested and now recovering, United States in 2015-2016. The state of the economy is very much reflective of the state of the Union with the socio-political factors too playing a meddling yet significantly transformative role in the developmental and growth indices of United States.

Also, the American economic crisis cannot be viewed in isolation from the global economic crisis or the European economic lag, as has been witnessed in the last few years. The *Yale Global Online* portal talks about the causes and the global ramifications of the economic crisis which permeated through the lax vigil of the American policymakers and the Federal Reserve and the lopsided and largely one-sided relationship and exchanges with the Chinese and others. Apart from that, lessons were never learnt from the other economic problems internationally.

The reputed *Yale Global Online* writes, "Over the past decade, Chinese trade revenues, savings and purchases of US debt increased. Low interest rates encouraged US consumers to spend and housing prices soared. But such imbalances could not be sustained and financial instruments containing mortgages for homes that have lost their value, have proven toxic for the world. Economists and central bankers are still struggling to find a way out of the subprime mortgage crisis. If Japan's lost decade offers lessons, then deflation must be averted at all costs if there is to be hope for a recovery. But for the long-run, one magical phrase emerges from experts and that's "stricter regulations for the banking industry."[8] Thus, the global repercussions of the American economic imbroglio have to be taken into account if the solutions have to be found out domestically. It is here that the virtual transactions and immediate impacts have become the hallmarks of the modern capitalist system. Some observers have also pointed out to the Chinese connection in the context of the US economic downturn, as all the economies of the world are now intertwined in a singular matrix. If China does not do well as it has not been doing well since October 2015, then the American and other international economic interests too get impacted. No economy can be treated as a singular case study, now. And, in the author's view, if the banking sector goes unnoticed and unregulated then the larger norm of the economics of a nation can get affected as it happened in the case of the South East Asian tigers economic crisis in the nineties and later on the American Banks in the 2008 scenario.

The Council on Foreign Relations has done a commendable study of the Great Economic Depression and the post-2007 economic downturn in the United States. If one analyses the graphical representation of the depicted data, then one can fathom a few deductions. For instance in the realm of the quantum of industrial production, the great depression times were the worst off with the 2007 depression times reflecting better circumstances. In the sphere of unemployment too, the Great Depression age soars much worse than the post-2007 times. Another graphical representation depicts that in the context of the Federal budget deficits, both the great depression times post-Lehman Brothers' crash were similarly poised graphically.[9] And finally, the real great difference was the difference in the home prices. It was here that the graphical representation posits that the home prices did not fall beyond a certain distress level but during the post-Lehman era of the current times, the house price levels witnessed a completely debilitating crash.[10] Thus, the historicity of the economic crash of the post-Lehman crisis can also go a long way in strengthening our understanding of the causes of the crash and can energise the American and other policy makers into creating creative solutions to stymie such future shocks to the global and the American economy. Lessons can be learnt from the Great Depression era and the seventies' challenges to mark the trajectory of the post Lehman era economic policy making and economic thought cumulatively.

The Marxist Take on the Surge and Annihilation of Capitalism... or America?

One observation in the entire ambit of the discussions and deliberations on the American economic crisis, can attain much of an academic girth, if one refers to Lenin's thesis of 'imperialism being the highest stage of capitalism'. In the Preface to the work, Vladimir Ilyich Lenin has contended that when he wrote the work in Zurich in 1916 there was not much of an availability of the French, British and Russian literature. Finally, he utilised the British author, Hobson's, work on Imperialism.[11] Thus, he wrote, keeping in view the limitations imposed by the Tsarist censorship on the Russian writings of the time.Still the pamphlet which Lenin wrote was not limited to the idiom of economics, the demarcation between the bourgeoisie and the Proletariat. It also included the political element of the entire narrative in the Russian and the global/internationalist context. It was the instrument of unbridled capital which was utilised as the mainstay of Lenin's narrative where an international clarion call was given in order to unite the working classes and the peasants of the international order. This was done in order to derive a universal convergence of the impoverished forces all across the world.

Lenin writes about the changing contour and the role of the banks, as, they transformed globally from their original simplistic functionality to being international monopolies. He writes, "As banking develops and becomes concentrated in a small number of establishments, the banks grow from modest middlemen into powerful monopolies having at their command almost the whole of the capital of all the capitalists and small businessmen and also the larger part of the means of production and sources of raw materials in any one country and in a number of countries. This transformation of numerous modest middlemen into a handful of monopolists is one of the fundamental processes in the growth of capitalism into capitalist imperialism; for this reason we must first of all examine the concentration of banking."[12]

Lenin further underwrites the prognostication about the future of the capitalist world and the future role and tenor of the financial market, where-in, the banker metamorphoses into an industrial capitalist. Lenin again enlarges upon the content of the financial project, when he refers to the rather ingenuous and a naturalised homegenisation of the banking sector with the manufacturing and the service capitalist which leads to the spawning of a financial oligarchy in the global international system; "A steadily increasing proportion of capital in industry," writes Hilferding, "ceases to belong to the industrialists who employ it. They obtain the use of it only through the medium of the banks which, in relation to them, represent the owners of the capital. On the other hand, the bank is forced to sink an increasing share of its funds in industry. Thus, to an ever greater degree the banker is being transformed into an industrial capitalist. This bank capital, i.e., capital in money form, which is thus actually transformed into industrial capital, I call 'finance capital'... "Finance capital is capital controlled by banks and employed by industrialists."[13]

Lenin finally writes about the debtor status of the entire gamut of the underdeveloped nations and the colonial possessions of countries such as Britain, France, Germany and the United States. It is the quantum of the global financial capital owned and run by these nations which regulates the global trade and earns for them the sobriquet of donor capitalist nations. Lenin writes about these nations and their over arching financial influence in the same phenomenal pamphlet. He writes,

> From these figures we at once see standing out in sharp relief four of the richest capitalist countries, each of which holds securities to amounts ranging approximately from 100,000 to 150,000 million francs. Of these four countries, two, Britain and France, are the oldest capitalist countries, and, as we shall see, possess the most colonies; the other two, the United States and Germany, are capitalist countries leading in the rapidity of development and the degree of extension of capitalist monopolies in industry. Together, these four countries own 479,000 million francs, that is, nearly 80 per cent of the world's finance capital. In one way or another, nearly the whole of the rest of the world is more or less the debtor to and tributary of these international banker countries, these four "pillars" of world finance capital."[14]
> Thus, during those times around 80% of the global finance capital was owned by these few countries which created a natural and synchronised domination of the entire world. Also, these nations were already the colonial masters of large swathes of international territory, so, they automatically controlled the maritime pathways and land trade routes all across the global firmament due to their outstanding reach. Also, in the present-day context of the twenty-first century, the United States contributes to 30% of the world's agri-industrial output while no other nation in the international system contributes even half—that is 15% of that huge quantum. This

brings to the fore, the centrality of United States of America inside the rubric of the global geo economic apparatus.

Still, it might be very much simplistic to intone the alternate logic that the United States is a crassly capitalist nation state, with a selected posse of corporate companies acting as the national and global monopolies. The traditional and established success stories of American companies such as General Motors, Chrysler, Microsoft, General Electrics, Disney International, etc, are, being considered as the finality, of commercialism and business interests, in the global economic context. These compassionate companies if they are truly human are part of the American way and the attendant dream where President Obama in 2015 has made honest attempts to include the American corporate world in the effort at improving infrastructure and general security in the nation. In the author's view, thus, one can safely argue that benign corporate and positive liberalism can take hold of an America-on-the-mend in 2015 and beyond. The American recovery has already begun as it was mentioned by the Chair of the Federal Reserve that the Federal Reserve will opt for an interest raise reflecting confidence in the improved economic and stock sentiment and the rise in employment opportunities in United States.[15]

William A. Gatston writes in a Brookings Release that, "As the New Deal took shape, Franklin Roosevelt was accused of undermining capitalism. His response was that he was saving capitalism, not least from itself. And he turned out to be right. Today, in the midst of another economic crisis, cries of 'socialism' once again abound. There is every reason to believe that these charges, too, will prove to be overwrought. Even if all of Barack's Obama's proposals were adopted, the United States would remain a capitalist country."[16] Thus, is it a retreat of the Big Business era which is the panacea for the American economic health? Can the Americans survive this lashing out at their capitalist and consumerist way of doing business with a socialism-tinged policy making with Government support to the ailing Industrial sectors? This refers to the Democrats stated lesser capitalist policy to support an ailing US economy. Is this the "Stimulus Socialism" which United States, can spawn as a policy, in order to set its house in order?

Governmental regulation might not be entirely tinged with the ethos of socialists and communitarians but it does play a concomitant role in the idea of living through the rough times with a human element. The Government of the day as espousing positive liberalism can serve as the saving grace for the troubled business and corporate world. Gatston writes, "Roughly speaking, capitalism implies that markets and market transactions are the principal drivers of economic activity. But this activity takes place within a system of public rules that define property, transactions, and everything else that gives shape to markets. And these rules must be enforced through public power. As we have seen recently, when the rules are inadequate, ill-conceived, or poorly enforced, markets malfunction badly, causing great damage. Regulatory institutions are not antithetical, but rather essential to a well-functioning modern capitalist system."[17] Thus, classical liberalism, if invoked through the vestiges of the thought of Lenin, would paint the Western world and United States of America in the twenty-first century with a broad brush of class based monopolies and class-based oligarchies, resulting in micro level and individually impactful exploitation. This approach might be a classical vituperation aimed at an ideal, stereotypical and quintessential capitalist set up. What needs to be taken into account in the case of countries such as the United States, is the idea that the so-called 'spiteful' march of rumbustious and rotund capitalism can be regulated and tempered down by the authorities. Then, the plane jane 'peripheral myth' of capitalism being all-subversive and inimical for humanity and the underprivileged classes, can be negated to a great extent. The Obama Stimulus is one such instrument of pacification and stabilisation not in the pacifying sense of the Vietnam War, but, in the stabilisation mode of an ' Economic Stimulus' which was meant to serve the sagging economic fortunes of the country.

The latest Post-Recession Vocabulary

What exactly was this 'stimulus'? And what was all of this talk about the "Fiscal Cliff" faced by the US economy not so long ago? Let us go into the brasstacks of these two idioms, which provide a fuller picture of the American Economic Downturn. These developments are also being related with the much larger imperative of the American Decline or the faltering of an Empire which does not take pride in itself being an Empire. Michael Mandlebaum refers to the historical imageries. He writes, "Empires are all about the Roman Legions replete with their Brass helmets, brass breastplates and sharp lances. Empires were all concerned with the bearded Hapsburg Grandees which rode on horse backs on the cobblestoned roads of Central Europe. Another vignette signifying an Empire might be the picturisation of British Officials riding on horsebacks wearing their pith helmets and red coats as they dwell upon their tea estates in the Caribbean and other tropical regions."[18] Thus, the question of an American decline only arises when it is to be categorised as an Empire In the author's view, the soft power and the cultural potency, the popularity of the American lore and the system is a matter of prestige, modernity and advancement for many significant corners of the world so how can the American recession be associated with a grandee phenomenon called as the American decline? The entire phenomenon can be construed as a 'Re-balancing', as a 'New Pivot', but not necessarily as the fall of the new Roman Empire which the United States has never been, in the strictest physical and territorial sense of the term. Michael Mandlebaum further defines the notion of an empire in his own manner. He writes, "America is known to provide governance to certain parts of the world and in its overarching definition, an Empire can be defined as being part of the notion of Global Governance or World Government which United States specialises in."[19]

What is the meaning of Obama's Stimulus package to the beleaguered business world of United States? The Cable News Network provided a pithy and factual definition of the Obama Stimulus package in 2011. The transcript of the report says, "A mix of $253 billion in tax cuts and $194 billion in new spending, the total bill for the plan is $447 billion. Given staunch Republican opposition to most new spending, the measure has almost no chance of passing the House in its current form."[20]

The report further states,

1 Democrats, and Obama in particular, love talking about investments in infrastructure. One top priority: a national "infrastructure bank."
2. Nodding to an **idea supported** by both the AFL-CIO and the U.S. Chamber of Commerce, Obama proposed $50 billion in immediate funding for highways, transit, rail and aviation.
3. Nearly 43% of the unemployed have been so for more than six months —a drag on the economy that Obama wants to soften by extending unemployment benefits once again.[21]
4. Lawmakers first lengthened unemployment benefits to the current 99 weeks in 2009, and then **reauthorized the measure five times since**. The White House estimates another extension would cost $49 billion.
5. Following the lead of a **job training program in Georgia**, Obama wants to offer the unemployed a chance to work temporarily as a way to build their skills while they search for a permanent job.
6. He also vowed to work with Fannie Mae and Freddie Mac to help homeowners refinance their mortgages at historically low interest rates around 4%.[22]

Thus, in more ways than one, the Stimulus package introduced by President Obama, in a way, advanced the solutions which can positively serve the American economic system. As an instance, the state of the American infrastructure might not be in complete shambles, but what the global audiences witnessed through the live telecast of the O.J. Simpson Trial was that the freeways, flyovers and the works were not in the same pristine shape as what an Americophile Hollywood watcher in India or Philippines, would think about.

The New Deal advanced by the likes of President Rooosevelt laid the stage of infrastructural uppage and construction in the United States even in the post war country. Slate, an alternative voice portal, commented about the crumbling state of infrastructure in the nation when it was posited by Jeremy Dennison that, "America's infrastructure is the backbone of its economy. If not for the United States' networks of roads and bridges, its waterways and sanitation systems, its power plants and electric grids, and its airports and harbors, trade and transport would vanish. The golden age of American infrastructure was during the post-World War II era."[23] The premise of the talk on American infrastructure was always on a sound footing. Yet, decades of neglect and a want of maintenance have led to a rot setting inside the entire system which has gone rather unnoticed as the other barometers and yardsticks of development and urban living standards have led to the basic necessity being given a short shrift by the American lawmakers. If one traverses across the motel-dotted surface of a barren Midwestern highway tract then it is like what the Hollywood Movie, Natural Born Killers showcases; a terrain dotted with a dry land surface with mirage like visions of heat and wet cars disappearing into furloughs. The rides by mad crazed teenagers and charged up crazy men with long hair and floral trousers, remains a memory etched as part of the mid western landscape. All this is far removed from the Manhattan skylines depicted in the film 'Ghost' starring Patrick Swayze and the film 'What women want' starring the popular actor, Mel Gibson.

Coming back to the ground of hard reality from the world of make-believe, the American Society of Civil Engineers has come out with a report which refers to the idea of a shortfall in industry investment which has tilted the developmental aspect surprisingly in the United States into a topsy-turvy state of affairs. This is deplorable but still not unredeemable. Jeremy Further writes, "The American Society of Civil Engineers documents these shortcomings of investment in its series of reports Failure to Act. The investment shortfall is forecast to be $1.1 trillion by 2020, increasing to $4.7 trillion by 2040. The bottom line, according to ASCE, is that if investments in surface transportation aren't made in conjunction with significant policy reforms, families will have a lower standard of living, businesses will be paying more and producing less, and our nation will lose ground in the global economy."[24] The international rate and pace of infrastructure developments in the Latin American and Asian nations and other regions are such that the unreachable and untouched pelf and the mirror like 'touch-me-not-sheen' of America does not go much out of the global imagination. The skyscrapers in Manila, Mumbai and Kuala Lumpur in Malaysia do not leave much to be desired by the end users. These are the symbols of a new found prosperity and the sheen of development which are very much Asian now in origin and sheen. The clean urbanization and the smooth-edged cityscapes of these Asian giants happen in a world which is being less and less ordained and calibrated by the Occident/West, now.

In a report in the *Huffington Post*, it is strikingly mentioned that when global travellers reach the United States then the sheen and the shine is conspicuous by its absence and the redundancy of the technological and urban advancement rubs off the people. What they had heard and seen about the land of milk and honey, all, seems to be a thing out of the past which is hallowed in its connotation and comprehension; "When travelers from abroad come to this city, the financial and cultural capital of the world's richest nation, two dilapidated and depressing airports greet them. The clogged runways, the leaking roofs, the maddening taxi lines, the lost travelers bumping into each other—all these depredations are just part of flying the friendly skies to JFK or LaGuardia."[25] The broadband network that United States utilises and the energy wastage in the nation all account for the decline which has not set in after the rogue non state actors began attacking the nation. It happens to be development and an exercise in the little rot in the infrastructure trails since the last two or three decades.

The same *Huffington Post* report further says, "Using data from the Bureau of Economic Analysis, Mandel has calculated that American highways and streets are an average of 25 years old, up from 23.2 years in 2000. The economic stimulus, meanwhile, did little to slow down that aging process, "perhaps because the amounts involved were too small. Despite the hundreds of billions of dollars in public stimulus that Obama pushed through in the Recovery Act of 2009, spending on public construction is still down by a considerable margin."[26] Thus, there happens to be a clearly delineated linkage between the idea of man, machine and the economy which gets reflected in the predicament which the United States finds itself in and the political debate which President Obama's stimulus provides for the American citizenry.

Another pertinent quest that the author engages in, is the attention of the political economists and global observers is whether the American economy can at least replicate other mild recoveries? And, can the robust appearance and apparent strength of the economic system be rekindled in actuality? A Council For Foreign Relations report by Dinah Walker contends that there are vast differences between the nature and the extent of recovery patterns and quantum between the earlier recovery characteristics and attributes in the context of the earlier economic depressions in the American economy. The report says, "The economic expansion following the 2008 recession has been the weakest of the post-World War II era. Four years after the start of the recovery, GDP has risen about half as much as in the average post-World War II era recovery. The federal budget deficit, which was larger than in any other post-World War II era recovery for much of the past four years, has shrunk rapidly in recent months and is now smaller than in the recoveries which began in 1980 and 1982. House prices rose again in the second quarter of 2013 but remain 5 percent lower than they were at the start of the recovery."[27] Thus, the report intends to stress and emphasise that though the fundamentals have not drastically improved since the year 2013, the idea of numbers and stats have improved since the initial economic crash.

What is the economic outlook and a forecast for the US economy in the year 2014? The quest needs to be revisited, if the future of a nation includes a withdrawal from the international flashpoints such as Iraq and Afghanistan. The US policy is undergoing a rebalancing to older pastures such as the Asian Pivot which has to be deciphered in the terms of an economic question and a sturdy, challenging and creeping poser before the American lawmakers. How does the Congressional Budget Office (CBO) feel about the US economic outlook in 2014? Pessimistic. The CBO expects the US economy in 2014 to remain moribund and the unemployment to remain near eight per cent. But, it gets better. It also projects that both the actual and the potential real GDP will eke out 2.25% annual gains between 2019 and 2023.[28] Thus, the fortune and the futuristic performance of the American economy, is, not too positive even after six years of the economic crisis. What can one make out is that since the United States faces an economic downslide after every four to six years, so in that context, is the recovery incomplete or is the idea of recovery, another stage for a forecasted downturn. The larger context of the market has improved a great deal, but the standard of life of the average American remains unchanged and the same maladies of household debts and disturbing and disconcerting unemployment rates, seem to abound in the national context. There has been a pessimistic and gradualist reading of the situation by most of the observers of the US economic scenario. In December 2015, the American economy has shown signs of improvement with the job seekers queuing up at the offices which expresses a new found confidence among the qualified youth that the economy in US is finally looking up and is on a mend.[29]

The US economic outlook summarises rather pithily the general fundamentals of the crisis, whether one calls it as the housing bubble or the Lehman Brothers' crash or the supreme and the prime mortgage crisis. After all, what's there in a name! It has been said that, "Since 2008, the actions of the Federal Reserve have put the U.S. on a path to economic failure. To stem the economic slide of the U.S. housing collapse that first surfaced in 2005, the Federal Reserve unveiled three different quantitative easing (QE) efforts. Since 2008, the Federal Reserve has printed off trillions of dollars, and it continues to add to that number at a staggering rate each month. The extra dollars pumped into the economy were supposed to spur economic growth. It had the reverse effect, shrinking the buying power of each dollar, the driving force of inflation. As the U.S. dollar continues to decline in value against other world currencies, goods imported into the U.S. become more expensive."[30] The idea is that America needs a sturdy visitation, where-in, the Dollar can become the real standard in the twenty-first century and that the imports are not very expensive for the American industry as the manner and the extent to which goods from the East such as the Chinese manufacturers enter the nation's market. This means a great deal for the health of the American economy. It also remains to be perceived that the age-old and now very common trajectory of universal entrepreneurship needs to be rekindled in the American context with its much maligned innovation finding a place in the reworking ethics of rebuilding a new America.

The idea of cloud computing and the works of the Indian-born American software developers leaving their companies in the United States and establishing parking shed companies in the Noida bungalows, is another pet refrain. How has the American exclusiveness been compromised, can thus be conveniently referred to. For instance, these India-born, US-educated engineers, work to establish a banking system through their web systems and through the conduits of NREGA, which is a Government Scheme in India pertaining to poverty eradication and employment generation. The interface with the local postal systems in the rural hinterland of the country which have been developed by these US return engineers cum entrepreneurs, is a steady development which cannot be ignored by the American lawmakers. With these America return entrepreneurs, the city employed people can send money back and forth between their city stations and the villages populated by their families which receive the money earned by them in the cities. This reverse brain drain that engulfs the US and the American resources, is, being mobilised globally and elsewhere. It is in such trying times that President Obama struggles with his economic recovery plan against an American Congress which is prejudiced and partisan in its approach.

The 2014 Fortaleza Declaration in Brazil after the 7-1 soccer drubbing of the Selecao in the FIFA World Cup 2014 semi-finals, sheds light on the challenges that are being attempted on the West. The new development patterns essayed by the BRICS is symptomatic of the alternate way of development and progression which is reflected by groupings such as the BRICS, IBSA community and others. These new communities place a challenge before the IMF and World Bank directed dominance in the larger global system. For instance, the spawning of the New Development Bank or the BRICS bank in Shanghai and the Presidency of the Bank going India's way, leads to a kind of reassertion of the realignment of forces against the Western modalities of the IMF and the World Bank. In a way, the idea that occurs temptingly is that with a combined working capital of 100 billion dollars with the newly spawned BRICS bank, the developing world can look at alternate sources of capital too apart from the IMF way. Thus, though not as yet an instrument pitted against the IMF and the World Bank, alternatives are being gingerly attempted in the light of the developments of the order of the global economic downturn. Where does America stand as the traditional regulator-provider nation state amidst its own difficulties, remains an untraversed trajectory which is yet to be honestly travelled on by Washington and the global geo-economic handlers.

INTERNATIONAL ECONOMIC SCANDALS: SYSTEMS, FAILURES AND A TRIUMPH OF GENIUS AND TECHNOLOGY

One can delve into a rank capitalist mode in South East Asia which has reached a crest and then a trough and then has once again balanced out on a stable growth and trajectory of development.

The Asian Economic Crisis, 1997–98

In the years following the Second World War, the emerging economies of East Asia showed rapid economic growth, high HDI standards and a standard of living comparable to that of the developed economies of the West. The high GDP growth rates of 8–12% in the Southeast Asian economies were widely acclaimed as the *Asian Economic Miracle.*

The economic crisis that began in Thailand in July 1997 raised fears of a global economic meltdown since the countries most affected by the crisis served as attractive foreign investment destinations and were well integrated into the global financial market. These included Thailand, Singapore, Malaysia, Indonesia, Philippines and South Korea.

Fall of the Asian Tigers: Background and Causes

In the 1990s, East Asia was one of the most attractive investment destinations, with a share of almost half of the total capital inflow into developing countries. High interest rates provided an incentive to investors seeking higher rates of return. Ever increasing inflow of money into the economies led to a skyrocketing increase in asset prices. With the onset of economic reforms in China in the 1980s, the export market of South East Asian economies suffered a major setback. Cheaper Chinese made goods flooded global markets, thus worsening the already deepening trade deficit of these countries. The worst hit economies of Thailand, Indonesia and South Korea followed a fixed or semi-fixed exchange rate system pegged to the US Dollar. In 1995, following a high appreciation in the USD, especially against the Japanese Yen, the exports from East Asian countries became relatively less competitive and the export driven markets were adversely affected.[31] Various other domestic and external factors exacerbated the crisis. Domestic currencies were pegged against the USD at unsustainable levels giving a false impression of the state of the economy on one hand, and encouraging external borrowings, on the other. A slump in the GDP growth rate, high interest rates and excessive and poorly supervised foreign borrowing and investment pulled up the current account deficit and public debt, leading to speculative attacks in the foreign exchange markets.

The crisis was mainly driven by the creation of a 'credit bubble', that is, easily available credit, that pushed up asset prices to an unsustainable level and in effect causing individuals to default on their debt commitments. A negative investor sentiment led to a further credit crunch in the economies, creating a ripple effect. Foreign debt to GDP ratios increased from 100% to 167%. Capital inflow into these economies was short term, expensive and aimed at making quick profits. The policy centres in these countries though aware of this situation chose to not act upon it. The corporate and financial systems were largely left unsupervised by the authorities even after signs of an economic fallout had emerged. Government-led lending, in fact, resulted in an increase in the non-performing loans of banks. Moreover, there existed an air of suspicion and lack of transparency on the part of the government, about the market and monetary policies. The crisis proved to be a classic example of how the ineffectiveness of the political leadership and poor standards of governance can affect the overall economic well-being of an entire region.

The depreciation of the Baht, Won and Rupiah against the US dollar raised the large amounts of foreign currency loans taken by the companies in domestic currency terms, thereby leading to more defaulting and rise in the number of non-performing Assets with banks, and an eroding investor confidence in the market. Subsequently, the International Monetary Fund proposed a bailout programme worth $36 billion to the three worst hit economies—Thailand, Indonesia and South Korea. It is imperative to analyse the implications of such an assistance for the international political economy.

The IMF, in its World Economic Outlook report, recognised the risks attached to such bailout programmes. The report refers to it as a 'moral hazard'. Provision of such an easily available assistance which might lead the creditors and lenders to default on their debt commitments without any major repercussions. To prevent such an easy risk-taking behaviour on part of creditors, the IMF bailout programme comes with a few conditionalities with respect to a monetary policy: to prevent further currency depreciation and domestic inflation; b) to address financial sector weaknesses; c) high levels of accountability, transparency and ethics to be maintained in public and corporate sector governance; and d) focus on asset creation and strengthening of social safety nets.[33] Secondly, since the disintegration of the USSR, the East Asian crisis was the first large-scale economic fallout. The assistance provided to these economies by the IMF further reinforced the importance of the west-led Bretton Woods institutions. This also meant a loss of bargaining power at multilateral finance institutions for these East Asian economies, which now relied on a financial assistance from the West.

Implications of the Fallout and the Way Forward

The economic policies of the East Asian region have mostly been guided by the results of the crisis. While most of these countries observe a large current account surplus, a fall in the number of Non-Performing Assets with banks and extensive foreign exchange reserves newer issues have emerged both in the political and the economic sphere having overlapping ramifications. Large holdings of US treasuries by Asian banks have translated into losses because of a large US current account deficit. While extensive financial sector reforms, fiscal consolidation and improved regulatory controls have been initiated, a dearth of investors still remains.

Thailand remains embroiled in a political crisis, especially after the 2006 military coup, thus eroding investor confidence and preventing accountable governance practices. In Indonesia, bureaucratic corruption has proved to be a roadblock in ensuring a business friendly environment. Exchange controls were put in place in Malaysia to cater to the weak external demand and a decrease in investment and household spending during the crisis. The government has now dismantled these controls and switched to a 'managed float' system of foreign exchange determination. South Korea, which was the recipient of the largest amount of IMF assistance of US$ 60bn, has managed to balance greater openness with better regulation, but it still struggles to deal with an over-accumulation of foreign exchange reserves and appreciation of the domestic currency, making its exports competitive in international markets.[34] Moreover, its rigid labour laws obviate the establishment of a healthy business-friendly environment.

The role of the Association of South East Asian Nations in intensifying economic cooperation to promote the region's interest was acknowledged at the ASEAN Ministerial Meeting held in Malaysia in 1997. The East Asian leaders must realise that prudent fiscal and monetary policies, greater unification of the Southeast Asian market, regional economic and political cooperation, transparent and ethical governance practices in the public and corporate sectors will go a long way in ensuring that the region recovers from the economic collapse and emerges as an attractive investment destination.

What the Greek Market Dependency Contends

One can also delve into the Greek economic crisis, which could be finally solved after the Eurozone agreed to part with an economic stimulus of 87$ billion in order to re-finance the Greek banks and re-start the payments in Greece and also re-initiate the pensions for the old and retired. The nations such as Italy, Spain and Ireland have been in the eye of the storm as they lurched on from one mini-bankruptcy and one currency devaluation to another in 2015. Finally, the saviours turned out to be the capitalist Eurozone which did not want a 'Grexit,' that is, a Greek Exit from the Eurozone in order to initiate the recovery in economically beleaguered nations such as Greece. The Greek Communist Party lead by Tsipras, was asked to tone down its communist and nationalist rhetoric as all the national banks had defaulted and despite a looming fall from power, the Greek President signed the Faustian pact with the Euro Zone in order to ascertain that Greece does not default on its immediate domestic and international payments. Thus, in a manner, the Eurozone stimulus package was a kind of American Marshall Plan after nations in the European continent had collapsed as an aftermath of World War II. Greece and Italy did not see a war, but, Greece had defaulted twice before in 2010 and 2012 and the much castigated European capitalists were the 'Avengers' who acted as the saviours of the beleaguered Greek nation State.

Harking back to the American context, one can dutifully adhere to the grandiloquent American Dream and its related serendipity. There have been much referred to instances, when immigrants have been able to raise their penury to prosperity or at least to a tenet of stability and good existence as part of the normalcy of the American narrative. When Jerus Serrato and his family came from America, then, home ownership was far from their minds. Considering the poverty they had known in Mexico, "Home ownership was the last thing on our minds." Dan Rather writes in the *American Dream* that, "When economic news turns to home ownership and housing starts, chances are that you will hear the latest figures put in terms of the American Dream. As in with real estate prices rising up, the American Dream reaching out for young couples, the kind of question you see in magazine headlines, the sort I have occasion to ask any number of times on evening news. Owning one's own home is like becoming one's own boss or coming to this country to escape oppression, something that is considered synonymous with the pursuit of happiness. It's one aspect of the Dream that is considered quantifiable."[35] Its also serendipitous for immigrants.

Despite the economic crisis witnessed through the tales of housing, sub-prime and mortgage crises, the Dream does not go sour. Any god-fearing and entrepreneurial American denizen is taught by his parents while he is growing up taming horse runs and shouting out aloud, "Here's, Muh Lasso!" in the true spirit of an American cowboy and the family Rodeo. Archibald MacLeish symbolically intones for the Republic that, "Because those who lived before us in this nation were able to imagine a new thing, a thing unheard of in the world before, a thing, the sceptical and tired man who did not trust in dreams had not been able to imagine, they erected on this nation the first free nation-the first society in which mankind was to be free and prosperous at last." Thus, the Republic endowed with a disdain for its successful growth story had to adhere to the negative ides of liberalism too which have been bravely depicted in the Hollywood movies like *The Gangs of New York*. The film creates a depiction of two gangs slugging it out in the big business era of New York where a wronged son at the hands of a ganglord, rises from his family's ashes in order to militate incognito against the Ganglord, who is played by Daniel Dafoe. At the end of the movie, the entire underbelly of New York erupts in an industrial riot and a sudden gang war which the Director Martin Scorcese depicts with aplomb and disturbing accuracy. Still, in the author's view, the entire argument about the dilapidating impact of a disabling capitalist system of development is too simplistic a narration of the American problems. The nation has a great deal of tensile strength and innate steadfastness with the dynamics of its economy which make every economic recovery, an agreeable development after a seemingly destructive economic crisis.

NOTES

1. Rajiv Bahel, *Superpower: The Amazing Race Between China's Hare and India's Tortoise* (New York: Penguin, 2010), pp. 146-147.
2. Marshall McLuhan, Lewis H. Lapham, *Understanding Media: The Extensions of Man* (MIT Press, 1994).
3. Allen Head, Ellis Llyod, Son Hongfei, "Search, Liquidity and the Dynamics of House Prices and Construction", *American Economic Review*, Volume 104, No. 4, April 2014.
4. Fred Moseley, "The US Economic crisis: Causes and Solutions", *International Socialist Review*, 2008.
5. Ibid.
6. Neil Irwin, "The Great Recession May Have Crushed America's Economic Potential", *Washington Post*, November 5, 2003
7. Ibid.
8. "American Economic Downturn: Solutions", URL: http://yaleglobal.yale.edu/special_report/732 (Online: Web), Accessed on 1 July, 2015.
9. Dinah Walker, "Quarterly Update: The Economic downturn in Historical Context" (Online: Web), Accessed on 10 April, 2014.
10. Ibid.
11. Vladimir Ilyich Lenin, "Imperialism: The Highest Stage of Capitalism," *Selected Works*, Progress Publishers, 1963, Moscow, Volume 1, pp. 667–766.
12. Ibid.
13. Ibid 1.
14. Ibid. 2.
15. *Indian Express* Report, December, 2015

16. William A. Gatston, "US is still a Capitalist Country", URL: http://www.brookings.edu/research/opinions/2009/03/11-capitalism-galston (Online: Web), Accessed on 1 April, 2014.
17. Ibid. 1.
18. Michael Mandlebaum, *The Case For Goliath: How America acts as the World's Government Twenty First Century* (New York: Public Affairs, 2005), pp. 12-20.
19. Ibid.
20. "Analayn Censky, Charles Riley, "What's in Obama's Stimulus Plan", URL: http://money.cnn.com/2011/09/08/news/economy/obama_stimulus_plan/ (Online: Web), Accessed on 1 August, 2015.
21. Ibid.
22. Ibid. 1.
23. Jeremy Dennison, "American Infrastructure is Crumbling", *The Slate*, October 7, 2013.
24. Ibid.
25. "Infrastructure Problems in US go far beyond Dollars", New York: *Huffington Post*, 2013.
26. Ibid.
27. Dinah Walker, "Economic Recovery in Historical context", URL: http://www.cfr.org/united-states/quarterly-update-us-economic-recovery-historical-context/p25774?cid=ppc-Google-CGS-chart_book-recovery-economic_recovery&gclid=CIzRlITD-b0CFdYNjgodkmsAOw (Online: Web), Accessed on March 1, 2014.
28. "The Budget and Economic Outlook: Fiscal Years 2013 to 2023", Congressional Budget Office website, February 2013.
29. *Indian Express* report, November, 2015.
30. "What is the US Economic Outlook for America in 2014: Not Good", URL: http://www.useconomicoutlook2014.com/ (Online : Web), Accessed on April 1, 2015.
31. "The Asian Crisis: Causes and Cures" International Monetary Fund 1998.
32. "Timeline of the Crash" (URL: http://www.pbs.org/wgbh/pages/frontline/shows/crash/etc/cron.html), Accessed on 10 March, 2015.
33. IMF World Economic Report 1998, "The Asian Crisis: Causes and Cures", International Monetary Fund 1998.
34. "Ten Years On: How Asia Shrugged off its Economic Crisis", *The Economist* (http://www.economist.com/node/9432495) Accessed on November 10, 2015.
35. Dan Rather, *The American Dream: Stories From the Heart of Our Nation*, (New York: William Morrow), pp. 50-65.

16

The Tell Tale Trajectory of "Indo-US Bilaterals": Amidst the American Myth

The Destiny Argument

The Hollywood movie, Million Dollar Arm, is an ecstatic incarnation of the Indio-US Relations in the cultural stratosphere. The narrative is woven around a sports agent, Bernstein, who is searching for the next great pitcher in the arena of American baseball. He finally zeroes in upon a cricket player from the land of Sadhus and serpents, that is, india, to groom him into an ace baseball pitcher. Reed Tucker reports in *New York Times* that, "When Rinku Singh and Dinesh Patel arrived in the United States for the first time in 2008, the two small-town Indian teens were shocked by what they saw. Coming from villages without cellphones, the Internet or flat-screen TVs, they were awed and baffled by the proliferation of technology."[1] This was the true but exciting story behind the presence of two talented pitchers who came from India as immigrants to the United States, as one of the most potent symbols of the Indo-American experience.

Apart from the cultural context of the relationship between India and United States, collective science games and projects, between both the nations, there are another key exchange and shared experiences through the instrument of community colleges in United States. The land of milk and honey still remains the most cherished destination for the students from India for higher education goals. Some of the same Indian students have chafed heavily through red sickle and star flag motifs but in the line of the search of a vocation they go on to endear themselves to the American way of life. These students once, were the alternate way of lifers in India. That is a strange accommodative exercise but that's how the India-US experiences have unfolded through the academic exchanges between both the nations which are gifted by the liberal and progressive traditions of their respective political cultures. In another literary metaphor, Amitav Ghosh's, novel, *The Inscrutable Americans*, paves the way for our male protagonist, to immigrate to an American Engineering College to obtain a bachelor's in engineering. The male protagonist always keeps his head dripping with oil and talks about the hair oil factory in Jajua in Madhya Pradesh, which, his father runs in India. In the author's view, various nations are there to be seen in the amalgam of myriad races and identities that US has become after waves of migrants have settled themselves comfortably and productively in United States. One can refer to quaint Diaspora experience which makes the male protagonist in, The Inscrutable Americans, talk about his hair oil production lineage with national pride and oriental aplomb. He manages to befriend the students of opposite sex with his innocent charm and vulnerable incandescence. But, what this chapter does is that it dismisses these Indian stereotypes and paints a more globalized and realistic picture of Indians in America where-in, the Indian community is the third largest immigrant community in United States after the Mexicans and the Philippinos. This is a predestination about the mixing of people and races which flourishes in the womb of American civilization, whether it be a baseball fixture or having Chole Bhature at Madison Square Garden. Thus, the experience of the migrants and the 'other' as they subsume the American nationality and identity, lets them extricate themselves out of the hyphenated existence as immigrants from some Asian country.

India and the United States have an intertwined destiny. This is not a value-laden assessment but a metaphor of the times for the present international system in which the historical, strategic, political and cultural factors bring both the nations together. This avowed convergence happens in a much divided international system which suffers with the global divisions in the World Trade organization and the United Nations. Many factors make India and the United States as ideal partners and the narrative is devoid of any 'Empire factor' or the 'quasi hegemonic' factors, debilitating the relationship for the times to come. Both of them are global nation states with hallowed traditions of liberal democracy and a deeply entrenched *do-gooder* and philanthropist national characters. Historical and cultural factors, still, remain the pegs which any assessment of any bilateral relationship is premised upon apart from the involved strategic, economic and the political factors. Both the nations, claim the high place for 'a coming together' in the specific matrices of strategy and global politics.

The American nation began with the Mayflower Pact of the 16th century, where-in, the British citizens of different denominations set sail across the Atlantic in the search for the new found land. They arrived amidst the land of Cherokees and Chenynes. Apart from the Eastern Coast land, the frontier typified by the

Oregon Trail across the Rocky Mountains, formed the constructing and founding ethos of the New American Republic. The neophytic settlements excelled through the instruments of Big Business, entrepreneurship and innovation which now in the 21st century, clinically forms the panacea for a stimulus driven Obama economy. In the author's view, the innate strength of the authentic American Republic lies in the varied experiences of the Immigrants as US has always been called as the "land of immigrants". These immigrants including the Indians have enriched the United States's immensely with their political allegiance and economic productivity.

In the more immediate context of the Indo-US biltaeral relationship,, the Komagatu Maru landings initiated the 'first contact' between India and the North American continent. The narrative of the Nehru visits to US, the food security crisis in India in the sixties and the umbilical years of the Indo-Bangladesh war, in the era of Ping Pong diplomacy and Gunboat diplomacy bring forth the new quintessence of an eventful 'bilateral' between both the nationalities of the world during the cold war. One nation's international perch reflects the era of a 'have been', that is, India and the other nationality epitomises the 'Foremost have' of the global order, which, perceived the other way round, stands true for India as a 'have not' nuclear power and United States being 'a have nuclear pontiff of the World'. Soon, were ushered in the irksome days of the civil nuclear cooperation agreement, along with domestic debacle of UPA Government and the counter proliferation activist theorists of the order of Michael Krepon, Richard Einhorn and the US Congressional distrust, which served as the points of divergence between the political classes in New Delhi and Washington. The Bush era in the 21st century ushered in an era of nuclear detente and camaraderie between the largest and the oldest democracy of the world. The shape of the relationship was further impacted by the defence and the nuclear aspect of the diplomatic exchanges in the 21st century.

The 123 agreement, Strobe Talbott talks, counter terror and home land security cooperation along with the idea of community colleges, cultural cooperation and the UC Berkeley's Spark toys Project, form the contemporary context of the 'bilateral relationship' betwixt the twin nation states, in, all its geo cultural and geo economic bloom. The quintessential attributes of the American Dream, along with the super hero and Bald Eagle imageries form the substratum of any quintessential narrative on United States. Furthermore in the much nearer present, the Indian launch of Chandrayaan-I and the aircraft acquisitions by India from the Americans, too constitute, an out of the way reference for Indo-US cooperation. Scientific and Defence cooperation between India and United States is far removed from the political and the cultural conduits which have been established between these twin nation states with a larger destiny to fulfil. One cannot leave out the Space and Defence cooperation, as, per the 2005 Defence framework agreement between India and US which too firmed up the seeds of future cooperation.

If we do not adhere to the strategic roadmap and factually dissect the bilateral partnership between New Delhi and Washington, a thematic percept and a conjoined narrative, can be conveniently created in the context of a cautious and withdrawing super power and an aspirant nation with impeccable peace credentials, that is, India. The Devyani Khobragade diplomatic fracas seemingly imploded the relationship, where-in, one can refer to the domestic help incident involving the Indian Foreign Service Officer, Devyani Khobragade. Added to the incident was the pent up enthusiasm of the US Attorney Preet Bharara, to interdict Khobragade in a class action suit despite being an Indian. Perceptually, not much should be read in the diplomatic incident which has been much avidly deliberated upon in the Indian Media. Even the attendant withdrawal of Nancy Powell, the US Ambassador to India, should not be perceived as a bottleneck of any denomination in the relationship. The twin incidents might make for swift news byte but the bite for the 'longer run of the bilateral partnership' might not be much of an ask in the light of the future of a liberally, geo economically and national interest oriented international system.

One can enunciate upon the theme of the significance of the soft power appreciation of US potential through an effective prism of culture, myth and lore too. Long since its inception as a responsible nation state actor, the idea of being a post modern Empire has been forcibly festooned upon United States of America. No individual can be perfect and kosher but one can attempt to be a faithful humanitarian functionary. The twirl of the hand in the Spidey dovey character bespeaks of a proletarian-out-of-work-next-door, American, who attains like the great nation itself, an accidental role of a perennial round-the-clock-national-mascot of hope, aspiration, love and most important of all, liberty. Now, in the contemporary and metaphorical narrative of United States, the myriad superheroes of the order of the Hulk, Superman and Captain America, tie up to meet up with messier foes in the magical reality concerning the American myth.

Thus, international cooperation, in a constructivist age, points at the great powers teaming up with each other to take up cudgels against the global ills. This quaint American narrative can form an ideal staple fare for deliberation and implementation. It is here, at, this interesting cusp of magical realism, that the centennial significance of a messianic zeal lies. There lies the visionary need for a developing world leader in a BRICS ordained world and a super power on a rebuild, which can take the world to the next level of prosperity, pelf, cohabitation and most important of all, security. The Asian pivot as posited by the American establishment, might be an old peeve in 2015, but, it need not be dismissed as a simplistic military redeployment between the European theatre, Iraq, Afghanistan and the Asia Pacific. Mark Twains' quote in the climactic moments of E.M. Forester's "Passage to India" that, "East is East and West and West is West and the Twain Shall Never Meet," is, a rote relic of a dissipative and an undecided past, clouded and mired in the deep freeze of a Cold War directed world order. A post-recession international order, devoid of a deft and critical statistical analysis, demands a much saner and realistic tryst with the destiny. Both India and United States form the twin pegs upon which the entire Global polity can revolve with China too being enmeshed in the narrative, with its aggressive perch. India with its Asian credentials, can be the fulcrum of the American friendship in the region and the larger international system. As a pessimistic theme, China still races ahead both with its super power ambitions and its domestic limitations.

The bilateral relationship between India and United States needs to be perceived through the perspective of 'Cooperative engagement,' where-in, the tiered and the balance of power defined relationship can be tailored through the prism of an international system perched upon the idiom of camaraderie and economic diplomacy. All was not well with the state of the relations between both the nations, since, the attainment of India's independence and the prolonged impact of the Cold War. The grand battle between the twin Cold war protagonists had lead to the inculcation of a confrontationist culture and a divisive mould in the functioning of the international system. The interactions which the Indian Prime Ministers such as Pandit Jawaharlal Nehru and Indira Gandhi had with the American Presidents such as Truman and Nixon, did not do much to initiate a wholesome relationship between the two nations. The Food crisis in India too led to the American help in the then ongoing Green revolution and the Americans seriously considered supporting India during and after the Chinese aggression in the Himalayan frontiers. Thus, the relationship even then did not have only negativities attached to it. Rather a circumstantial miscomprehension of each other's national interest along with ideological predispositions of Panchsheel, Non Alignment and third World solidarity ideals, were the cornerstones of the discomfiture in the relationship. These developments and global realities made the two nations part ways which culminated with the nadir in the relationship being reached. This culminated in the interruption of the US supply of nuclear fuel to the Tarapur Nuclear reactor in the late seventies.

The Attendant Historicity in the Relationship

The United States was the first country to exchange ambassadors with India. K. Asaf Ali presented his credentials to President Harry Truman in February, 1947. In an excerpt of his speech to the American establishment, he stated that "this is the first time after centuries that India at the dawn of her renewed freedom, has entered into a direct diplomatic relationship at the highest level with a power and people of the Western hemisphere who occupy a unique place in history in every sense of the term. He went on to express the profound appreciation of Indians, for, the American decision, to be the first in the world to establish diplomatic relations with their country."[2] It appeared that "the bilateral relationship" between India and United States was initiated in a sentiment of bonhomie imbued with mutual respect for each other's histories and traditions. But, as it is said, all that ends well is considered to be a fruitful outing so the cold war permutations and combinations with the Indian socialistic perch mildewed the 'candy' of a prospective relationship.

Foreign aid, in the form of the famed Marshall Plan, became a significant foreign policy tool for United States in the aftermath of WWII. Food, as an integral part of the international aid framework, figured prominently in Washington's policies towards India. [3]In light of the fact that the U.S. had made repeated attempts to secure the alliance with India during WWII, many Indians perceived the Truman administration's extension of aid to their food crisis in 1946 as a way for the US to compel their country to accept the American political and commercial policy and to widen its involvement in South Asia.[4] In fact, they believed that these "pressure tactics" had started as early as 1943, when the United Nations Relief and Rehabilitation Administration (UNRRA) came into existence.

The emergence of a bipolar world during the Cold War, between the superpowers enhanced the importance of the various developing countries in foreign affairs.[5] The concept of economic aid, as, a worthy goal in its own right, was soon replaced under the pressures of the Cold War by the notion of mutual security through alliances and alignments.[6] The initial contact between the US and India started on a positive note, when, in 1942, President Franklin Delano Roosevelt needled Britain to consider the Indian aspiration for freedom and independence in a sympathetic manner.

However, after Independence, India's presence at the forefront of non-aligned movement (NAM), which ran counter to Washington's desire for establishing a cold war alliance with New Delhi, created a distance between the two countries. Despite the effort of Jawaharlal Nehru, who, was the first Indian Prime Minister to visit the U.S. in 1949, the Truman administration's subsequent decision to sell arms to Pakistan planted the seeds of discontent and suspicion among Indians about the American superpower. All this had the negative impact on India-Pakistan relations. When Nehru visited America for the second time in 1956 and protested to President Dwight Eisenhower against the U.S. decision to supply arms to Pakistan, he was informed that arms had been given to Pakistan to defend itself against any Soviet adventure that might come through Afghanistan. In response, Nehru cleverly quipped, "I have never heard of a gun that fires only in one direction."[7] Thus, the seeds of circumstantial discord within the ambit of both the nations had been sowed between both the nations. Both the nations embarked on a confrontationist trajectory in their initial odyssey of the relationship with the cold war and the liberation of Bangladesh amounting to a severance of western Pakistan from Eastern Pakistan leading to a full-fledged war between India and Pakistan in South Asia. This sowed the seeds of the furtherance of the conflict over Kashmir and nuclear stand offs, along, with the initiation of Pakistan led cross-border terrorism in India. The Chinese idiom of containment of India through the doctrine of Pakistan being 'An All weather friend' too queered the pitch for South Asia. Thus, United States too with its nuclear non proliferation idiom and its support for Pakistan as a 'frontline state' for waging its war against the Soviet Union in Afghanistan, invited strategic and diplomatic distrust by the Indian establishment.

The Non Proliferation Fusillade

Another theme which is of paramount concern, happens to be that of the non proliferation concerns of United States, where-in, India exploded the nuclear device in Pokharan in 1998 with reciprocal nuclear responses in the form of its own tests by Pakistan. This invited a slew of American sanctions on India. Still, India after weathering the storm of the US economic sanctions, entered into the much debated 123 civil nuclear cooperation agreement with the President Bush's Regime, in the initial decade of the twenty first century. What is to be interestingly noted, is, that despite the non proliferation hawks in the American Congress and the civil societal clamour, President Bush manifested personal diplomatic and administrative interest in the entire deliberations leading to the firming up of the 123 civil nuclear cooperation agreement between the twin democracies in the international system.

The entire discussion on the firming up of the nuclear deal depended upon the domestic constituencies of both the nations. The domestic constituencies had to be deftly and strategically withered away before a semblance of an understanding, could, be reached between the two nation states. Secretary of state, Condoleezza Rice, refuted the American contention, that, with the help of the nuclear deal India would arrive in a prime and practical position to spawn a nuclear weapon. She testified in a Congressional testimony, "This is just not the case. The initiative does not cap the Indian nuclear weapons production but nothing under this initiative will directly enhance its military capability or add to its military stockpile. India could already build additional weapons within the limits of its capabilities if it so desired, with or without this deal. But, the

Indian Government has repeatedly confirmed to public that it intends to expand only its civil nuclear energy capacity."[8] Thus, the Indian standpoint of non-military gains from the civil nuclear cooperation deal, was reinstated with the official American viewpoint that India was to be helped as it was bestowing upon itself any kind of nuclear weapons potential as a consequence of the inking of the 123 agreement between India and United States of America. The anti India and the proliferation hawks in the American establishment were firmly answered by the official American speak thus alleviating all the doubts about an Indo-US nuclear rapprochement.

Congressional acquiescence was repeatedly sought by the American government and as part of a Congressional testimony carried on by Senator Lugar, a Senatorial enquiry ensued, which says the following. "Senator Lugar asked about the Status of India's violation of its peaceful use undertakings in the 1956 Heavy Water Contract and enquired whether these violations are ongoing or are they as a result of the termination of India-US Nuclear cooperation, no longer operative. Under Secretary Joseph replied, "The outcome was that a conclusive answer is not possible due to the factual uncertainty, as, to whether US supplied heavy water contributed to the production of plutonium used for the device and the lack of a mutual understanding about the scope of the 1956 contract language."[9] India did not consider that its usage of the heavy water supplied by United States, in any way contravened the idea of American statutory norms of nuclear cooperation with nations which had not signed the Nuclear Proliferation Treaty. These were aimed for castigating nations such as India for being the violators of the Global non-proliferation Regime. Thus, the US establishment, particularly, the Bush denomination faced several such investigative exercises from the US Congress before the American policy to sign the energy deal with India could be finalised in letter and spirit.

Scholars such as Michael Krepon, Leonard Spector and Robert Einhorn[10] were part of the US non proliferation experts and traditionally critical voices, which, had always militated against the have-nots voice of the non nuclear power nations. Their state of not being in possession of the nuclear related technologies, fuel, technologies and the attendant networks and influence with the global nuclear watchdogs and the United Nations, kept these nuclear have-nots in a perennially deprived situation and at a decided disadvantage. In the author's view, privileged and such more independently minded and capable nations, such as India could manage to gain a lateral entry inside the dynamics and the structure of the Global Nuclear regime. These nuclear energy institutions were already historically manipulated and reflected 'strategic and diplomatic legerdermian'. And, with nations of the stature of United States, accommodating, India in their norm setting and global strategic dimensions the manifold opportunities for both the nations in the larger context of the international system, opened up. It's an altercasted world, where-in, during a bilateral tryst, both the partnering nations tend to learn from each other as part of a strategic transaction. This 'learned behaviour' turns out to be a changed policy manoeuvre, as, a consequence of the bilateral interaction and engagement. The Indo-US bilateral case study, pinpoints towards this shared existence.

Much in the context of the larger role played by newer legislations and follow up acts, the Civil nuclear legislation passed in 2010, also, became a bone of contention between the two nations. The UPA Government succeeded in getting the Civil nuclear Legislation passed only after it was able to get rid of the domestic political dissent and get the Bharatiya Janata Party on board in the national Parliament. Thus, the debate working up to the Civil nuclear Bill was akin to a run up and a natural continuation of the 'works' related to the 123 agreement. The passing of the bill was seen by many as a watershed in Indian Politics as the BJP cooperated with the ruling party in getting the bill through the Parliament. The Government backtracked on numerous clauses to accommodate the main opposition party."[11] The conditionality of the civil nuclear liability bill also led to the coalescing of the domestic political dissent.

C.G. Manoj contends in *Indian Express* that, "The Government agreed to address a range of major concerns of the Bharatiya Janata Party and make significant amendments in the draft legislation. There was to be initiated a threefold increase in the operator's liability ceiling from 5000 to 15000 crore adding a new clause that the bill would only apply to nuclear plants owned and operated by government and increasing the compensation claim period from 10 to 20 years and setting up a nuclear liability fund."[12] Also, India remains one of the few countries in the world, which imposes stringent conditions of operation of plants and supply and management of fuels in the context of moderating the raging ambitions of nuclear power suppliers and the plant operators in India. Still this ideal attached to the sovereignty argument cannot be of much utility in the hour of globalization and the convergence of Regimes. Thus, India remains rigid but arrangements are being worked out with the operators and the corporates residing in United States. In April 2016 nuclear security summit also brings out a convergence in the realm of nuclear terrorism.

The Diaspora Linkages

The Indian Diaspora too has played a significant role in the firming up of the nuclear cooperation agreement between both the nations. The Diaspora factor stands true in the larger context of the relationship covering its entire ambit. The Indian Diaspora has acted since the recent years as a strong and an effective lobby group, in order to market and solidify the Indian stance in the United State's socio-political and cultural firmament. It is reported that, "The US is home to about 1.6 million Indian origin people making them the third largest immigrant group in the country after Mexican and Filipino immigrants. Between 2007 and 2008, the number of Indian immigrants surpassed the Chinese and Hong Kong born immigrants for the first time since at least 1960."[13] As Robert Hathaway suggests that, "Today India can identify scores of US members of the House and Senators, who publicly and proudly declare their friendship for New Delhi. More than a quarter of the members of the House of Representatives have joined an informal Congressional Caucus, one of whose principal goals is to promote close Indo-American ties."[14] Maria Kamder gets it right when she contends in the US national daily, *Washington Post*, when she says, "The nuclear pact got together an Indian Government that is savvier than ever about playing the Washington game, an Indian American community that is just coming into its own and powerful business interests that see India as perhaps the single biggest money making opportunity of the 21st century."[15] The idea of the Patel community as an instance who own the motley motels in the entire sunscape of United States, is a visible instance of how entrenched are the Indians in the American community scenario. An Indian immigrant who owns acres of lady finger farms and earns millions out of them, or an Indian scientist from University of Rajasthan in Jaipur who already has a laboratory under his name in United States, are some of the instances of the Diaspora's entrenchment in the American firmament. There is also a flip side to the entire immigrant experience in the United States. The movie "My name is Khan" goes a long way into reminiscing about the experiences of a South Asian who only speaks two sentences with clarity and aplomb which are, "My name is Khan and I am not a Terrorist." The South Asian context has received a slight socio-cultural beating in a one-dimensional way of sorts since the September 11 attacks on the World Trade Centre towers. Still, in the author's view, the sentiment of tolerance in US remains an abiding norm. The 2015 declaration by Donald Trump, a Republican Presidential hopeful might be similar to an aberration. Donald trump during his campaigning called out to the national leadership to prevent the Moslems to enter United States before the American authorities clear the doubt about the role of the Moslems in United States. Such aberrations cannot be read for much at they amount to a gimmick to garner political support for the candidate, Donald Trump.

Still, specifically speaking of the Indian community, it happens to be one of the most law abiding communities in the homeland with the preserve of doing well vocationally and professionally. Indians only 'work' in United states to live a dream as pithily and cinematically picturised in the realm of bollywood such as in, "Kabhi Khushi Kabhi Gam", where-in, the hard working affluence and advancements of the Indian expatriates in United States makes them part of the moral fibre of the kind and welcoming nation. It is here that, they excel as professionals and wear long embroidered Kurtas in zany dance numbers all the way to prosperity, pelf and a resultant Indo-US bonhomie.

A Post September 11 Neo Age and the Indo-US 'Bilateral'

Both, India and United States are a classical instance of "Altercasting," as, both the nations have seemingly gotten over the ides of the cold war's hallowed past and are past the murky diplomacy and strategic skulduggery, which was symptomatic of the surreptitious Cold war years. The relationship has now graduated on to become a strategic relationship in the truest and the most advanced sense of the term. The post Cold war, a post september 11 and a post American recession, world is going to augur well for both the liberal democracies of the world. New challenges of the order of global terror modules, climate change and energy challenges, mar the international environment in an impactful manner. President Obama made a policy change during his the first term.He deleted the American insistence of mediating on Kashmir as part of the official American policy. He rekindled the American interest in India, when India was to be given a frontline role in the Af-Pak region with the already realised play acting by Pakistan.[16] Thus, India had reservations about the internationalisation of the Kashmir issue, which the author does not refer to as a dispute, led to the timely realisation by President Obama that India prefers to tackle Kashmir bilaterally devoid of any international mediation and arbitration edifice.

The general academic perception and informed analysis, about the India-US relationship is that of a hegemonic state with its quasi-imperialistic ambitions, scheming to ground India into economic and strategic gains. What is seldom understood is the much too apparent fact that India is no Iraq and Afghanistan. It's a different parallel Universe that India subsists in. There are different "EARTHS," and, India and US, seem to be subsisting somewhere near to each other on the same "EARTH". That perception set me thinking and moved me onto a messianic search for the quality of the psyche in India. I assiduously floated an questionnaire which quizzed the various target groups about the idea of being impressed by an American and the global visage of Superman, the Man of Steel who largely represents the liberal and justice and humanitarian credentials of United states as a super hero since its creation by DC Comics in 1938. Most of the respondents did not evince a hatred or distaste or any iota of political incorrectness about the origin myth and the symbolic significance of the steely and messianic figure of Superman. They did not identify with the American and the Christian myth of Superman as they alluded to Indian figures such as Lord Hanuman, who flies across oceans and the Indian Hindi comic figures of Nagaraj, Fauladi Singh and Super Commando Dhruv, and, off course the Indian-spiritual version of Superman, the Shaktiman!

The questionnaire bore a few simple posers. It went on like this:

Is Superman your favourite Superhero? Yes or No.

Which is your favourite superhero?

What qualities, habits, powers and what part of the storyline make Superman your favourite superhero?

Do you think that the character of superman reflects the true essence of United States of America, its culture and its Foreign Policy?

Does the character of Superman reflect American Hegemony or dominance or American generosity and benign pelf?

The author invited the readers to fill in the questions for a better comprehension of what United States is all about and how significant is the American Dream for the Indian rise?

Thus, some respondents wrote about the the pristine attributes of liberty, equality, egalitarianism along with the philanthropic zeal of a light hearted but determined and supine super hero. Xenophobia and a distrust of the Occident happen to be the twin parts of the vile concoction which makes some sections hate America. Distrust, is, a much smaller and limited nomenclature. Add another element to the heady Indian brew, that is Jealousy with a capital "J" which makes United States of America every 'classy souls' and 'fashionable elites' bug bear and an eternal punching bag for the humanist thinker. There is no nation in the entire ambit of the international polity which has grown and prospered in the absence of the single minded devotion to the idiom of national interest. Be it Realism or randomization, all the tides of arguments originate in the non American world which the "Super State" has to guard against. It's not a polemical argument or a indigestible platitude, but, plane jane Realism which is characteristic of what Asian nations such as China and India have been attempting to do. Emulate United States of America. What else can account for the existence of Bollywoods and Tollywoods, in, sync with the hagiographic, "Hollywood."

The Contemporary context in the 'India-US Bilateral Partnership'

In the context of changes in the tenor of the relationship after President Obama's visit to New Delhi on India's Republic Day, a great deal of takeaways can be fathomed out for both the nations. One of the achievements of the summit was the Indian agreement on softening the Civil Nuclear Liability Bill. The Civil Nuclear liability extant in India, aims at attaching a major compensatory liability, on the investor and the provider of the nuclear fuel and technology on the firm which supplies a nuclear energy reactor/plant in India. The legislation has been promptly criticised by the American establishment and the nuclear firms which have gone on to demand that a certain iota of liability in the event of an accident, has, to be borne by the regulator, which is an Indian Public sector firm. Thus, this point in the relationship has been a significant bone of contention between the twin negotiating sides which was solved to a great extent during President Obama's state visit to New Delhi on 26th of January, 2015.

Other 21st century issues, which remain as a fly in the ointment, in the relationship are that of Intellectual property rights and the issue of castigating India as the "Nation of great concern" in the itinerary of the US domestic intellectual property law. It is a widely acknowledged fact, that, India's laws on the issue of trade related Intellectual property Rights are arcane and need urgent upgradation and amendment if India can hope to do unrestricted and liberal trade with the rest of the World. In a report, written by Ankit Panda, in the Diplomat, Climate change was one of the chief agenda items. The report relates that, "Modi seems to have partly revised India's position. India will expand its use of renewable energy and move toward joining an international deal on global warming that would see developed and less-developed countries alike cap emissions. The development is a coup for the United States, which had similar success with China late last year."[17]

Other path breaking and impactful, issues which were discussed and deliberated upon between P M Modi and President Obama were the themes of, "Bilateral Investment Treaty" (BIT) and the Defence Technology and Trade Initiative (DTTI). The Diplomat reports that "Back in September 2014, the two leaders noted that their countries would "treat each other at the same level as their closest partners" on issues including "defence technology transfers, trade, research, co-production, and co-development." The DTTI is poised to increase co-production, co-development and partnership in U.S.-India military-industrial matters. The initiative is line with the Modi government's plans to increase India's defense self-sufficiency and increase the share of India's military hardware that is manufactured on the Indian soil."[18] The partnership has been further cemented by the Indian decision to buy the Javelin anti-tank missiles from United States but a divergence has been observed pertaining to the issue of the buying of MMRCA, that is the Medium Multi Role Combat Aircrafts. This contract for the Aircrafts has been denied to the American firms and the French Rafales have been preferred over the American fighter craft option. Thus, even the India-US Defence relationship is a mixed bag punctuated with a variegated mixture of agreements and disagreements. P M Modi has made the Indian stance clear that merely, the import of foreign technology in the Defence sector is not enough but the higher national objective is to, attain self sufficiency through an indigenous production of the American and other imported defence technology and know-how. Recently, according to an August 14, *Indian Express* report, the nomenclature of the Bilateral Investment Treaty with America and other Western nations would undergo a vast change and India and US are presently re-negotiating the Treaty, (BIT). The November, 2015 pact of joining the Commercial Dialogue with the Strategic dialogue is one of the recent achievements in the radar of the relationship between both the nations.[19]

The relationship received an impetus in September 2014, with Prime Minister, Narendra Modi's visit to US when he deliberated upon a whole plethora of issues straddling the set piece of the India-US Relations. The Ministry of External Affairs Report contends that, "Key outcomes of Prime Minister's visit include new mechanisms to enhance trade and investment, particularly in infrastructure; new modalities to implement cooperation in energy, including nuclear and renewable energy, and climate change; new initiatives in knowledge, education and skill development; new approaches to defence trade, security and counter-terrorism collaboration; and new areas of cooperation between India and the U.S. in third countries."[20]

With the global political and strategic developments such as the rise of Asia, China's assertiveness in the South China sea and the on-going negotiations between Taliban and the Kabul Government, a whole host of negotiations and dialogue has ensued between Prime Minister Narendra Modi and President Barack Obama. India has had several rounds of Strategic dialogue with United States. The recent strategic dialogue between India and US covered a few significant issues. They were, "There have been regular contacts at political and official levels on bilateral, regional and global issues. Foreign Office Consultations, at the level of Foreign Secretary of India and US Undersecretary for Political Affairs, are an important part of the dialogue structure. The last round of Foreign Office Consultations was held in Washington D.C. in December 2013. India and US, have, in the recent years instituted structured dialogues covering East Asia, Central Asia and West Asia, and have agreed on strategic consultations covering Latin America, Africa and the Indian Ocean Region."[21] Thus, what all these deliberations and higher level summitry, reflects is the idea that India is rising as a great power in the Asiatic geo political and geo economic space and has to be co opted with the sole surviving super power which is the United States of America. Thus, the centrality and the essentiality of the role of India in the global power and diplomatic equations has been realised by US. Very rightly, President Obama calls the India-US Relationship as "the defining relationship of the 21st century" just as he calls Af-Pak as "the most dangerous place" in South Asia.

As a figment of factual information, one of the recent developments between India and United States has been the signing of the Income Tax sharing agreement. The Embassy of United States reports and the Revenue Secretary, Shaktikant Das commented that, "Signing the IGA with U.S. to implement FATCA, today, is a very important step for the Government of India, to tackle offshore tax evasion. It reaffirms the Government of India's commitment to fight the menace of black money. It is hoped that the exchange of information on automatic basis, regarding offshore accounts under FATCA would deter tax offenders, would enhance tax transparency and eventually bring in higher equity to the direct tax regime which is necessary for a healthy economy."[22] Thus, it was one of the central election planks of Prime Minister Modi's political party, Bharatiya Janata party to locate people who have stashed away black money in foreign accounts. Thus, in tandem with that domestic poll promise to the Indian electorate, this Tax declaration can go a long way into Indians and others escaping their tax liabilities.

Ambassador Richard Verma, once again belonging to the Indian Diaspora, showered encomiums at the richness and the girth of the India-US 'Bilateral partnership'. He too has roots from the city of Jalandhar, that is the pristine and sunny sun scape of the Indian state of Punjab. He was speaking at the Centre of Strategic and International Studies. He spoke that, "This "strategic plus" relationship has blossomed in the last year, highlighted by the two Obama-Modi summits. The roots of this relationship go much deeper, however. They grow from the Diaspora community, which stretches back to farmers from the Punjab who came to work the Californian soil in the 1800s, to help build railroads and work in lumber mills. They were strengthened by the thousands of scientists and doctors who traveled to the US in the 1950s and 60s, bringing our research and academic communities more closely together."[23] Thus, the concept of, "Strategic Plus" happens to be one of the most recent tenets of the India–US relationship in 2015. The concept is a very wide and holistic comprehension of the relationship, where-in, cultural, political, diasporic, economic-commercial and defence relationships all tend to construct the larger relationship between the two liberal democracies. Referring to the instigations of a cold war's staid mentality and harping upon an anti-convergence and domestically embedded mindset of Sovereignty, leads one to a simplistic stance. The standpoint is that a defence of what United States is all about and where India figures in the entire rubric of the bilateral relationship, is not at all required.

With United States figuring, as the second largest trade partner of India after the People's Republic of China, the byte and the analysis becomes a conveniently easy task. India being a rising power with a huge business market and an eligible-skilled work force can devote much prosperity to Washington's business and economic interests when US finds itself in the fag end of an economic recovery. President Obama, too, in his 2010 visit to India and specially in his speech at the St. Xavier's College, invited the Indian youth and the corporate sector to invest in America and its people's interests. Then, President Obama came on an emergency mission in order to resuscitate the American dream which was slightly wobbly after the economic recession. Now, US has recovered by leaps and bounds and despite the fact that President Obama is a lameduck plenipotentiary, India and US can cooperate with each other. In author's view, this cooperation will lead to an emergence of a scintillating synergy and symbiotic convergence which will outshine other allies which United States has had to live with since the times of the Cold War. In the author's view, both the nations are already brothers in arms and part of a Global band of brothers which reflects in the various significant summits and diaspora exchanges. The China factor and the Pakistan factor, have been de-hyphenated, out of the relationship, long time back. The stereotypical and the beaten-track narrative of the India-US relationship being dependent upon the India and Pakistan relationship and the Sino-Indian skirmishes, is a mythical and backlog discourse now. It's the grandiloquent American dream and how that draws a natural parallel with the India's democratic and liberal-progressive thought structure, which is important now. The attendant open political culture makes dialogue and altercasting between the new bird India and the grand Bald Eagle, United States, as a nature corollary to global politics. In the author's view, India ought not to perceive the American visage as a, "Bald Eagle" or the "Great Indian Bustard," which is a bird of prey and swoops down upon the lazy lizard and a rotund and helpless mouse, crawling in the great American canyons. The American bird can also be the Turkey which is sacrificed on the day of the Easter in the Presidential House. President Obama knows better going by the photograph of the American President pardoning the white Turkey, '***Popcorn***', in the historic North Portico of the White House in the fag end of 2015.

In accordance with the Democratic Peace theory's tenets, too, two democracies have always been generally friendly to each other and have seldom militated against each other. These are not platitudes but part of a Dream which every nation dabbles in-order to shine alone at the elite stable of global one-upmanship. An Asian nation such as India is no exception to the global power rule. To offer another argument, the economic relationship between both the nations serves as the driving factor into serving the cause of the larger partnership. A recent instance in 2015 is the dialogue on Intellectual Property rights being carried on between both the nations along with the clubbing together of the Defence and the Commercial part of the diplomatic parleys between both the nations. All in all, both the democracies with a liberal bias, have a plural, assimilative and a bright future ahead of them with instances of bilateral convergence being more often than not. In conclusion, much water has flowed under the bridge, and the skies of cooperation have been opened up after the dark clouds and shrouds of cold war era confrontations have been removed from the firmament in the context of India-US ties. Recently, Prime Minister Narendra Modi visited Washington in June 2016 and addressed the US Congress. The Indian giant gave a herculean but pragmatic clarion call that the "shadows of hesitancy" which have generally mired the India-US relationship, have become part of the hoary past and it has been supinely replaced by the three C's of, "convenience, candor and convergence". This forms the essential amalgam between the India-US detente in the 2016 furlough and for the time to come.

NOTES

1. Reed Tucker, "The Wacky But True Story Behind Million Dollar Arm," *The New York Times*, 11 May, 2014.
2. See *Indo-American Relations: From Emergence Into Strength*, online at http://74.125.153.132/search?q=cache:ngR0MmVaWOEJ:span.state.gov/wwwfspjulyaug072.pdf+US+GOVT.+DOCUMENTS+ ON+INDO+US+ RELATIONS+DURING+THE+TIME+OF+RICHARD+ NIXON&cd=8&hl=en&ct=clnk&gl=in (visited on Feb 1, 2015).
3. Allen J. Matusow, *Farm Policies and Politics in the Truman Years* 45 (Harvard University Press 1967), See also Henry Chalmers, *World Trade Policies* (UCLA 1953).
4. Shrinivas Cherry, *The Eagle and the Peacock: US Foreign Policy Towards India since Independence* 12 (Greenwood Press 1995).
5. Irving L. Horowitz, *Three Worlds of Development* (Harper 1966).
6. See *Zee Exclusive, (2007)"Indo-U S Relations: A Timeline"* Online at http://www.zeenews.com/znnew/articles.asp?aid=278513&sid=ZNS, (visited October 28, 2009)
7. Ibid.
8. See, "Remarks of Secretary of State Condolezza Rice at the Senate Foreign Relations Committee on the Indo-US Civil Cooperation Initiative," Wednesday April 5, 2006, p. 13, URL: http// foreign. Senate. Gov/ testimony/ 2006/ Rice Testimony 064045 pdf (accessed on 18 May, 2014)
9. Harsh V Pant, "Indian Foreign Policy in a Unipolar World," (New York: Rutledge, 2009), pp. 154-155.
10. Ibid.
11. Coomi Kapoor, "When Two Become One", *Indian Express*, 2 September, 2010.
12. C G Manoj, "Govt. BJP seal their Nuclear deal", *Indian Express*, 18 August, 2010.
13. Aminah Mohammed Arif, 2002, "L Inde Et Sa Puissance," AFRI, Vol. No.3, URL: www.diplomatie.gouv. Fr (accessed on May 19, 2015).
14. Robert M Hathaway, 2002, "Coming of Age: Indian Americans and the US Congress," in A Kapur, Y K Malik, Harold A Gould and Arthur G Rubinoff (eds), India and the United States in a Changing world," New Delhi: Sage Publications, p. 386.
15. Maria Kamder, "Forget the Israel Lobby, The hill's Next Big Player is Made in India", *The Washington Post*, 30 September, 2007.
16. Harsh V Pant, "The US India Nuclear Pact: Policy Process and Great Power Politics," (New Delhi: Oxford University Press, 2011) pp. 63-65.
17. Ankit Panda, "Nine Takeways on India-US Ties After Obama's India Visit," URL: http://thediplomat.com/2015/01/9-takeaways-on-us-india-ties-after-obamas-india-visit/ (Online: Web), accessed on August 15, 2015.
18. Ibid.
19. US Embassy Website in India.
20. "Overview of the India-US relations",URL: http://www.mea.gov.in/Portal/ForeignRelation/USA_Dec2014.pdf (online: Web), accessed on August 15, 2015.
21. Ibid.
22. Embassy of United States, Media Centre, "India and United States sign agreement to share Tax information," URL:http://newdelhi.usembassy.gov/pr070915.html (Online: Web), accessed on 15 August, 2015.
23. Ibid.

17

To Conclude

The lyrics of the ditty, You are a Grand Old Flag, run like this only to inspire the American citizen and universal humanist in the larger international system:

> There's a feeling comes a-stealing,
> And it sets my brain a-reeling,
> When I'm list'ning to the music of a military band.
> Any tune like "Yankee Doodle"
> Simply sets me off my noodle,
> It's that patriotic something that no one can understand.
> "Way down South, in the land of cotton,"
> Melody untiring,
> Ain't that inspiring?
> Hurrah! Hurrah! We'll join the jubilee!

The work attempts to argue the notion that can a nation such as United States rise above the cumulative angst and criticism which confronts it in the international system. It's not a counter critic but an enunciation of the way the American Dream works and functions and reflects itself in the international firmament in the context of US Foreign policy. The work argues that by a coincidence of history and power equations, United States has developed as the most powerful and influential nation in the international system. The age of the rise of the American Republic after the initiation of the Big Business era and the ending of the Civil war, meant a lot for United States. Harking back to history, the advent of the European settlers through the Mayflower pact, the Salem witchcraft as mentioned in Arthur Miller's play, "The Crucible" and the revolution aimed at ending the British Colonial rule, initiated the eventful odyssey of United States as an independent nation. The United States evolved as a super power after its period of industrialization, modernization and urbanization largely on the Eastern seaboard. Interwoven inside the matrix of modernization and gilded age development in the 19th century, the Japanese attack on Pearl harbour during World War-II made United States leave its isolationist foreign policy. Interventionism emerged as the prime driver of US foreign policy along with a historical pre-emption of war. Debates have engulfed the nation that the American war of independence had nothing to do with the Colonial rule of the British, but the author has attempted to argue that it was definitely the British rule characterised by its exploitative and discriminating legislations and policies which made the patriots take up arms against the British crown.

The trail of events which followed amounted to the Cold War years, where-in, the communist and closed political system of Soviet Union emerged as the adversary for United States. These cold war developments ushered in the events in Korea, Vietnam and Nicaragua, where-in, the concept of pre-empting Dominoes became the core policy of both the arch adversaries, that is, United States and Soviet Union. Both the nations went on from one Cuba to another as part of a conventional, inter-continental and nuclear arms race in order to retain dominance over the other foe. The fall of the Soviet Union with the collapse of the Berlin wall separating the two Germanies, ushered in a new age of post globalization and post cold war era. It was in these challenging times that United States was confronted with lethal non state actors in the form of global terrorists with actual global reach, kill potential and international funding mechanisms. This new age led to a re-ordering of the American foreign policy which included forging new alliances and coalitions in order to thwart the 'risks' of terrorism, Climate change, arms trafficking and drug laundering, which had their own global ramifications. Old foes such as Cuba and Russia were made into coalition partners and new foes such as Iraq and Iran emerged with changing volatile power equations in the crucial region of West Asia. The taint of pre-emption of wars and aggression by the United States establishment was embalmed upon the nation. Little forgetting the incident of the burning of the White House in 1815 by the British Royal Navy, which ushered in the lore and practice of "Pre-emption" in the American grand strategy. It also avidly reflected the National Security Strategies of an ever challenged America. The international lawyers have grave procedural and substantive difficulties in agreeing to the American rationale of sending "boots on grounds" in conflict zones such as Vietnam, Iraq and Afghanistan. Still, the American notion of being a Global-Regulator nation remains an unflinching idea about the vision of American foreign policy. In the author's view, the most powerful and the most visible nation in the World Politics is United States which has lived in tandem with the principles and values enshrined in the American constitution and the American declaration of independence. The ideals of liberal democracy, justice, egalitarianism and humanism have been the guiding lights of the American Empire which is very "non-Empire-like" in its functioning and global reflections. The work also utilizes the variegated and colourful imageries from the mainstream Hollywood constructs, art and literature to drive home the point of American super-puissance and its stature as a hyper power with a coincidental role of a Regulator nation and the sole power in the international system. The imageries and the narratives of comic books are there but, very much meaningful and impactful superheroes such as Superman and the Avengers have been included in the narrative of the work in order to distill the message of the work. The work takes regular and repetitive recourse to comic book super heroes and other Cultural-Cinematic precepts in order to lighten the broodiness and the overtly sincere veneer of the work. As any nation's art, literature and Cinema reflect the actual state of the nation, the present work also attempts to drive home the same message of being a narrative positing the largeness of the American Dream in the context of the US foreign policy in a few conflict ridden terrains of the international system. Thus, the character and the stereotypical persona of "Superman" which is quintessentially American in origin and conception, serves, as one of the anchors for the entire narrative along with the landmarks and symbols such as the Oregon Trail and the Star spangled banner in a symbolic American narrative. Apart from the utilization of super hero characters and the symbols of the pride of US, the work has attempted an analysis of the Hollywood constructs in order to enliven the tenor of the work with arguments from popular works, too. The Super hero's blue super suit, the red cape and the "S" insignia is more than a "non-sincere comic book" strip to regale children. The character stands for the proud pantheon of the superlative patriotic, nationalist and cosmopolitan oeuvre that US has managed and attained for itself over the years. The work demands of the reader to move beyond the sincere academic interpretations into the realm of contemporary affairs and take a meaningful flight of fancy into the myth and lore of United States.

There ought to be no quotes and citations from other sources in a book's conclusion. But, I cannot prevent myself from referring to an article from the American national daily, the *Atlantic*. The author of the article is troubled by the bleakness and the brooding visage of the Man of Steel, in the last Superman biopic. When the caped crusader rises up defying gravity or alights on a skyscraper next to the iconic Statue of Liberty, then, the global community swoons and ratchets up a great deal of an identity storm, often resulting in the super hero's canonization. Superman's, Smallville world is a bright world infused with the basketball heroes and the lush green lawns in front of brightly painted wooden houses without the Vietnam war guilt and the laconic and dark sky's silhouette out of which emerges the 2013 Superman only to thank the American Brigadier to let him be himself after the arch adversary, Zod has been annihilated in the 2013 release, *Man of Steel.* Mark Waid, a Superman comic creator, writes longingly, "With the exception of the first-flight beat—the smile Superman gets when he first takes to the air—it's utterly joyless. From start to finish. Utterly. Joyless. And I just have no interest in relentless joylessness from a guy who can fly."[1] This amounts to a negation of the American Dream and a negation of what being an American and a humanist is all about.

The talk of the American decline is another infringement belittling the grandiloquent American Dream which finds an echo in the darker and devilish demeanour of a quintessentially bright and sunny Smallville which epitomises the regular American life and all that's positive about the founding ideals of United States. Some critics have pointed out that due to the passionate idealism of the American revolution, rhetoric became a mainstay of the American narrative. Words such as liberty, fraternity, equality in the disbursement of the Public goods, and egalitarianism formed the undercurrent of the American way of doing politics and carrying on governance. These larger words and slogans not only make for enlightened governance and politics, but, they also reflect the ideals of participative narratives by the commoners which is the neglected part of the academic discourse. Apart from coincidence being a reason behind the quintessential "Surge" of American power in World Politics, the 'antiquity of benevolent rhetoric' placed behind the American discourse, also concretizes the entire dynamics and the functioning of the American dream. It is in the antiquity of "Cato" and the sacrifice of the private goods by the citizens in order to achieve the public goods, that, the driving idiom of the American dream lies. The author would argue that though the American ascendance might not be a self fulfilling prophesy, but, the internal girth of the nation shines through its incessant stress on Democracy and public good.

In the twenty-first century, the growth indicators might have been out of sync from what China had achieved or what the South American geo-economics were up to in 2015. Still, great nations such as United States, too have their laudable and epitomised crests and introspective troughs. Troughs might include the debates over Preemption to war and humanitarian interventions in nations such as Iraq and Afghanistan. The bright sunny scapes of Hollywood and the global tourists walking in the Hollywood hills in tanned skins wearing military jumpers in the Griffith Park is a quintessential imagery which one associates with the American Republic dreaming on to perfection and perpetual betterment. The author would argue that this idyllic satiation is a noble and innocent state of affairs that all progressive nations strive to attain. The Dark Knight's Gotham City's stylistic gloom has never been the embodiment of the American city as the Smallvilles and Archie's hometown have been the regular staple of the American barbecue. Thus, brightness and a garish routine of self-seeking behaviour, has been the symptomatic part of the American myth and lore which reflects the humdrum routines despite the irritants of gun violence, race related conflict, over-commercialisation and others. The author has argued that the cinematic moments with an imbued comicality and light-heartedness, have to be roped in for illustration's sake. The *Superman* I, movie picturises the *Daily Planet* journalist, Lana Lang, falling from a chopper. Suddenly, the caped crusader, Superman, arrives in the limelight and catches her. A surprised, fazed and hazel-eyed, Lana Lang asks Superman as he carried her to the ground. "You have got me alright, but, who has got you?" The superhero merely smiles. Such is the regulating and Don Juan like 'role-playing capacity' of the United States as a nation as it can hurtle unintended aid to the suffering nations and their populations and emerge as the quintessential do-gooder country. This is the core argument of the work which takes recourse to Hollywood productions as part of the theory making exercise in the realm of Cultural Studies and International Relations Theory. Cinema has its own tale to tell in the context of US foreign policy and the philanthropic zeal of United States as a Regulator nation!

Leaders are not born but made, while, an alternate school of thought might perceive the scenario in a perverse manner. To some, extent of the 'rise and surge' of the United States of America is not all about a calibrated Pax Americana, but, it all amounts to a kaleidoscope of assumptions and rationales. The nation was not always great and powerful, but, the exigencies of the post-American revolution era along with the cleansing achieved through the perniciously violent and bloody Civil War in the United States, transformed the nation into a seething and vibrant nation. This transformed the nation into the age of Big Business, which refers to the era of industrialization and urbanization in the US. The country entered the era of Big Business and industrialisation, which catapulted the United States on to the road of pelf and stolidity. Once an acceptable iota of utility, pelf and influence was attained by the country, it unshackled itself in the 20th century, with the Teddy Roosevelt's Panama Canal Treaties and further interventions in the global happenings.

The decision of the founding fathers to stay away from the 'Entangling alliances of the European theatre' was soon cast away. A contrary approach to intervene in nations such as Vietnam, Iraq and Afghanistan, perched United States atop an engine of military and economic growth. The author has argued that it is through these interventions that United States festooned itself on the world stage and it was essential for them to do so. The work primarily argues that it became a realism driven necessity for United States to intervene in far off lands which were strategically important regions for an embattled America with direct linkages to the security of its homeland. This new World Power could compete seriously with the European powers of the order of the United Kingdom, the Soviet bear, a phoenix-like Germany and a stately France (though an ally). Thus, the nations were surprised with the international community witnessing a new upstart with global ambitions and with an equal reasoning to back its moderate claims to superpower status. The intertwined politics of the two World Wars, along with the idiom of a modernist self-doubt perceived and universally felt across the entire post-World War II international system, launched United States into a permanent perch atop Mount Sinai, as the American myth refers to the perceived "Greatness of their nation". All these narratives might seem essayist in nature and content, but, the discourse of the 'American rise' leading to the entire international system subsisting within the rubric and the staple mantle of 'Uncle Sam,' soon became a global reality after World War-II.

The idiom that 'With Great power comes Great Responsibility' runs true to the American tale in a post-Appalachian and post-Oregon trail world. The cultural matrix of the public sphere, as elucidated by the indubitable Habermas along with his idiom of communicative rationality, too, serves as a creative methodology in order to decipher the myth and lore of United States of America. The nation has a hallowed past, but the upstart country's tale is similar to a Cinematic construct, Spiderman and serendipitous Superman.

What is the significance of this often narrated comic book tale about America? The author would argue that Cinema and Cultural representations reflect the actual social-political and external characteristics of a society, a nation and a region. This is the rationale why the author has attempted to argue through the constructs of Hollywood and art in order to clarify the American firmament with its varied domestic and external ramifications. It is not about a childhood fantasy but it is about the fantasy of being a great nation which cannot be challenged in whatever manner by any other state on the face of the Earth in a perfunctory manner. That is where the quest of the American Dream begins from. It reflects a fundamental truth about the United States of America and its American Dream, as, it gets manifested universally and globally through its cultural and cinematic precepts and through its foreign policy events across the international system. We are talking about a nation akin to a metaphorical superhero making personal sacrifices in order to attain a higher and super power perch for the hoi polloi of the nation. The nation believes itself to be akin to Peter Parker who finds his destiny with the attainment of splendid super powers, which he utilises with a moral principle of being a philanthropist and a do-gooder nation state with a global mission and a special zeal to democratize the world's challenged countries.

The nation akin to a superhero plays a vigilante and a veritable Don Juan, in order to universalise the new-found land's idiom of democracy, human rights, rule of law and international economic brotherhood. Similar to the archetypal superhero, the nation, too gets vilified with the ogre of rising expectations and falling dividends. Thus, emerges the norm of global talk on the post-economic recession America.

The quintessential superhero similar to the super state is often castigated by the public opinion wielders in being inimical to the moral constraints of a larger unprivileged section of the world. The author would argue that the ides of supreme jealousy could be one factor or else the suspicion of the bravado and exemplary superior strength might wean away the hoi polloi away from the innocent and 'plain-jane do-gooder rationality' of the super state which America had become after the dissolution of the Soviet Union. Even the superhero, Superman in the Hollywood construct, Superman Part III of the eighties is made out to be schizophrenic, who, at times of internal crisis, oscillates between his philanthropic self and the vile stranglehold of his baser self, which a nation and a personage might be inclined to gravitate to, in the hour of personal weakness and tumult. Can the nation and Kal-El be pardoned? The author here harks back to the introductory chapter of the Book premised upon the American Dream. The author would argue that when objectivity too can be part of a manufactured consent with the argument of the Military-Media-Industry complex, then why cant the Cultural imprint of a nation be given a generous reading which is its due after phenomenal castigation and criticism. Maybe because it is Mainstream.

The character of Clark Kent, as the bumbling but talented newspaper correspondent lives a worldly life and mutates into the 'MAN OF STEEL' Superman to save the souls in distress and a planet in need of super protection from the vile pyrotechnics of the likes of Lex Luthor and other sundry threats which the modern day technology of the STATE cannot tackle and requires super intervention. Thus, here too in this selective and subjective argument and metaphor, the male protagonist of 'Dear Ol Supes' lives as a metaphor for the stately and super power persona of United States and for the attendant symbols of the order of Statute of Liberty, Arlington cemetery, White House, Mount Rushmore and the Brookyln bridge, often deconstructed by the American Godzillas and King Kongs. The King Kongs and the Godzillas stand for the attractive and insidious, "Other" which have to be liquidated through the 'splash' of the American civilization and the attendant Dream.

Thus, the messaging through the American mainstream creativity industry is clear and definitive. The nation gets catapulted as the 'Ubermensch' to shoulder unprecedented responsibilities in the global firmament. The American military and economic overarch, is there to reside in the sphere of Global affairs and foreign Policy.The status and the fungible reality being that the country occupies the 'one to ten positioning' in the pedestal of an international power sprint. The nations of the order of People's Republic of China and the Russian Republic, achieve the '11th and onwards slots' in the global power paradigm. Thus, the 'extreme powerfilled heft and the amalgamated principled standpoint,' displayed in United States foreign Policy, hews together, a geo economic, strategic and geo political perch for an already anointed United States of America. The author has attempted to argue that every progressive nation worth its salt attempts to progress and communicate through its founding myth and it is an ingrained thesis that if the nation and its cultural representations have the strength of purpose and the convincing stealth, then such artefacts travel into the sphere of practical International politics. The soft power which the Americans have utilised so successfully had to be convincing and belief worthy only then it managed to enter the national and global myth. This myth once again amounts to the ideals of liberty, fraternity, egalitarianism and constitutionalism which are the core tenets of the American Dream and philosophy. It's no serendipity after all.

The nation firms up an ethos for others and messages/communicates and diplomatically propels on, the grand idiom of a 'glad strategy,' which is non hierarchic and is as Flat as Milton Freidman gets. The 'Glad paradigm' is very much gladiatorial in nature and its multifaceted ramifications, depend upon the global idiom of 'Global Governance' and 'responsibility for the greater world, 'where-in, the travails, trials and tribulations of the international actors are accounted for to the maximum humanly extent possible. The author too argues that there are sad and unhappy instances of American inaction and want of valuably quick policy action which has mired a few of the Global nationalities in intractable morasses. All this cannot be explained away through the instrument of foreign policy ordained, 'national interest'.

United States can gobble up the vicious vortex of criticism of its foreign policy in some quarters such as in the muddle of West Asia and in the context of its avowed 'Global War on Terror' (GWOT). The global overarch, can be further translated into an internationally contagious institutionalism of norm setting and global convergence, through allocating ample space for the non state and the civil societal actors. Thus, the world warrants 'a responsive and risk rider' which needs to function as a World Government or the 'Planetary Legislature' in the lingo of the Star Wars metaphor. It has be a "Joker balancer player," who can stabilise the world politics and the attendant system of nations. It is only an able bodied super hero, who can take on the mirth of the destabilising Joker antagonist with its own humanist sense of humor and a scintillating and picture perfect 'boom of a timing'.

The soft power projection by the Global power, too, can be better comprehended in a bipartisan manner, where-in, the Cinematic, Media and the larger Cultural contexts of the nation can be utilised diligently as reflectors of Foreign policy. The larger understanding of security, thus, ensures a new role for a taciturn United States as the 'Regulator' nation state which can run the entire show within human and possible means at its disposal. The tenor of the nightangle's 'star spangled banner' can serve the global polity's resources. This is the catch world which the entire ambit of Governments and Corporates hanker after. The enviable pelf of United states of America is historically endowed with the correct admixture which has been assiduously developed and utilized during the supreme pressure of a powerful Cold War in the form of a state threat and in the face of a later day menace of religious fundamentalism. Thus, Global governance has been diligently realised through the best practices of superiority, globally spread out alliances, control over the world's resources, geo economic entanglements and a principled stand point to be with the 'Right' and not with the forces of the 'non-Right.' Thus, the International system has largely been within the confines of an 'American Cycle' for long despite the proud palaver of an 'Asian century' and various other formulations. The wars in Iraq, Afghanistan and now the advent of Daesh, are an ample reflection of this fact.

In a post-Globalization and post interdependence world, the American nation has reinvented itself with the general wisdom being that the framing of sound foreign policy is sound economics. For instance, the trade and investment entanglement of Washington and Beijing and India, leaves the containment doctrine defanged and the Asian pivot and the rebalancing foreign policy thought of a second Obama term to be redefined. In a way, the preponderance of the mantra of money and investments, is a significant part and parcel of the American rebuilding strivings in a post global recession years as the contagion is yet to be completely tamed by the Federal Reserve in totality.

Thus, the economics-centric world, too, has a place in a post American decline world, which, is all set to strike back with new age allies and coalitions, with the multiplicity of new actors. The American empire also has a 'non-empire and non-impish' functionality, with the idea of nation building and reconstructing any host nation's infrastructure and getting involved in its multi sectoral development, being some of the facets of a 'regulator-developer state.' The sustainable face of the efforts in Iraq, Afghanistan, Haiti, Somalia, Yugoslavia, Kosovo and other international stations underline the true intent of the American foreign policy over the years. Whenever terror and insurgency have struck the American allies and other non allies have been impacted with instability, the American establishment on most of the occasions has worked hard to ameliorate the 'troubles' of that nation. Iraq, Afghanistan, Somalia being instances in the same American narrative. It would be a completely far fangled position to adopt if every American action is reviewed through an idealist prism, which cannot be the way in which any country can function in the present day dangerous and changing international system. Most of the nations, big and small, major and minor, great powers and minuscule powers, have to function keeping in view the mainframe of national interest and the wishes of the domestic interests. United States does the same round and gets castigated by the liberal bias. It's again a serendipity.

Another scenario which filters through the prism of history is the figurative faltering of the grand American Dream. The American hyper puissance after the heady World War-II victory, the dynamics of the Club of victors (United Nations and Bretton Woods) along with the Fukuyama ordained 'End of Ideology/Anti-Communism' discourse, all pinpoint towards an abiding American strategic crest. But, the rise of non-state and non-traditional security threats, have led to a redefinition of the US policy with initiatives such as the GWOT, Space warfare, the practice of the New American century ideals coupled with the Revolution in Military affairs. These are the pertinent cases in point, which, circumvent a traditional and quintessentially global reading and interpretation of World Affairs.

Wars are fought and some of them leave an indelible imprint upon the character of nations. The dynamics of the Vietnam War and the attendant pyrotechnics of the American war effort against the communist Viet Cong in Hanoi had a far reaching and path changing influence upon the hallowed and warm ideal of a picket fenced American Dream. The rest of the world tends to relate to the dream through the soft instruments of power. The tangled ethics of a robotic Forrest Gump who plays ping pong till kingdom come in a war ravaged Vietnam to the portrayal of a handicapped Tom Cruise, who ceases to be a self believing and patriotic Vietnam war veteran, all highlight the plight of what happens if a Citizen Cain turns critical of his alma mater. Thus, the American denizens witnessed a vitriolic backlash in the form of a post Vietnam war Counter culture, with the advent of the Hashish and drug infected University youths and the rebellious medley of Timothy Leary's flower children. The breaking up of faith in the justness and the correctness of distributive justice in United States and the faltering of the ideals of egalitarianism and equity tore apart the socio-political fabric of a questioning America in the tumultuous decade of the scandalous sixties and the supine but equally transformative seventies. Still, the author has argued that the idea of America is also about the exchange of opposite views and lines of thinking, which qualifies United States to be a true blue Democracy where people argue and interest groups clash. Alex De Tocqueville had said that the American political system is similar to a mortar grinding machine which has two sections where the sludge and the finally prepared mortar get separated. Thus, the clash of approaches is a quaint characteristic of the

American dream which demystifies the counter culture movement in the times of American interventions in Vietnam, Iraq and Afghanistan.

The entire context of the present day American scenario in the larger world, seems to be posited for a change. The episode of Edward Snowden, who was a contractor for the Central Intelligence Agency, has lead to the idea of a repercussion to get built up against the United States, all across the international firmament. The exposes of the surveillance which have been taken into account for have led to a global informational and diplomatic avalanche to be built up against the White House and the Foggy bottom. Also, the May 2014 palaver about an American Sergeant Bergdahl, who was posted in Afghanistan and was declared as the first prisoner of war from America, too, has created a tumult in the entire American edifice.

As it was deliberated upon in the American war on Iraq, Private Jessica Lynch, was wounded during an Iraqi attack and was elevated to the pedestal of an American martyr and a patriot. In the similar vein, various reports have indicated that Sergeant Bergdahl was a deserter in the state of Afghanistan which lead to the idea of his being anointed as a patriot coming through as a non starter. Thus, the American Dream takes a beating every now and then which needs a far greater academic and learned deliberation. The counter culture movement which was initiated by the likes of Timothy Leary and the American music and aesthetic groups, needs to be re examined which became the cynosure of all eyes in the light of the American debacle in Vietnam. Still, the public sphere and the cultural context of the idea of the 'American Dream' is a spill over from the post World War II years, where-in, the US Television precepts such as the 'Wonder years' posit the male protagonist as a teenage boy who is witnessing the critique of US foreign policy as the American military casualties mount in the badlands of Vietnam. Also, the teenage-child witnesses the massive and impactful Anti-war rallies and protests which undulated and more than shook the fundamentals of the American socio-political and cultural system. And, he has a lady classmate in the town's only school, who hates war and mutilated limbs!

Thus, the American mantra led by the nation's founding fathers along with entrepreneurs and innovators par excellence, has received a hefty international criticism. Other geo-economic centres, such as the guileful and cosseted People's Republic of China and the smaller giants of the Asiatic space, have firmed up a new Asian pivot in the larger global space. The rise of China with its larger maritime ambitions and economic and business forays into Latin America and Africa, have inevitably broadened the working space of the larger global firmament. Thus, in Kishore Mahbubani's terminology, the Asian century, has definitely arrived warranting a re-look by the Occident and the American nation state which they have happily and gainfully accomplished as a strategic transition keeping

India in the lead. All these developments have taken place after the trenchant debate surrounding the American interventions in Vietnam, Iraq and Afghanistan.

The author has attempted to argue that the American enmeshing of its ideals with the Wilsonian, 'Fourteen points' and the attendant notion of Idealism, gels with the idea of the Realism directed real politick, which United states assiduously follows. This tenet is similar to the dynamics of the rest of the international community. Somebody has observed that United States should not be any longer perceived as a Global giant, which has gone berserk in a closed hall which flings its tail to break all the room's furniture. In a way, the United States policy has led to the development of the need to trust the intentions of United States, so, that the world at large can learn from the benign co-operator. The objective of American Public Diplomacy is not to be considered as 'a Benign Hegemon' anymore. Hegemony is a chilling relic of the historic past. The nation has learned its lesson. The entire idea of America has been well elucidated by President Obama as he addressed the larger Arabic and Moslem world in his Cairo address during his initial visits to West Asia. President Barack Obama congratulated the Arabic world into adopting the Cairo University and AL Azhar as the anointed seat of Islamic Learning.

He spoke that, "We meet at a time of tension between the United States and Muslims around the world – tension rooted in historical forces that go beyond any current policy debate. The relationship between Islam and the West includes centuries of co-existence and cooperation, but also conflict and religious wars. More recently, tension has been fed by colonialism that denied rights and opportunities to many Muslims, and a Cold War in which Muslim-majority countries were too often treated as proxies without regard to their own aspirations. Moreover, the sweeping change brought about by modernity and globalization led many Muslims to view the West as hostile to the traditions of Islam. Violent extremists have exploited these tensions in a small but potent minority of Muslims." Thus, the global criticism of the American intent and the instruments of foreign policy and governance, has, led to a great deal of internal deliberation and churning in the nation's establishment. This has lead to a 'Change' which was a byword in the Obama Election campaign, to initiate a more friendlier and assimilative face of the American nation and its foreign policy.

Apart from the idiom of, "Yes, We can: Change", the cultural arc of America, too, needs to be delved inside with some incisive detail which refers to the Mainstream Media coverage of American interventions all across the global firmament. All these developments include the Hollywood's Cinematic portrayal of American wars and American episodes of glory and eulogisation themes. The American interventions, in the wars in Iraq both in the 1991 and 2003 witnessed something which had not been experienced since the heady days of Vietnam war. The tradition of Pentagon and the Public Affairs Department of the US State Department was that reporters were made part of designated, 'pools of reporters' which were permitted to receive and transmit daily evening snippets of news capsules about the war from the Department of state which were 'gatekept' by the American military at Doha. All this was managed near the immediate battle stations in Iraq beyond 2003.

The practice of giving access to war correspondents in the battlefield, was, further changed to the idea of embedding the war correspondents as the 'Embeds' with the American Defense forces as the US forces led the incursion inside mainland Iraq in March 2003. Soon, the American war effort led to the capitulation of the capital city of Baghdad. Thus, the role played by the Public sphere consequently spawned public opinion in United States as a result of coverage of the war in CNN, NBC, etc. The national dailies such as Washington Post, New York Times and Wall Street Journal, led to the firming up of both the criticism and praise of the US Government. Still, the Media moved beyond the "Patriot Frame" of reference in the context of the American interventions abroad and its Domestic challenges. The blatant oil factor was held up as a factor leading up to the American military involvement in Iraq. The rationale of United States going to war in Iraq was avidly and widely questioned by the American and the global public opinion makers alike.

The rise of factors such as the 'CNN Effect' and the 'Rally Around the Flag Phenomenon' were the abiding vantage points through which the US war effort was widely analyzed and discussed in the Fourth Estate and the national drawing rooms alike. The notion of 'Rally Around the Flag Phenomenon' spelt doom for the alternate doomsday nay-sayers in the American political and social firmament. The brass-tacks of the 'Rally Around the Flag phenomenon' contended that whenever the national forces fight a war then the situation is connoted as a national crisis and a national emergency which it actually does amount to. The Government's decision to enter the far off war, leads to a surge in empathy for the White House's decision to march on with or without a Congressional war decision. The initial surveys have always posited in the American domestic situation, that, the citizens and the civil societal actors, have always supported such contingent wars. But, once the casualties of the American GI's start getting reported from the far flung and alien battle fields of Vietnam, Panama, Korea, Iraq and Afghanistan, then the public opinion takes a negative turn around. This is a quaint American phenomenon which goes hand in hand with the grandiloquent American Dream.

As part of the churning that a nation goes through, an internal chasm is reflected in the nature and content of popular representations in the country. Without being retrogressive about the American phenomenon, the unprecedented success of the 2014 Hollywood film, The Purge: Anarchy, and its sequel in 2015, can provide the critics with a useful insight into the internal dynamics of what US is challenged with largely like any other progressive nationality. The Purge: Anarchy, is the highest grosser in United States. It's a Hollywood film released in 2014. The manner in which the nation allows a 12 hour purge for all is a disturbing sign for the times to come. The turpitude of what ails mankind is staggeringly brought forth in the narrative. The connection between the Columbine massacre, the school violence, and gun running instances which have taken place in San Bernardino, Colorado and South Carolina in 2015, showcases the gory state of affairs in its all prognosticative detail. This is part of a larger churning, which, every nation has to pass through in its larger odyssey across the pyrrhic developmental pathway. The idea that only 'significance' attracts criticism and universal questioning merits attention which is a test case for the manner in which United States has been treated globally. It's now the victimhood trajectory for United States where they can too intone with the rest of the international community as being the victim of Global terror and environmental challenges getting manifested domestically, too. It's no more a serendipity that US is a great nation adjusting to multi-polarity.

Now, the public through interviews and candid protests, begins to clamor for the American withdrawal from these foreign battle stations such as Somalia, Haiti, Iraq, Afghanistan or Eastern Europe. The expressed hope is that the number of body bags arriving at Fort Sumpter and other places will only die down if the war ends. Thus, soon the anti war voices and protestations gain ground in the American sphere which makes for a negative publicity for the overall trajectory of American foreign policy and its attendant decision making process. Even Presidents such as George Bush have been lampooned with aplomb as being blood thirsty and brutalized war mongers. Such a narrative is an quintessential American discourse which runs through the life blood of the American nation including its people. The author has argued in the narrative that, no finality can be drawn out of this narrative as America happens to be a democracy where the visceral ideological and political counter views, are debated and discussed threadbare very naturally and conveniently in the nation's public sphere. The author's argument is that these plural narratives rampant in United States might surprise a closed polity and society and make "Them" jittery, discomfited and overtly aggressive. The climatic moment of "Batman vs. Superman" displaying the "demise of Superman" is not a reality after all.

One of the core arguments of the Book is that dissent and the alternate way of life and politics, too, has an eminent standing in the entire foreign policy making process in the nation. The establishment rightly prides itself atop the humanitarian mound displaying the genial characteristics of democracy, human rights, rule of law, egalitarianism and justice. Also, as it has been often narrated and recorded,, that United States cannot afford to be a disinterested Goliath and a superhero who has taken off his super suit and cape only to surreptitiously applaud the new state actors from amongst the crowed in a confetti lined promenade like the flick, megamind. The super hero and the super state has to re-ignite his larger-than-life-force, and, learn to desist from self doubt about the efficacy of continuing to don the super suit in the larger interest of an embattled and easily endangered humanity. The rule of law's maintenance, has, its embedded costs. The super states themselves might be an embattled lot, but, the clarion call of the hour amounts to a convenient resuscitation of the Great powers to cobble together a Justice league and avenge the ills done to the larger human species. United States of America, has, borne the burden immaculately and can do so even more effectively in a multipolar international system looking askance for a superhero and his equally potent sidekicks in larger human interest. It's a predestination that Washington cannot escape by calling its international interventions as its, "Ever-Gnawing Overarch". But, the serendipitous rise is imminent.

Samuel P Huntington writes in his seminal work, Who We Are, "Charles Street, the principal thoroughfare on Boston's Beacon Hill is a comfortable Street bordered by four storey brick buildings with apartments over Antique stores and other shops on the ground level. At one time, on one block, American flags regularly hung over the entrances to the United States Post Office and the liquor store. Then, the post office stopped displaying the flag and the flag stood alone on the liquor shop on September 11, 2001. Two weeks later, seventeen flags flew on this block in addition to a huge stars and stripes suspended across the street a short distance away. With their country under attack, Charles Street denizens rediscovered their nation and identified themselves with it." Thus, the people residing in Charles Street were at once with the rest of the American denizens. This 'unflagging enthusiasm for the flag', has been the cornerstone of the American theme and the Dream, as, it reverberates and resonates throughout the nook and cranny, mall and ice peaks in the nation's firmament since the glacial ages, to utilize an over exaggeration and off course it runs thus throughout the entire narrative of the Book. It is here, where-in, lies the American call for forming the stately and all encompassing, then, and an all participatory, World Government. It can also be argued that the hyperbole and the value laden approach of the American founding fathers needs some deft trimming. But, reason and rationality alone cannot account for the progress which United States has achieved in the years after the war of independence. Values if not systematically propagated domestically and globally will amount to a whimper with the world citizens reflecting no "significance" for United States and any other great and progressing nation.

The argument can be further enlivened by referring to a Cinematic construct. The all-for-your-eyes-only, visage of Mel Gibson as he delivers death blows with his saber riding atop his mutineer/militia horse along in the flick, 'Patriot' along with the forlorn and embattled figure of the American President astride a F-16, in the film Independence day, form memorable vignettes for the rasping and ungrudging patriot. The speech which the US President delivers from his precarious perch in a F-16, invigorates the rag tag bunch of Airforce pilots and the civilian survivors, as they mount a successful counter attack on the Alien, 'Mother Nest Space Ship' in the popular Hollywood construct, Independence Day. The author would argue that an informed yet interestingly ebullient analysis of the 'American Project' doesn't seem very much different than the idea of nationalism and cosmopolitanism, as, practiced in other nations and by their people. Today, the need of the hour as the narrative suggests has to be a new cosmopolitanism. This theme resonates with the new version of the science fiction and alien films in Hollywood. In the 2015 release, Star Wars: The Force Awakens, the straight-jacketed black and white coloring of god and the bad jedis has evaporated into oblivion. The new nature of the international system is very pithily depicted by the multi-racial and the multi planetary cosmos of quaint characters as they vividly populate the cinemascope of the 2015 Star wars film. The same space has been nearly replicated in the international system as an old and wizened, Luke Skywalker, receives his battling saber from the new age troopers of "Good."

There has been a slight erosion inside the rationale of the American Dream in a study undertaken by the newspaper, Atlantic, especially amongst the youth in the country. Jon Pinsker writes that, "There's been extraordinary examples of people that have been poor and stuff that have risen to the top just from their personal hard work...not everybody can do that, I realize, but I think a lot of people could if they just tried."[2] This was the perception in 1996. But a difference has been observed when the same question was asked to a sample group of young Americans in 2011." The 2011 survey informs that, "You can always work hard, but if you aren't given the opportunity or you don't have the funds to be able to continue working hard, then, you never get the chance to get out of where you are," said one student respondent.[3] The study which has been carried on by Carol Hostetter, Sabrina Sellenberger and Leila Wood, has reached a conclusion that the belief of the Young Americans in meritocracy has faltered in the idiom of "Americo-cracy". The young ones now call the entirety of the phenomenon as the "American Dream-2.0".

Some larger issues have fared well in the context of the external visage of United States and the American Dream stands vindicated. The various Regimes such as the climate change Regime along with the human rights turnpike and the Macdonaldization process, all converge in the American highway arch of the Yellow lined Macdonalds. It is here, on this twilight zone cafeteria and universally loved eatery that all and sundry, monks and men in Ferraris, people with their filial baggages and the teeny bloopers with their yellow top cars cruise through to the parking lot and enjoy the sentiment of being a true blue American. 'The work argues that the American Cycle' as the driving sentiment of the work suggests, has the influence and the halo to shine amidst all and sundry nationalists and ingrained national interests of concerned countries. The universally felt and practiced pathos of being true to one's nation and involving oneself for uplift during national emergencies, is a concept alien to no nation and their people, with United States of America being no exception to the idea, 'with all the works.' Still, the ascent is definitively, serendipitous.

Its the Army Again! Soldiers we swoon for U.... This happens to be an Indian refrain too. Being an Indian writer, I can serve up umpteen instances when the threats to a nation are ably and wholesomely reciprocated by the denizens.

26th July, Kargil divas. 4th of July: American Independence day. No astute comparisons can be drawn and attempted. The tantalizing and not-for-us-torturous heights of Tololing and the million dollar "snap" at Tiger Hill (when the Indian army vacated the Pakistani incursion in Kargil) and Point 5102, reflect the boisterous bravado of the brave soldier being immortalized in the 'upward crawl'. I am fortunate to move around greens named after the war heroes and ply on ways named after the 'self less smarties'. The swoon of staccato of the radio, the boom of the Howitzers and the uncertain greys of the Leh road are broken in the narrative by the facts of the Kargil war. The same can be the tell tale story of the "Patriot's" Mel Gibson as the American patriot creates a trap for the British Colonists who have recently ravaged his home and are moving away with his family. The manner in which the Patriot hides a few rifles in a grove overlooking the Redcoat advance and flits from one tree to the other, remains etched as the turnpike symbol of the Oregon trail without its belittlements and self doubts as discussed in the Book. Chris Kyles, the American Sniper who has toiled hard in the Iraq wars too maintains the stately and patriotic order of his life's preferences, that is, God, Country and Family which heavily disturbs his better half, Taya, somewhere down in the security and safety of the hearth in the cotton fields of United States of America. Still, the American Dream, lives on and '***seethes and froths***' with life and warm proactivity, to cast asunder the self doubt, which is an inalienable spec out of a nation's life and its jaunty race of people and related global criticism. The argument that how can the world's largest debtor compete with primacy with the Globe's largest creditor beyond 2009 does have some girth in its entrails. Still, austerity has been an avidly adhered to solution in US which has made the American Union extricate itself out of the debacle of a crash. The idea of the American decline is the most fashionable one in the international system. One can recriminate against a President in disrepute or one can castigate an unpopular policy and both can find a heuristic convergence in the "Johnson's Vietnam war" and the "Bush's Iraq War," as, everybody's pet peeve. The slime and the sludge of the Jealous and castigating majority will always romp home for the collectivity in the form of the byte on the, "American Decline" which has been the proud palaver of the collectivity. This debilitating talk which argues against the American Dream and the Oregon trail never seems to arrive in the 'Real world in the Real time.' The author finally argues that the lofty ideals such as liberty and egalitarianism which are not lofty after all, lead to the myth being challenged academically as being rhetoric and narcissistic. Still, the author argues that the passion of the founding fathers and the tradition of the American Revolution led the United States to adopt "a larger-than-life" visage and vocation for itself. The argument is furthered when it can be said that greatness in nationhood and progress in the external scenario by powerful nations with potential, is definitely a national objective which is practically, collectively and universally adhered to by the entire gamut of the international system with national and regional adaptations. Long live the Oregon Trail and the grandiloquent American Dream!!!!!!! It's a serendipity that America beckons!

NOTES

1. Charles Moss, "Superman's Dark Past", The *Atlantic*, May 24, 2015.
2. Joe Pinsker, "Teenagers are Loosing Confidence in the American Dream," *The Atlantic*, June 15, 2015.
3. Ibid.

Index

PENTAGON PRESS

COMMITTED TO SERVE THE ARMED FORCES